AN UNCOMMON CRIMINAL

The Extraordinary Life of Edwin Turner Osbaldeston

A Biography by

Noël G. Siver
and
Kenson J. Siver

18410 Magnolia Parkway
Southfield, Michigan 48075 USA

Printed in the United States of America
by
Johnston Lithograph, Inc.
11334 Hunt Street
Romulus, Michigan 48174 USA

ISBN-13: 978-0-9982981-0-8 (cloth)

AN UNCOMMON CRIMINAL

The Extraordinary Life of Edwin Turner Osbaldeston

CONTENTS

PREFACE

Growing up we occasionally heard stories about our great-grandfather Edwin Turner Osbaldeston from his surviving children and our father. In retrospect the stories were highly sanitized, "G" rated accounts of life in another age. They were devoid of sex, profanity, scandal, and crime, with only a hint of violence.

Our paternal grandmother, Normandie Alice Turner Osbaldeston Siver, with whom we had the most contact, told us how we were descended from British aristocracy. The Osbaldestons, she liked to remind us, had been landowners and lived in a castle. Our ancestors had been a higher class of people, she said. As proof of this, Normandie presented a British magazine with an article on the remains of an ancient Osbaldeston castle. The photographs of the ruins were underwhelming. What we saw did not fit our youthful definition of a castle.

In addition to tales of visiting relatives in the English countryside when they were young, Grandmother and her sister, our great-aunt Ethel Monica Turner Osbaldeston Groves, also gave us copies of the Osbaldeston family crest as further proof of noble lineage. Always critical of her grandchildren's behavior, it appeared Grandmother was attempting to impress upon us the need to carry ourselves with greater dignity while clinging to the belief of her lineage. In truth, our Osbaldeston ancestors fell squarely in the working class.

Our father spoke of his grandfather as a man who was restless—who could never stick with any pursuit for long or stay in one place. He believed that his grandfather's restlessness had undermined his success in life and that of his family. As children we did not know a great deal about the *real* Edwin Turner Osbaldeston. We knew he was born in England, had been a ship's surgeon, promoted the art of massage in America, and had lived in New York City and Asbury Park, New Jersey.

We assumed Edwin had a medical degree and came from a good home. In photographs we always saw a well-dressed gentleman with a handlebar moustache. Likewise, in family photos he stood as a proud papa with his brood, all appearing nicely dressed in well-appointed surroundings. Given the training required and stability a medical career provided, it always struck us as odd that our great-grandfather did not maintain his medical practice.

As the children of Edwin Turner Osbaldeston passed on, we inherited boxes of family photo albums, mementos, books, and the family Bible. Among the items was Edwin's handwritten journal, spanning approximately forty years of his life. Great-aunt Ethel, the custodian of the English family history material for many years, had carried out some research on the families of both her parents.

In 1962, at the age of eighty-one, she transcribed her father's journal into thirty-three single-spaced typewritten pages and sent carbon copies for us to read. The boxes from our elders containing the final remnants of their lives lingered among us. Great-grandson Kenson Siver sorted, preserved, and stored the materials. As we were preoccupied with building our own lives and establishing careers, the stories, photographs, mementos, and the journal were set aside but not forgotten.

In the 1980s, Noël Siver, the eldest daughter of Kenneth Siver (son of Normandie), began to research her great-grandfather's life. She had read his journal with its many tales of adventure and travel and the harrowing experiences he had had in various places across the globe. A number of the stories she suspected were too good to be true.

When Noël resumed her family history research in earnest in 1996, her first task was to re-transcribe the handwritten journal into an electronic format and, in places, correct Ethel's transcription. The journal entries began in 1860, and the last dated entry was from 1899. We believe it was in the 1890s when Edwin copied the material from the original journal (or journals) into a new one. At the same time, he added new information. For instance, he recorded recollections of his early childhood and his parents and revised earlier entries to include more flattering reflections. In the course of copying information, he recorded dates that were not accurate and misspelled names of people and places. It is altogether possible that Edwin reproduced this notebook with his children in mind. He came from a very troubled background and had numerous difficulties during his life but wanted to give them the impression that his early life had been grander than it was in reality. It is also possible that he wrote this notebook to soften his children's opinion of their autocratic, and at times tyrannic, father. Clearly, Edwin wanted to be remembered in a heroic light. While the journal does contain some accurate details, in many ways it is a work of fiction and fantasy.

Label on the cover of Edwin T. Osbaldeston's journal

The journal has been a less-than-satisfactory source of information regarding the life of Edwin Turner Osbaldeston. Most of the entries in the first section are undated. In those instances where there are dates, many of the dates are incorrect, often off by a year. The notes in the second section are often cryptic, and it has not always been possible to understand their meaning. The finding of alternative—and mostly contradictory—sources for some of the incidents described in the notebook created a credibility gap and made us wonder just how much stock should be placed in the descriptions of incidents for which no other sources have been found.

In the course of her early research, Noël unearthed aspects of Edwin's life that he had not mentioned in his journal or that had not been told to us by our grandmother or great-aunts and great-uncles. These new details took her on interesting detours, pushing her to mine new veins of information and further piece together the unrecorded and more delicate details of his life.

If it weren't for the existence of Edwin's journal, there are certain details of episodes in his life that she might never have discovered. For example, it was an entry in the address book section of his journal that prompted Noël to search for and find his mother in the records of the Bristol Lunatic Asylum. On the other hand, there were numerous occasions when she was led on paper chases to nowhere while trying to verify information. For example, the assertion by Edwin that he was related to English sportsman and politician Squire George Osbaldeston proved to be totally false. Research on incidents described in the journal has shown that just as the stories that Edwin told reporters in 1926 contained many exaggerations and distortions of the facts and omissions of unsavory truths, so does the journal. In a number of cases, alternative sources have been found that contradict or downplay the information given by Edwin.

Once she had completed the transcription, Noël began the lengthy task of doing research in archives, libraries, and family history centers in the United States, England, and Australia in an attempt to confirm the veracity of events described in the journal, learn about people mentioned, check the spelling of names of persons and places, etc. She found the search for traces of his exploits to be most enthralling!

Noël's background in library science and archaeology greatly assisted her search for information as she went about validating the contents of the journal. Her research took her to churches in England to scour parish records; cemeteries in numerous countries to check burial records; a host of libraries for local histories; county and other public record offices for official documents; and national and state archives in the United States, England, Germany, and Australia for correspondence and records.

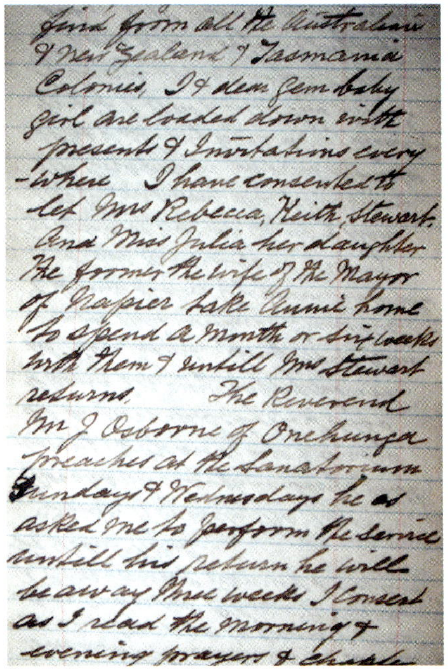
Send from all the Australian
& New Zealand & Tasmania
Colonies, I & dear Gem baby
girl are loaded down with
presents & Invitations every
-where I have consented to
let Mrs Rebecca, Keith, Stewart,
And Miss Julia her daughter
The former the wife of the Mayor
of Napier take Annie home
to spend a month or six weeks
with them & untill Mrs Stewart
returns. The Reverend
Mr J Osborne of Onehunga
preaches at the Sanatorium
Sundays & Wednesdays he as
asked me to perform the service
untill his return he will
be away three weeks I consent
as I read the morning &
evening prayers & [illegible]

A page from Edwin's journal

The more she researched, the more intrigued she became. Facets of Edwin's life were like a puzzle to be solved, a mystery to be resolved. Noël's quest for answers grew from a hobby to a near obsession.

Through census data; ship passenger manifests; police, court, and military records; city directories; and a myriad of other sources, she was able to verify some of what he recorded, disprove some of his claims, or correct the dates and particulars of certain events that Edwin referenced in his notes. For example, in his journal entries from the fall of 1875, Edwin wrote in some detail the names of people he met or lodged with and specific places he frequented during his stay in San Francisco. He had sailed there from Australia, serving as a ship's surgeon. The people and places proved to be accurate. However, several events in which he played a role were likely exaggerated and biased by the author's telling. Likewise, some of his accounts could not be disproved because documentation could not be found or the records no longer exist. There were any number of dead ends.

Among the memorabilia that were passed down to us were newspaper clippings from the time of Edwin's death. Most of them were from the *Asbury Park Evening Press*. Edwin spent the last years of his life in Asbury Park and died there. When Noël began her research, the vast majority of newspapers did not have indexes going back to the date on which they began publication. However, the *New York Times* did have such an index in bound volumes. Noël went through its index year by year from 1880, the year Edwin arrived in New York, copied down all the references to him, found the articles on microfilm, and printed out copies. If a *New York Times* article was datelined Asbury Park, it indicated to her that she would find the same or a similar article in the *Asbury Park Evening Press.* Once she had compiled a list of articles, she used interlibrary loan to borrow microfilms of the *Asbury Park Evening Press* from the Asbury Park Free Public Library.

Then came the discovery of extensive reporting of Edwin's activities in a great many newspapers. In the twentieth century, many newspapers were microfilmed. Initially, researching news articles was a tortuous process requiring one to sit before a microfilm reader and sift through pages upon pages, reel after reel of filmed editions of newspapers. With the advent of Internet databases, websites, search engines, and the digitization of newspaper archives, a virtual landslide of information about Edwin was uncovered. In the past few years, the number of websites that permit the user to search these millions of pages and download articles or entire pages has multiplied greatly.

From 2007 onwards, Noël found and downloaded dozens of articles about Edwin from free and pay-per-view websites. Membership in genealogical societies and Ancestry.com produced additional material about Edwin and family members.

So in fact, Edwin's journal serves as a starting point for this biography. The authors acknowledge that it contains many factual inaccuracies and numerous omissions. However, it provides a framework of the life of a man who truly had a troubled but extraordinary existence. The authors quote the journal to appropriately reflect the character of Edwin Turner Osbaldeston and his view of the times, people, and places he encountered. Other sources are referenced to set the story straight. In some instances it is left up to the reader to decide what to believe.

Edwin's published and unpublished letters illustrated that he had a strong vocabulary and could compose well-constructed prose. Many of his letters were extravagantly rich in hyperbole. His journal, on the other hand, was rather informally composed and riddled with run-on sentences, misspelled words, and inconsistent application of the English language. In quoting the journal, the authors have standardized spellings and punctuation and edited for clarity and brevity. His choice of words and the thoughts expressed were not changed.

Similarly, the authors relied heavily on newspaper accounts to advance Edwin's life story and to relate another perspective on the incidents he recorded. So much is known about the life of Edwin Turner Osbaldeston because his exploits were widely reported in newspaper articles around the world for most of his adult life. The amount of coverage he received in the press was extraordinary, and much of it of his own making. It was extraordinary in that Edwin was neither a world leader, a captain of industry, nor someone who would normally be associated with celebrity. Edwin was keenly aware of the power of the press and frequently used it to further his own ends. He routinely befriended editors and reporters. When friendship with newsmen didn't produce the desired results, he took to placing advertisements in newspapers and wrote letters to the editor. And he created his own news. Conversely, because of his notoriety, his deeds and misdeeds were covered extensively as well.

In this volume, newspaper articles have also been edited for the sake of brevity. Since Edwin was frequently quoted by reporters, his quotes have been lifted (with attribution) from articles to further illuminate the man, his thoughts, and his personality. Many, many news reports misspelled "Osbaldeston." So frequent were the misspellings of his surname that the authors decided to spare the reader of having to be told repeatedly of the error. Thus, "Baldeston," "Osbaldistone," "Osbaldston," "Osbaldiston," and any other derivation of the name will not be followed by "sic." It should also be noted that at times he went by his middle rather than his last name.

Edwin's life is a rich reflection of the times in which he lived. In many respects he was not a spectator of the times but rather a participant. Growing up he experienced the harsh realities of the life of the working class in Victorian England. Fascinated by medicine and emerging health sciences, he gravitated to trends in health care and physical fitness and applied them in his work life. He was part of the nineteenth-century expansion of the British Empire, having spent years in the new settlements in Australia and New Zealand. Ocean travel changed dramatically in his lifetime. As an enlisted man, passenger, and crew member, he experienced the advances in sailing through his extensive travels. As a resident of New York working in a field that attracted people of means, the Gilded Age enriched his life. In turn he came to experience many of the finer things in life and was in contact with a host of luminaries of the day.

Edwin Turner Osbaldeston (1916)
The "Doctor" or "The Professor"

A nicely matted, framed photograph of our great-grandfather that our great-aunt kept among her possessions was handed down to Kenson Siver. The photograph is a headshot in profile of Edwin taken when he was seventy-eight years old. Edwin is looking to the right, dressed in a light-colored suit, a shock of white hair gracing his collar, head tilted slightly upward, and face distinguished by a thick, white moustache that covered his lips. To the unfamiliar eye, Edwin could be mistaken in this photograph for Mark Twain. Although Twain was taller and stockier of build, Great-Grandfather bore a resemblance to the accomplished American writer and humorist. Not to suggest that Edwin Turner Osbaldeston came anywhere near the accomplishment, wealth, and fame of Samuel Clemens, but there are some remarkable similarities between the two men that went beyond physical appearance.

Although they led very different lives and were born an ocean apart, Edwin Turner Osbaldeston and Samuel Clemens had much in common. Born in the 1830s, they were contemporaries. Both grew up in families gripped by poverty. When Clemens was a boy, his father declared bankruptcy. During his youth, Edwin's father was sent to debtor's prison. Both men were tireless wanderers who continually reinvented themselves throughout their lives. They traveled, albeit at different times, to many of the same places in the world. They shared an affinity for new inventions and trends. In finance, neither man had a head for business. Each made considerable sums of money and lost it all to extravagances and poor investments, only to repeat the boom-to-bust cycle several times over.

Samuel L. Clemens "Mark Twain"

Perhaps most of all, Clemens and Edwin craved the spotlight. They both took to wearing white suits year round. Twain said dark colors depressed him. Edwin did not say but favored the color. They were eccentric characters that would talk to anyone who would listen and were frequently quoted in newspapers in New York and in other parts of the country. Reporters regularly sought comment on current events from Twain. They could count on him for a humorous quip or colorful insight. Edwin either made news or inserted himself into public affairs. A reporter for the *Asbury Park Evening Press* said Edwin made "good copy." Unquestionably, Clemens was the superior performer with an international following. Edwin had a much smaller international following and not for the same reasons. Where Twain needed no introduction, Edwin at times had to inform new acquaintances of his claims to fame. However, once one met Edwin, a second introduction was not necessary. With oversized personalities, each man enjoyed being at the center of attention and reveled in their celebrity. Yet privately, they both were wracked with despair and loss.

The most striking similarities the men shared had to do with the contrast between their public personalities and private lives. Although Edwin would survive Clemens by two decades, their final years followed a similar pattern. Clemens and Edwin were widowers who had outlived a number of their children. Edwin was estranged from his surviving offspring, while Clemens's only remaining daughter was distant. Faced with loss of family, declining health, and career accomplishments behind them, they fought to remain relevant. They took solace in their public personas. Life was more enjoyable when they inhabited their alter egos. In the years before his death, it was as if Samuel Clemens ceased to exist. Mark Twain greatly overshadowed the man who had been his creator. Twain served as an escape from the depressed and lonely Sam. Meanwhile, Edwin glorified in being the distinguished war hero who had fought bravely in many a battle. His careers in medicine, massage therapy, and hydrotherapy were mostly forgotten. In news articles and conversation, he was addressed as "Doctor" or "Professor" Osbaldeston and was universally defined as the old veteran with the distinguished war record and a medal to prove it.

Did Twain and Edwin ever meet? Edwin claimed they did. That has not been proven, but both men resided in New York City at the same time and traveled in some of the same social circles. If they had met, Clemens might very well have enjoyed the character Edwin had become and would probably have lampooned him for his many foibles.

ACKNOWLEDGMENTS
& Sources of Information

Our initial sources of information regarding our English great-grandfather, Edwin Turner Osbaldeston (1838–1929), were his grandson, our father Kenneth Ludbrooke Siver (1909–1984), and his daughters—our great-aunt Ethel Monica Turner Osbaldeston Groves (1880–1968), and our grandmother Normandie Alice Turner Osbaldeston Siver (1887–1965), all of whom were either born in or grew up in New York City.

Ethel Turner Groves was the family historian of her generation. It was she who kept the collection of family history material relatively intact, wrote letters seeking information about her parents and their ancestors in England, related family history anecdotes in letters to our generation, and late in life, transcribed a journal written by her father.

In September 2006, thanks to a ship's passenger list seen on www.ancestry.com, Noël Siver discovered that her great-aunts, great-uncles, and grandmother had a younger half sister whom they had never mentioned. Louisa Mascot Osbaldeston (1896–1980) was the daughter of Edwin Turner Osbaldeston and his German mistress, Louise Weiss (1876–1951).

In 2008 Noël made contact with Edwin's youngest granddaughter, Patricia During Dawson (1929–2010). She was born a few months after Edwin died but had heard stories about him from her mother, Louisa Mascot Osbaldeston Drukker and her maternal grandmother, Louise Weiss Lucas. In letters and phone conversations Patricia shared what she knew of her grandparents and her parents. Her desire to know more about her English ancestors is what sparked Noël to begin work on a first draft of a biography of Edwin Turner Osbaldeston.

Annie and George Rossi of Ormond Beach, Florida, members of Random Acts of Genealogical Kindness, sent photographs of the gravestones of Mascot and her mother and copies of Daytona Beach newspaper articles about Mascot.

On February 20–21, 2009, Noël Siver and her sister Judith Siver visited Patricia During Dawson at her Columbia, South Carolina home. Noël presented Patricia with a rough draft of a biography of Edwin Turner Osbaldeston. In return Patricia very kindly allowed Noël to take digital photographs of her mother's two photo albums that contained photographs and newspaper clippings from Mascot's international career as a ballerina.

The source material for this biography came from years of research in family history centers, archives, county record offices, and libraries in the United States, England, and Australia. Initially the information was found on microfilm; in census records, parish registers, city directories, and a few reference works; and in a small number of documents such as vital records and military service records.

In the first decade of the twenty-first century, more and more material became available on the Internet. From 2005 onwards Noël downloaded dozens of newspaper articles about Edwin. Later, historical newspapers had been digitized from microfilm.

Noël found numerous newspaper articles about Edwin on the free websites www.fultonhistory.com, a site with scans of millions of pages of New York State newspapers; nyshistoricnewspapers.org, which contains digitized images of historical newspapers from New York State's northern counties, including Franklin County, where Edwin spent three years; www.loc.gov/chroniclingamerica, set up by the Library of Congress to assist access to historical American newspapers published through 1922; paperspast.natlib.govt.nz, which consists of digital images of newspapers published in all the regions of New Zealand between 1839 and 1945; and trove.nla.gov.au, the website of the National Library of Australia, which includes digitized Australian newspapers from 1803 to 1954.

Noël also downloaded Edwin Turner Osbaldeston-related newspaper articles from the pay-per-view websites www.genealogybank.com and www.proquest.com. Membership in the New York Genealogical and Biographical Society and the California Genealogical Society provided free access to www.newspaperarchive.com. A subscription to www.ancestry.com produced additional material about Edwin and family members.

A September 2006 Google search for "Osbaldiston" (a variant spelling of Osbaldeston) and "Adelaide" retrieved the website www.victorianturkishbaths.org. The creation of retired English librarian and social historian Malcolm Shifrin, the website listed Edwin T. Osbaldiston as operating a Turkish bath in Adelaide in 1867. Noël corresponded with Malcolm and contributed background information about Edwin to his website. Malcolm, in turn, introduced Noël to another contributor to the website, Australian historian Susan Aykut, who, after completing a PhD on the role of the bath in Ottoman society, had begun researching Turkish baths in Australia.

In the course of her research, she had come across Edwin Turner Osbaldeston working in Turkish baths in three different Australian cities during the years 1866–1867. Susan was in the process of writing an article about Edwin when Noël contacted her. This contact resulted in a mutually beneficial exchange of information. Noël provided Susan with background information about Edwin, and Susan very kindly shared archival material relating to him that she had found in the files of the Public Record Office of Victoria, Australia.

An archivist who went out of his way to be helpful was Manfred Rauscher of the Stadtarchiv Idar-Oberstein, the municipal archives of the town formerly known as Oberstein, in Western Germany. When Noël e-mailed the archives in February 2008, asking if it held any information regarding an incident in the town in which Edwin Turner Osbaldeston was involved in May 1902, Rauscher found four articles in the local newspaper. Because the newspaper had been bound, it was not possible to photocopy or scan two of them. Herr Rauscher very kindly transcribed those articles.

The receipt of those articles was followed by a visit to the National Archives and Records Administration (NARA) in College Park, Maryland. That branch holds records from the US State Department, including key material from the US Embassy in Berlin and the US Consulate in Mainz.

The military careers of Edwin and his older brother Frederick Turner were traced using Royal Artillery records at The National Archives, Kew, Surrey, England. Likewise, Admiralty records relating to their maternal grandfather, Royal Navy lieutenant Charles Pye Turner, and his widow were also consulted at the UK's National Archives. Records relating to Edwin's father, Josiah Scudder Osbaldeston, were seen at Oxfordshire History Centre in Oxford, England; Soldiers of Oxfordshire Research Centre, in Woodstock, Oxfordshire, England; and Gloucestershire Archives, Gloucester, England. Bristol Record Office in Bristol, England, holds records pertaining to Edwin's mother, Mary Ann Turner. Additional information about Edwin's ancestors was found in the library at the Society of Genealogists in London.

In Australia, records were consulted at the State Library of Victoria and the Public Record Office of Victoria in Melbourne, as well as at State Records of South Australia and the State Library of South Australia in Adelaide.

Since 2002 Noël has been in touch with English family historian Peter Osbaldeston, who is an authority on the Osbaldestons of the world. Peter has uploaded some of the results of Noël's research to a family tree on www.ancestry.com, entitled "Edwin Turner Osbaldeston (1838 Cheltenham UK to 1929 USA) his crazy but fantastic life story."

Collaboration with our Australian fourth cousin, retired University of Queensland librarian John East, did not turn up any new information about Edwin, but it did result in the addition of two more generations to Edwin's family tree.

After the 1968 deaths of Ethel Osbaldeston Groves and her brother Francis Osbaldeston, Kenson Siver collected and organized the majority of the family history materials. He acted as the "keeper" of the photographs, letters, documents, artifacts, etc. He provided Noël with these materials during the early days of her family history research, and as she began piecing together a first draft of the Edwin Turner Osbaldeston biography in late 2008.

In November 2013 Kenson began reworking Noël's first draft. He expanded the biography to place Edwin Turner Osbaldeston in his world surroundings. The movements of Edwin Turner Osbaldeston were placed in the broader context of the times in which he lived and societal settings and circumstances. Kenson conducted research on the places his great-grandfather had lived, the things that he had experienced, and some of the people he encountered. He also looked into what made Edwin Turner Osbaldeston "tick." Kenson blended his research with the massive amounts of data that Noël had previously unearthed. He and Noël then reassessed the contents, and Kenson produced a second draft.

Individuals who proofread Kenson Siver's second draft of the biography and offered constructive comments were our sister Judith Siver, who has long been interested in the research on our ancestors; retired English and French teacher Darla Van Hoey of Southfield, Michigan; and retired Southfield librarian Laurie Penn.

A third draft was then produced and shared with librarian Sandra Novacek of Detroit, who has published her late husband's memoir. Their suggestions for improving the flow of the life story were invaluable and greatly appreciated. Further, the perspective of reviewers not familiar with Edwin T. Osbaldeston was very helpful. From there, yet another draft of the biography was produced.

And finally, it should be noted that Berkeley, California, clinical psychologist Dr. Jonathan Rousell provided clinical insights that support the evidence of Edwin Turner Osbaldeston's narcissistic character structure.

With Kenson's background in journalism and desktop publishing and Noël's in library science and academic research, the story of their great-grandfather has been a very rewarding collaborative effort.

Noël G. Siver, Berkeley, California
Kenson J. Siver, Southfield, Michigan

WHO'S WHO

Relationship to Edwin Turner Osbaldeston

FAMILY MEMBERS

Josiah Scudder Osbaldeston	....	Father
Mary Ann Lewis Turner	....	Grandmother
Maria Osbaldeston	....	Half sister
Mary Ann Turner	....	Mother
Frederick Turner	....	Brother
Emma Osbaldeston Vernon	....	Sister
Oscar Vernon	....	Nephew
Charles Osbaldeston	....	Brother
Francis Osbaldeston	....	Brother
Julian Osbaldeston	....	Brother
William George Osbaldeston	....	First cousin
Alfred Osbaldeston	....	First cousin
Ann Pratt	....	First wife
Frederick Josiah	....	First son by Ann Pratt
Annie Mabel Knowles	....	First daughter by Ann Pratt
John Frederick Knowles	....	Annie Mabel's husband
Alice Agnes Moore	....	Second wife
Ethel Monica Turner	....	First daughter by Alice Agnes Moore
Donald Duncan Stewart	....	Ethel's first husband
Arthur T. Groves	....	Ethel's second husband
Edwina Agnes	....	Second daughter by Alice Agnes Moore
Edwin Julian Turner	....	First son by Alice Agnes Moore
Donald Turner	....	Grandson
Geneva Agnes Miller	....	Third daughter by Alice Agnes Moore
Frederick B. Miller	....	Geneva's husband
Normandie Alice Siver	....	Fourth daughter by Alice Agnes Moore
James H. Siver	....	Normandie's husband
Kenneth Siver	....	Grandson
Francis Scudder Osbaldeston	....	Second son by Alice Agnes Moore
Olive Teel Osbaldeston	....	Frank's wife
Alberta Plaistridge	....	Fifth daughter by Alice Agnes Moore
Philip Plaistridge	....	Alberta's husband
Louise Weiss	....	Mistress
Mrs. Metzgar	....	Alias of Louise Weiss
Louisa Mascot	....	Daughter by mistress

ACQUAINTANCES

Timothy Ahern	....	Binghamton cellmate, 1880
Alfred, Duke of Edinburgh	....	Employer in Adelaide in 1867
Thomas Allen	....	Utica farmer, 1880
Ballarat Corporation Baths	....	Baths in Ballarat, Victoria
Louis C. Bartlett	....	Binghamton sheriff, 1880
Thomas Bastard	....	Adelaide baths manager
S. Foster Black	....	Broome County lawman
James Penn Boucaut	....	Adelaide lawyer
John Boyce and wife	....	Employees of the Ballarat baths
George Brown	....	Broome County detective, 1880
Joseph Burton	....	Turkish baths owner, London
Roscoe Conkling	....	US senator from New York
Charles E. Cook	....	Asbury Park attorney
George Coppin	....	Politician, actor, owner of the Olympic
Sir Charles Darling	....	Governor of Victoria
Martin Donohoe	....	Malone lawman, 1896
Thomas Doyle	....	Adelaide policeman
James Dwyer	....	Utica police chief, 1880
Irwin W. and John W. Fay	....	Malone store owners
John Foley	....	Utica livery stable owner
Edwin Ford	....	Binghamton doctor
Robert Graham	....	Waiwera Hot Springs spa owner
Ulysses S. Grant	....	Former US president
Wilton Hack	....	Adelaide pastor
Clarence F. Hetrick	....	Asbury Park mayor, 1926
George Hufford	....	Wyoming County, PA farmer
J. Lyle Kinmouth	....	Publisher of *Asbury Park Evening Press*
Frank (Franz) Lucas	....	Husband of Louise Weiss
Urbane C. Lyon	....	Broome County district attorney, 1926
James MacGeorge	....	Adelaide architect
Edward J. Mannix	....	Malone justice of the peace
William Martin	....	Utica livery stable owner
Harry A. Moore	....	New Jersey governor, 1926
Thomas Moore	....	Artist
J. S. Oliphant	....	Adelaide Destitute Asylum official
Frederick G. Paddock	....	Franklin County district attorney, 1897
Ferdinand Pietriche	....	Turkish baths operator, Melbourne
Richard Propsting	....	Hobart, Tasmania police superintendent
Edward Bates Scott	....	Yatala Labour Prison superintendent
Alfred E. Smith	....	New York governor, 1926
K. D. Sykes	....	Auckland baths operator
Charles Watson	....	Broome County sheriff, 1926
William Alfred Wearing	....	South Australia Supreme Court justice
Eduard Wild	....	German carbine manufacturer
Edward J. Wivell	....	Dance instructor, Adelaide

CHAPTER ONE

The Media Storm ~ 1926

A throng of reporters, supporters, and onlookers gathered outside the small clapboard house at 801 Railroad Avenue in Asbury Park, New Jersey, on Saturday, March 27, 1926, to shake hands with and speak to Dr. Edwin Turner Osbaldeston. The ninety-three-year-old doctor, with a wiry frame, shock of white hair, and bushy mustache and beard, reveled in the attention.

Wearing a tam-o'-shanter cocked to the side of his head, he spent most of the day on the porch of the weather-beaten house greeting visitors as car after car rolled up to his home. The cause of the excitement was Dr. Osbaldeston's arrest the night before for allegedly stealing a horse and buggy and allegedly escaping from jail forty-five years earlier in Binghamton, Broome County, New York.[1]

His accuser was the legendary lawman Deputy Sheriff S. Foster Black of Binghamton, who newspapers of the day mistakenly reported as being ninety-one years of age. The jailing the night before of the ninety-three-year-old retired physician, who had been pursued and arrested by an aged marshal for crimes committed nearly a half century earlier, was great human-interest fodder for reporters.

The media played up the story of the two dueling nonagenarians. For days the struggle between the old sheriff and the elderly doctor appeared on the front pages of newspapers across the country and had been picked up by the international media. Stories appeared in Canadian, British, and Australian newspapers. A film crew for the fledgling newsreel media even made its way to Railroad Avenue in the seaside resort town to interview the accused doctor.[2] Dr. Osbaldeston gladly obliged the crew by posing and pacing back and forth in front of his home.

Left: This photo in the Sun *(Binghamton, New York) caught the eye of Deputy Sheriff S. Foster Black.*

How the arrest of Dr. Osbaldeston came about was a bit of a fluke. The previous Wednesday (March 24), the pictorial section of Binghamton's *Sun* newspaper had carried a photograph of Dr. Osbaldeston with the following caption:

> Hale and hearty at 93, Dr. E. Turner Osbaldistone (above) of Asbury Park, N. J., believes himself the oldest living survivor of the Crimean war. He also fought in the Boxer rebellion, Boer war and under Garibaldi. Though he smokes and drinks, he has never had a sick day in his life.[3]

Born in England and having served in Britain's Royal Artillery, Dr. Osbaldeston claimed that he had fought in the British army alongside soldiers from France and the Ottoman Empire against Russia. (The British and French engaged in the Crimean War between 1853 and 1856 to block Russia's attempt to gain control of the Holy Land that at the time was part of the declining Ottoman Empire.)

Dr. Osbaldeston stated that he was a captain in the artillery, directing eighty men and the fire of six guns, which supported the Light Brigade at Balaklava.[4] Following Crimea, he spoke of serving with Garibaldi in the struggle for the unification of Italy

Dr. Osbaldeston stands outside his modest home at 801 Railroad Avenue in Asbury Park, New Jersey (circa 1926).

(1860), fighting in the Boer War (1880–1881), and the Boxer Rebellion (1899–1901).

Some months earlier Dr. Osbaldeston had written to the War Office in London, requesting a veteran's pension. In reply the War Office asked him to provide documentation of his military service. When Dr. Osbaldeston complained to a friend about the matter, the friend thought it would make an interesting news story and arranged to have a photographer take the old doctor's picture. The photographer, sympathetic to the aged veteran's plight, contacted a New York newspaper.[5] A brief news item with photo appeared about the man believed to be the oldest surviving veteran of the Crimean conflict. Numerous other papers followed in carrying the captioned photograph.

Meanwhile, in Binghamton, New York, S. Foster Black, who had never fully retired from law enforcement, picked up a copy of the *Sun* newspaper and saw the photograph and its caption. A distinguished Civil War veteran who had served in the Twenty-Seventh New York Volunteer Infantry, Black was known for his sharp memory.[6] He was well respected in Broome County for his fifty-plus years of service in law enforcement and service as the president of the Broome County Veterans Association. He had also worked as a private detective and US marshal. During the Civil War, he had been captured by Confederate forces in the Battle of Petersburg, Virginia, and held at the infamous Andersonville Prison in Georgia.[7]

Although forty-five years had passed since the arrest, Black was certain from the photo that he had found the man who, in 1880, had stolen a horse and carriage, escaped from the Broome County Jail, and fled a second time after being rearrested. Surely the humiliation of losing his prisoner twice created an indelible memory of the face of a man who went by the names of E. T. O'Shaughnessy and Edward Turner.

The horse and rig, belonging to Dr. Edwin Ford of Binghamton, was stolen on October 30, 1880, from a nearby stable.[8] Undersheriff Black was assigned to the case. O'Shaughnessy/Turner was arrested on November 6 in Utica, New York, while driving the rig into a livery stable and taken back to Binghamton, where he was arraigned and jailed for the theft. The horse and rig were valued at $200, and thus,

O'Shaughnessy/Turner was charged with grand larceny. He was held in Broome County Jail while awaiting trial.

On December 4, 1880, Black went to New York City on business. In the early morning hours of December 6, O'Shaughnessy/Turner managed to saw through bars of the door to his cell, saw the hasp off another door, and make his way to the jail yard with cellmate Timothy Ahern. From there the pair scaled a high wall to freedom.[9]

Left behind in the empty cell in the Broome County Jail was a long letter simply signed "A Sinner." The letter writer began by professing a love of liberty as the reason for fleeing. It read in part, "Under every circumstance happiness has been long a stranger to me. I have suffered terribly in mind and body and stand this hour a completely ruined man in wealth and reputation. I am heartily sorry for any wrong that I may have thoughtlessly done any one." The letter went on, "I have said that I am not the actual guilty party. I told the police of a younger erring brother, who brought this, as before, trouble on members of his indulgent family."

The letter writer closed with, "I may leave my place without legal authority—if so fortunate. Let me here tender my best thanks to the sheriff and others for their care of me and kindness toward myself and family, and in conclusion I apologize for taking leave in this rude manner. Reward me with your indifferences, pray my very bitter prosecutors to exercise a trifle of the milk of human kindness and that charity towards their fellow men, which so well graced the character of the Great Master whom those profess to serve and whose sovereignty they proclaim as influenced by you. You have all my parting blessings."[10]

When Black returned on Monday morning, he discovered the jailbreak. Not to be outdone, the deputy sheriff sent out circulars with descriptions of both escapees to law enforcement in the surrounding area and offered a reward of one hundred dollars for the capture of either man.[11]

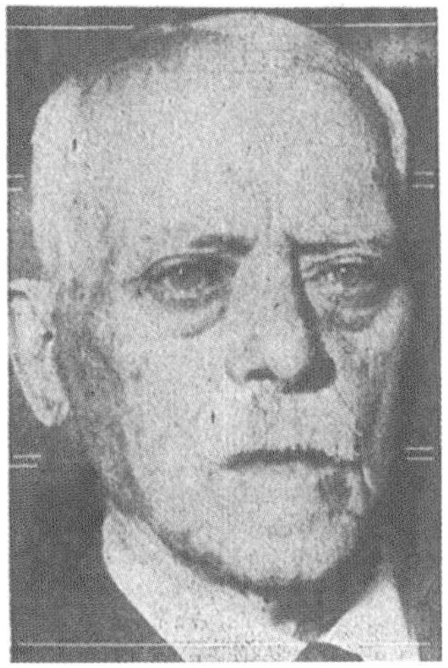

Broome County, New York, Deputy Sheriff S. Foster Black

Six days later Black heard from detective George Brown that officers had arrested the pair at a farmhouse near Scranton, Pennsylvania. In seeking shelter they had told the farmer they were hunters.

O'Shaughnessy/Turner and Ahern were taken to the Forest Hotel in Scranton and held there while waiting to be transported by a morning train to Binghamton.[12] About 10:00 p.m., as one officer stood guard over Ahern, O'Shaughnessy/Turner asked to use the washroom. Detective Brown accompanied his prisoner into the lavatory. Suddenly, O'Shaughnessy/Turner opened a ground-floor window, jumped out, and disappeared into the night.[13] Although a search was immediately conducted, O'Shaughnessy/Turner was not found. On January 7, 1881, O'Shaughnessy/Turner was indicted in absentia in Broome County on the added charge of jail breaking.[14]

Years went by before Black heard anything more about O'Shaughnessy/Turner. In January 1897, the district attorney in Malone, New York, wrote to Black asking him if O'Shaughnessy was still wanted in Binghamton as he was being held in Malone on a new charge.[15] Black made a beeline for Malone, only to arrive there and learn that O'Shaughnessy/Turner had posted $700 bail on a shoplifting charge and skipped town. Foolishly, the Malone district attorney had asked O'Shaughnessy/Turner how he would like to return to Binghamton.[16] Again, Black was left empty-handed.

Thus, convinced that the Crimean War veteran calling himself Dr. Edwin T. Osbaldeston of Asbury Park was indeed the horse thief and escaped prisoner O'Shaughnessy/Turner, Black went to the current sheriff of Broome County, Charles Watson, and district attorney Urbane C. Lyon with the news item and firm assertion that at last he had found his man.[17] Some concern was expressed over issuing a warrant given the advanced age of the veteran, the possibility that Black might have the wrong man, and the amount of time that had passed since the charges were filed.

Black insisted that he had the right man and that his age didn't matter. He asserted that the law had been broken and the guilty party must be brought to justice. Furthermore, Black felt that an example should be made of Dr. Osbaldeston so others would not think they could run from justice.[18] Clearly, the arrest of the old doctor was a personal matter for Black. "I want to show people around here that Foster Black never misses his man," he said.[19] After a search of old records, Lyon issued a bench warrant for the arrest of Dr. Osbaldeston on the charge of escaping jail. The statute of limitations on the theft charge had run out, and all of the witnesses were deceased. However, the statute did not apply to jail breaking.[20]

Black and Broome County deputy sheriff W. Ray Elwood took a train to Asbury Park. Arriving in the city at 7:00 p.m. on Friday, they went directly to the Asbury Park police headquarters and presented the warrant to the desk sergeant on duty. At first the desk sergeant was reluctant to act given that forty-five years had passed. Further, he felt an arrest could wait until the next day when a judge would be available. Black responded that he had been waiting forty-five years and would not wait another day longer.[21] With Black and Elwood in tow, a patrolman was assigned to go over to the house on Railroad Avenue to make the arrest. Dr. Osbaldeston was taken into custody and spent the night in the Asbury Park lockup with several miscreants. The next step for the Broome County prosecutor would be to seek extradition to New York. That would not be so simple.

The following morning Dr. Osbaldeston was arraigned and, with great indignation, pled not guilty. His attorney, Charles E. Cook, secured his release. Dr. Osbaldeston was to remain in the custody of his attorney for thirty days pending extradition.[22] Word of Dr. Osbaldeston's arrest spread quickly. The aged doctor would later state that he had been "bad for two days, down on my back, and I was undressed when they came. Pushed right in. I never lock my door. Often folks come in on me that way to bring a gift or say hello."[23] Dr. Osbaldeston went on, "They humbugged me into that cell. I demanded to see the chief of police. They said, 'Right down here, come on.' And when I looked ahead I heard a click and was locked up. Well, it's hard on old bones to be in a cage without a blanket."[24]

Edwin T. Osbaldeston was well known in the seaside community for his attention-getting antics. He was an affable fellow and a teller of big tales. He embarrassed his adult children when they visited by picking up discarded cigar butts on the street and smoking the remains.[25] He made little gardens for neighborhood children who liked to come by his house and sit on his lap.[26] Others who had been patients of long standing knew Dr. Osbaldeston for the school of scientific massage he had founded in New York City.

He was known for walking about town with a gnarled hickory stick, wearing a Crimean War

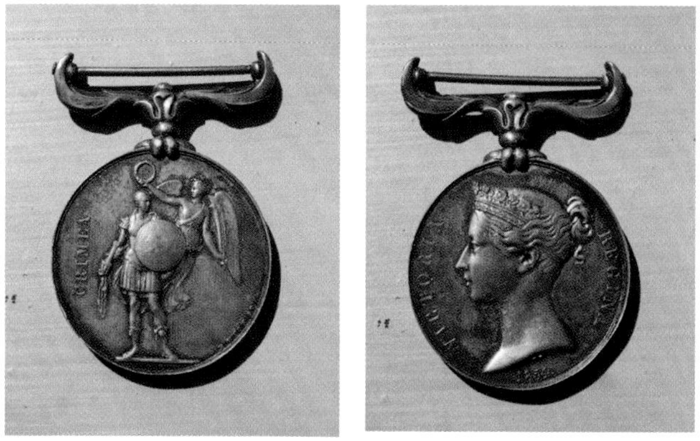

The reverse and obverse of the Crimean War medal that Dr. Osbaldeston wore for many years

medal on his chest. By some he was considered a town character who had fought in many wars and even been a part of the famous rescue party that went in search of members of the Burke and Wills Expedition that was lost while crossing the Australian bush country.[27] [28] He regaled listeners with stories of fighting in the Crimea, being wounded in the Battle of Alma, and witnessing the Charge of the Light Brigade. "That was a real war, boys," he said of the Crimean War. "This last war [World War I] which you hear so much about nowadays was a war of cowards. Everybody hid and kept under cover. We fought out in the open. We rode 'em down wherever we saw 'em," Osbaldeston said.[29]

He had vacationed in Asbury Park for many summers prior to moving there in 1919. At first he stayed at the New Tenney Hotel on Grand Avenue. When rates increased he moved to the one-room house on Railroad Avenue.[30] Some would recall a visit in 1920 by the Reverend Donald Stewart. Reverend Stewart had come to the New Tenney to ask Dr. Osbaldeston for his blessing to marry his oldest daughter Ethel. According to reports, a stormy session ensued, and the doctor called Stewart a "damned, swindling rascal" and chased him out of the hotel at gunpoint.[31] It turned out that Dr. Osbaldeston was right about Stewart. Ethel married him that year, and two years later Reverend Stewart was arrested for bigamy in Los Angeles. Reverend Stewart met women through the Temperance Movement, married them, and ran off with their money. He reportedly had wives in Indianapolis, Detroit, Boston, and New York.[32] Stewart's arrest in 1922 was reported in the *Asbury Park Evening Press* complete with mention of the 1920 confrontation he had with his future father-in-law.[33]

When word got around that Dr. Osbaldeston might be extradited to New York, there was an immediate outcry. With the support of local residents, J. Lyle Kinmouth, publisher of the *Asbury Park Evening Press*, launched a drive against extradition and petitioned New Jersey governor Harry A. Moore to deny the request.[34] Kinmouth was joined by Asbury Park mayor Clarence F. Hetrick, who declared the arrest and possible extradition "an outrage." Hetrick vowed to enlist civic groups to petition for a denial of extradition. The mayor issued a statement that said in part, "Up in Binghamton there are probably scores of serious criminal cases unsolved . . . yet this deputy sheriff and his district attorney are expending their valuable energy to bring a harmless and very lovable old man of ninety-three to the bar of justice. It is contemptible!"[35]

Shortly after his arrest, the Asbury Park City Commission approved a resolution condemning the action of New York authorities in regard to Dr. Osbaldeston by causing him an "unpleasant notoriety."[36] The community uproar was so great that the Asbury Park police chief said the old doctor should not have been jailed and shifted the blame to the desk sergeant who took the complaint.[37] Even the *New York Times* weighed in with an editorial on April 1, opining that the matter should be forgotten as it would be next to impossible to extradite "the ancient doctor."[38] There was outrage in Broome County, as well. The Binghamton mayor criticized Black and District Attorney Lyon for pursuing this case and felt the arrest was more of a personal matter for Black.[39] Under public pressure, Lyon backpedaled a bit at having issued the warrant but claimed it was his duty to do so.[40]

Back at 801 Railroad Avenue, Dr. Osbaldeston was steadfastly denying the charge to all who would listen. He said he had traveled the world over but had never been to Binghamton and never met Deputy Sheriff Black.[41] Dr. Osbaldeston claimed that it was a case of mistaken identity and that the sheriff had confused him with a wayward half brother who looked like him.[42] He scoffed at Black's assertion that O'Shaughnessy/Turner was Osbaldeston because they both had British accents, sarcastically noting that of course Englishmen have English accents. His alibi was that he was miles away in a suite of offices at Eighty-First Street and Broadway in Manhattan, practicing medicine when the crime was committed, but also said that he was traveling in the Adirondacks.[43]

As for Black, Dr. Osbaldeston had many choice comments. To a *New York Times* reporter, he commented that Black may be younger than he but he looks older. "Let him keep up his dastardly joke and I'll knock the lights out of him," he declared. "I could do it, too!" he said for added measure.[44] To the same reporter he claimed to have no hatred for Black. "He is too old to have any sense."[45] Black's actual age, which went uncorrected in news accounts throughout most of the ordeal, was eighty-two.

In his indignation on being arrested, Dr. Osbaldeston wanted to assure people that he was a man of high character and breeding. His credentials included graduating from the Royal Military Academy at Cheltenham, England. He said his great-grandfather was Admiral Charles Pye Turner of the British Navy and his father was the Earl of Onslow.[46] The doctor studied medicine for four years and was a physician for the British government and in private practice. He also had been a ship's surgeon and physical training instructor and had practiced medicine in Australia and New Zealand.[47] His patients had included the Rockefellers, Vanderbilts,[48] President Ulysses S. Grant, and even Oscar Wilde.[49]

> ***"My escutcheon has been marred by the charges brought against it by this gang up in Binghamton. I do not believe that they should be permitted to go unscathed. The charges against me are nebulous and entirely unfounded."***
>
> **— Edwin Turner Osbaldeston**

Public opinion was running high in favor of Dr. Osbaldeston. Letters and telegrams streamed into his one-room home that he referred to as his "den." People came by to offer encouragement and to pledge their support. To shield him from the media and scores of visitors, he was invited to stay at the city hospital for a few days, a local hotel offered to put him up, and his attorney tried to persuade him to relocate to a private home in nearby Ocean Grove.[50] Dr. Osbaldeston declined the offers, stating that an old soldier never retreats.

New Jersey Governor Moore acted quickly, announcing on Monday, March 29 that he would not honor a request by New York authorities to extradite Dr. Osbaldeston. The governor issued a statement that said, "I will not sign extradition papers for this man if such a request is made. If this crime was committed forty-five years ago it is time to forget it. I understand that Dr. Osbaldeston's life in Asbury Park has been exemplary and there is no reason why any action should be taken against him. There is another phase of the case, too, and that is the trip and ordeal he would undergo. It would probably mean his death."[51]

In Binghamton there was still talk of filing an extradition request. Deputy Sheriff Black hadn't changed his mind about bringing the escapee to justice. He said, "I don't care if this man never serves a day."[52] He just wanted him held accountable. When Governor Moore was informed that Broome County officials would continue to fight to have Dr. Osbaldeston extradited, Moore was quoted in the *New York Times* as saying, "If it becomes necessary I will throw all the legal machinery of the State into the fight to keep Dr. Osbaldeston in New Jersey."[53]

Naturally, reporters turned their attention to New York governor Alfred E. Smith. Governor Smith, who would become the Democratic Party's nominee for president in 1928, was silent on the matter. It was reported unofficially that governor Smith dismissed the idea.[54] On April 1, 1926, District Attorney Lyon said he wouldn't have time to file the extradition papers for at least a week.[55] Nine days later Lyon called attorney Charles Cook with an offer to drop the indictments. This would occur if his client would sign a release absolving Deputy Sheriff Black and all other law officers of Binghamton and Broome County of liability.[56]

Dr. Osbaldeston responded to the offer in an interview he gave to the *Asbury Park Evening Press* on the morning of Monday, April 12. "My escutcheon has been marred by the charges brought against it by this gang up in Binghamton. I do not believe that they should be permitted to go unscathed," he said as he considered filing a lawsuit. "The charges against me are nebulous and entirely unfounded. This Deputy Sheriff Black who started all the rumpus realizes now . . . that it isn't so easy to substantiate charges as it is to make them. Everyone who knows me knows that I am a man who has never committed a dishonest act in my life. I have sought to do charitable acts. I have had the interest of others paramount in my mind all the days of my life."[57]

The civil action would be based on false arrest, libel, and defamation of character. "The authorities up there in Broome County are beginning to realize that the unjust charges they brought against me may get them into very serious trouble," Dr. Osbaldeston said. "My record as a soldier and a gentleman has remained untarnished through my entire life. The whole gang up in Binghamton seem to be getting nervous." He and attorney Cook discussed seeking $500,000 in damages.[58]

Could Dr. Osbaldeston win a civil suit against the Binghamton officials? In the court of public opinion, the answer would be most certainly. The public, media, and elected officials had been willing to overlook holes and contradictions in Dr. Osbaldeston's stories since coming under the media spotlight. For example, in interviews the aged doctor variously had said it was a younger brother, half brother, kin, and then a nephew who stole the horse and buggy.[59] His alibi had two versions as to his whereabouts. Several reporters interpreted the note left in the Broome County Jail as proof that it was a younger brother who was the culprit rather than proof that Osbaldeston had been in Binghamton.[60]

When his arrest for shoplifting in Malone, New York, in November 1896 came to light several days after the initial story broke on the forty-five-year-old charge, Dr. Osbaldeston again claimed it was the deed of his wayward brother. But as more details came out about that arrest and his life in Malone, he dismissed that incident as covering for his secretary who had stolen the goods.[61] He did admit to jumping bail in Malone, however.[62]

The public and media readily believed he had fought in the Crimean War, the Boer War in South Africa, and the Boxer Rebellion in China. They believed he had marched with Garibaldi in the struggle for the unification of Italy and had been part of a rescue mission in Australian bush country. They also accepted his explanation of the mysterious disappearance of his first wife in Australia and the killing of two men in duels of honor in Germany in 1902. Of his first wife he claimed that kangaroos had taken her.[63] The duels of honor involved defending himself when his secretary embezzled $5,000 from his practice and ran off to Germany. The (unidentified) man who she was with said he would kill Osbaldeston if he came looking for her. Dr. Osbaldeston recalled that they taunted him by claiming that Americans cannot fight. He said he laid them out in ten minutes, shooting the first right through the heart.[64]

So charismatic and colorful was the doctor that the stories were rarely questioned and the discrepancies were brushed aside. Even the venerable *New York Times* took a charitable stance, ending its editorial on the matter with "Whether his tales owe a little to imagination is a question nobody seems inclined to press. There is no particular reason for doubting any of them, for what couldn't happen in ninety-three years to an adventurous person?"[65]

As the media attention began to fade and with firm assurances from Governor Moore that extradition would not take place, a sign appeared in the window of 801 Railroad Avenue. Written on a piece of cardboard were the words, "All's Well."[66]

In a telling footnote, none of Dr. Osbaldeston's surviving six children (of ten) were heard from during the debacle. His daughters Normandie and Geneva lived about sixty miles away—Normandie Siver in New Milford, New Jersey, and Geneva Miller in upper Manhattan. Frederick Miller, Geneva's husband, told reporters that his wife had no plans to go to Asbury Park. "He is well able to take care of himself," Miller said.[67]

NOTES

1. "Former Sheriff Black Causes Arrest for 45-Year-Old Crime," *Binghamton Press* (NY), 27 March 1926, p. 5.
2. "All Other Joys Tasted, Doctor Is Now Movie Actor," *Asbury Park Evening Press* (NJ), 1 April 1926, p. 1.
3. "Veteran Warrior," *Sun* (Binghamton, NY), 24 March 1926, p. 13.
4. "Doctor, 93, to Fight Extradition as Thief," *New York Times*, 29 March 1926, p. 1.
5. "All Other Joys Tasted, Doctor Is Now Movie Actor," *Asbury Park Evening Press* (NJ), 1 April 1926, p. 1.
6. "Sheriff Noted for Memory," *New York Times*, 28 March 1926, p. 12.
7. "S. Foster Black 83 Years Old Sunday," *Binghamton Press* (NY), 21 October 1926, p. 1.
8. "New Jersey Governor to Deny Extradition of Black's Prisoner," *Binghamton Press* (NY), 29 March 1926, p. 1.
9. "Black Insists That Doctor Is Thief Who Escaped Him in 1880," *Oneonta Daily Star* (NY), 29 March 1926, p. 1.
10. "Note Left in Cell Voices the Plea of Osbaldeston," *Asbury Park Evening Press* (NJ), 3 April 1926, p. 1.
11. "Broke Jail. Successful Escape of Two Jail Birds—They Saw Their Way through Iron Bars Undiscovered—Climb a Tree and Scale the Jail Yard Wall—'Gone Where the Woodbine Twineth'—One Hundred Dollars Reward for the Capture of Either of Them," *Broome Republican* (Binghamton, NY), 8 December 1880, p. 8, col. 2.
12. "The Jail Breakers Caught. A Dispatch Announcing Their Arrest at Scranton," *Broome Republican* (Binghamton, NY), 15 December 1880, p. 8, col. 2.
13. Ibid.
14. "Black Wants to Show People He Never Fails to Get Man," *Oneonta Daily Star* (NY), 30 March 1926, p. 1.

15. "New Jersey Governor to Deny Extradition of Black's Prisoner," *Binghamton Press* (NY), 29 March 1926, p. 1.
16. Ibid.
17. "Former Sheriff Black Causes Arrest for 45-Year-Old Crime," *Binghamton Press* (NY), 27 March 1926, p. 5.
18. "Aged Doctor Held for Ancient Crime is Hotly Defended," *Daily Sentinel* (Rome, NY), 29 March 1926, p. 2.
19. "Black Wants to Show People He Never Fails to Get Man," *Oneonta Daily Star* (NY), 30 March 1926, p. 1.
20. "Former Sheriff Black Causes Arrest for 45-Year-Old Crime," *Binghamton Press* (NY), 27 March 1926, p. 5.
21. "Aged Doctor Held for Ancient Crime Is Hotly Defended," *Daily Sentinel* (Rome, NY), 29 March 1926, p. 2.
22. "Doctor, 93, Seized as Robber of 1881," *New York Times*, 28 March 1926, p. 1.
23. "Aged Doctor Held," *Daily Sentinel* (Rome, NY), 29 March 1926, p. 2.
24. Ibid.
25. Kenneth L. Siver, personal communication to author.
26. "Doctor, 93, Seized as Robber of 1881," *New York Times*, 28 March 1926, p. 1.
27. "Doctor, 93, to Fight Extradition as Thief," *New York Times,* 29 March 1926, p. 1.
28. "New Jersey Governor to Deny Extradition of Black's Prisoner," *Binghamton Press* (NY), 29 March 1926, p. 1.
29. "Doctor, 93, to Fight Extradition as Thief," *New York Times,* 29 March 1926, p. 1.
30. "Nonagenarian Doctor Tells Many Stories of an Adventuresome Life," *Binghamton Press* (NY), 30 March 1926, p. 5.
31. "Dr. Osbaldeston's Cremation Wish to Be Carried Out," *Asbury Park Evening Press* (NJ), 19 February 1929, p. 1.
32. "Reformer Is Jailed; Stewart Held as Bigamist," *Los Angeles Times*, 21 June 1922, sec. 1, p. 1.
33. "Crimean Hero's Daughter Is Held with Bigamist," *Asbury Park Evening Press* (NJ), 22 June 1922, p. 1.
34. "Doctor, 93, Denies Charge of Horse Theft 46 Years Ago; His Accuser Is 91," *Syracuse Herald* (NY), 28 March 1926, p. 12.
35. "Hundreds Offer Aid to Accused Doctor," *New York Times*, 31 March 1926, p. 3.
36. "Nonagenarian Doctor Tells Many Stories of Adventuresome Life," *Binghamton Press* (NY), 30 March 1926, p. 5.
37. "New Jersey Governor to Deny Extradition of Black's Prisoner," *Binghamton Press* (NY), 29 March 1926, p. 1.
38. "Much Fame and No Peril," *New York Times*, 1 April 1926, p. 24.
39. "Doctor, 93, Seized as Robber of 1881," *New York Times*, 28 March 1926, p. 1.
40. "New Jersey Governor to Deny Extradition of Black's Prisoner," *Binghamton Press* (NY), 29 March 1926, p. 1.
41. "Doctor, 93, Denies Charge of Horse Theft 46 Years Ago; His Accuser Is 91," *Syracuse Herald* (NY), 28 March 1926, p. 1.
42. "Black Insists That Doctor Is Thief Who Escaped Him in 1880," *Oneonta Daily Star* (NY), 29 March 1926, p. 1.
43. "Doctor, 93, to Fight Extradition as Thief," *New York Times,* 29 March 1926, p. 1.
44. "Hundreds Offer Aid to Accused Doctor," *New York Times*, 31 March 1926, p. 3.
45. Ibid.
46. "Doctor, 93, Seized as Robber of 1881," *New York Times,* 28 March 1926, p. 1.
47. "Doctor, 93, Denies Charge of Horse Theft 46 Years Ago; His Accuser Is 91," *Syracuse Herald* (NY), 28 March 1926, p. 1.
48. "Strain Telling Upon Old Crimean Veteran," *Asbury Park Evening Press* (NJ), 30 March 1926, p. 2.
49. "Doctor, 93, to Fight Extradition as Thief," *New York Times,* 29 March 1926, p. 1.
50. "Doctor Refuses to Retreat Under Fire," *Asbury Park Evening Press* (NJ), 31 March 1926, p. 1.
51. "New Jersey Backs Accused Doctor, 93," *New York Times*, 30 March 1926, p. 3.
52. "Black Wants to Show People He Never Fails to Get Man," *Oneonta Daily Star* (NY), 30 March 1926, p. 2.
53. "New Jersey Backs Accused Doctor, 93," *New York Times*, 30 March 1926, p. 3.
54. "Smith May Not Ask Extradition," *Asbury Park Evening Press* (NJ), 2 April 1926, p. 2.
55. Ibid.
56. "Overtures to End Osbaldeston Case," *Asbury Park Evening Press* (NJ), 12 April 1926, p. 1.
57. "Overtures to End Osbaldeston Case," *Asbury Park Evening Press* (NJ), 12 April 1926, p. 2.
58. "Osbaldeston To Sue Over Arrest as Thief," *New York Evening Post*, 12 April 1926.
59. "New Jersey Backs Accused Doctor, 93," *New York Times*, 30 March 1926, p. 3.
60. "Note Left in Cell Voices the Plea of Osbaldeston," *Asbury Park Evening Press* (NJ), 3 April 1926, p. 1.
61. "New Jersey Backs Accused Doctor, 93," *New York Times*, 30 March 1926, p. 3.
62. "Strain Telling upon Old Crimean Veteran," *Asbury Park Evening Press* (NJ), 30 March 1926, p. 1.
63. "Doctor, 93, to Fight Extradition as Thief," *New York Times,* 29 March 1926, p. 3.
64. "Strain Telling upon Old Crimean Veteran," *Asbury Park Evening Press* (NJ), 30 March 1926, p. 2.
65. "Much Fame and No Peril," *New York Times*, 1 April 1926, p. 24.
66. "Smith May Not Ask Extradition," *Asbury Park Evening Press* (NJ), 2 April 1926, p. 2.
67. "Daughter Here Is Married," *New York Times*, 30 March 1926, p. 3; *Asbury Park Evening Press* (NJ), 30 March 1926, p. 2.

CHAPTER TWO

The Master of Self-Promotion

Asbury Park flourished in the 1890s and after the turn of the century. Grand hotels were built and amusements were installed. In the summer hordes of visitors from northern New Jersey, Philadelphia, and New York City came to the seaside resort by train. It was estimated the summer population swelled to 200,000. By the 1920s a casino, theater, carousel, and convention hall had been added to the boardwalk.[1] The city became known as "the Jewel of the Jersey Shore."

Dr. Osbaldeston had been a summer visitor since 1905. Among his many activities in Asbury Park, he enjoyed going for long walks to the boardwalk, the municipal pier, and also to local cemeteries. Gregarious and friendly, Dr. Osbaldeston came to be known by residents of the resort community from his walks about town and the stories he told them when they stopped to chat.

The Osbaldestons lived in New York City for many years. As Dr. Osbaldeston's practice and training school grew, he became comfortable enough to afford to take leave of the city for what might be called "working vacations." Wealthy New Yorkers frequented resorts during the summer months. Dr. Osbaldeston went where the money went.

For a number of summers, he packed up his family and headed to resort towns in Upstate New York to escape the noise, heat, and pollution of the city. Some summers he took his wife Alice Agnes and children to stay in Newport, Rhode Island.

He discontinued frequenting upstate resorts and Newport after he discovered Malone, New York. He originally went there to treat a patient but became involved in the town and bought a summer cabin on a lake nearby. A few years later, he was forced to abandon Malone after he and an associate became ensnarled in difficulties.

Instead, it was Asbury Park that became his summer haunt and then his year-round home. Ever the extrovert and the performer, he jumped into community activities. In the 1905 Asbury Park Summer Festival, he appeared as the court jester. The festival also included a "baby parade," an annual event since 1890, in which Dr. Osbaldeston was a participant. His role in the festival was reported in the *Philadelphia Inquirer* and subsequently carried in other newspapers. (As a three-year-old, grandson Kenneth Siver appeared in the 1912 baby parade.)

At left: The Asbury Park, New Jersey Boardwalk in 1905

Below: Edwin participated in the 1905 Asbury Park baby parade.

Postcards reprinted with permission of Jack D. Mount, Antique American Postcards, www.nostalgia.esmartkid.com

Edwin loved to dress up. In this photo (circa 1890s) Edwin is dressed in a naval uniform. He frequently looked for opportunities to appear in front of an audience.

> **Queen's Reception To-night.**
> Following the announcement of the Court Jester, Dr. E. J. Osbaldeston, of New York, merry maids and little men from Sunset Hall, Columbia Hotel, Lafayette, St. Charles, Coleman House, Monmouth, Brunswick, West End and Plaza trooped in and rendered a program of songs and dancing. . . .[2]

News of his appearance in the parade also appeared in a Malone, New York newspaper. "Among the photographs of some prominent figures in the Asbury Park baby parade," the *Malone Palladium* reported, "is one of a gentleman well, if not favorably, known in Malone."[3]

By the decade of the 1910s, Dr. Osbaldeston fought valiantly to remain relevant and respected. He had entered the stage in life where he was transitioning from older to elderly. Age was undermining his self-worth, and he pushed hard against it. He had been a man who loved adventure. Starting in his late teens, he began a life of travel, never staying in one place for long, and had sailed around the world several times. Few of his contemporaries had traveled as extensively as he had or seen as much of the world.

Family and age slowed his wanderlust. New York City and Asbury Park were the two places he had come to live the longest. His last long-distance journey took place in May and June of 1910. He sailed to England to see family, visiting his older brother Frederick Turner and nephew Sydney in Southhampton.

As much as he loved adventure, Dr. Osbaldeston loved the spotlight more. He wanted—no, he *needed*—to be viewed as a person of status and accomplishment. A master of self-promotion, Dr. Osbaldeston reported his presence to newspaper reporters and editors everywhere he went. Often his first stop upon arrival in a new town was at the local newspaper office. He regularly used newspapers to advertise his talents and services. He regaled all who would listen with his experience, credentials, and expertise. He carried written testimonials of his accomplishments and skills with him. He unabashedly dropped the names of prominent and famous persons whom he had met and/or treated.

For a number of years Edwin stayed at the New Tenney Hotel in Asbury Park. He later moved to Railroad Avenue when he could no longer afford the hotel.

Although his globe-trotting days were behind him, he continued his habit of seeking out reporters. In August 1917, accompanied by two of his daughters, Dr. Osbaldeston visited Newport, Rhode Island.[4] He had previously spent summers there in the 1880s. He made sure the local newspaper was aware of his arrival. The *Newport Journal and Weekly News* reported on his visit, complete with untruths, career highlights, and the names of Newportonians that he had treated.

> Among the many visitors to Newport this summer is one who half a century ago was a familiar figure on the streets, for several years a resident and for many summers a habitué of the old Ocean House. He is Dr. Edwin Osbaldeston of New York. Now 84 years, but still vigorous and capable of walking many miles a day; with clear eyes, able to read newspaper print without glasses; and generally a robust, stirring

The 1914 edition of Empire State Notables *listed Edwin under the heading of "Physicians & Surgeons."*

> man. He has been in practice in this country since 1867. . . .[5]

As in this case, frequently reporters and editors found Edwin charming and interesting and played into his hands with glowing reports.

He found other media outlets for self-promotion as well. The 1908–1909 edition of the vanity publication *Who's Who in New York* listed Dr. Osbaldeston as among the elite of the city. This two-hundred-word biography credited him with introducing scientific massage and home medicogymnastics to the United States.

The account of his life listed his parents, wife, and children. Under education it stated that he was a graduate of Gower Street University Hospital in London and earned an MD degree from University of Carlton, Melbourne, Australia. Inclusions under military service noted that he had been an officer in Garibaldi's army in Italy and a member of a search party in the Australian bush country, but interestingly, it failed to mention his service in the Crimean War. However, in this same section it stated, "Served for a short time in the U. S. Secret Civil Service during the Civil War at Bermuda and at London, England."[6]

The annual *New York City Directory* listed him as a physician. He appeared in the 1914 edition of *Empire State Notables*, under the heading of "Physicians & Surgeons." His name was listed for many years in the *Medical Directory of the City of New York* and in the *American Medical Directory: A Register of Legally Qualified Physicians of the United States* published by the American Medical Association. In the latter it stated that Edwin was not practicing medicine but had earned his degree in 1862 in Australia.[7]

As he was always ready to talk of his military record, World War I provided Dr. Osbaldeston with a new platform. The entry of the United States into the war in 1917 saw patriotism on the rise. In October that year, a procession was staged on New

Edwin proudly displayed his family crest and had stamps made with his photograph.

York's famous Fifth Avenue to promote the war effort. Dr. Osbaldeston commanded a leading role. He marched with a squad of Red Cross nurses dressed in white uniforms. The nurses carried a banner reading "Red Cross Nurses to Service in Rough Places in Rough Weather." Dr. Osbaldeston walked in front, wearing white flannels, a Red Cross armband, and his Crimean War medal. Alongside was Tristain, a German police dog that had seen service in France.

Naturally, Dr. Osbaldeston caught the eye of spectators. For those who inquired of his military service, he went into great detail about his combat experience in the Crimean War and marching with Garibaldi. He told reporters that he became friends with Florence Nightingale at the Barrack Hospital in Scutari (Istanbul), where she attended the Crimean War wounded. "I frequently walk five miles a day to keep limbered up," he proclaimed. "I am good enough to be of use in our present war, but cannot make our government think so."[8]

Having told the story so often of marching with Garibaldi in the struggle for the unification of Italy, he visited the Order of the Sons of Italy in Manhattan in June of 1918, where he gave a speech on his combat experience. Duly impressed, the organiza-

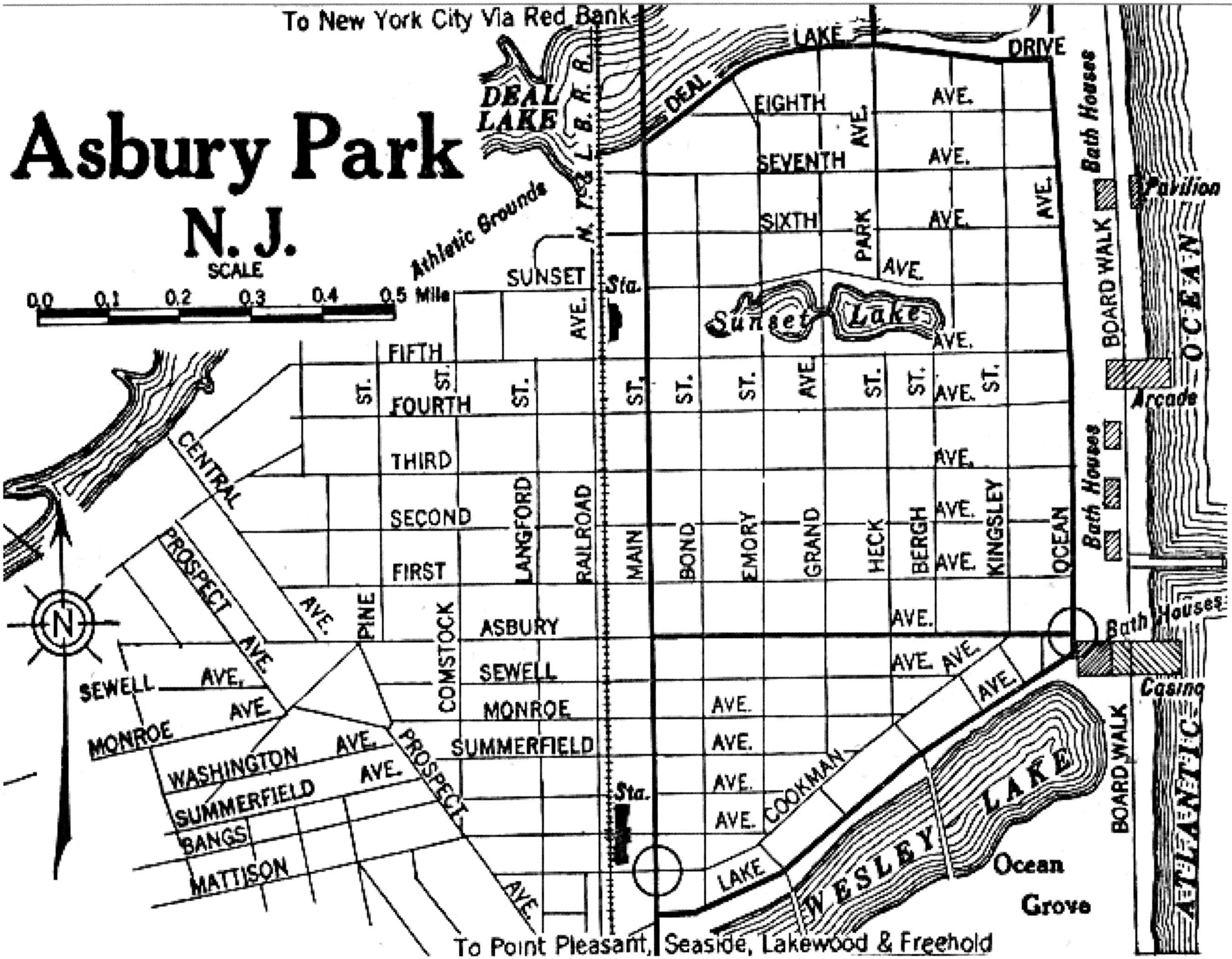

1920 map of Asbury Park, New Jersey

Edwin lived at 801 Railroad Avenue where it intersects with Asbury Avenue.

(www.lib.utwexas.edu/maps/historical/asbury_park_nj_1920.jpg)

tion's newsletter included an article on his presentation.[9]

As the 1910s drew to a close, Dr. Osbaldeston was separated from his wife, his contemporaries were dying off, and his children were grown and going about their lives. Edwin continued his fight to hold on to his dignity and self-respect. The Crimean War medal that he proudly wore served as a visual symbol that he indeed was somebody.

Although his clothing was dated and showed signs of wear, he remained well dressed and well mannered. The many acquaintances he made and the people he encountered on the streets of New York City and Asbury Park may have viewed him as a harmless eccentric or an entertaining character, but very few really knew much about him. Some sensed he was a lonely man in the sunset of his life and were protective on that basis alone. Many Asbury Park residents and a surprising number in the media bought into the image of the man he pretended to be. They wanted to believe he was who he said he was.

Through his engaging antics and frequent retelling of his adventures and military record, Dr. Osbaldeston had marketed an image for himself that gave him a protective following. His self-promotion and self-advertising had created a brand loyalty as if he were a favorite breakfast cereal or pack of smokes. The stories had been told so many times that they went unquestioned. Further, his age and transient past left little room for anyone to refute the image. On those occasions when that image came under attack, numerous persons rushed in to protect it. With the exception of his immediate family, no one fully knew the real Edwin Turner Osbaldeston in his naked totality.

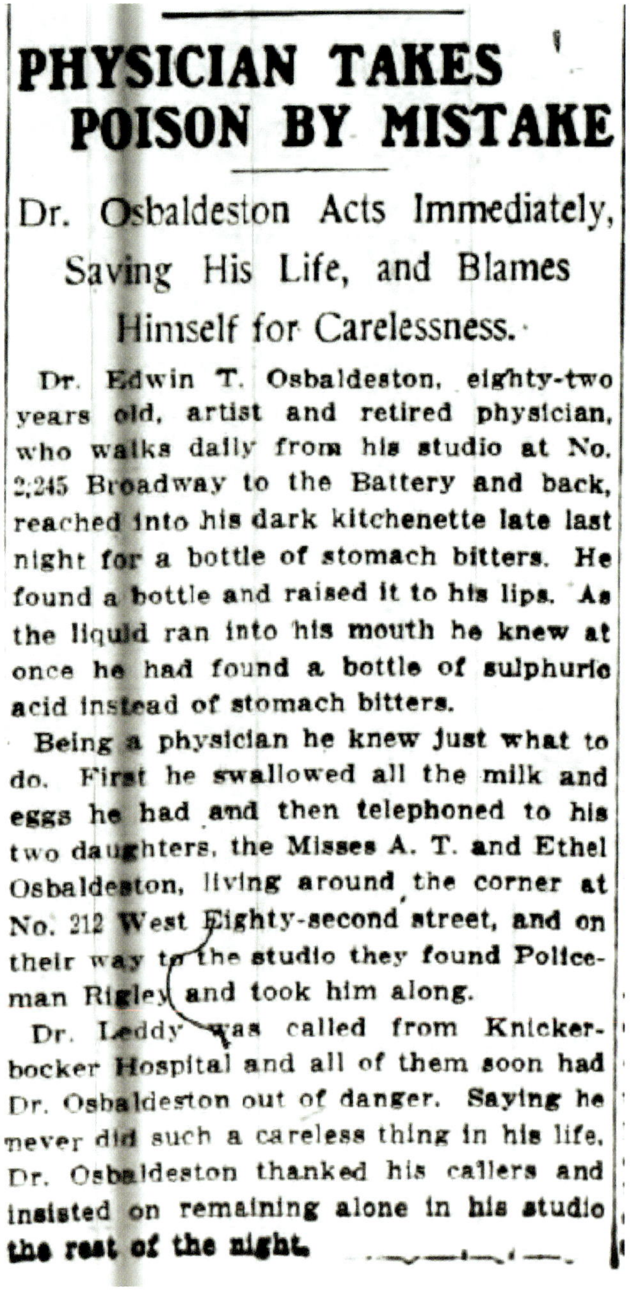

PHYSICIAN TAKES POISON BY MISTAKE

Dr. Osbaldeston Acts Immediately, Saving His Life, and Blames Himself for Carelessness.

Dr. Edwin T. Osbaldeston, eighty-two years old, artist and retired physician, who walks daily from his studio at No. 2,245 Broadway to the Battery and back, reached into his dark kitchenette late last night for a bottle of stomach bitters. He found a bottle and raised it to his lips. As the liquid ran into his mouth he knew at once he had found a bottle of sulphuric acid instead of stomach bitters.

Being a physician he knew just what to do. First he swallowed all the milk and eggs he had and then telephoned to his two daughters, the Misses A. T. and Ethel Osbaldeston, living around the corner at No. 212 West Eighty-second street, and on their way to the studio they found Policeman Rigley and took him along.

Dr. Leddy was called from Knickerbocker Hospital and all of them soon had Dr. Osbaldeston out of danger. Saying he never did such a careless thing in his life, Dr. Osbaldeston thanked his callers and insisted on remaining alone in his studio the rest of the night.

This article appeared on page 1 of the New York Herald *on April 18, 1916. It speaks to the celebrity following that Dr. Osbaldeston had. The status of his health was regularly reported upon by the New York newspapers and the* Asbury Park Evening Press.[10]

NOTES

1. http://en.wikipedia.org/wiki/Asbury_Park,_New_Jersey, accessed on 4 April 2014.
2. "Queen Titania Is Crowned at Asbury; Consort of Oberon Arrives in Magic City-by-the Sea, That Was En Fete for Her Coming—Picturesque Exercises," *Philadelphia Inquirer,* 29 August 1905, p. 4.
3. *Malone Palladium* (NY), 7 September 1905, p. 1, col. e.
4. "Lived Here 50 Years Ago; Dr. Osbaldeston, Once a Habitue of the Old Ocean House Returns," *Newport Journal and Weekly News* (RI), 24 August 1917.
5. Ibid.
6. *Who's Who in New York*, 1908–1909 ed., p. 202.
7. "Physicians of New York City," *American Medical Directory: A Register of Legally Qualified Physicians of the United States,* 3rd ed. (Chicago, IL: American Medical Association, 1912), p. 870.
8. "Fifth Avenue Sees the Red Cross Nurses March," *Evening Post* (New York, NY), 4 October 1917, p. 6.
9. "La visita di un veterano inglese agli uffici del nostro ordine," *Ordini figli d'Italia in America—Bollettino ufficiale* (New York, NY), 8 June 1918.
10. "Physican Takes Poison by Mistake," *New York Herald*, 18 April 1916, p. 1.

CHAPTER THREE

The Early Years ~ 1838–1858

At the time of his arrest in 1926, Edwin Turner Osbaldeston was actually eighty-seven years of age, not the ninety-three years that was widely reported. He may have grown up not knowing his birth date or his true age. He told reporters that he was born on December 27, 1832.[1] His actual birth date was July 11, 1838.[2] He came into the world on Gas Green (or Gas Light Green) off Gloucester Road in Cheltenham, Gloucestershire, England, under unusual circumstances. His life began as a lie to avoid family scandal.

His father, Josiah Scudder Osbaldeston, was baptized in 1797.[3] (The exact date of Josiah's birth is unknown.) As a young man, Josiah made his living as a glove cutter. Records show that he had had several run-ins with the law, having been arrested and fined for assault[4] and for vandalism.[5] Josiah married widow Mary Ann Lewis Turner, ten years his senior, in 1825 in Oxford.[6] Lewis Turner had been married to British Royal Navy lieutenant Charles Pye Turner.[7] There were two children from this marriage—Mary Ann Turner, born 1815,[8] and Charles Pye Turner Jr., born 1817.[9] Edwin would sometimes include the name Pye when giving his full name.

Josiah and Mary Ann Lewis Turner (the elder) had four children—Maria, baptized 1825; Henry William, baptized 1828; Bridget, born circa 1832; and Joseph, baptized 1835. By the time Joseph was born, the family had moved several times—from Woodstock to Witney to Oxford, all in Oxfordshire, and then from Oxford to Gloucester in Gloucestershire. Bridget was not the only addition to the

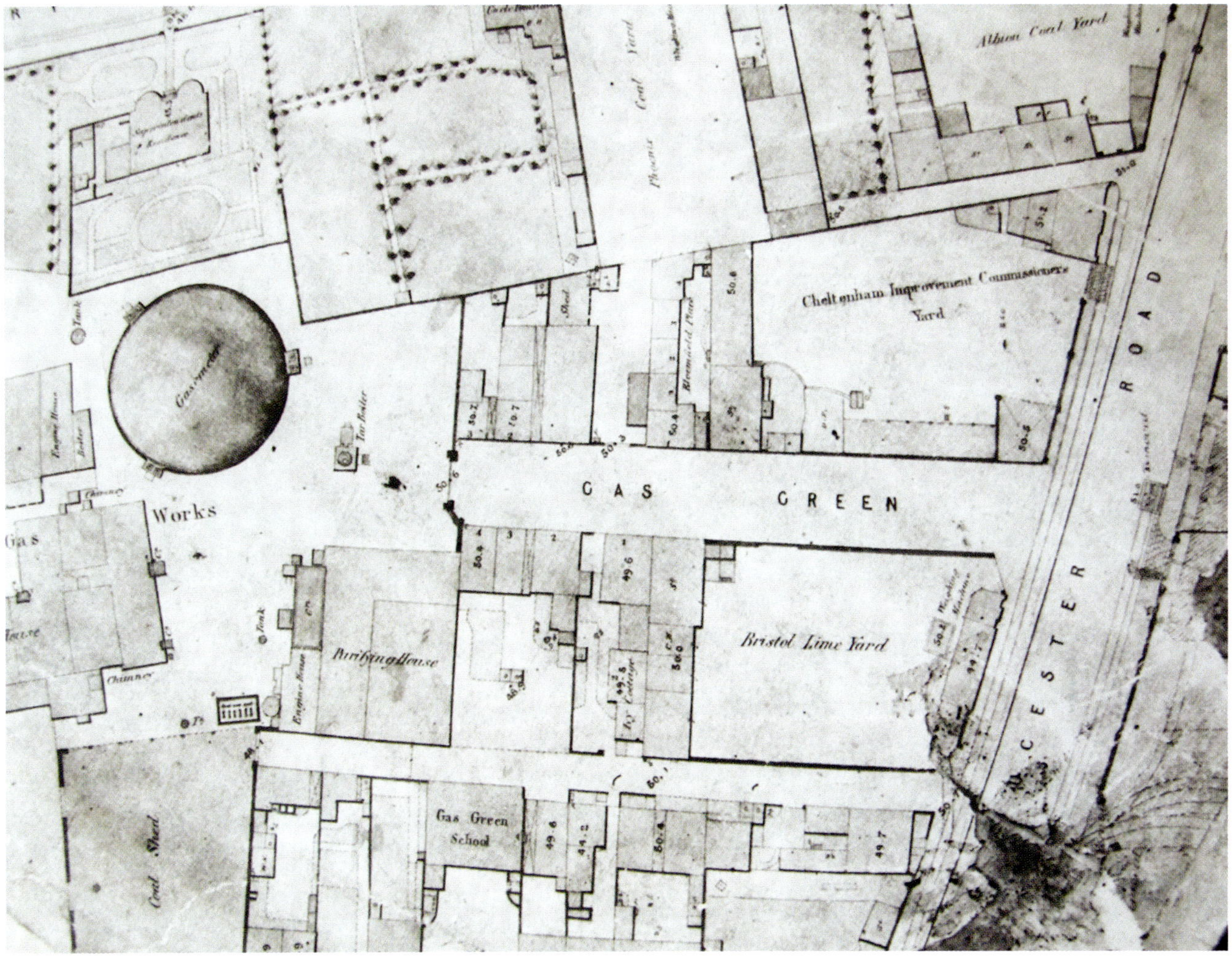

Detail from the plan of Cheltenham showing Gas Green (a.k.a. Gas Light Green) off Gloucester Road where Edwin was born and lived for approximately six years. (Board of Health, Sheet 28, 1852. Ref. No. PC767, Gloucestershire Archives, Gloucester, UK)

household in 1832. Seventeen-year-old Mary Ann Turner (the younger), daughter of Mary Ann the elder, gave birth to Frederick, who was fathered by Josiah. Frederick did not remain in the home as he was shunted off to be raised by relatives.[10] Frederick was christened at St. Thomas the Martyr Church in the historic Jericho neighborhood of Oxford. The parish register noted "son of Mary Ann." No father's name was given.[11]

At this time a child born out of wedlock was considered scandalous, bringing shame to the mother and "bastard" child. Illegitimate births represented only 6 percent of all live births in England in the mid-nineteenth century and dropped to 4 percent by the dawn of the twentieth century as societal condemnation increased.[12] Thus it was that the family sent Frederick to live with relatives. When Josiah's liaisons with his stepdaughter resumed (or if they ever stopped) is unclear. However, Mary Ann the younger gave birth to six more children fathered by Josiah—Edwin Turner (1838), Emma (circa 1841), Charles (circa 1844), Francis (circa 1849), Ann Maria (circa 1851), and Julian (1854). Their mother was also their stepsister.

Civil registration of births, marriages, and deaths had begun in England and Wales on July 1, 1837, a year before Edwin was born.[13] From the start, civil registrations were plagued by inaccurate and incomplete information. Illiteracy was partly the cause as well as a lack of standards for the data to be recorded. It was not uncommon to find in the census enumerators' books from 1841 to 1851 or 1851 to 1861 that people had not aged ten years in a decade.[14] (The accuracy and completeness of civil registries of births, deaths, and marriages improved in the later years of Victoria's reign, as did the census data.)

And so it was that Mary Ann the younger gave false statements to the registrar that went unchecked. She reported her son's name as Edwin Turner and that his father was Charles Pye Turner. She listed the father's occupation as bookbinder. A few years earlier, Josiah had become a hawker of books and now was a bookbinder. She repeated the same untruths when Edwin was baptized on December 30, 1838, in St. Mary's, the parish church in Cheltenham, Gloucestershire. St. Mary's register of baptisms listed his parents as Charles and Mary Ann Turner.[15] The baptismal records for Ann Maria and Julian also listed the father as Charles Turner.[16] Mary Ann was actually using the name of her own father, Charles Pye Turner, who had died on August 12, 1820.[17]

Edwin was baptized in St. Mary's Anglican church in Cheltenham, Gloucestershire on December 30, 1838.

Gas Light Green, also known as Lower Gas Green, was so named due to its close proximity to the gasworks on the outskirts of Cheltenham. Cheltenham was an elegant spa town in southwest England. The Turner-Osbaldeston home was in a working class neighborhood. Among their neighbors were laborers, a cordwainer (shoemaker), gardeners, smiths, publicans, laundresses, etc. Edwin recalls his family's home as "a large, old fashioned mansion laying back in the midst of an immense, lovely garden on Gloucester Road. The house of old Elizabethan style, [was] covered with ivy, [had] church-like windows, some with small, square panes of glass; some leaded in diamond shape. In the centre of the large windows . . . four of those in the dining room with its immense, old fashioned fireplace, [were] larger panes of glass bearing royal and family arms."[18] Edwin's description of this childhood home was most certainly exaggerated.

During the Victorian era (1837–1901), Great Britain was the wealthiest nation on earth. Yet a great number of the populace lived in poverty or near poverty. A very small percentage of the citizens controlled most of the nation's wealth. Seven thousand people owned 80 percent of the land in England and Wales.[19] Land and wealth were passed down from generation to generation with little chance for upward mobility for those in the labor class. Wages for unskilled and casual workers were generally very low. Tradesmen and artisans faired better.

The larger the family, the more likely there was insufficient income to provide food, clothing, and shelter. Spending money on drink or other pleasures could break a family financially.[20] Most working class families lived in cramped quarters. Children were expected to devote a good deal of time to household chores until they were old enough to go to work (at age twelve or thirteen). Most children were born at home rather than in hospitals. The rate of infant mortality was 25 to 28 percent. Many of the deaths were due to poor nutrition and hygiene and infectious diseases.[21]

People of the Victorian era lived a mostly unspoken double standard. In this age a premium was placed on respectability or the appearance of respectability. However, a class system thrived that divided the population, imposing cruel living conditions on those on the lowest end of the social spectrum. People were expected to "know their place."

Even in the working class, a social divide existed between the artisans and skilled laborers and the nonskilled.[22] The bar on social standards, decorum, and manners was raised. Sex was not to be discussed. Euphemisms replaced words for things that were considered "indelicate." Clothing was formal and the body was well covered, even in the privacy of one's home.

In family roles, fathers were encouraged to be authoritarian and unemotional, and mothers were to be submissive and frail. The father was to be obeyed and children not to be seen or heard. In the upper classes, children might rarely be seen by their parents as they were raised by nannies and sent to boarding schools. Corporal punishment of children in school or at home was acceptable. Respectable persons did not swear, drink, or gamble—at least not publicly.

The population of England and Wales nearly doubled during the Victorian era due to rising fertility rates, medical advances, and greater immigration. It was also a time of great change and rapid industrialization. The increase in population brought with it a rise in social ills, mainly tied to poverty. The masses of people looking for work drove down wages. Housing in cities was expensive, causing entire families to live in a single room. The moneyed class looked upon poverty as a crime and penalized those whose circumstances—be it poor health, lack of education, limited mental ability, misfortune, or just bad luck—meant they could not support themselves. A system of workhouses created by law in 1834 was expanded during the era. The workhouse, or poorhouse, in most cases made life more miserable for those who were sent to them.

What evolved during this period has been referred to as "the Victorian compromise"—a system of differing public and private behavior. The morals, values, and social standards espoused by the Victorians were more likely a reflection of the world that they would have liked to live in rather than the world they were in. To be sure, there were social reformers, but much of Victorian society looked the other way at the conditions that many of their countrymen were living under.

Edwin Turner grew up in this social environment. In an account that he wrote years later, Edwin spoke very fondly of his mother (Mary Ann Turner) and grandmother (Mary Ann Lewis Turner Osbaldeston). His recollections of childhood appear to be a look back at simpler times in his life, recalled with a good dose of nostalgia. Perhaps they were a reflection of the Victorian compromise. "Childhood with pleasant surroundings cannot be prolonged too much." In his journal Edwin wrote the following:

> As I pen these lines they call me a young gentleman now and my elder brother Fred a young man, and my then three-year-old darling sister Emma, a young lady. She was my constant playmate and companion and her joys and her sorrows were equally mine. A cross word or wrong done her by others of our playmates would drive me into a fury with them and I can well recall the many battles I had with others on her account. I used to love to see her getting her strings of pretty boots and shoes, and doll like hats and dresses. Whatever I had pretty or nice to eat . . . was considered by me as much hers as my own. We were inseparable in every thing even in our prayers as we knelt at the feet of Angel Mother or Grandmother at the diamond-shaped, glass leaded bedroom window with white curtain drawn on one side so that we could see the twinkling stars which we in our childish innocence thought were holes leading into heaven & the twinkling caused by angels passing in and out.
>
> It was considered by us a great thing to be allowed to sleep in Grandmother's bed with its elaborate canopy and tent like hangings, the whole standing on a one step, raised platform. Whenever it came my turn it was my pleasure to jump into bed before Grandmother and watch her take off the wonderful wardrobe women wore in those days. The white silk or satin cape like shawl, the dress with its high balloon like hip flounces and then the bustle, a kind of small pillow with strings to tie it round the small of the back. . . . Ah, to me the best article of all [was] the great white pocket with strings to tie it on with. I would keep my eye on that chiefly and just watch where it was hung, generally on a chair. But under the pillow it would go if she caught me watching.
>
> As soon as I noticed her asleep I would steal softly out of bed & having possessed myself of that coveted prize would push aside the window curtain a little so as to let in the moon's rays. Then sitting down upon the carpeted floor would satisfy my childish curiosity by overhauling its contents which were numerous—my much prized rubber ball, some of my best marbles that had been taken from me temporally because I had been naughty. . . . Sometimes Grandmother would wake up and catch the "young pirate" as she would afterwards describe my act to mother. I would leave the things as they were all scattered on the floor and by a gentle command hasten into bed and cuddle up to Grandma who would never rebuke me but ask if I did not think I was a rogue of a boy. My arms round her neck and a kiss & I was forgiven.
>
> But if I had tried that on with father, I would not have been able to sit down com-

fortably for a week no matter how much healing salve mother used.[23]

In his journal, Edwin made the following remarks about his parents:

> Of Father I have only my childhood knowledge. . . . To me he appeared then a giant in size. Mother was a blond with a luxuriant growth of extra long, beautiful, brown hair which I would . . . see her carefully brush and comb out daily, sometimes falling over me like a great silky veil as I sat on a low stool with my head nestled in her lap, awaiting my turn for she loved to fondle me in that manner and pass her tapered fingers through my own light curly locks. A charm to me I am still ever missing and a thousand other delightful mother pleasures, even in preparation of foods I particularly was partial too. Mutton broth as only she could make it, Yorkshire batter pudding, plum pudding cakes, meat and potato rolls, and lovely home-made bread. I wonder if I get married if I shall ever meet another woman like Mother & Grandmother. I fear not.
>
> Father had regular well-formed features; medium dark hair, a tall military bearing. Strong, active, and muscular, a most determined will of his own—a born commander. As I now remember he must have been about five feet, ten inches high, was a careful dresser and in business a real hard worker and pusher. Never idle, his word was his bond and woe unto anyone who disobeyed his commands or did him a willful undeserved wrong. He was expert in the use of military arms especially with the cavalry sword.[24] I remember to have seen him many times before visitors draw his sword and in a flash cut the top of a lighted candle off and sticking against the wall [it] would still continue to burn so quick were his movements and so sure his aim.
>
> I remember his betting a wager that he would split down into two halves a live Conger eel [large species of eel] suspended by a cord from its mouth and awaiting the proper moment he accomplished the difficult task. Another feat was the placing of a piece of broom handle, both ends resting on wine glasses filled with wine, and cutting the stick in two pieces by a lightening like stroke without spilling the wine.
>
> He was equally expert with the use of the military lance on horseback & could ride a horse bare backed standing, turning round & round several times, & on the side of the animal holding on to mane and tail.
>
> Like Mother and Grandmother, he was a great churchgoer (Episcopalian) and would never miss a service if possible or let one of his children [go without] morning and evening prayers and reading a chapter from the Bible. . . . A terror of a religion to me for it meant a most unmerciful punishment if during the week besides long rows of spelling set me on the Monday morning . . . and sometimes a whole chapter of the Bible to learn and repeat after morning school on Sundays. The marvel is that father did not make an Infidel of me by his process. And with all this outward show of religion, [in] the fashion of the age, he could when mad do as good a turn at cussing as the Bishop or Parson at a dinner or fox hunt.
>
> One great overwhelming fault above all others he possessed. [Although] a lover of his family, a good home, eating, and dressing, he would boast that he was a three-bottle man meaning that at a jolly meeting of friends for an evening's social he could drink his companions under the table where they would find themselves in the early lights of the morning. Trying their thick wine paralyzed voices on "He's a jolly good fellow," etc.
>
> Happy of nature . . . good-hearted [and] ever wishing his fellow beings well when sober . . . [but] under the influence of those drinking bouts every member of the family suffered and even at times ran [the] risk of their lives. It was my misfortune to be singled out to have the greatest share, too awful to dwell upon. . . . He was simply insane at those times. The marvel is that I survived.
>
> I think it was owing to my father's drink habit and its attendant baneful results, and my being so absorbed by my mother & grandmother [that] I know so little about him or his family. He was a man who never talked of himself to anyone.[25]

Edwin's father, Josiah Scudder Osbaldeston

Edwin may have been singled out by his father because he was, in effect, the eldest son as his older brother Frederick spent most of his childhood living elsewhere. Additionally, Edwin may have known less about his father as his father's trade was selling books and stationery. He was away from home as an itinerant salesman for periods of time. Furthermore, Victorian and Edwardian Britain was an authoritarian society where corporal punishment was used to enforce obedience and to act as a deterrent, both at home and at school.[26]

In spite of the glowing memories of his childhood that Edwin wrote years later, the family was not well off. Given that Josiah had a fondness for drink and there were many mouths to feed in the blended Turner-Osbaldeston household, it can be safely assumed that the family struggled financially.

One saving grace was the officer's widow's pension that Mary Ann (the elder) received due to her first husband's service in the Royal Navy. In November 1820 widow Mary Ann Lewis Turner applied to the Royal Navy's Compassionate Fund for financial support for her two children. In the column of the fund's register headed "Circumstances under which the Widow or Orphan has Applied, or been recommended for Relief," the entry was as follows: "Lieut Turner had been for many years on Half Pay. His widow represents that he had been long subject to Epileptic fits, and for the last four years had laboured under occasional fits of insanity. She has been allowed the pension of £50 per ann & has no other means of support. She states that she & her children have frequently been without the necessaries of life & that the expenses of her husband's illness have left her much involved in difficulties." The decision of the Admiralty on this case was that they should receive £6 each.[27]

Shortly after the 1841 census was taken, Josiah Scudder Osbaldeston was declared an insolvent debtor and committed to Gloucester Gaol on July 7.[28] In mid-November 1841 Josiah Osbaldeston was released from prison after a hearing in Insolvent Court.[29] [30]

Family members appear to have undergone an acrimonious parting of ways in 1844. Records show that Mary Ann Lewis Turner Osbaldeston began receiving her naval officer's widow's pension in Oxford from October 1844.[31] At the time of the 1851 census, Mary Ann (the elder) and her daughter Maria were recorded as living together in the St. Giles neighborhood of Oxford.[32]

At some point between 1844 and 1849, Josiah Scudder Osbaldeston, his stepdaughter Mary Ann (the younger), and their children went to live in the city of Birmingham. Josiah Osbaldeston may have thought that business would be better in this bustling industrial city. Also, in a large city such as Birmingham, it might be easier to conceal their illicit relationship and the fact that he was not married to the mother of his younger children.

Edwin's mother Mary Ann Turner (the younger)

By the time of the 1851 census, Josiah Osbaldeston and Mary Ann (the younger) had five children. Their eldest son, Frederick Turner, eighteen, was back living with them in Birmingham along with Edwin, twelve; Emma, ten; Charles, six; and Frank, two. They told the census taker that their last name was "James" rather than Osbaldeston. Edwin's occupation was listed as "errand boy."[33] He appears to have left school at age twelve or possibly earlier, as was the case with most children in Victorian working class families.

Following this census Mary Ann the younger gave birth to a daughter named Ann Maria. Then in December 1854 Mary Ann gave birth to her son Julian, the last of her children by Josiah Osbaldeston.[34] Ann Maria and her brother were baptized on January 21, 1855.[35] Ann Maria died of scarlatina [scarlet fever] in the General Hospital on Summer Lane in Birmingham on October 18, 1858. According to her death certificate, she was seven years old.[36]

Edwin's older brother Frederick enlisted in the Royal Artillery in Birmingham in April 1855 and was sent to Royal Artillery headquarters in Woolwich near London for basic training.[37]

On December 11, 1857, Edwin's maternal grandmother, Mary Ann Lewis Turner Osbaldeston, died in Oxford.[38] Even after the death of his wife, Josiah Scudder Osbaldeston was still not free to marry his stepdaughter. Since 1560, the Church of England's "Table of Kindred and Affinity" had specified that a man may not marry his stepdaughter and that a woman may not marry her stepfather.[39]

As Edwin matured, was it nature or nurture that

caused him to exaggerate his accomplishments and circumstances? Are his warm reflections of home life more wishful thinking than reality? Was his personality more like that of his father than his mother? Did the state of family finances, mobility, social class, and the circumstances of his birth generate feelings of insecurity, inferiority, and low self-worth? Was he heavily influenced by Victorian values? Or was it all of the above? The pages that follow will shed more light on Edwin's complex personality and what shaped him as the man he became.

NOTES

1. "Doctor, 93, Denies Charge of Horse Theft 46 Years Ago. His Accuser is 91," *Syracuse Herald* (NY), 28 March 1926, p. 1.
2. England, birth certificate for Edwin Turner, born 11 July 1838; citing XI/11/208, Cheltenham registration district; General Register Office, Southport, UK.
3. Priory Church (Great Malvern, Worcestershire, England), *Registers of the Priory Church, Great Malvern, Worcestershire.* Part Two: *Baptisms & Burials, 1709–1837; Marriages, 1754–1837.* Society of Genealogists, London, UK, WO/REG/46914.
4. Canon W. J. Oldfield's Calendar to Oxfordshire Quarter Sessions Rolls, 1687–1830, Vol. II, Depositions, Recognizances, Indictments, Easter 1783–Mich[aelmas] 1830. Oxfordshire County Record Office, Cowley, Oxfordshire, UK.
5. Canon W. J. Oldfield's Calendar to Oxfordshire Quarter Sessions Rolls, 1687–1830, Vol. IX, Certificates Conviction by Magistrates, Grand Jury Presentments, Petty Constables, Recusants. Oxfordshire County Record Office, Cowley, Oxfordshire, UK.
6. St. Mary Magdalen (Oxford, England), Transcript of parish registers, vol. 5, Marriages, 1813–1851, Osbaldeston–Turner marriage (27 April 1825). Society of Genealogists, London, UK, OX/R/261.
7. St. Mary (Lambeth, Surrey, England), Register of Marriages, August 1810–December 1817, p. 318, Turner–Lewis marriage (31 December 1814). London Metropolitan Archives, London, UK, microfilm X38/18.
8. The National Archives (UK), "Register of officers' widows & orphans applying to the Compassionate Fund," catalog reference ADM 6/326.
9. Ibid.
10. Edwin Turner Osbaldeston (hereafter ETO), "Journal" (unpublished manuscript), 18, Siver family history material.
11. St. Thomas the Martyr (Oxford, England), Parish register, Society of Genealogists, London, UK, OX/R204.
12. David Hey, *How Our Ancestors Lived: A History of Life 100 Years Ago* (Surrey, UK: National Archives, 2003), pp. 28–29.
13. Hey, *How Our Ancestors Lived*, p. 24.
14. Ibid.
15. St. Mary (Cheltenham, Gloucestershire, England), Baptisms register, p. 160. Gloucestershire Archives, Gloucester, UK, ref. no. PFC 78/1 IN 1/12, microfiche no. 9.
16. St. Thomas (Birmingham, Warwickshire, England), Baptisms register, p. 89; Birmingham Archives and Heritage, Birmingham, UK.
17. The National Archives (UK), "Register of officers' widows & orphans applying to the Compassionate Fund," ADM 6/326.
18. ETO, "Journal" (unpublished manuscript), 2, Siver family history material.
19. Hey, *How Our Ancestors Lived*, p. 3.
20. Hey, *How Our Ancestors Lived*, p. 9.
21. Hey, *How Our Ancestors Lived*, pp. 30–31.
22. Hey, *How Our Ancestors Lived*, p. 11.
23. ETO, "Journal" (unpublished manuscript), 4–7, Siver family history material.
24. Registers of the Oxfordshire Yeomanry regiment in which Josiah Osbaldeston was enrolled from 1820 until 1835 are held by Soldiers of Oxfordshire Research Centre, Woodstock, Oxfordshire, England.
25. ETO, "Journal" (unpublished manuscript), 19–25, Siver family history material.
26. Hey, *How Our Ancestors Lived*, p. 29.
27. The National Archives (UK), "Register of officers' widows & orphans applying to the Compassionate Fund," ADM 6/326.
28. *The London Gazette*, Issue 19997, 9 July 1841, p. 27.
29. "Minutes of proceedings in case of insolvent debtors under Acts of 5 George IV, c.61, and 7 George IV, c.57." Gloucestershire Archives, Gloucester, UK, ref. no. Q/RID/2, pp. 122–23.
30. "Insolvent Court," *Gloucester Journal*, 20 November 1841.
31. The National Archives (UK), "Paymaster General's Office: Widows of Naval Officers Pensions, 1842–1845," PMG 19/6.
32. Census Returns of England and Wales, 1851, Kew, Surrey, England: The National Archives of the UK (TNA): Public Record Office (PRO), 1851, class HO 107, piece 1727, folio 495, page 36, FHL microfilm 193636.
33. Census Returns of England and Wales, 1851, Kew, Surrey, England: The National Archives of the UK (TNA): Public Record Office (PRO), 1851, class HO 107, piece 2058, folio 434, page 12. The family was found by searching an index of the 1851 census for Warwickshire on CD-ROM under the terms name "Josiah" and birthplace "Malvern."
34. England, birth certificate for Julian Alexander Turner, born 12 December 1854; citing 6d/48, Birmingham registration district, General Register Office, Southport, UK.
35. St. Thomas's, Birmingham, Warwickshire, England. Information found on International Genealogical Index, British Isles, www.familysearch.org.
36. England, death certificate for Ann Maria Turner, died 18 October 1858; citing 6d/125, Birmingham registration district, General Register Office, Southport, UK.
37. The National Archives (UK), "Description Book, Royal Artillery, Battalion 7, Recruits," WO 54/297.
38. England, death certificate for Mary Ann Osbaldeston, died 11 December 1857; citing 3a/355, Headington registration district, subdistrict of Saint Clement, County of Oxford, General Register Office, Southport, UK.
39. "Forbidden Marriage Laws of the United Kingdom," accessed 6 February 2014, http://www.genetic-genealogy.co.uk/Toc115570145.html.

CHAPTER FOUR

Military & Marriage ~ 1859–1864

For centuries, military service has offered young men (and women) an opportunity for employment, education, travel, and adventure. This was especially true in Victorian England, where upward mobility was difficult to achieve. Following in his older brother Frederick's footsteps, Edwin enlisted in the Royal Regiment of Artillery, a branch of the British army commonly known as the Royal Artillery, on January 22, 1859.[1]

He gave his name as Edwin Turner and his age as nineteen, but he was actually twenty years and six months old on that date. According to Royal Artillery documents, Edwin was a shoemaker at the time of his enlistment.[2] From Birmingham he was sent to Royal Artillery headquarters at Woolwich, near London, for basic training.[3] Additionally, he received training at the Royal Artillery's School of Gunnery at Shoeburyness in Essex. The school had been established in 1859 and was where his older brother Frederick had begun his tenure as an instructor.[4]

Horseshoe Barracks, Shoeburyness Garrison in 1879 (www.shoeburyness.qinetiq.com)

Brothers Frederick and Edwin were polar opposites when it came to military service. Frederick took to army life and made a career of it. He enlisted in April 1855 and by July had been promoted to bombardier. Frederick rose steadily through the ranks. He was assigned to the Adjutant's Detachment of the Fourteenth Battalion in April 1857 and promoted to sergeant the following December. He attained the rank of captain in 1872 and was granted the honorary rank of major in 1886. For a man from the working class, this was about as far as he could go in those times. Frederick was held in high esteem by fellow officers and his superiors and well regarded for his abilities. Much of his service was with the administration of the First Northumberland Artillery Volunteers as an instructor. He retired in 1890 upon completion of thirty-five years of service.[5]

Frederick Turner

Edwin, unlike Frederick, did not enjoy being in the military and was not a good soldier. While at Woolwich in March 1860, he committed an offense that caused him to be put on trial. As a result of his court martial, Edwin was demoted from bombardier to gunner.[6] (The court martial, but not the offense, appeared in the records.)

In May 1860 Edwin's unit, the Royal Artillery's Sixth Brigade, Fourth Battery, was sent to Portsmouth. Portsmouth was the first naval port of the British Empire and of great strategic importance due to its location in the center of the English Channel on Britain's southern coast.

From there the Fourth Battery was transported on the troopship HMS *Megaera* to the Mediterranean

Royal Artillery headquarters and parade ground, Woolwich, England. Photo: Noël Siver, September 16, 2007

island of Malta.[7] The battery was stationed at the Grand Harbour at Valletta.

Malta, located in the center of the Mediterranean Sea, south of Sicily, had become part of the British Empire in 1800. From ancient times the island had been under control of passing empires beginning with the Phoenicians, Carthaginians, and Romans. Due to its location and its fine natural harbors, Malta was militarily a significant position to hold. In 1798 Napoleon seized the island on his way to conquer Egypt. The Maltese did not like French rule and revolted with the help of the British. The French retreated when the British fleet entered the Grand Harbour. British military presence remained there for the next 164 years as Malta had become part of the empire. For much of the time, military personnel stationed at Malta had little to do other than serve as a defense presence and maintain the fortifications. For Edwin, his experience on Malta would be woven into many of his tales of military service.

The Royal Artillery's quarterly pay lists recorded that gunner Edwin Turner was on the island of Malta from May 26, 1860, until August 29, 1861. The pay lists also indicated the number of days a soldier spent in the hospital in each quarter. Edwin's pay records revealed that he spent time in the fort's hospital in every quarter except one. His longest stay in hospital was thirty-five days during the quarter of July 1–September 30, 1860.[8]

Edwin later claimed that he began writing in a notebook during that time. On the first page of the notebook, he wrote the following:

> Accident Ward No 2. Bed 31.
> Case Sunstroke
> Ricasoli (Napoleon's) Hospital
> Malta in the Mediterranean[9]

Edwin recalled being in Ricasoli Hospital, Valletta, Malta, recovering from a fall of three or four

Modern map of the Grand Harbour at Valletta, Malta
Credit: Google Maps

Bighi Hospital, Valletta, Malta

The troopship HMS Himalaya *(Illustration from www.keepmilitarymuseum.org)*

hundred feet from the ancient lantern of Fort St. Anthony. His fall was the result of passing out from sunstroke.

> My first [sunstroke] occurred July 3rd, 1862 [actually 1860] at Malta. I was looking out through what is called the lantern, a projecting ornamental building built at the top of Fort St. Anthony [should be Fort St. Angelo], Cottonera side of Valletta harbour, & facing the entrance. In ancient times the Knights Templar of Malta & Jerusalem used to light their signal fires in these lanterns which are the size of a small room. There I got my first sunstroke & was a patient in Napoleon's Hospital, Ricasoli, a long time.[10]

Edwin may have actually been in Bighi Hospital, the British Royal Navy hospital that was built in the early 1830s. It was situated between Fort Ricasoli and Fort St. Angelo.

In August 1861 Edwin's Royal Artillery battery was transferred from Malta back to Portsmouth. He was on board the troopship HMS *Himalaya* from August 29 until September 7, 1861.

> When on board the "Himalaya" on my way from Malta I was fairly well posted in *Materia Medica* and had had some practical experience in surgery and was kindly allowed to assist the doctors aboard the vessel . . . the largest in the Royal Navy was carrying many hundreds of men back to England from India, Ceylon, Aden, Corfu, Malta, and Gibraltar. I spent much of my time in the dispensary where six chemists were constantly employed night and day. Whilst there I had an opportunity to study the effects of certain chemicals upon diphtheria membrane that I had cut from a dead soldier's throat who had died of the disease & put overboard. . . . [My] result is highly satisfactory and will be useful to me in years to come if I practice as a doctor or even as a Clergyman. One or other I am sure to be if I live.[11]

In Portsmouth the battery was mustered at Haslar Barracks in Gosport on the western side of the entrance to Portsmouth Harbour. Between October 1 and December 31, 1861, Edwin spent thirty-nine days in the hospital.[12] He may have been malingering.

On December 31, 1861, the battery was mustered on the Isle of Wight.[13] From January 1 to July 9,

Edwin's mother, Mary Ann Turner, gave him this compass. The compass foreshadowed a life of travel and adventure.

1862, Edwin was stationed at Fort Victoria, located on the north shore of the Isle of Wight. The fort had been built in the 1850s to help strengthen England's coastal defenses. Portsmouth was said to be the most fortified city in Europe. The Isle of Wight is approximately seven miles southwest of Portsmouth. Osborne House, the Royal Family's beautiful seaside residence, was located on the Isle of Wight. Queen Victoria spent summers there.

Instead of idling his time in the hospital at Fort Victoria, Edwin was recorded in the Royal Artillery's pay lists as earning good conduct pay.[14] It appeared that he had a plan. Edwin received a pass for leave from July 9–15. When he did not reappear at Portsmouth on July 16, 1862, it was recorded that he had deserted from the Royal Artillery—thus ending the military career of Edwin Turner Osbaldeston.[15]

In one of the many interviews that Dr. Osbaldeston gave after being hunted down by Deputy Sheriff Black in 1926, he made a rather revealing comment about military life to a reporter for the *New York Times*. The reporter wrote, "Although he said he was the son of the Earl of Onslow, the old man declared he quit the British army because he could not stand the peacetime frivolity of army life." Directly quoting Dr. Osbaldeston, "It was no life for a serious man," he said. "The British Army was just a social organization, and you soon tire of it."[16] His disdain for the "peacetime frivolity of army life" was probably one of the most truthful comments he made during the media storm.

In that same interview, Edwin mentioned being in Malta. However, it was not for guard duty. He gave a more thrilling version of his stay on the island. During the Crimean War battle at Balaklava, he was wounded while trying to ride down four Russians in a thicket. His horse pistol was knocked from his hand, and then he fought with a sabre. The next thing he said he remembered was waking up on the island of Malta with a nurse looking into his eyes.[17]

Marriage and Life in London

Leaving the Isle of Wight, Edwin made his way to Birmingham to visit his mother and siblings. In addition to his dislike of life in the Royal Artillery, there appear to have been family reasons that compelled Edwin to desert and return to Birmingham.

His father, Josiah Scudder Osbaldeston, and his mother Mary Ann, had parted company. At the time of the 1861 census, Josiah Scudder Osbaldeston was living in a lodging house in Wolverhampton, northwest of Birmingham.[18] Because he was an itinerant bookseller and stationer, at first glance it did not seem unusual that Mary Ann Turner and their children were not enumerated with him.

However, Mary Ann had met and become betrothed to another. On August 24, 1862, James Hubbard, who was about thirty-eight, a cane chair maker, and illiterate, married forty-seven-year-old Mary Ann Turner at St. Jude's parish church in Birmingham.[19]

Edwin wrote that it was on September 1, 1862, that he met his future wife, Ann Pratt, in the Acock's Green area of south Birmingham. They were married by banns three weeks later on September 21, 1862, in All Saints Church, Hockley, Birmingham. On the marriage certificate, his name appears as Edwin Turner Osbaldeston rather than Edwin Turner.[20] Witnesses to their marriage were James and Mary Ann Hubbard.

In his journal Edwin recorded the following about his new bride and her family:

> A new life has just opened up to me shared by one I regard as beautiful in heart & body and soul. Annie P. . . [Pratt] age 16 years & 4 months. But I gave the Curate an age one year older to make things suit his notions of propriety so it appears 17 & 4 months instead.[21]

Ann Pratt was actually eighteen at the time of her marriage. Perhaps, like Edwin, she did not know the year of her birth.[22] He described her in his journal.

> Pretty, dark-eyed Madonna like Valletta of Malta is not in it with fair Annie the bright, dancing & singing romp of an English maid. Born of a four generations back, very wealthy & prominent land owning family but now comparatively poor at Haycock Green, Warwickshire.
>
> Now the family father Thomas P— [Pratt] Harriet his wife, father a Railway Superintendant at a nearby small Depot. Broth-

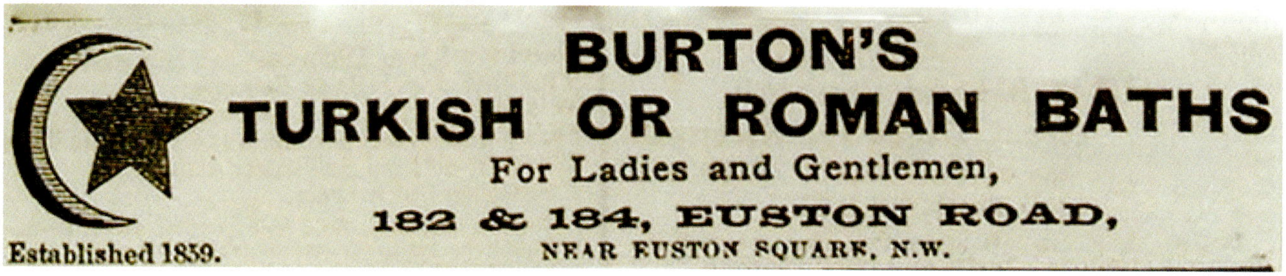

Advertisement for Burton's Turkish baths in London where Edwin worked as an attendant

ers, Joe 1, William 2, James 3, Thomas 4, Sisters Harriet 5, Elizabeth 6, Alice 7, Annie 8. Helen the youngest. Residing 1 Blue St, West Hockley. Eight out of the nine children now married. Helen is 14 years of age.[23]

Edwin Turner and Ann Pratt Osbaldeston moved to London after their marriage. Edwin noted the following in his journal:

> He who tied the knot was our guest here in London [at] Mrs. Coles, 53 Whittleberry Street. Just returning this morning after a course of treatment to cure him if possible [of] the drink habit at which times he would do more at cussing than preaching to his parishioners. The Reverend J. T. Brian Curate of All Saints Church Hockley, he a dear old fellow, could not resist the temptation of kissing Annie, now my wife on September 21st 1862. Mr. & Mrs. James & M[ary] A[nn] Hubbard were witnesses as he finished tying the nuptial knot. Copy of certificate applied for 1863. N° of Register 447, Page 224.—N° 6 & Reverend J. W. Daline 1863. All's well if it ends well. If lots of prayers & good wishes by friends there & here will make it so Annie & I are in for a good time together until one or the other falls out of the ranks.[24]

To support his new bride and himself, Edwin began working at Joseph Burton's new Turkish and Russian baths on Euston Road at Euston Square. He and Ann were renting a three-room apartment for fifteen shillings a week off Euston Square from Mrs. Coles.[25]

He said that he was volunteering at a public dispensary and "occasionally running up to London to study surgery under Professor Ives at the Gower Street University Hospital. He [Ives] and Dr. Wilson Fox, the chief physician, have taken a great liking to me and persuaded me to give up ideas of the ministry in the Baptist Church. . . . Both these gentlemen refuse to accept any fees and have presented me with books I require and free passes to lectures."[26]

He claimed to be the manager of the baths but was more likely a bath attendant. According to his journal, he found working at the baths to be an interesting and educational experience.

> I am however compelled to do some kind of work for a living & have mastered scientific massage & medico gymnastics & offered an appointment through the interest of Surgeon Ives as manager of Mr. Joseph Burton's new Turkish & Russian Baths 135 [should be 184] Euston Road, Euston Square where I hear Mr. Charles Dickens, Mr. Thackeray, Sir Edwin Lanseer & Machoriniti [Baron Marochetti] the famous sculptor, the Rothschilds and the Earl of Onslow & many other eminent personages patronize & assemble for social chat. I have been introduced to Mr. Burton, a Yorkshire man, tall & stately with a splendid physique, light brown, curly hair and full beard with clear complexion & blue eyes.
>
> I have been studying phrenology by [George] Combe & phrenology & physiognomy & mesmerism by [Lorenzo Niles or Orson Squire] Fowler so can well judge of a person's make up & describe their appearances & disport and character. Very useful things to be acquainted with I find.
>
> But of mesmerism I think it is wrong to try & influence any one against their free consent & that the law should intervene to punish all who do for I have personally witnessed some vile abuses of the power on young girls & two boys under 16 [who] were made to submit to hypnotic influence & undergo several surgical operations. There was no pain & no ill effects followed but neither their parents' or guardians' consent was previously obtained. And as for the girls I cannot write the scenes the principals being in one case a doctor & clergyman combined the other a doctor.
>
> I enter on my duties as manager of Burton's Bathing House & find it exceedingly interesting & profitable employment. I am styled "doctor" by courtesy. It possesses the advantage so of meeting & mingling with a very learned & eminent class of patrons ever ready to enter into conversation on matters that interest them so I glean much valuable information I think on various topics than I would be able to learn even in College. I am as usual regarded as smart & already have earned the confidence & good will of Mr. Burton & his sister Beatrice, the Manageress for the Ladies Department, although I find I am in as much requisition there as elsewhere in the establishment.[27]

"I am styled 'doctor' by courtesy. It possesses the advantage so of meeting & mingling with a very learned & eminent class of patrons ever ready to enter into conversation on matters that interest them so I glean much valuable information I think on various topics than I would be able to learn even in college."

— Edwin Turner Osbaldeston

The Turkish bath was introduced to the British Isles in 1856. The British Victorian adaptation of the baths employed dry heat as opposed to steam used in other cultures. The patrons of the Victorian baths stepped into a room that was heated with dry air and then into rooms that were progressively hotter, which was followed by a full-body wash, massage, and relaxation in a cooling room. Another variation was a plunge in cold water before the body wash.[28] In 1860 a number of Turkish baths had opened in London, and by 1865 there were thirty-seven bathhouses operating in the city.[29] Besides the hygienic benefits of the baths, they also became a place to socialize.

The Euston Road Turkish or Russian Baths was opened in 1861 by John Maxfield, and within a few months, it was sold to Joseph Burton. A newspaper review of the bath noted it "was well attended and the Turkish crescent now graces the front garden leading to it."[30] Burton hired Edwin to work in his establishment. Edwin remained in Burton's employ until 1864.[31] Again it was unlikely that he managed the bathhouse as he was learning the business during his employ.

Two things emerge from Edwin's tenure at Burton's Turkish baths: his attraction to people of wealth and fame and his wanderlust. Until settling in New York and Asbury Park, he rarely remained in any one place for long.

NOTES

1. The National Archives (UK), Commissary General of Musters Office and successors: Artillery Muster Books and Pay Lists, Field and Garrison, Gosport: Brigade 6: Battery 4, "Pay List for the Quarter Ended 30th of September 1862, Form 35," WO 10/2534.
2. Ibid.
3. The National Archives (UK), Commissary General of Musters Office and successors: Artillery Muster Books and Pay Lists, Field and Garrison, Detachment Woolwich: Depot, Battery 3, "Pay List for the Quarter Ended 31st of March 1860," WO 10/2747.
4. Family information states that ETO trained with his older brother Frederick Turner. This would mean that he was transferred to Shoeburyness in Essex in the latter half of 1859, when his brother Frederick was a sergeant on the staff of the newly established Royal Artillery School of Gunnery. According to M. E. S. Laws, compiler, *Battery Records of the Royal Artillery,* Vol. 1, *1716–1859;* Vol. 2, *1859–1877* (Woolwich: Royal Artillery Institute, 1952–1970), Royal Artillery muster rolls and pay lists for the period from October 1858 through December 1859 have not survived.
5. "Late Major F. Turner, Military Funeral at Boscombe," *Bournemouth Daily Echo*, 18 November 1919, p. 2.
6. The National Archives (UK), Commissary General of Musters Office and successors: Artillery Muster Books and Pay Lists, Field and Garrison, Detachment Woolwich: Depot, Battery 3, "Pay List for the Quarter Ended 31st of March 1860," WO 10/2747.
7. The National Archives (UK), War Office and predecessors: Secretary-at-War, Secretary of State for War, and Related Bodies, Registers, "Embarkation Returns, 1860," WO 25/1170.
8. The National Archives (UK), Commissary General of Musters Office and successors: Artillery Muster Books and Pay Lists, Field and Garrison, Malta: Brigade: 6, Battery 4, "Pay List for the Quarter ended 30th of September 1860," WO 10/2532.
9. ETO, "Journal" (unpublished manuscript), 1, Siver family history material.
10. ETO, "Journal" (unpublished manuscript), 108–9, Siver family history material.
11. ETO, "Journal" (unpublished manuscript), 40, Siver family history material.
12. The National Archives (UK), Commisssary General of Musters Office and successors: Artillery Muster Books and Pay Lists, Field and Garrison, Malta: Brigade: 6, Battery 4, "Pay List for the Quarter ended 31st of December 1861," WO 10/2533.
13. M. E. S. Laws, compiler, *Battery Records of the Royal Artillery* (Woolwich: Royal Artillery Institute, 1970), vol. 2, *1859–1877*, n. 150.
14. The National Archives (UK), Commissary General of Musters Office and successors: Artillery Muster Books and Pay Lists, Field and Garrison, Isle of Wight: Brigade: 6, Battery 4, "Pay List for the Quarter ended 30th of June 1862," WO 10/2534.
15. The National Archives (UK), Ordinance Office, Military Branch, and War Office: Royal Artillery Records of Service and Papers, Indexes to Non-Effectives: Brigades to 1877, "Brigade 6," WO 69/845.
16. "Doctor, 93, to Fight Extradition as Thief," *New York Times*, 29 March 1926, pp. 1 and 3.
17. Ibid.
18. Census Returns of England and Wales, 1861, Kew, Surrey, England: The National Archives of the UK (TNA): Public Record Office (PRO), 1861, class RG 9, piece 1996, folio 135, page 7. His name was mistakenly recorded as Joseph. FHL microfilm 542900.
19. St. Jude's Parish (Birmingham, Warwickshire, England), Marriages 1851–1864, p. 129, Hubbard–Turner marriage (24 August 1862); FHL microfilm 918917.
20. All Saints Parish (Birmingham, Warwickshire, England), Marriages, 1856–1867, p. 224, Osbaldeston–Pratt marriage (21 September 1862); FHL microfilm 918921.
21. ETO, "Journal" (unpublished manuscript), 50, Siver family history material.
22. "England & Wales, Free BMD Index: 1837–1983," *FreeBMD*, birth entry for Ann Pratt; citing September [quarter], 1844, Solihull, vol.16: 439, acessed 17 November 2008, http://freebmd.org.uk/cgi/search/pl.
23. ETO, "Journal" (unpublished manuscript), 50–51, Siver family history material.
24. ETO, "Journal" (unpublished manuscript), 51–52, Siver family history material.
25. ETO, "Journal" (unpublished manuscript), 44, Siver family history material.
26. Ibid.
27. ETO, "Journal" (unpublished manuscript), 41–44, Siver family history material.
28 . Malcolm Shifrin, "The Victorian Turkish Bath Arrives in 19th Century London, 1. Introduction," accessed 6 February 2014, http://www.victorianturkishbath.org/2history/atozhist/monument/1monumentsf.htm.
29. Shifrin, "The Victorian Turkish Bath Arrives in 19th Century London, 3. The First in London," accessed 6 February 2014, http://www.victorianturkishbath.org/2history/atozhist/monument/3monumentsf.htm.
30. Shifrin, "Burton's Turkish Baths," accessed 6 February 2014, http://www.victorianturkishbath.org/_6DIRECTORY/AtoZEstab/London/Euston/EustonEng.htm.
31. Ibid.

CHAPTER FIVE

A New Life in the Australian Colonies ~ 1865

In February 1865 Edwin and Ann visited Cheltenham, his birthplace, and made a farewell visit to Ann's family in Birmingham. Their first child, Frederick Josiah Obsbaldeston, had been born on May 12, 1864. The infant died twelve days later of an imperfect formation of his heart.[1 2 3] Edwin recorded that he quit his job at the baths on the day his son died. The couple made plans to relocate to Australia. Edwin noted in his journal, "February 7, 1865—Visited Annie's home and parents. It may be many, many years before she ever sees them again, possibly never."[4]

With the Civil War raging in the United States, Australia had become the place for Englishmen to look for adventure and economic opportunity or to start a new life. The Dutch had been the first Europeans to reach Australia, landing in 1606. They named the southern and western coasts New Holland. Ships from the Dutch East India Company occasionally sailed to this remote corner of the world in the years thereafter. In 1770 British Royal Navy lieutenant James Cook reached Australia. He charted the east coast of the continent, and by order of King George III, Cook claimed the territory for the Crown.

Interest then came about for settlement and penal colonies.[5] Beginning in 1788 and continuing until 1868, the British government, as a way to relieve its prison population, shipped convicts to Australia. Most of the people sent to the penal colonies had been convicted of thievery, although some were soldiers who had been convicted of desertion, mutiny, or insubordination. In the course of eighty years, Great Britain relieved itself of 162,000 convicts by banishing them to Australia.[6]

Others emigrated from England and Wales of their own free will, looking to start a new life in a far-off land. The discovery of gold in Victoria in 1851, and two years later in Queensland, opened the floodgates of immigration. In 1852, 370,000 immigrants arrived in Victoria. In two years the population of that state went from 77,000 to 540,000.[7] The image of life in Australia had changed dramatically in a decade. Primitive frontier settlements turned into thriving towns.

On Friday, March 10, 1865, Edwin and Ann boarded the emigrant ship SS *Lobelia* at Plymouth and set sail for the colony of Queensland, Australia. In his journal Edwin wrote the following:

> We sail, having received an appointment to the emigrant sailing vessel, *Lobelia,* as Assistant Surgeon in charge of the dispensary. The vessel of 850 tons to carry 830 [sic] first class emigrants, chiefly well-to-do farmers with their implements, for Brisbane, Queensland. From there I propose to go to Sydney & take passage back to the US from which I have been longer than I intended—all my interests are there but I may decide to spend a year or two in Queensland or New South Wales, or Victoria. If I see a chance to earn money quickly, I may—
>
> Am here waiting to sail as soon as the vessel is ready. . . . Emigrants & Dr. Black, Senior Physician & Surgeon, are busy examining & classifying them & appointing a schoolmaster & 12 men as a police force on board under my command. The emigrants all look grand & are happy in contemplation of their hoped for good prospects.[8]

Even though Edwin claimed to have been appointed assistant surgeon on the *Lobelia*, he and Ann sailed for Queensland under an assisted passage program.[9 10] Their fare was probably paid for by the Queensland Immigration Society. The Society was originally founded by Irish Catholics in Brisbane "to alleviate the misery" of people in Ireland who were suffering from the potato famine. In order to avoid creating antagonisms with people of other faiths and nationalities, the Society did not limit assisted passage to just the Irish. The mission of the Society was expanded to bring more young, single women to Australia and to anyone in "every part of the continent of Europe who understood the cultivation of cotton, the vine, the olive, and other products congenial to our soil."[11]

Later the program was expanded further to assist unemployed textile workers. Due to the American Civil War, exports of US cotton to English textile mills had dried up, causing what the British termed a "cotton famine." Many people lost their jobs when the factories were forced to close. In response, spinners, weavers, and others needing work were offered free passage to Australia.[12]

The assisted passage program was funded by donations. Emigrants were expected, once they were established, to reimburse the Queensland Immigration Society and to make donations beyond that if they were able. Some were given free passage if they were deemed "eligible or desirable emigrants."[13] For Edwin assisted passage to Australia was a means to reach America, which he had stated in his journal was his ultimate goal.

The *Lobelia* was of the wooden clipper ship variety with high masts. The ship weighed 823 tons. It had cabins on the top deck for persons of means. Most of the passengers were assigned to the lower deck or steerage section. From floor to ceiling, the lower deck measured seven feet and two inches in height and contained double rows of bunks on either side of the boat. Children were assigned two or three to a bunk. Down the middle ran a long table with fixed seats. This area was for meals and socializing. There were latrines or water closets for the passengers that had to be emptied by hand. The *Lobelia* lacked portholes. Fire was an ever-present concern, so lanterns were few and most light came from the rectangular scuttles or hatches in the ceiling. During storms and rough seas, the hatches were closed. Ventilation was extremely poor. Steerage passengers had little privacy and suffered in the heat of the tropics, in the cold of the South Pole, and from the turbulence of rough seas. Movable partitions separated the single men (assigned to the bow), married couples, and single women (assigned to the aft).[14]

Edwin overstated the number of passengers on the ship by about 460. Given the crowded conditions and the length of time the passengers were confined, it may have seemed as though there were a greater number of people on board. The *Lobelia* carried a crew of 29 and set out with 342 passengers. The vast majority of the 336 persons who landed in Brisbane were in their twenties. Only 8 of the passengers were forty years of age or older. Among the passengers there were 7 infants and 55 children age twelve and under. Four births were recorded during the voyage.[15 16]

Passage to Australia took nearly four months.

Places where Edwin Turner Osbaldeston lived in Australia

After leaving Plymouth, the *Lobelia* sailed south to the northern coast of Africa and then steered across the Atlantic Ocean toward South America to take advantage of westerly winds as it prepared to round the Cape of Good Hope. In the South Atlantic the *Lobelia* encountered intermittent rough seas. At one point the ship was struck by a violent squall that carried away the topmast, topgallant, and jibboom.[17] With a barrel-shaped bottom, the ship swayed back and forth, particularly in high winds and rolling seas. After reaching the Cape of Good Hope in mid-May, the ship sailed east toward Australia. As the *Lobelia* sailed along the southern coast of Australia, light winds extended the voyage. The ship finally entered Moreton Bay at the mouth of the Brisbane River on July 2. The voyage had taken 114 days.

The journey was not over, however. Because there had been a number of deaths on the ship and many cases of ship fever, the passengers were ordered quarantined for thirty days. On July 6, after some bureaucratic delays, the tugboat *Platypus* attempted to tow the *Lobelia* to the quarantine station but failed due to adverse weather. Three days later, the steamer *Kate* towed the *Lobelia* to Dunwich on North Stradbroke Island. Finally, on July 10 the passengers were allowed to disembark. The single men were housed in fourteen tents. The buildings for the others were cramped. Tempers flared and patience wore thin among the passengers. Two more people had died since the ship's arrival in Moreton Bay.[18]

In his journal Edwin recorded a gallant account of his service to his fellow passengers on the *Lobelia*.

> Dunwich [on North Stradbroke] Island, July 2nd. Quarantined until August 2nd. Then to proceed by government boat *Platypus* up the River Brisbane to the city. Have had an awful long, tedious voyage, lost many passengers, nearly all the children & old people aboard through Black Cholera breaking out after a month out.
>
> I have been & still am until we reach Brisbane & deliver the emigrant doctor, [the] chief constable, parson & frequently nurse. Bodies put over board, sometimes three or four a day. At times [they] would float about the ship in a calm with the upper portion [of the body] bobbing up & down from careless packing & not putting sufficient weight to sink them. . . . All our medical comforts gave out & we had to resort to the use of strong coffee for the sick and burning the same between decks which completely stayed the plague & saved many lives. Annie & I worked hard among the sick & never took ill for an hour. We always kept bags of fresh roasted coffee about us, even washed our hands & faces in it.
>
> [North Stradbroke] Island presents a fine field for hunters. I come in daily with two natives loaded down with game I shoot & curiosities I find by their aid. They give corroboree dances to amuse us at night & show their skill in throwing the boomerang which is wonderful indeed. I must now, August 2nd, suspend note making. Shall be very busy for a time.[19]

A very different account of the arrival and quarantine of the *Lobelia* was published in the *Brisbane Courier* on July 6, 1865. The story on page two of the newspaper read as follows:

> A disease of the typhoid class existed on board the ship Lobelia, recently arrived from London via Plymouth, with government immigrants. On Monday she [the ship] was visited by the Health Officer, Dr. Purdie, from who we learn the following particulars:
>
> The disease made its appearance soon after the sailing of the ship, and in a much milder form than that which it subsequently assumed. In all, there were between 50 and 60 cases, of which nine proved fatal. There were also two deaths from other causes—one from bronchitis, and the other, an infant, from dentition. The last death occurred on the 28th June, and on that day the only remaining patients were discharged from the hospital as convalescent. Since then no other persons have been taken ill. Under these circumstances, the ship was declared to be in quarantine. . . .
>
> This morning the *Platypus* [a tugboat] will leave town for the purpose of towing the ship to the Quarantine Station at Dunwich. . . . The immigrants—338 in number—will then be landed, and no doubt in the course of a few days will be released, and allowed to come up to town.[20]

In an updated article on the *Lobelia* that appeared in the *Brisbane Courier* on July 18, much of the same information was repeated, but the story amended the onboard death count to twelve, adding a case of dropsy.[21]

Common ailments of passengers on long-distance voyages were diarrhea, seasickness, and ship fever. Several weeks into the journey, a twenty-year-old passenger succumbed to ship fever.[22] As the voyage progressed, many more passengers became ill. Ship fever (also known as jail fever) comes in several varieties of typhus. It causes headache, muscle ache, a prolonged high fever, and a rash or spots on the skin. In its various forms typhus is spread by flea, body lice, or rodent feces. Typically a person becomes infected after a flea or louse feeds and defecates on their skin. When a person scratches the bite, the bacteria-laden feces is rubbed into the wound.

Throughout history, outbreaks of typhus have occurred in places where people have lived in overcrowded, dirty conditions and were unable to bathe regularly and wash their clothing.[23] With the high concentration of people in the steerage section, sanitation was a serious issue.

The quarantine was well intentioned but of little help in curbing typhus. Typhus is infectious but not transmitted from person-to-person. It wasn't until 1916 that the cause of typhus was discovered by Brazilian doctor Henrique da Rocha Lima.[24] Living conditions in the quarantine station at Dunwich on North Stradbroke Island were in some respects worse than in the steerage section of the *Lobelia*. The emigrants would have been better off had they been allowed to disperse.

At the end of July, a number of the single men threatened mutiny if they were not released. A standoff lasted for two days between the passengers and the government officials.[25] Edwin did not record any hardships or mutinous behavior while he and Ann were in quarantine. Finally, on the morning of August 2, the passengers and their belongings were loaded on the *Platypus* and taken to Brisbane. They had landed at last.

Soon after his arrival in Brisbane, Edwin was reunited with his younger brother Charles. Charles had arrived in Queensland in March of 1862. In his journal Edwin described meeting Charles.

> Met my brother Charles Edward at Hotel George South Brisbane last night. In splendid condition but acts & talks queer. Has made a pile of money, is married & has one child. Says he is Edwin & I am Charley. Queer fellow* & yet I find on enquire he does not either drink or smoke. Talks of going to Melbourne shortly. I may decide to go with him. His wife a fine, handsome young Englishwoman, thinks his mind is giving way through hard work & the heat & [thinks] that the Melbourne climate, which is cooler, will be best for him & hopes I will accompany them. I will try to if possible.
> *He is 6 years younger than me.[26]

In another journal entry from his time in Brisbane, Edwin wrote, "In our cottage I invented a self-acting punkah [large ceiling fan] to keep rooms cool and insects out for the climate is like a furnace from 12 to 4 p.m. and those who can, indulge in a siesta."[27] In mid-November 1865, several articles appeared in the local papers noting the introduction of the punkah. The *Weekly Herald* reported the following:

> We have often expressed our surprise that the adoption of that luxury Indian existence—the punkah—has not, ere this, become universal in this country. We are glad to learn that its introduction has taken place. We owe this to a Mr. Osbaldistone, who, an old resident of the East Indies, has lately arrived from Calcutta with a quantity of punkahs, which he is disposing of at reasonable prices. He intends, we believe, to import periodical assignments of these luxuries, and we little doubt that they will speedily become as common in Queensland as in Hindostan.[28]

Edwin stated in his journal, "The punkah sold very readily and I made money fast by it. Sold out the idea and the right to manufacture to Lieutenant Lewis."[29] Where and how Edwin came in possession of the punkahs is not known, but he was never a resident of the East Indies, nor had he been to Calcutta at that time.

Edwin and Ann did not stay long in Brisbane. From there they moved to Sydney.

> Have drawn up plans for converting Mr. J. Stuart's large house 158 Pitt Street [Sydney] rear of the General Post Office into a Turkish & Russian Bath. It will be the first of the kind in these colonies. I also supervise its furnishing & fitting on my return. He has two charming daughters Annie, age 26, and Tilley, age 16. The latter acts very silly [and] I think is non compos mentis. Also one son William who keeps a paint store on the premises. . . .
>
> Am cultivating my voice as a ventriloquist. Since I was a boy I have had this gift & in years past took part in public entertainments. Have been offered one hundred pounds sterling (£100/-) per week as an engagement under the name of Val Vose. Have given six pounds £6/- for old man & woman figures & a boy & girl almost life size & with moveable jaws. Annie does not like the idea and tries to persuade me out of it. She may succeed—[30]
>
> We remained in Sydney sufficiently long to see the J. Stuart baths finished. I was offered the management but declined it.
>
> I gave several exhibitions of ventriloquism in the theatre but declined offers of permanent engagement & to travel with the troupe. My entertainments drew large houses & were well received. I introduced there for the second time my talking hands. Scene one representing Mr. Cordel, the other Mrs. Cordel in the curtains. Lectures a grand success. I first gave this illusion . . . in London at Highbury Barn, Russell Square & Holborne Hill and New Cut Music Halls. . . .
>
> Mr. Wilson & Mr. Stuart have obtained for me an appointment to the Paramatta convict prison as assistant physician if I will stay for it but I fear the Sydney heat & shall leave for Melbourne where a man of the name of Hosie on Burk St. has made me a very fine offer to come & supervise the erection & furnishing of what he proposes to be Turkish & Roman baths & their management. He says it shall become one of the finest bathing houses in the world.[31]

When she transcribed her father's diary in 1962, Ethel Turner Osbaldeston Groves confirmed her father's ability as a ventriloquist. "We, his offspring, well remember his ability as a ventriloquist: He had a dummy named 'Johnny' a small boy type, well-dressed, movable jaw, wooden hands which we particularly recall because our own small hands were sometimes rapped with these hard hands."[32]

When he wrote in his journal in the 1890s about his appearances as a ventriloquist, Dr. Osbaldeston gave himself the stage name "Val Vose." The real Val Vose was Irishman Henry "Valentine" Vousden, who had an international following. Vousden performed his variety act that included song, stand-up comedy, and ventriloquism in New Zealand in 1874 and 1875; in South Africa in 1876 and 1877; in Australia from 1873 to 1879; in Singapore, India, China, and Japan in early 1880; and in New York City, New York State, and Europe in the 1880s.

More than likely Edwin attended one of his performances or had read about Vousden and co-opted the name. Edwin mounted a stage act with ventriloquism in Melbourne. Evidence of Edwin's performances as a ventriloquist in Sydney has yet to be found. Similarly, evidence that Edwin designed Turkish baths for Mr. J. Stuart in Sydney has not been found. Two things are certain, however. Edwin loved to perform and he was highly prone to exaggeration.

NOTES

1. "England & Wales, Free BMD Index: 1837–1983," *FreeBMD,* birth entry for Frederick Josiah Osbaldeston, citing June [quarter], 1864, Pancras. vol. 1b: 95, accessed 17 November 2008, http://freebmd.org.uk/cgi/search.pl.
2. "England & Wales, Free BMD Index: 1837–1983," *FreeBMD,* death entry for Frederick Josiah Osbaldeston, citing June [quarter], 1864, Pancras. vol. 1b: 78, accessed 17 November 2008, http://freebmd.org.uk/cgi/search.pl.
3. ETO, "Journal" (unpublished manuscript), 52, Siver family history material.
4. ETO, "Journal" (unpublished manuscript), 56, Siver family history material.
5. www.australia.gov.au/about-australia/australian-story/european-discovery-and-colonization, accessed 8 February 2014.
6. www.australia.gov.au/about-australia/australian-story/convicts-and-the-bristish-colonies, accessed 8 February 2014.
7. www.australia.gov.au/about-australia/australian-story/austn-gold-rush, accessed 8 February 2014.
8. ETO, "Journal" (unpublished manuscript), 56–57, Siver family history material.
9. Queensland State Archives, digital image ID 8369, Register of passengers on immigrant ships arriving in Queensland, pp. 226–228, Lobelia, 2 July 1865, accessed 10 February 2014.
10. http://www.archives.qld.gov.au/Researchers/ImmigrationIndexes/Documents/Assisted-Immigrants-1842-1912-0, accessed 26 October 2014.
11. "Prospectus of the Queensland Immigration Society," *Courier* (Brisbane), 8 October 1862, p. 3.
12. James Jupp, *The Australian People: An Encyclopedia of the Nation, Its People and Their Origins* (Cambridge: Cambridge University Press, 2001), p. 301.
13. "Prospectus of the Queensland Immigration Society," *Courier* (Brisbane), 8 October 1862, p. 3.
14. Lyall Ford, *Below These Mountains: The Adventures of John Henry Mills—Pioneer Photographer and Gold Miner* (Freshwater, Queensland, Australia: Taipan Press, 2001), pp. 9–11.
15. Ibid.
16. http://www.archives.qld.gov.au/Researchers/ImmigrationIndexes/Documents/Lobelia_1865_QSA_Item_ID-18474, accessed 26 October 2014.
17. [Report of *Lobelia's* journey], *Brisbane Courier*, 1 August 1865, p. 2.
18. Ford, *Below These Mountains,* pp. 18–19.
19. ETO, "Journal" (unpublished manuscript), 58–60, Siver family history material.
20. "The Lobelia," *Brisbane Courier*, 6 July 1865, p. 2.
21. "The Lobelia," *Brisbane Courier*, 18 July 1865, p. 2.
22. Ford, *Below These Mountains*, p. 13.
23. "Typhus," medical-dictionary.thefreedictionary.com/Typhus, accessed on 27 October 2014.
24. "What is the history of typhus?" http://www.medicinenet.com/typhus/page3.htm, accessed on 27 October 2014.
25. Ford, *Below These Mountains*, pp. 20–21.
26. ETO, "Journal" (unpublished manuscript), 60, Siver family history material.
27. ETO, "Journal" (unpublished manuscript), 79–80, Siver family history material.
28. Untitled notice, *The Weekly Herald* (Brisbane), 4 November 1865.
29. ETO, "Journal" (unpublished manuscript), 79–80, Siver family history material.
30. Ibid.
31. ETO, "Journal" (unpublished manuscript), 83–84, Siver family history material.
32. Ethel Turner Osbaldeston Groves, "Notes by Transcriber, E. T. G. 1962." A single page of notes precedes her transcription of her father's journal.

CHAPTER SIX

Moving on to Melbourne & Ballarat ~ 1866–1867

With the steady expansion of settlement in Australia, new business opportunities continually presented themselves. If a venture did not pan out in one colony, a person could try in another. A man like Edwin T. Osbaldeston, who welcomed adventure and sought wealth, was well positioned to improve his fortunes in Australia. The year 1866 would prove eventful for him. Leaving Sydney behind, Edwin and Ann sailed on January 13 in steerage class to Melbourne on the ship *City of Melbourne*. Their names appeared on the passenger list as Edwin Turner and Mrs. Turner.[1] At the time of their arrival Ann was five months pregnant with their second child.

Edwin reunited with his brother Charles in Melbourne. In his journal he unloaded his thoughts about Charles. "[I] find my brother all right but he still insists that his name is Edwin. When I asked him what mine is he tells me anything I like to call myself. I find it very awkward his assuming my name. It has already caused serious complications and in two instances trouble. . . . He talks of going to Western Australia. He loves to move around from place to place like myself. Annie does not."[2]

There is some evidence that Charles Osbaldeston was using his brother's name. In mid-March 1867 articles appeared in two different newspapers in Ballarat, in the colony of Victoria, describing the successful efforts of Mr. E. T. Osbaldeston of that city in raising rare breeds of chickens. It is far more likely that it was Charles who was the breeder rather than Edwin.[3] There was no record of Edwin having been in Ballarat as yet.

At some point during the first two and a half years that Edwin lived in Australia, he had been contacted by his two first cousins, William George and Alfred Osbaldeston. William had arrived in Australia in 1852, and Alfred had been there since at least 1864. During their early years the two brothers were involved in gold mining. William George was the manager of the Crœsus Gold Mining Co. in Sebastopol, near Ballarat, Victoria.[4] The brothers persuaded Edwin to invest in their mining ventures. Edwin claimed that he had "lost a little fortune" in mining speculation at the hands of his cousins.[5]

Coppin's Olympic Theatre ("the Iron Pot") in Melbourne
State Library of Victoria P.326/NO.113

To support himself and his wife, Edwin sought work in another Turkish bathhouse. The Turkish bath movement had reached the shores of Australia in 1859 with the opening of a bath in Sydney. Concerns for health and sanitation helped the movement take root in this developing part of the world. There were claims that the baths could cure a host of ills from hysteria to halitosis to kidney disease. The belief was that the heat applied in the baths flushed out impurities from the body.[6]

Melbourne's first Turkish bath was established in the failed Olympic Theatre in 1860. The theater had opened in June 1855 on the corner of Lonsdale and Exhibition streets. Nicknamed the "Iron Pot," the Olympic was constructed of prefabricated iron commissioned from Manchester by noted local actor and political figure George Coppin.[7]

From the start the Olympic Theatre had struggled financially. A week before its first drama season began on July 30, 1855, the Theatre Royal opened. The competition proved to be too great, causing the Olympic to close after five seasons. The Royal was more centrally located and was cooler in the summer.[8] Ferdinand Pietriche was the operator of the bath at the Olympic when Edwin was hired in 1866 as a shampooer. In the lexicon of the baths, to shampoo was to massage.

> The *Illustrated London News* (26 July 1862) describes a shampoo at the newly opened London Hammam: As soon as the skin of the bather exhibits a flow of gentle perspiration a tellak, or bathman, commences the manipulation. . . . We are softly handled instead of being violently pinched. The bathman follows the line of muscles with 'anatomical thumb' to render them supple and to ascertain that they are so before the next operations are proceeded with. With a camel's-hair glove on his hand he sweeps over every inch of the body from the neck to the heels, starting the skin and planing it off in successive rolls, his dexterous hand missing no portion of the body. Legs and arms are cleared of every superfluity. Every part of your body is then cracked with surprising skill—an alarming operation to

a novice, but a perfectly safe and necessary one when performed by experienced tellaks.[9]

On May 18, 1866, Ann gave birth to a daughter they named Annie Mabel. Edwin, Ann, and their newborn were registered as living in the Melbourne suburb of Collingwood.[10] However, given their work schedule, they actually lived at the baths in rooms at the rear of the building. The former theater was also leased in part to the Turn Verein, a German social club founded to promote physical development and mental enrichment through literature, music, and social entertainments.[11] The Turn Verein was associated with a German gymnastics program.

Ann Pratt Osbaldeston and her daughter Annie Mabel (Melbourne, 1866)

Edwin, in his telling of events, claimed to be the person who established and operated the baths and who leased the building.

> The side rooms I have fitted as a Turkish Bath establishment & let to a Frenchman of the name of Pietrietch. The large front rooms [are let] to the members of the Turn Verein Association of which I am the only non-German member. The main portion I let as a Variety Theatre or Circus as occasion may require. I do a great business at both places. I am also Masseur to Sir Charles Darling the Governor of Victoria, treating him for gout.
>
> Have appointed Annie Lady Superintendant of the ladies baths. It is a very easy & light duty & she makes three pounds £3/- per week & takes her meals at the baths which are sent to her from the restaurant.
>
> When I have time I go up to the University at Fitzroy, a suburb, to refresh my memory as a postgraduate. Dr. McCrae, Chief of the Surgical Department, & many other doctors come to the baths where I spend most of my time so I have splendid opportunities of acquiring valuable medical information. Occasionally, I go to Hood & Cos., chemists on Elizabeth Street, to help & work free in their laboratory. [With] an epidemic of diphtheria having broken out and carrying off dozens of children, I brought forward my cure I discovered some years ago on my way from Malta. I have already by it made over seven thousand pounds sterling.[12]

Edwin also spent some of his hours away from the baths performing. On July 19 and 24 and August 14, he placed ads in Melbourne's *Argus* newspaper announcing that he would be performing a "Grand Drawingroom Entertainment" at three different venues. The *Telegraph* of August 18 described his performance as follows:

> On Tuesday evening last, Mr. Osbaldeston, late of the Davenport Brothers, gave his entertainment at the St. Kilda Town Hall under the patronage of W. Ford, Esq., the worshipful mayor and others. Besides the "Rope Tying Illusion" the entertainment consisted of a Polytechnic Display and the exhibition of the "Talking Hand" both of which afforded considerable amusement; but Mr. Osbaldeston astonished his audience most by the dexterity with which he freed himself in a very short time, without assistance, from a rope with which he had been bound hand and foot by a gentleman who was called from the body of the hall for that purpose. Mr. Osbaldeston then bound a lad, who, after having been told the secret, very soon released himself from his bonds. Mr. Osbaldeston disclaimed any connection with "spirits," and stated that he was willing to impart the secret to any of the audience.[13]

On November 29, 1866, an event occurred that had a profound effect on the lives of Edwin and Ann. A fire broke out in one of the rooms of the former Olympic Theatre building. In his journal he recorded the conflagration this way.

> Trouble. The Turn Verein Association gave an entertainment in their rooms last night & the place caught fire & the great theatre on Great Lonsdale Street is burnt to the ground. My losses are quite twenty one thousand pounds sterling. My insurance expired just three days before. I was notified but forgot the matter. My menagerie alone was worth three thousand pounds. All my fine collection of birds & animals destroyed. Much clothing & furniture & trunks full of rare curiosities & a two thousand pound theatrical wardrobe gone up in smoke through persons' carelessness & the vile habit of beer drinking for the sheer useless pleasure of it. I heartily mistrust &

dislike a drinking man & drunkard & have made it a life long rule not to do any kind of business with such people.[14]

The newspaper account of the fire in the *Argus* told a different story.

> The site of the old Olympic Theatre—which was destroyed by fire at an early hour yesterday morning—was visited during the day by large numbers of persons. The place was burned entirely out, and little but the smoke-blackened brick walls of the front and back now remains standing. The interior is strewn with the wreck of the iron roof, lying in shapeless disorder. . . . The fire . . . was discovered shining through the windows of the front of the building, at about a quarter past one, and, upon observing it, Constable Delaney burst open the door of the Turkish Baths . . . and alarmed the persons who were living there. The other part of the old theatre was occupied by the German Gymnastic Association, and a man was sleeping in one of the back rooms. He endeavoured to make his way out by the front, but finding that to be impossible, he escaped by the back. . . .
>
> The building being but of light construction (principally wood and iron), the fire blazed up very brightly, and illuminated the whole neighbourhood; the tall white spire of the adjoining Wesley Church being rendered visible to a considerable distance by the ruddy glare reflected upon it. Large masses of burning material were borne upwards by the strong indraught caused by the flames, and were carried far and wide. Some degree of apprehension was felt that these fire-flakes would ignite some of the neighbouring roofs; but owing probably to the fact that a slight rain had fallen some little time previously, no damage resulted from that cause. Although the fire occurred at so early an hour, a dense crowd of spectators speedily collected. The brigade, on arrival, soon got to work, and six streams of water were brought to bear upon the flames. However, from the hold which the fire had obtained of the building in which it arose, all hope of saving any part of it was soon seen to be fruitless, and the firemen directed their efforts mainly to prevent the flames from extending to any of the neighbouring houses. . . . The fire was not actually extinct till about five o'clock in the morning. The theatre was the property of the Hon. J. M'Crae, M.L.C., and was insured.
>
> Amongst the losses incurred by the destruction of the Turn-Verein, we learn that Mr. C. E. Horsley has severely suffered. A large proportion of choral music and scores intended for the future concerts at the Exhibition, the rehearsals for which were held at the building destroyed, have been annihilated.[15]

On December 6, 1866, the caretakers of the German Association, a constable, Edwin, and Ferdinand Pietriche gave testimony to the Melbourne coroner's inquest regarding the fire at the former Olympic Theatre building.

> **Dr. Youl, city coroner** . . . building known as the old Olympic theatre, Lonsdale Street, part of which was used as a gymnasium by the Deutscher Turn-Verein, and the other portion as Turkish baths.
>
> **Constable Patrick Walsh** deposed, that at about ten minutes past one o'clock on Thursday morning, [November] 29th, while on duty in Lonsdale Street, he observed a fire in the second story of the building in the part occupied by the Turn Verein. He took a cab and called the fire brigade. On his return the fire had extended to the whole building, and hundreds of people had assembled.
>
> **Carl Heintz** deposed that he resided in the building as care-taker for the Turn Verein, and was sleeping there on the night of the fire; also his wife, son, and daughter. The place was all right when he went to bed at a quarter past twelve. He was awoke by his wife, and heard the people in the Turkish baths calling out, and saw that the front of the place was on fire. It appeared to come from the part over the baths. He and his family had to hurry out as quickly as possible, and were unable to save anything, the fire extended so rapidly. They had no fire in the front part. The Verein had lost about £1,000, and were, he believed, insured for £700. He was sure that the fire had not originated in their part of the premises. The people from the bath premises were out before him, and had three boxes out. Had his wife not been aroused by a shout, and by calls of "fire" in the baths, they could not have escaped. Theresa Heintz, wife of last witness, gave similar evidence.
>
> **Edwin T. Osbaldeston** stated that he had been in charge of the Turkish baths, and lived in apartments at the back of those premises. The part which they occupied was all at the back and ground floor, except one room, which was upstairs at the back, and was used as a cooling-room for the bathers. There was no fire there. The fires were all at the back and ground floor. He went to bed about midnight. The gas had been turned off since seven o'clock. He was awoke by his wife at about a quarter past one. She asked him to take down his revolver, as she heard a noise upstairs as though some one was moving about the furniture. He then went into the tepidarium, when he observed the windows illuminated by a strong light, and saw that the place was on fire. The flames were coming out of the sitting-room of the German Association. It was then confined to those premises. Seeing this, he gave the alarm to

the persons there. With the assistance of a police constable he secured a portion of his goods. He believed that the fire originated in the sitting-room of the association. The members were accustomed to sit and smoke there. Witness's goods were not insured.

Ferdinand Pitriche, owner of the baths, said that when he left the place at seven o'clock on the evening before the fire, the gas was extinguished. His place was insured for £200. He had applied to insure it for £200 more, and his proposition had been accepted, but he had neglected to pay the premium (30s.) on the day before the fire, as he had intended, but forgot to do.

Constable Michael Delaney proved discovering the fire when on duty in Little Bourke Street. He gave the alarm, and tried to break open the door of the German Association's premises, but was unable to do so. The fire seemed to have originated in the upper portion of the premises of the German Association. He then went to the door of the baths, and broke that open, when he found the people up. He helped them to get out some of their things. The fire, at the time when he first saw it, was confined to the place of the German Association. In a few minutes it had extended to the whole building. Nothing could be saved.

The coroner, having summed up the evidence, the jury found that the premises were burned by a fire which originated accidentally in the premises occupied by the German Association.[16]

Clearly, from the testimony, it was Pietriche who was insured, not Edwin, and it was Pietriche who had meant to increase his insurance but had neglected to do so. The loss of his place of employment meant that Edwin had to quickly make other arrangements to guarantee his future and that of his wife and baby daughter.

The Osbaldestons Move to Ballarat

Pietriche stated that it was his intention to rebuild the Turkish baths in Melbourne. (He did three weeks later.) Edwin either felt he could not take the chance that this would happen or did not want to wait for it to occur. Thus, he decided to seek his fortune elsewhere. On December 7, 1866, the day after he gave testimony to the coroner's inquest into the fire at the former Olympic Theatre building, Edwin sent the following letter soliciting for a position to the Town Clerk of Ballarat, a gold-mining town northwest of Melbourne:

> Sir,
> I take this opportunity of forwarding to you a newspaper containing the account of the inquest held upon the late fire here. Also a copy of a testimonial presented to me by my late employer. The latter I shall be obliged if you lay it with my testimonial brought before the Corporation.
> Yours most respectfully,
> E. T. Osbaldeston[17]

Following a visit to the Turkish baths at Ballarat on December 17, Edwin wrote the following letter to the editor of the *Ballarat Star:*

> Sir,—Having had much experience, extending over fifteen years, in that most luxurious and health-giving establishment, the Turkish bath, it gives me much pleasure to bear my testimony to the scientific and skilful manner in which the establishment has been introduced into your township. During the fifteen years of my experience I have had the pleasure of seeing them in their native state in the East, also as they have been adopted by Europeans in the United Kingdom and other colonies in Australia. When I was in London some few months ago I was told that the Hammam or Turkish bath had been introduced into the Australian colonies, but in a very imperfect state. Guess my surprise upon my arrival here some few days back to find a Turkish bath equal, if not superior to anything of the sort I have ever met with, and I am sure it must be very gratifying to the public to know that they have now amongst them an establishment which may vie with any in Europe or Australia, including the much-approved Oriental system of treatment. What I here state I do so from experience, and may add that this, amongst other useful establishments in and about Ballarat, bears testimony to the enterprising and benevolent spirit of the inhabitants. What more is wanted to complete the comfort, add to the health and the enjoyment of the

Edwin Turner Osbaldeston (1866)

public than this luxury of all luxuries, the Turkish bath?
E. T. Osbaldeston, late Turkish Zelikah.
17th December.[18]

Edwin definitely exaggerated the length and breadth of his experience with Turkish baths. Fifteen years earlier, in 1851, he was a thirteen-year-old errand boy living with his parents in Birmingham, England. In Ballarat the officials must have been swayed by his complimentary assessment of their facility as, later that month, Edwin and Ann were hired by the Ballarat Corporation Baths. Ballarat began operating the baths as a municipal service in 1863 and hired people to operate the facility.[19] When Edwin and Ann were hired job descriptions were drawn up. Their duties were described in a hand-written document entitled "Duties of the Several Attendants employed by the Bath Committee" as follows:

Mr. Boyce—Will take charge of the keys of the front doors, boiler house, and swimming bath. Attend to boiler, getting up steam & consistent supply of hot water, look after swimming bath, & assist to give common warm water baths and will take charge of swimming baths every third Sunday.

Mr. Osbaldeston—Will take charge of [the] keys [to the] Turkish Baths [and] look after them. Keep the whole [facility] clean including the Frigidarium, Dressing Boxes, Lavatarium, Tepidarium, Calidarium warm bath & closet. . . . Shampooing on Gentlemen's days. Give Scicillian or warm douche baths & when convenient assist to give common warm water baths. Every third Sunday take charge of swimming bath.

Mrs. Boyce—Will do the laundry work. Keep a constant supply of clean linen for the Turkish, warm water, and swimming baths and will keep clean the passages leading to the baths.

Mrs. Osbaldeston—Will shampoo the ladies on their respective days and keep repair of the cushions, curtains, etc.

Duties of Clerk—Will take cash, issue tickets, show bathers into the bath, & assist to give common warm baths. Will take charge of swimming bath every third Sunday.

Besides the above duties, every person will be expected to cooperate & make themselves useful about the building. Civility, attention, and cleanliness will be expected from all. A complaint book will be kept in the cooling room of the Turkish Baths. All complaints by the attendants to be made to the General Manager.[20]

While the delineation of duties was fairly clear, the corporation did not direct who was to be ultimately in charge of the total organization. The failure to put in place a hierarchy of command would soon lead to problems in the operation of the baths.

Edwin wrote a letter on December 20, 1866, to the Bath Committee and chairman, stating that he would like to rent two shops located in front of the Turkish baths. He wanted to convert them into living quarters for himself and his family.[21] The corporation rented only one of the shops to him. On January 3, 1867, Edwin wrote to the mayor of Ballarat regarding his wish to rent both of the shops. As he and his wife were expected to work long hours in the baths, he wanted their accommodation to be conveniently close to their workplace. However, there was another contender for the other shop. Jane Cullen, a young single mother, was awarded the space. She planned to serve coffee and other refreshments in the second storefront.

Even though he had earlier remarked how exceptional the Ballarat Corporation Baths were, he found them lacking in many ways. On January 6, 1867, Edwin sent another letter to the chairman and members of the Bath Committee with a list of equipment and materials he wanted for the Turkish baths. Among other things he asked the committee to provide were a shampooing bench, large wooden bowls, oil cloth, scrubbing brushes, common soda or washing powder, two divans, and several small, round tables.[22]

A third letter on January 25, 1867, was addressed to the mayor requesting permission to prepare and sell coffee and tea to bathers. He stated, "Burning the coffee is not only the bather's luxury but the bath purifier, therefore this Coffee Question is one of importance acting as it does in so many beneficial ways to the edification of this glorious institution."[23]

Apparently, that letter went unanswered, so Edwin wrote again on February 11, raising the subject of wanting a small place to make coffee or tea for the bathers. He mentioned that he had asked Cullen, the occupant of the other shop in front of the Turkish baths, to provide these refreshments for the bathers. She had refused him on the grounds of lack of space. She also told him that it would interfere with her duties as a private tutor.[24] (It is not known if these were her true reasons as to why she had refused his request or if Edwin had antagonized her in some way.)

In his letter of February 11, 1867, Edwin included a well-thought-out list of equipment that he felt would improve the comfort of the bathers. He also included some good ideas for attracting more customers to the baths. He suggested a flag for the roof and a limited free pass for a few influential residents so they could attest to the experience and make endorsements. He knew that previous attempts to make the baths a paying proposition had failed. He also knew that the more customers there were, the greater economic benefit there could be for him personally.[25]

Relations between Edwin and his fellow employees Mr. and Mrs. Boyce soured quickly. The two strong personalities clashed and a turf war ensued. Surely, Edwin's self-aggrandizement annoyed the Boyces. John Boyce may have felt threatened by Edwin's suggestions for improving the operations of the baths. Petty arguments and actions followed.

On February 14, 1867, Boyce sent a letter of complaint to the Bath Committee. Edwin retaliated in a letter he sent to the mayor on February 18. "My wife and I," he wrote, "have been badgered by an everlasting series of petty annoyances from the man Boyce & his wife; & these have now become so aggravated that I can no longer bear them."[26]

His lengthy letter cited other grievances.

> My terms with the Committee are to be at the baths nine hours per day and six days in the week . . . but I have always made it a rule to work 2 or 3 hours per diem over my time. . . . I made great improvement in the appearance & comfort of the place & always kept it clean. Yet it is by no means fair that I should have to clean up candle grease from the floor of my bath rooms, evidently placed there by intention, or sweep & scrub up the dirt & filth that may be left from the various folks who it would seem hold their nocturnal revels in the apartments I am expected to keep in nice order—Nor is it by any means pleasant to find that my bathers are also subjected by certain hints & winks on their way to & from the Bath Rooms that lead them to believe they are not properly dealt with, while submitting themselves to my system of treatment I who after fifteen years experience in the East, England & the Colonies.
>
> . . .
>
> When I have ventured to suggest he [Boyce] should leave me to manage my own department [he] has only hinted at a pugilistic settlement as also his Amazonian wife has shown similar symptoms towards us both. She actually had the impudence to send one of her minions into the Bath to threaten & insult my wife.

Edwin closed his letter by denying that he had sold spirits in the baths, making it known that he would not be subjected to such treatment and stating that he had offers of other employment.[27]

Replies to Edwin's letters to the mayor and members of the Bath Committee (if there were any) have not survived. In spite of his problems with the Boyces, Edwin persevered in his efforts to improve the Turkish baths and the services offered. On February 20, two days after he wrote his letter of complaint, Edwin sent yet another letter to the chairman and members of the Bath Committee with suggestions on changing the operations and requesting advertising.[28]

On March 4, 1867, John Boyce wrote a letter to the mayor of Ballarat in response to the complaints Edwin had made against him and his wife. In his letter he denied some of the charges and offered his version of the events described by Edwin. Boyce retorted that it was Edwin who admitted bathers free of charge and introduced hard liquor into the baths. Boyce said Osbaldeston had told him that he was able to clear "eight pounds per week in Melbourne by so doing." Boyce also claimed, "[Osbaldeston] asked me to go hand and glove with him to make money. I refused. I told him I would have nothing to do with him whatever. Since then he has tried every means to make mischief."[29]

Some baths did permit the consumption of spirits on their premises. Such baths were not conjoined with swimming baths. In Ballarat the corporation forbade alcohol because of the obvious dangers of mixing swimming and spirituous liquors. Further, the baths were considered to be an alternative to the saloon and for some served as a promoter of temperance and healthy living.[30] Edwin maintained that he only sold tea, coffee, and lemonade to bathers.

As troubling as his barrage of requests and his squabble with the Boyces may have been to the mayor and members of the Bath Committee, Edwin's tenure in the Ballarat Corporation Baths would be brief. His employment ended as a result of an altercation with a customer named Timothy Foley.

On March 12, 1867, Mr. Foley sent a letter of complaint about Osbaldeston to the proprietors of the baths, the mayor and councillors of Ballarat.[31] In his letter he recounted his visit to the Turkish baths earlier that day where he had purchased a ticket for a bath and a massage. After having done this, he was told that the shampooer, Mr. Osbaldeston, was at lunch and it was not known when he would return. Deciding he was unable to wait for Osbaldeston's return, he exchanged his ticket for a shilling hot bath.

While his bath was being filled by Mr. Miller, another bath attendant, Edwin returned, prompting Mr. Foley to ask him what his hours were. To this question Edwin replied "it was no business" of his. No doubt greatly taken aback by such a response, Foley sought to justify his inquiry by explaining that this was his third visit to the Turkish baths and on none of those occasions was Osbaldeston in attendance. This response, if Foley's words were an accurate account of what followed, sent Edwin into a fury.[32]

> [Osbaldeston] then commenced abusing me and calling me abominable names. I told him he had better go away that I would get my satisfaction. He then shook his fists and said he was not afraid of any man and struck and cut me in the face and tore my shirt and clothes. I caught him and turned him over into the bath. When down he said he would cut my liver out then put his hand in his pocket. Thinking he was getting a knife I went off. The old man Miller was present at the whole. The boy [an assistant] and Mrs. Boyce heard him making the threats. In fact, Mrs. Boyce insisted on my going into the wash house for fear he would use a knife.[33]

Rather than fire Edwin, the Bath Committee asked him to resign. He did so in a letter dated March 15, 1867, in which he intimates to be the victim.

> To the Bath Committee
> I am sorry to say I feel bound in justice to myself to resign my position as Manager of your Turkish bath. I do this with regret but with perfect confidence in the fact that did you thoroughly understand the peculiar position I am placed in at the Bath you could in no wise attach blame to my actions. I have always been thought hither too capable of managing my own peculiar department in the Baths and I will not here in Ballarat be subjected to further annoyance from those who think proper to annoy me. I beg you will consider that my long experience as a shampooer and the numerous testimonials I have received, I have no right to refuse the office of manager of the New Melbourne baths. To stay longer in a place where it would seem I am looked upon by the people in charge and their peculiar friends in the light of an interloper and a nuisance. To be got rid of anyway by fair or foul means would only be to subject myself again to those unjust annoyances which I justly complain of. In conclusion, I may add I shall be happy to prove my respect for yourselves by giving lessons previous to my departure to any gentleman who may be appointed by you as my successor.
>
> Respectfully,
> E. T. Osbaldeston[34]

A week later he wrote a letter to the Mayor of Ballarat from Melbourne in an attempt to clear his name.

> To his Worshipful The Mayor of Ballarat as Chairman of the Bath Committee:
>
> Sir, I take this opportunity of writing to you for my discharge from the employ of the Committee. In complying with my request I hope they will take into consideration my former good character, and my endeavor to please while in your service.
>
> With regard to Mr. Foley, I beg they will consider that I was justified in doing as I did under the aggravating circumstance.
>
> Most respectfully,
> Edwin Turner Osbaldeston[35]

If John Boyce's claim that Edwin had attempted to introduce bathers free of charge as his personal friends was true, the friends involved may have been his first cousins, brothers Alfred and William George Osbaldeston.

Having lost two positions in less than a year, Edwin packed up his family and moved to another Australian colony to start over again. Would he make a fresh start, or would his difficulties follow him?

Edwin's cousin, William George Osbaldeston, manager, gold mining company, Happy Valley, Victoria, Australia, age 30, Tuesday, 20th February 1866

NOTES

1. Public Record Office Victoria (PROV), "Inward Passenger Lists (Australian Ports)." Series VPRS 944/P, Box 23, July 1865–March 1866.
2. ETO, "Journal" (unpublished manuscript), 85, Siver family history material.
3. *Ballarat Evening Post,* 16 March 1867, p. 2, col. f; *Ballarat Star*, 23 March 1867, p. 2, col. d.
4. ETO, "Journal" (unpublished manuscript), 78, Siver family history material.
5. ETO, "Journal" (unpublished manuscript), 131, Siver family history material.
6. "You Must Use the Bath!" Radio National: *Hindsight*, 16 July 2006, accessed 14 February 2014, http://abc.net.au/radionational/programs/hindsight/you-must-use-the-bath/3320140.
7. Elisabeth Kumm, "Olympic Theatre," accessed 12 February 2014, http://www.emelbourne.net.au/biogs/EM01089b.htm.
8. Ibid.
9. Malcolm Shifrin, "The Victorian Turkish Bath Arrives in 19th Century London, 1. Definitions," accessed 14 February 2014, http://www.victorianturkishbath.org/_3TOPICS/AtoZ-Topics/Social/Performance/1StagesEng.htm.
10. Victoria, Registry of Births, Deaths and Marriages, "Births in the District of Collingwood in the Colony of Victoria," entry for Annie Osbaldeston, born 18 May 1866, Melbourne, Victoria, Australia.
11. "The Melbourne Turn Verein: Fifty Years of History," *Argus* (Melbourne), 20 August 1932, p. 6.
12. ETO, "Journal" (unpublished manuscript), 86–90, Siver family history material.
13. "Memoranda," *Telegraph and St. Kilda, Prahran and South Yarra Guardian* (Melbourne), 18 August 1866, p. 2, col. d.
14. ETO, "Journal" (unpublished manuscript), 91–92, Siver family history material.
15. *Argus* (Melbourne), 30 November 1866, p. 5, col. a.
16. "The Fire at the Old Olympic Theatre. Coroner's Inquest," *Argus* (Melbourne), 7 December 1866, p. 5, col. d.
17. PROV, VPRS 2500/P0000/Unit 13 (October-December 1866 folder), "Letter to Town Clerk [of Ballarat] from Osbaldeston, 7 December 1866."
18. "Turkish Baths," *Ballarat Star*, 21 December 1866, p. 3, col. a.
19. Malcolm Shifrin, "The Victorian Turkish Baths Directory," accessed 14 February 2014, www.victorianturkishbath.org.
20. PROV, VPRS 2500/P0000/Unit 13, "Duties of the Several Attendants Employed by the Bath Committee."
21. PROV, VPRS 2500/P0000/Unit 14, "Application to the Chairman and the Bath Committee from E T Osbaldeston, 20 December 1866."
22. PROV, VPRS 2500/P0000/Unit 14, "Application to the Chairman and the Bath Committee from E T Osbaldeston, 20 December 1866."
23. PROV, VPRS 2500/P0000/Unit 14, "Osbaldeston to the Mayor of Ballarat, 25 January 1867."
24. Ibid.
25. PROV, VPRS 2500/P0000/Unit 14, "Osbaldeston to the Mayor of Ballarat, 11 February 1867."
26. PROV, VPRS 2500/P0000/Unit 14, "Osbaldeston to Mayor of Ballarat, 18 February 1867."
27. Ibid.
28. PROV, VPRS 2500/P0000/Unit 14, "Osbaldeston to chairman and members of Bath Committee, Ballarat, 20 February 1867."
29. PROV, VPRS 2500/P0000/Unit 14, "John Boyce to Mayor of Ballarat, 4 March 1867."
30. Susan Aykut, "'A Lot of Hot Air,' The Turkish Bath in Nineteenth-Century Australia," *Mt Wilson & Mt Irvine Historical Society, Historical Papers* 6 (2007), p. 8.
31. PROV, VPRS 2500/P0000/Unit 14 "Timothy Foley complaint against shampooer, 12 March 1867."
32. PROV, VPRS 2500/P0000/Unit 14, "Timothy Foley complaint against shampooer, 12 March 1867."
33. Ibid.
34. PROV, VPRS 2500/P0000/Unit 14, Osbaldeston's resignation, 15 March 1867.
35. PROV, VPRS 2500/P0000/Unit 14. Osbaldeston's resignation/discharge. Melbourne, 22 March 1867.

CHAPTER SEVEN

Adelaide & the Visit of Prince Alfred ~ 1867–1873

With an eye on his future and a nod at self-promotion, Edwin wrote a letter to the Adelaide newspaper the *Observer* in mid-February 1867 while he was still employed by the Baths Corporation in Ballarat. He had read that the Adelaide Municipal Council was considering opening a Turkish bath. Because he still had his position in Ballarat, he signed his letter "Sympathy" rather than giving his own name. The letter read in part as follows:

> To The Editor:
> Sir—I notice by your columns that a fresh trial is to be made to establish Turkish baths in Adelaide; and knowing as I do the immense advantages to be derived from them, I sincerely trust Mr. Bastard [lessee of the baths] may be more successful on this than on former occasions.
>
> That the Turkish bath is a most useful auxiliary to the curing of very many diseases is a fact so well known and so universally admitted by medical men that it does not allow of a doubt; but apart from that it is about the greatest luxury . . . in a climate like that of Adelaide, which is well known to me. . . .
>
> When for the first time a man has sat for an hour in the hot rooms of a Turkish bath and is well shampooed, and he sees the quantity of dirt and filth that is rubbed off him, he never afterwards fails to pay occasional visits, and be again made clean.
>
> After the actual bath comes its peculiar luxury—the quiet couch in the "frigedarium," the newspapers to his hand, the "cup of mocha" by his side, and if he be a smoker, the enjoyment of the fragrant weed. . . .
>
> [From] a sanitary point of view a Turkish bath in a city like Adelaide should certainly be considered a necessity. . . .
>
> Here, on Ballarat, the Borough Corporation have provided the baths, and I think we are lucky in having the services of a first-class man, Mr. Osbaldistone, who formerly managed the Melbourne baths, recently burnt down. Would this not be a hint to your own "regulators" to prevent the falling through of Mr. Bastard's present plan? I hope they may take it, and that when I come over to Adelaide next time, which will be in a month or two, I may find a well-conducted Turkish bath with its appropriate motto—"Be clean."
>
> I am Sir, &c,
> Sympathy[1]

Following the debacle in Ballarat, Edwin decided to move forward with his plan to relocate to Adelaide. He had been in communication several times with Thomas Bastard, the man who held the lease on the city baths of Adelaide. On March 27, 1867, Edwin; his wife, Ann; their baby daughter; and two friends, musician E. J. Wivell and artist Thomas Moore, departed from Melbourne. They were listed as sailing on the *Coorong*, a wooden barque of 359 tons built in 1864.

When they arrived in Adelaide on March 30, Edwin immediately went to the office of the *South Australian Advertiser* to inform the newspaper of his arrival.

> TOPICS OF THE DAY. . . . We understand that Mr. E. T. Osbaldiston, the late Manager of the Melbourne and Turkish Baths, arrived by the *Coorong*, for the purpose of assisting in the establishment of a Turkish Bath in the city of Adelaide.[2]

By Wednesday, April 3, 1867, Edwin had worked his way into the discussion with the municipal council on developing a Turkish bath at the rundown city baths.

> THE PROPOSED TURKISH BATHS.—On Wednesday morning the members of the Municipal Council, accompanied by the Town Clerk and Surveyor, met Mr. Osbaldiston and Mr. Macgeorge [architect] at the City Baths, and proceeded, with the lessee (Mr. Bastard), to make an inspection of the premises with a view of deciding upon the course to [be] adopted in reference to the erection of the necessary additional rooms for the Turkish baths. . . .[3]

Bastard had been operating the bathhouse since February 1866. At this meeting, the parties discussed whether to tear down the existing bath and build new or to add to the structures that were there to accommodate Turkish bath facilities. One consideration was to raise the roof of an existing building to sixteen feet. Edwin assured the councillors that sixteen feet would suffice although he had seen rooms in baths in Turkey that had ceilings as high as one hundred and one hundred and fifty feet. The councillors also reviewed a proposal to improve the swimming bath.[4] The discussion at the meeting centered on the cost of, and financing for, construction of a Turkish bath. The council was willing to cover half the expense. The other monies would have to be raised through subscriptions.[5]

At a special meeting of the municipal council held on Monday, April 8, the councillors learned that renovations to the existing city baths (including the creation of the Turkish bath) would cost over £700. The council decided not to take any action until £400 had been guaranteed in private subscriptions.[6] In the weeks that followed the funds were raised and the renovations of the existing baths took place.

It came as no surprise that relations between Edwin and Thomas Bastard became strained. By the second half of May, Bastard had come to the conclusion that he could not work with Edwin. Realizing this, Edwin wrote a letter to the municipal council in an attempt to secure a stronger foothold in the Adelaide bath. In this letter Edwin said that Bastard had induced him to leave a good situation to come to Adelaide with the promise that he would be employed in the construction and management of the bath and now was reneging on that promise.

In its weekly report on the activities of the Adelaide Municipal Council, the *South Australian Register* mentioned that a letter Edwin had sent to the council was read into the record on May 20. The council declined to get involved as it had nothing to do with the matter and moved that the letter simply be received and acknowledged.[7] The Adelaide town clerk forwarded the correspondence to Bastard, also known as "Cockney Tom," for a response.

Bastard saw things much differently. Although Cockney Tom misspelled Edwin's name, he certainly remembered the audacious fellow who had caused him so much grief. In his 1881, sixty-six-page autobiography, Cockney Tom devoted six pages to his dealings with the man he mistakenly called "Edward Baldiston." He recalled the situation thusly:

> At this time the then town clerk received a letter from a man calling himself Edward Baldiston, stated to be manager of the Turkish baths in Melbourne, giving a long account of his experience at Constantinople, and other places in Turkey, and applying for the management of the Adelaide Turkish baths. The town clerk sent his letter on to me, and advised me to answer it. I did so, but was sorry for it afterwards. The baths in Melbourne were burnt down shortly after that, and Baldiston found his way to Adelaide, and presenting himself and wife at the baths, gave me to understand that he had come over at the request of several gentlemen to superintend the Turkish baths department.
>
> I disabused his mind at once, and told him that no one had any power to engage him but myself; whereupon he said, "I'll see about that." He called on several of my friends and made out that I knew nothing about keeping baths, and in every possible way tried to injure my character. He did not, however, succeed as well as he expected.
>
> The next thing he did was to prepare a document for me to sign, appointing him shampooer, and came down to the baths with this document while no one but the boy was about. When he saw me he said: "Will you sign this?" "No!" replied I, "I will have nothing to do with you." He thereupon struck me a blow in the face, which knocked me into the water. I called for help, and my wife came to my assistance, and found Baldiston, who was a powerful young man, trying to hold me under water.
>
> "You wretch!" said she, "you are trying to drown my husband." "Yes!" he answered, "and I'll drown you too," and the next moment in she was sent likewise. Hearing the noise, some passersby came in, to whom he declared that the swimming master and his wife had been trying to drown him, and in the struggle we had all slipped into the water together. I went for a policeman and gave him [the] charge, but the policeman refused to take the charge on account of not having seen the disturbance, and before I could change my clothes and get to the Police Court, Baldiston had anticipated my action, and taken out a summons against me for an assault with intent to drown.
>
> All that I could then do was to issue a summons against the bad man, and employ a respectable solicitor. . . . Baldiston engaged Mr. Downer, who, of course, came down like a thousand bricks on me for the alleged attempt to drown his most respectable client. My solicitor, however, gave a very different version of the whole affair, and called my wife, who declared that Baldiston was holding me under the water when she came to my assistance, and that before she knew where she was she found herself floundering about in the bath, with Baldiston threatening to drown her and her husband into the bargain. Roars of laughter came from everybody in the court. My daughter also gave evidence that she saw her father and mother both in the water at the same time. (More laughter.)
>
> Mr. Beddome, and the Commissioner, gave their joint opinion that all parties were in the wrong, and inflicted a fine of five shillings on each, with costs, and I and my family and friends left the Court disgusted; but, nevertheless, felt glad to be rid of a man who had taken his Maker's name in witness to a most deliberate falsehood.
>
> A few days after that I received a letter from Baldiston, in which he confessed that what he had stated in Court was untrue, and begged me to forgive him and forget the past, and that he would endeavor to make amends to me by working the baths into such a state of

Professor Bastard.

Thomas Bastard (Cockney Tom), the manager of the Adelaide City Baths, devoted pages of his autobiography to his experiences with Edwin Osbaldeston.

> perfection that I would be sure to make my fortune out of them in a very short time. "All my eye and Betty Martin,"* thought I, "I will have no more truck with you." But, alas, I did have, and that in such a manner as will astonish the reader.[8]

**The expression "all my eye and Betty Martin," meaning total and complete nonsense, can be traced back to the eighteenth century. The exact origin of the phrase is unknown but there were several variations of it including "all my eye" and "all my eye and Tommy." The expression fell out of popular use. (www.worldwidewords.org)*

Even before he ruined his chances of operating a Turkish bath at the Adelaide City Baths, Edwin had set about earning his living and furnishing his home by a variety of other means. He taught calisthenics at eleven schools in Adelaide. Edwin placed ads in the *South Australian Register* as a chiropodist—one who treats corns, bunions, and troublesome nails.[9] He also appeared as a "subject" when English phrenologist and mesmerist Dr. Thomas Guthrie Carr lectured in Adelaide. Besides mesmerism and phrenology, Dr. Carr also lectured in Australia and New Zealand on electropsychology and electrobiology and held séances.

Edwin attended Dr. Carr's lectures at White's Rooms in Adelaide on June 28 and 29 and worked his way into Dr. Carr's performances by serving as a subject under mesmerism. Edwin also demonstrated his rope-tying feat. "He was securely fastened with a long rope by two well-known gentlemen from the audience, and in less than two minutes freed himself entirely and was rewarded by loud applause."[10]

Many of Edwin's future lectures would draw upon Dr. Carr's performances. Dr. Carr had numerous complaints filed against him by persons he "treated" while under mesmeric trances.

Edwin set up a Turkish bath in his own home and advertised this service in the *Register.* A gentleman, probably a reporter or editor of the newspaper, responded to the ad and then published a humorous account of his experience on September 23, 1867.

A TURKISH BATH ON A SMALL SCALE

An advertisement has several times appeared in the *Register* informing the public that Mr. E. T. Osbaldiston was prepared to give Turkish baths in his own house. Mr. Osbaldiston having been several years connected with baths in Constantinople, he may be supposed to have a thorough practical knowledge of the art of bathing and shampooing in all its branches.

Having heard a great deal about the luxury of a Turkish bath, the writer of this article thought he would avail himself of the opportunity afforded by Mr. Osbaldiston's establishment to obtain a new sensation so that he might judge for himself whether this famous institution which has become so popular during the last few years was all that it was represented to be.

An engagement was therefore made with the obliging "demonstrator," and on a certain morning lately, about quarter before 11, I presented myself at the door of Mr. Osbaldiston's modest and unpretending establishment in Grenfell Street. . . . At present he labours under considerable disadvantage in consequences of the smallness of his premises, but his experience and ingenuity have enabled him to make the most of his appliances.

I was first ordered to strip and was soon *in puris naturalibus*, and of course felt myself very much at the mercy of the operator, who took possession of me there and then. I was placed unresistingly on something that had the appearance of an altar covered with a blanket. I was then wrapped up in a series of blankets, one piled over the other to the number of some half dozen. The face only was left uncovered. I had not sat there more than a minute or two when I began to feel that I was pervaded and surrounded by an unknown heat, which crept up my legs, spread itself around my body, and penetrated under every nook and cranny of my manifold coverings. The heat increased and I became somewhat uneasy; it increased more and I became downright uncomfortable. The operator seemed as if he meant to make a burnt offering of me now that he had got me on his diabolical altar.

At last flesh and blood (or cuticle either) could stand it no longer and I roared out, "Murder!" "Is it getting rather warm?" said my inhuman persecutor. "Warm!" I exclaimed, "I am roasting." "All right," said he, "you will be easy just now," and so I was. I burst out into a profuse perspiration; I felt I was fast resolving into a dew, or something not quite so poetical. The perspiration trickled down my body and ran off my nose. Don't let the courteous reader suppose this was the result of fear. It was the hot air with which I was surrounded. After remaining in this state, I know not how long, the operator insinuated his hand under the blankets and began pinching and kneading my arms, hands, legs, and feet, pushing his capable thumb and pliable fingers into every cavity, boring, squeezing, and thumping me as if I were a dog or his bitterest enemy.

During the whole of this process, Mr. Osbaldiston was as calm and good-natured as a man generally is when watching the sufferings of his friend. He regaled me with scraps of his personal history, which under other circumstances might have been amusing enough. Altogether he was as jolly as Mark Tapley [a Charles Dickens' character] could ever desire to be.

Strangely enough, the more I was squeezed, pinched, kneaded the less became my inconvenience. I was like the skinned eels—getting accustomed to the process which I began to enjoy. My feelings towards the operator underwent a gradual change. He appeared less of a sacrificing priest and heartless executioner and at last stood out before me as a gentle, good-hearted, highly benevolent young man who instead of having spent half an hour in torturing me had been trying to promote my comfort.

After more roasting, more pinching, and squeezing I was ordered into a warm bath; and then the squeezing-cum-pinching-cum-kneading was repeated until it struck me that I must be getting as "fair as a lily." This was succeeded by a rough coating of soap which was followed by the application of the flesh brush, which until I obtain further evidence on the subject, I will persist in believing was made of brass wire, finely sharpened to a point. Didn't it scrap and rasp me! More hot water [was] dashed over me.

I was then placed in a squatting position with my head drawn down over my chest. While meditating on what the object of this new move could be, splash-dash came a bucket of ice-cold water over me. For a moment I gasped for breath and just as I was recovering, splash came another bucketful and I was told to jump out—a command which I obeyed with joyful alacrity. The moment I was out the world seemed to have grown brighter and lovelier to me. I was light and cheerful and at peace with myself and with all the world. My bitterest enemy might have borrowed five shillings from me on the spot without even an I.O.U.

Here I was carefully rubbed down, feeling the while [that] I could have jumped and danced for joy. The sensation was new, strange, and delightful beyond conception. I consider myself to be very clean in my habits, going in for a cold bath and scrubbing with a rough towel every morning in the year, winter and summer. I was therefore somewhat disgusted and humiliated to see the quantity of dirt which the shampooing brought out of me. Where it came from I could not understand, but there it was to my utter confusion. Let no man believe he is clean until he has been to a Turkish bath and been half-roasted, half-drowned, pinched, squeezed, kneaded, soaped, rasped. . . , and well thumped from top to toe.

All I had gone through up till this moment was stern business on the part of the operator and the passive patience and endurance on the part of the subject. Now the artistic part of the process came. We had got up from rough utility to sublime aesthetics. Mr. Osbaldiston took a snowy white sheet and with which he draped me in the manner of an antique statue. Though by no means such a specimen of manly grace and symmetry as a Phidias could have desired for a model in the palmy days of Grecian art culture, I flatter myself that as I stood there with my snowy mantle gracefully thrown around me, I was worth looking at!

In this fairy garb I was laid down on a sofa, door and window were thrown open, and as the cool air played around me a dreamy feeling of infinite content and satisfaction stole over me. I could not think; I had no desire to move; I could only luxuriate in the indescribable joy of the present moment. I had attained the *summum bonum* [highest good]. Something had gone from me in the last hour which had left me light, content, and invigorated.

After a while I began to dress and the momentary Elysium was over, but its effects remained with me during the whole of the day; and as I left the house of the clever and courteous operator I resolved that before long I would visit him again.

Alas! There I erred. Had I been content with one bath I should have done well but I went again two days after my first visit and I certainly had too much of a good thing. Turkish baths, even on a small scale, are to be taken in moderation. Like Oliver Twist, having enjoyed one taste, I asked for more and got it and with it something I did not bargain for. I acknowledge that Mr. Osbaldiston was not very cordial about giving me a second dose so soon after the first and it was unwise on my part to take it. The night after my second bath I was seized with violent rigors accompanied with a splitting headache and for a day or two was confined to bed. So I have learned that while one Turkish bath may be good, another two days afterwards may produce serious effects.

Courteous reader, if you want to know what real enjoyment is try a Turkish bath even on the small scale at present attempted by Mr. Osbaldiston, but be content with one, and don't be over-greedy of new sensations as I was.[11]

Prince Alfred and the crew of the frigate Galatea *(State Library of South Australia)*

Edwin's home Turkish bath business did not fare well even with his "experience and ingenuity." However, as the writer attests, Edwin went to great lengths in order to provide his client with the quintessential Turkish bath experience.

Turkish baths tended to attract a more sophisticated and learned class of people. More than likely Edwin met people of wealth and status while employed in the baths. He plied the rich and famous with charm, attentiveness, and compliments while gaining their trust and confidence. Edwin claimed that one of his clients while working in Melbourne had been

Prince Alfred was the first British royal to visit the Australian colonies.

Sir Charles Darling, the governor of Victoria. Somehow he became known to Sir Dominick Daly, the governor of South Australia. Governor Daly helped secure for Edwin an appointment to the staff of Prince Alfred, Duke of Edinburgh, while the prince visited Australia. He served as a temporary valet and masseur to the prince and his entourage while they were in Adelaide.

Prince Alfred was the second son and fourth child of Queen Victoria. He had joined the Royal Navy when he was twelve years old. By 1866 he was captain and commander of the frigate *Galatea*. In January 1867 he sailed from Plymouth on a trip around the world. Prince Alfred docked his ship in Gibraltar, rounded the Cape of Good Hope in July, and visited Cape Town in August. The twenty-three-year-old prince landed in Glenelg, South Australia on October 31 and remained in Australia for five months, paying visits to Adelaide, Melbourne, Sydney, and Brisbane. There was great excitement in Australia over the arrival of Prince Alfred as he was the first royal to visit the Australian colonies.[12]

For months prior to the prince's arrival, Adelaide and North Adelaide had been plagued by a series of robberies. Edwin wrote a letter to the editor of the *South Australian Advertiser* complaining about the inability of the police to end the crime wave.

PETTY ROBBERIES.
TO THE EDITOR.

Sir—Having for some short time been a resident in North Adelaide, and subject, like my neighbours, to the nightly annoyances of marauders, I resolved to keep watch, and if possible, make the acquaintance of these gentry, who consider it no sin to enter our homes during our absence, and carry off clothing, &c.; and pay nocturnal visits to our hen roosts and wood pile. But although I have been on the look out nightly, for the last month or so, I have not had the gratification of meeting them; and have been equally as unsuccessful in finding one of our paid guardians of our homes—until the other night for the first time since my residence in North Adelaide.

Now, what I wish to draw your attention to, is the serious want of police protection here; for this last week or a fortnight, scarcely a night has passed over without some one losing something. And although myself and neighbours have looked out for a constable on duty we could never succeed in finding one. The constable I met the other night bears a good name amongst the oldest inhabitants here as a man who strictly does his duty. But what can one man do in so large a district against (as there appears to be) a regular organised band of these petty robbers.

I am informed upon good authority that there are only four constables doing duty for the whole of North Adelaide; no wonder, then, with so small a police force dishonest persons are able to carry on their work unmolested. But as we pay our rents and taxes I see no reason why we should not expect our homes properly protected by a sufficient number of constables.
I am, Sir, &c.,
E. T. OSBALDESTON.
Ward Street,
North Adelaide.[13]

Before moving to the house on Grenfell Street in Adelaide, Edwin, his wife and daughter, and their friend Edward J. Wivell had lived in North Adelaide. It was from that address that Edwin had written the letter to the press in early May. Edwin was either taunting the authorities or making a clumsy attempt to explain crossing paths with a policeman on patrol.

Prince Alfred's visit to Adelaide coincided with the culmination of the investigation of the robberies by corporal Thomas Doyle of the North Adelaide Police. Thomas Bastard of the city baths recorded his role in the investigation and a second incident with Edwin in his autobiography.

> The Duke of Edinburgh arrived in the colony on a second visit to Adelaide and about the same time the new Governor, Sir James Fergusson, arrived. Now, at this stage of my history something connected with the celebrated Baldiston occurred which is worth mentioning.
>
> Through the interest of the late Governor Daly he had been appointed valet-de-chambre to the Prince and had been recommended to him as a smart man, and in a very short space of time Baldiston sustained his reputation in this respect, for whilst the Duke was staying at Government House he wantonly robbed him of his linen and other valuables; and not being content with that, he forthwith fell in love with the Governor's property, and not only stole his plate, but had the audacity to appropriate the Governor's under-garments.
>
> Housebreaking at this time was quite common in Adelaide, so much so that the Government had to increase the police force; but with all their sagacity the police could not detect the thief.
>
> Now, amongst my acquaintances at that time was one Tom Doyle, a corporal in the detective department of police. He called on me one morning and said, "How are you, old fellow?" "Quite well," said I. "Have you heard of the numerous robberies that have been committed lately, Tom?" said he. "I saw a letter in the newspaper," said I, "complaining of the police, and making out that they could not be over smart, or they would long since have discovered the thief; but don't you suspect any one?"
>
> "Well," said he, "as you are a sworn constable, I'll tell you in confidence that I suspect that fellow that tried to drown you and your wife. So keep your eyes open, and if you hear anything let me know at once. A family in North Adelaide of the name of Fitzpatrick had their house robbed while they were at church. The thieves took Mrs. Fitzpatrick's dresses, the child's clothes, and a musical-box that was on the table. Now, as you are fond of music, should such a thing as this be brought here for sale, make some inquires about it and let me know the result."
>
> I kept a good look out and it so happened that I was destined to be the means of bringing the thief to justice. One of my friends kept a watchmakers shop in Rundle Street, and I cautioned him that if any person called to sell a musical-box, or to have one repaired, to take down all [the] particulars. "'Well, I shall have enough to do," said he, "for every day I have repairs to make of that kind." I, however, kept calling on my friend every day, as we were very great chums and sang together at the cathedral, and other places not worth mentioning, and on one of these occasions my friend said, "Do you remember speaking to me about a musical-box?" "I do," said I, "what about it?" "Nothing particular," said he, "only a woman came in today with one to have a new frame made for it. The instrument is good, but there are one or two teeth broken; I never had a job like it before."
>
> "What is the name of the person that brought it?" asked I. He looked in the book, and read as follows:— "Mrs. Baldiston, Grenfell Street, Adelaide." "Good-bye," said I, "I will see you this evening." The first thing I did was to see my friend, Tom Doyle, whom I soon found.
>
> "My boy, I have got a scent, and believe I can put you on to the man who stole the musical-box." And with that, I told him all I knew; and when I mentioned the name, Doyle was ready to jump out of his shoes. "That's the man at Government House," said he, "and we will soon have him. The first thing to be done is to see Mr. Pfaendler, the watchmaker, and then to call on Mr. Fitzpatrick and arrange with him to meet us at Pfaendler's, to swear to the box. If he can do so, I'll get out a warrant to arrest my man, and search his house."
>
> We met at the appointed time at Pfaendler's, set the musical-box going, and before it had finished the second tune, Mrs. Fitzpatrick exclaimed, "That is my box, and I will swear to it in any court of justice!" "Sign this paper, then," said Doyle, "and I will see you tomorrow morning."
>
> Doyle immediately took out a warrant and sent a policeman to Baldiston's house. He then walked down to Government House to inquire, when who should answer the door for him but Baldiston himself in full livery. "I want you," said the detective. "Want me! What for?" asked the indignant valet. "Here is my authority," said the detective, showing his warrant. "If you will be good enough to wait till I change my clothes," said the valet, "I will go with you. I won't be long."
>
> The detective was taken off his guard by this little stratagem, for his prisoner quickly made tracks for the back door, bolted down the garden, jumped the wall, and made straight for his house. As soon as the detective discovered the trick, and fearing the escape of his man, he also proceeded to Baldiston's house in Grenfell Street, to catch him there. As soon as he found the detective was at his heels, he made his escape at the back door, mounted the fence, got into Rundle Street, and crossed North Terrace, followed by a crowd of men and

boys who had heard the cry of stop thief from the detective who was not far behind him in the chase. As they neared the Botanic Gardens they lost sight of Baldiston for a short time, but a boy having given information that he had seen a man get over the railing into the stableyards of Sir Henry Ayers, the detective, and the mob that had gathered, besieged the yard and stable.

Doyle got into the hayloft, turned over the hay, and found the wretched man rolled like a dog. The detective pulled him out, ornamented him with the bracelets, and took him first to his own house, where he took Mrs. Baldiston also in charge, and marched both of them off to the station. He had also taken the precaution to leave a policeman in charge of the house, where the thief had an immense lot of stolen property stowed away. The next day they had their hearing, and the wife was discharged; but Baldiston was committed and afterwards tried at the Supreme Court, and was sentenced to seven years penal servitude.

I never appeared as a witness against him, for although he had robbed and maltreated me and my wife sorely, yet I bore no malice towards the poor fellow, but left him to his fate; neither were the Prince or His Excellency the Governor called at the trial. This evil disposed man had robbed so many people that at least a hundred charges could have been laid against him, and there was a perfect dray load of stolen property taken to the Police Station to be claimed by the owners.[14]

Some details of Edwin's arrest as reported in the *South Australian Register* differ from Bastard's recollection, but for the most part, the recounting of the story is the same. It was the Kirkpatricks, and not the Fitzpatricks, who owned the musical box. When Corporal Doyle armed with a search warrant went to the Osbaldeston home, he recognized the jacket that Ann was wearing from a fabric sample that Mrs. Kirkpatrick had given him after they were robbed in April.

Edwin fled first from Government House, was captured, brought to his house on Grenfell Street and fled a second time, from where he ran for several blocks and through backyards, and hid in a haystack.[15]

Following Edwin's arrest on Friday, November 15, 1867, the police searched his house and discovered just how many thefts he had committed.

According to the *South Australian Register*, "On a thorough search of the premises being made, a vast number of articles of all descriptions was found, all of which are supposed to have been stolen. The lot, consisting of two drayloads, was taken to the police station for identification."[16]

The inventory of the stolen goods included clothing and an embroidered pillow belonging to Prince Alfred and apparel belonging to several officers of HMS *Galatea*. It also included a great number of articles, including dinnerware, belonging to Government House for which no prosecution was initiated. The property stolen from residents of Adelaide and North Adelaide was extensive and constituted in part the following:

- Insignia, jewelry, and clothing from Dr. H. T. Wittell on North Terrace
- A gold watch, rings, and assorted jewelry from Mr. R. Minchin living at the Bay
- Assorted jewelry, combs, and spectacles from Mrs. E. Chapman on Grote Street
- A railway rug belonging to the Methodist New Connexion Church
- A pair of muslin window curtains belonging to Mrs. M. Routledge
- Gold watch and apparel from Mr. W. Kay on East Terrace
- An English concertina and pair of burlesque shoes belonging to Mr. A. Dymond from White's Rooms
- Five chairs from Mr. Schultz on Flinders Street
- Three chairs from Mr. Gale of Nailsworth
- An American oven from Mr. Lallemann of North Adelaide
- A military uniform belonging to Major Lucas from White's Rooms
- A number of maps and anatomical and physiological charts from Pulteney Street School
- Quantity of linen and apparel marked "R. and K. Baker"
- A similar amount marked "R. C. Baker"
- Flags honoring the visit of Prince Alfred from Messrs. W. D. Allot, J. Calder, C. E. Tidemann.[17] [18]

Edwin, Ann, and their friend Wivell were brought before the police magistrate on Monday, November 18, on charges of housebreaking during the seven and a half months that they had lived in Adelaide.

Members of the Duke of Edinburgh's party and some Adelaide dignitaries were present. Lawyer James Penn Boucaut, an English immigrant who would go on to a distinguished career as a judge, politician, and premier of South Australia, was appointed to defend the prisoners. At the end of the proceedings, charges against Ann and Wivell were dropped for lack of evidence, and they were given their liberty.[19]

Following his release, Wivell wrote a letter to the editor of the *South Australian Register,* denying that he had anything to do with the robberies and that he considered Edwin only an acquaintance.[20] Yet he had traveled to Adelaide with Edwin and lived under his roof!

Edwin was returned to the Adelaide Police Station to await trial. The next night he attempted to hang himself in his cell. An officer intervened and frustrated his attempt. Edwin was then placed in a straightjacket.[21]

Additional theft charges were leveled against Edwin on November 21 when more stolen items were identified. Also found in his Grenfell Street home were the following:

Government House in Adelaide (1864) where Edwin had been employed as a temporary valet and masseur to Prince Alfred

- Three shirts, seven chemises, and fabric from the Wesleyan Church on Pirie Street
- Two books and a plan for a Turkish bath from architect J. MacGeorge
- A piece of gutta-percha pipe, fifteen pounds of horsehair, a table cover, and curtain from Mr. J. Saxby
- A wool mattress, three pillows, and two blankets from Mrs. F. Frearson of Kent Town
- A counterpane and trinkets from Mrs. M. McEvoy.[22]

The Adelaide Police reported that, in total, the stolen items taken from his house connected Edwin "with no less than forty robberies, and it is highly probable that the unclaimed articles still in the hands of the police will connect him with several others." The estimated value of the property returned to their rightful owners exceeded £208 14s. 8d.[23] [The value of these goods in 2013 equaled £16,070.]

After the last of the charges was filed against Edwin, he was transferred from the police courts to the Adelaide Gaol. His sentencing took place on December 3.

He was taken to the Supreme Court, where he appeared before Justice William Alfred Wearing. Since Edwin had pled guilty to three of the charges, the prosecutor decided not to bring the other offenses forward at the trial.

When asked why a sentence should not be passed upon him by the court, Edwin was silent, having previously submitted a letter to the judge asking for leniency.[24]

> Your Honor:
>
> Having lately occupied a position in this city commanding the respect and admiration of all, it is with painful feeling of shame and regret that I now find myself at this bar with such dishonouring charges against me, suddenly dashed from the pedestal of fame and honour that I had built for myself, and on which all my earthly hopes were planted. . . . Lost, lost forever to all respectable society, an outcast with a felon's brand, what earthly punishment can be greater?
>
> Were I to attempt, your Honor, to explain the manner in which I came in possession of those articles found at my house, it might appear as though I would excuse my conduct and sound more like romance than reality; but I will atone to society by an acknowledgement of my offense and humbly pray its forgiveness, for I am sure that there is not an eye in this Court but is moist, and not a heart but aches to see me in this dishonourable state.
>
> In passing judgment, your Honor, I pray you to remember my hitherto respectable position in society and that amongst the numbers who know me, and with whom I have done business, not one can come forward and say I am guilty of a single dishonourable action towards them.
>
> I pray, your Honor, to deal with me as leniently as the case will permit—mercy with judgment. Consider my youth, and the dread consequences of a schooling in a convict establishment; but more for the sake of the two poor innocent and helpless beings—my wife and child—who, with an aged father and mother, have been entirely dependent on me for support for this last five years or more. They have committed no offence, yet, through my indiscretion, must be made past sufferers.
>
> In conclusion, your Honor, I plead guilty, humbly asking your leniency, and praying forgiveness of an offended God and society.
>
> E. T. Osbaldiston[25]

Edwin's admission of guilt, coupled with his promise to atone for his sins and plea for forgiveness, did not produce the desired outcome. Justice Wearing said that it was with regret that he saw a young man with his abilities come before him, especially given that he occupied a position of some respectability in the community and that he was in the employ of Prince Alfred. Further, he had the means of earning a livelihood for himself and his family by legitimate means. Instead, the judge noted that Edwin chose to steal, his crime made worse by the fact that he was not a person thrown out of employment.

As for the consequences of his actions inflicted upon his wife and child, Justice Wearing said that he felt deep sorrow and regret that Edwin had brought this upon his family and that the innocent had to suffer for the guilty. In the end the judge did show some leniency. Each of the charges could have brought eight years of imprisonment per offense. Justice Wearing ordered Edwin imprisoned to hard labor for seven years.[26]

The *South Australian Register* reported that upon hearing his sentence, Edwin shrieked, "Oh, my wife and child! What will they do?" and fell down on the dock and had to be forcibly removed from the courtroom. The paper also reported that he tried to cut his throat with a knife after he left the court. Officers prevented the suicide and properly secured him.[27]

Following his sentencing the *South Australian Register* couldn't resist publishing an editorial mocking Edwin's remarkable plea for leniency. "This offender pleaded guilty to numerous charges," the editorial stated, "and by so doing he evidently thinks . . . that he has 'atoned' to the public for the injury he has committed. That statement, indeed, is about as remarkable a piece of Newgate logic and penitentiary bunkum as the public have seen for some time past."
Continuing, the editorial skewered Edwin for his inflated sense of position in the community. "[His statement] contains expressions of regret that the writer has been 'suddenly dashed from the pedestal of fame and honour,' which as a chiropodist, shampooer, and livery servant, he had built up for himself 'to the admiration of all who knew him,' and then it goes on to rebut the charges of robbery but to admit the crime of receiving stolen property, though it is attempted to surround even this admission with a halo of poetry and romance. . . ."[28]

The *Register* also theorized that Edwin must have had accomplices. It reported that there was evidence that stolen items had been sent to Melbourne to be disposed of. Many items went unidentified because they were "disfigured, altered, or broken." Sarcastically, the editorial noted, "No doubt 'society' will feel deeply this condescension and humiliation of the great shampooer. But it would have been much more to the purpose if, instead of playing the part of an injured man of honour who had accidentally 'fallen among thieves,' that he had made a clean breast to the authorities as regards [to] his accomplices. . . ."

The editorial concluded that "nothing was too large and nothing too small for his insatiate maw" and "he must have been miserable whenever his fingers were idle."[29]

As for Prince Alfred, his five-month visit to the Australian colonies ended in March 1868 after an assassin shot him in the upper back, just missing his spine. At the time Alfred was in Sydney for a second visit to New South Wales. The prince had recovered enough by April to take command of his ship for the return trip to England. Certainly he would remember the warm welcome he had received in the colonies, the theft and shooting aside.

Incarceration in Yatala Labour Prison

On Tuesday, December 3, 1867, Edwin was transferred from Adelaide Gaol to Yatala Labour Prison, also known as the Convict Stockade, seven miles north of Adelaide near Dry Creek.

Opened in 1854 to alleviate overcrowding at Adelaide Gaol and to house convicts serving longer sentences, the prison was situated next to a quarry at which inmates were required to work. Originally built to house 120 convicts, the prison was constructed of locally mined stone. Each cell contained only a wooden trestle bed and a mattress of straw. Blankets were distributed at night and were collected in the morning. Light was provided by a small, rectangular window. The prison had a school room, chapel, infirmary, library, kitchen, and mess hall. Convicts were allowed to read one book per week.[30]

Inmate's sketch of Yatala Labour Prison, 1877
(State Library of South Australia, B21925/1)

"In its early years rock-cracking, hard labour, and solitary confinement were the notable features of life at the prison. It was seen that hard-worked prisoners would not wish to return to the prison, with solitary confinement giving them time to reflect on past misdeeds. From inception the prisoners' main task was the breaking of one cubic yard of rock per day to be used for building roads and in construction. Until the middle of the twentieth century the prison department's philosophy remained punitive with much reliance on obedience to rules and regulations."[31]

The quarries were located outside of the stockade in a large gully. Immense, semicircular openings had been cut into the face of the gully. Crews of thirty to thirty-five prisoners worked at extracting the stone and carting it down the gully to another crew that worked at stone cracking. Guards with loaded rifles stood on a cliff above the gully. Violent and insubordinate inmates were kept in shackles, even while working in the quarries.[32] Through hard, physical work and good behavior prisoners earned marks, which in turn earned them remissions of their sentences.

Inmate's sketch, "Smoko" in the Quarries, *Yatala Prison, 1877*
(State Library of South Australia, B21925/8)

Clearly, Cockney Tom took satisfaction that the man who had abused him had received his comeuppance. He followed Edwin's imprisonment and wrote the following in his autobiography:

> Whilst in prison his conduct at first was fearful, he even attempted to cut his own throat, but after a time finding it was no good to be stubborn, he got to be as quiet as a lamb, and became very pious, he even preached to the prisoners on Sundays when he could get a chance, and wrote a long letter making full confession of what he had done and left undone. Amongst the latter was a design to blow up the City Baths. He stated in his letter that he intended getting on to the roof of the baths and dropping down the chimneys sundry bags of gunpowder, so that when the strings got burnt the bags of powder would fall, and a general blow-up of the whole place would have been the *happy* result.[33]

When Edwin entered Yatala Labour Prison, the following information was recorded in the prisoners' register:

Name	Edward Turner Osbaldeston
Number	842
Alias	
When received	3 December 1867
Where from	Adelaide Gaol
Class assigned to	
Date of Conviction	26 November 1867
Offence	Larcenies
At what Court	Supreme
Judge or Magistrate	Justice Wearing
Sentence	7 Years H[ard] L[abour]
Native Place	Corfu [incorrect]
Date of Arrival	April 1867
Name of Ship	Cooreng
Where from	Melbourne
Previous Convictions in the Colony	None
Last Employer	H. R. H. Prince Alfred
Friends in the Colony	Wife & Child
Where residing	Adelaide
Married or Single	Married
Religious Creed	Wesleyan [incorrect]
Education	Good
Occupation	Valet
PERSONAL DESCRIPTION.	
Age	25 [he was 29]
Height	5 Ft. 7 In.
Weight	9 St. 12 lbs. [138 pounds]
Make	Stiff, wiry, active
Complexion	Fair
Face	Long & Square
Hair	Brown, neither Dark nor light
Forehead	Wide Hew
Eyes	Blue
Nose	Small and pointed
Mouth	Medium
Teeth	Good
Chin	Square
Whiskers	None; Moustache;
Expression	Determined
Marks or other particulars	None [34]

The daily duties of the superintendent of the prison included attending at least one of the muster rolls of the prisoners that took place at 6:00 a.m., 9:00 a.m., and 2:00 p.m.; inspecting the prison cells, workshops and outbuildings; inspecting the prisoners' food, bread, and tobacco; visiting the gangs working in the quarries; recording credits for work performed, and writing down infringements of regulations and punishments meted out.

Glimpses of Edwin's life in Yatala Prison were found in several entries in the handwritten journal of Superintendent Edward Bates Scott that has survived for the period from December 1, 1869–December 31, 1872, and January 1–October 9, 1873.

15 Dec 1869	Infringement Prison Regulations. Osbaldiston, Williams, O'Donnell & Toombs—fighting and disobedience
23 Aug 1870	Infringement of Regulations. Prisoners Osbaldiston and Morris were accused of making noises in their cells.

24 Aug 1870	Infringement of Regulations. Prisoners Osbaldiston & Morris were taken before the Comptroller for making noises in their cells last evening. Punishments. Prisoner Osbaldiston was sentenced to 48 hours solitary confinement & prisoner Morris was mulcted [fined] in 24 Marks.
22 Mar 1871	Remarks. Prisoner Osbaldiston sent stonebreaking by Comptroller on recommendation of Medical Officer.
17 Sept 1872	Infringement of Regulations. Prisoner Osbaldiston (calling Guard Sunderland a liar)
18 Sept 1872	Punishments. Prisoner Osbaldiston fined 48 marks by Comptroller for making use of abusive language
25 Nov 1872	Infringement of Regulations. Prisoner Osbaldiston (charge disobedience)
30 Dec 1872	Remarks. Mr. Oliphant [officer of the Destitute Asylum, Adelaide] had a private interview with Osbaldiston in my office by permission of the Hon. Chief Secretary.
31 Dec 1872	Remarks. Prisoner Osbaldiston wished to make a statement to me having reference to his wife & a Government officer. Superintendent declined hearing statement. Prisoner also wanted a character [reference] on discharge = not required.[35]

Added information regarding Edwin's life in prison appeared in the Medical Officer's Journal (special diets) that exists for the years 1870–1874.

8 Aug 1870	To be allowed to wear the drawers supplied by his friends when the others are worn out.
2 Dec 1870	No. 3 [Diet] & gruel & exempt [from work] for two days
18 Mar 1871	Recommended to be sent to the works two or three days a week
29 Mar 1871	Infirmary [After injuring an eye while breaking stone ETO was admitted to the prison infirmary for five days]
3 Apr 1871	Discharged [from infirmary] for light labor in a shady place
14 Aug 1871	[Diet] Gruel for three nights
11 Sept 1871	Requires warm water twice a day
1 Oct 1871	No. 3 [Diet] & gruel. Exempt to his cell for the day, to have his bedding
14 Oct 1871	Requires his suspensory bandage altered by the Tailor
27 Dec 1871	[Diet] Gruel for two nights
25 Jan 1872	No. 3 [Diet] & gruel. Exempt to his bed for two days
29 Feb 1872	No. 3 [Diet] & gruel. Exempt for the day.
22 Mar 1872	[Diet] 2 oz Lime Juice, 1 oz Sugar daily for ten days
28 Apr 1872	[Diet] Lime Juice & Sugar for ten days
28 May 1872	[Diet] 2 oz of Lime Juice & 1 oz Sugar in lieu of Potatoes

Cell Block B of Yatala Labour Prison

19 Sept 1872	Requires his suspensory bandage altered by the Tailor
6 Nov 1872	[Diet] Pint of milk in lieu of half his rations.—Lime juice to be discontinued.[36][37]

Due to the marks he had earned for his labor and for good behavior, Edwin's original seven-year sentence was reduced to five years, one month, and ten days. He was released on January 13, 1873.[38] Before leaving Yatala, Edwin asked the warden to provide a character reference. The superintendent declined his request.[39] In its issue of January 8, 1873, the *South Australian Police Gazette* published Edwin's release under the heading "Prisoners Discharged from Yatala Labour Prison."

During the five years that Edwin was in prison. it appears that his wife and child were in the Destitute Asylum in Adelaide. The asylum was an institution set up to house deserted and destitute men, women, and children who were unable to support themselves. Evidence that Ann Pratt Osbaldeston and her daughter Annie Mabel were in the asylum appears in the journal of the superintendent of Yatala Labour Prison.
Some idea of what became of Edwin following his release from prison can be found in the following excerpt from the autobiography of Tom Bastard:

> The Rev. Wilton Hack [a pastor who regularly worked to reform prisoners], a good man and a minister of the gospel, used to visit the prison. This gentleman took a liking to the prisoner, and is said to have converted him, and after a time baptized him in the presence of all the prisoners. He was relieved from hard labor and appointed attendant in the sick ward. His general behaviour was so good that at the end of four [should be five] years he was released. Mr. Hack helped to set him up in business in North Adelaide as a green-grocer [seller of fruit and vegetables]; his wife rejoined him, and all seemed to go well for some time. He held prayer meetings and occasionally preached on Sundays, sometimes at one place and sometimes at another; but his wickedness could not have been thoroughly eradicated, and an evil fate seemed to have cast its shadow over his life.
>
> Truly the way of transgressors is hard. His wife left him, and he mixed himself up with some old chums from the stockade. At this

> time a cart and horse were missing, and somehow or other he was summoned as a witness in the case, and when asked his name he said it was Edward Turner; but the judge remembered him as the notorious Baldiston who had robbed the Prince. The indefatigable detective Thomas Doyle was promoted to the rank of sergeant, with a reward of twenty pounds for the zealous performance of his duty to his Queen and country in the celebrated Baldiston case.[40]

In his journal Edwin wrote that he was in New Zealand in mid-1873 and that he had sailed on a couple of different ships. No evidence has been found to substantiate these claims. There are no entries in his notebook with dates between September 2, 1873 and November 2, 1874.

Not surprisingly, Edwin's journal made no mention of committing burglaries in Adelaide, nor did he record his stays in Adelaide Gaol or incarceration at Yatala. However, he did leave a few clues in his notebook. Page 150 contains eight references to newspapers in Australia and New Zealand. Among them were the following:

Register	16.11.1866 [should be 18 November 1867]
Register	Nov. 16
Argus	Friday, Nov. 22
Herald	Sat. 16 [Nov.][41]

Written on page 130 are these simple notations:

Doyle	Nov. 15 67
Wearing	26 [Nov.] 67
Howell	4th 12 67[42]

Doyle was the corporal in charge of the North Adelaide police station, Wearing was the justice of the South Australian Supreme Court, and Howell was the superintendent of Yatala Labour Prison during the first two years that Edwin was an inmate there.

NOTES

1. "Turkish Baths," *Observer* (Adelaide), 9 March 1867, p. 5, col. a.
2. *South Australian Advertiser* (Adelaide), 1 April 1867, p. 3, col. a.
3. "The Proposed Turkish Baths," *South Australian Register* (Adelaide), 4 April 1867, p. 2, col. e.
4. *South Australian Advertiser* (Adelaide), 4 April 1867, p. 2, col. g.
5. *Observer* (Adelaide), 6 April 1867, p. 3, col. e.
6. The Turkish Baths," *Observer* (Adelaide), 13 April 1867, p. 3, col. b.
7. "Mr. Osbaldiston," *South Australian Register* (Adelaide), 21 May 1867, p. 3, col. e.
8. Thomas Barnabas Bastard, *The Autobiography of "Cockney Tom," Showing His Struggles Through Life, and Proving the Truth of the Old Saying "That Honesty Is the Best Policy"* (Adelaide: McClory & Masterman, Printers, 1881), pp. 56–57.
9. "Professional & Trade Addresses," *South Australian Register* (Adelaide), 17 June 1867, p. 1, col. f.
10. "Topics of the Day," *South Australian Register* (Adelaide), 29 June 1867, p. 2, col. d.
11. "A Turkish Bath on a Small Scale," *South Australian Register* (Adelaide), 23 September 1867, p. 3, col. c.
12. *Wikipedia*, s.v. "Alfred, Duke of Saxe-Coburg and Gotha," accessed 12 February 2014, https://en.wikipedia.org/wiki/Alfred,_Duke_of_Saxe_Coburg_and_Gotha.
13. "Petty Robberies," *South Australian Advertiser* (Adelaide), 4 May 1867, p. 2, col. h–p. 3, col. a.
14. Bastard, *The Autobiography of "Cockney Tom,"* pp. 56–57.
15. "The Late Robberies in the City," *South Australian Register* (Adelaide), 18 November 1867, p. 2, col. g.
16. Ibid.
17. Ibid.
18. "Police Courts," *South Australian Register* (Adelaide), 20 November 1867, p. 3, cols. e-f.
19. Ibid.
20. "The Charges of Theft," *South Australian Register* (Adelaide), 19 November 1867, p. 2, col. h.
21. *South Australian Register* (Adelaide), 20 November 1867, p. 2, col. d.
22. "Police Courts," *South Australian Register* (Adelaide), 22 November 1867, p. 3, col. c.
23. South Australia, Parliament, *Proceedings of the Parliament of South Australia; with Copies of the Documents Ordered to Be Printed, 1872* (Adelaide: By authority: W. C. Cox, Government Printer, 1873) vol. 3, p. ix, "Appendix to Minutes of Evidence on Metropolitan Police Force, Letter from Police Inspector T. W. Bee to the Honorable Chief Secretary, 5 December 1867."
24. "Law and Criminal Courts. Supreme Court—Criminal Sittings," *South Australian Register* (Adelaide), 4 December 1867, p. 3, col. f.
25. "The Prisoner Osbaldiston," *South Australian Register* (Adelaide), 5 December 1867, p. 2, col. e.
26. "Law and Criminal Courts. Supreme Court—Criminal Sittings," *South Australian Register* (Adelaide), 4 December 1867, p. 3, col. f.
27. Ibid.
28. "The Criminal Sittings," *South Australian Register* (Adelaide), 9 December 1867, p. 2, col. d.
29. Ibid.
30. "The Stockade," *South Australian Register* (Adelaide), 27 December 1865, p. 4.
31. *Wikipedia*, s.v. "Yatala Labour Prison," accessed 16 November 2008, https://en.wikipedia.org/wiki/Yatala_Labour_Prison.
32. "The Stockade," *South Australian Register* (Adelaide), 27 December 1865, p. 4.
33. Bastard, *The Autobiography of "Cockney Tom,"* pp. 58–60.
34. State Records of South Australia GRS 2412/1 (book) or GRG 54/41 (microfilm) Yatala Labour Prison, Prisoners' register, vol. D, 1866–1871, folio 165.
35. State Records of South Australia GRG 54/33 Yatala Labour Prison, Superintendent's Journal, vol. 1, 1 December 1869–31 December 1872, 12 September–23 November 1874.
36. State Records of South Australia GRG 54/35 Yatala Labour Prison, Medical Officer's Journal (Special Diets), 1870–1874.
37. State Records, Adelaide, South Australia, GRG 54/38, Yatala Labour Prison, Dry Creek, South Australia, Medical Officer's Journal (Prisoners under Treatment), vol. 1, 1869–1873.
38. State Records of South Australia GRG 54/33 Yatala Labour Prison, Superintendent's Journal, vol. 2, 1 January–9 October 1873.
39. Ibid.
40. Bastard, *The Autobiography of "Cockney Tom,"* pp. 60–61.
41. ETO, "Journal" (unpublished manuscript), 150, Siver family history material.
42. ETO, "Journal" (unpublished manuscript), 130, Siver family history material.

CHAPTER EIGHT

Moving on to Sydney, Tasmania, & San Francisco ~ 1873–1875

Following his release from Yatala Labour Prison in January 1873, Edwin managed to maintain a low profile for some time. His journal contains few entries for 1873 and 1874, and there was no mention of being incarcerated for the five years prior. In one entry he wrote, "1869–1870 back in lovely Melbourne again many flattering newspaper notices of me. Have decided upon a sea life as ships surgeon. Have received an offer from Captain Scott, sailing ship *Glasgow* of Scotland loading with tan bark and wool."[1] Clearly, this was fantasy or a cover for the truth.

From the autobiography of Tom Bastard and court testimony in Adelaide, it is known that he supported himself as a greengrocer in 1873. For what duration is not certain, and given his temperament, it was unlikely that this occupation would have held his interest for long. Following his release from prison, he went by the name Edwin Turner rather than Edwin Osbaldeston or Osbaldiston. Edwin was reunited with his wife and daughter for a time. There is a hint in the Yatala Prison records that Ann may have had another man in her life. Just prior to his release, Edwin was visited by a Mr. Oliphant, an officer from the Destitute Asylum in Adelaide. Following the visit, Edwin asked to speak to the prison superintendent about his wife and a government officer. The superintendent declined to discuss the matter.[2]

Edwin was called to Supreme Court in Adelaide on May 13, 1873—this time as a witness rather than as the accused. Judging by his court testimony, he could be described as "uncooperative." Edwin appeared for the defense of Robert Marshall, who stood accused of selling a horse, bridle, and cart that had been leased to him. Ironically, Edwin objected to taking an oath to affirm that he would give truthful testimony.

"I want my word taken as a man, conscious of the true dignity of man," Edwin explained.[3] After an exchange with Judge William A. Wearing, he agreed to make a declaration to be truthful. For his defense Marshall maintained that the owner of the horse and cart had sold all three to him. Edwin supported Marshall's claim. Edwin noted that he had known Marshall for some time and that it was Marshall's wife who had leveled the charges so that as an imprisoned man she might see her husband more often.

The cross-examination provided a telling exchange between Edwin and the crown solicitor (prosecutor) as he tried to discredit Edwin as a witness.[4]

> **Crown Solicitor:** How long have you known the prisoner?
> **Edwin:** Declined to answer
> **CS:** Is your name Edwin Turner?
> **Edwin:** Yes.
> **CS:** How long have you borne that name?
> **Edwin:** Throughout my life.
> **CS:** Have you never borne the name Osbaldistone?
> **Edwin:** Declined to answer and appealed to the Court
> **Judge:** The question is a fair one.
> **Edwin:** Yes, I had gone by that name.
> **CS:** Were you not convicted of stealing the Duke of Edinburgh's jewels?
> **Edwin:** No.
> **CS:** Were you not convicted and imprisoned in the Stockade [Yatala]?
> **Edwin:** Declined to answer
> **CS:** Did your first acquaintance with [the] prisoner commence in the Stockade?
> **Edwin:** Declined to answer
> **CS:** Where did your first acquaintance with him commence?
> **Edwin:** My first acquaintance with him as a free man was at Hilton.
> **CS:** Did you never see him at the Stockade?
> **Edwin:** I might have seen him there as a visitor.
> **CS:** Which was the visitor, he or you?
> **Edwin:** I visited him.
> **CS:** Was it not while you were incarcerated in the Stockade that you became acquainted with the prisoner who was then confined there?
> **Edwin:** Declined to answer[5]

In giving instructions to the jury, the judge cautioned the panel that it would have to be careful when considering the testimony of Turner. He added that there was direct falsehood on one side or the other. In referring to Turner, Justice Wearing frequently used the name "Osbaldistone." He apologized for that, explaining that he knew the witness from a previous case. It would seem that Edwin's testimony was of little or no help. Nonetheless, the jury found Marshall not guilty and he was discharged.[6]

How long before Edwin's wanderlust struck again is uncertain. He noted in his journal that in 1873 and 1874, he worked on SS *Nubia* and SS *Ceylon*, sister ships of the Peninsular and Oriental Steam Navigation Company. These ships carried mail, passengers, and cargo from Australia to Bombay,

Edwin was a crew member on the Nubia, *part of the Peninsular and Oriental Steam Navigation Company's fleet.* *(Printed with permission from the P. & O. S. N. Co.)*

Calcutta, Singapore, Hong Kong, and other points in the Pacific and Indian oceans. In an entry dated June 14, 1873, Edwin wrote that while on a stop in New Zealand, he had been introduced to Sir George Grey, governor of New Zealand. The governor invited him to join a shooting excursion at his island home.[7] (Grey served two terms as governor of the colony—1841–1845 and 1861–1868, and one term as governor of the Cape Colony [South Africa]—1854–1861. Grey also served in the New Zealand Parliament from 1875 to 1895.)

By January 1875 Edwin was back in Sydney, where he placed advertisements in the *Sydney Morning Herald* for Turkish and hydropathic baths at 160 Pitt Street using the surname Turner. His advertisement offered a new technique whereby the bather, after undressing, sat in a large box filled with steam and sulfurous vapor. The bather's head protruded from the box so that he might breathe easily. From there the treatment proceeded to follow the steps of the traditional Victorian Turkish bath. He also offered first class accommodations for invalids wishing to reside on the premises.[8] It was at this point that he expanded his role from advocate of good hygiene and stress relief to that of healer. At the same time Edwin was also offering treatment for corns, bunions, and painful nails.[9]

Edwin did not remain in Sydney for long. His next port of call was Tasmania. In a journal entry dated March 20, 1875, he claimed to have taken on the case of a woman with breast cancer who lived in Hobart.[10] In another entry dated later that year, he noted, "Lost a case. The first in all my years of practice." The patient was a seventeen-year-old boy suffering from pneumonia.[11]

In late April he set up shop in Launceston, Tasmania. In an advertisement, he announced that he was establishing a hydropathic practice. "Mr. Turner was patronized in Sydney by His Excellency Sir Hercules Robinson [governor of New South Wales] and his certificate book contains numerous records of cures effected by his Turkish baths and Hydropathic treatment," the notice read.[12] A second ad followed on May 3 advising that he was holding consultation hours from 10:00 a.m. to 6:00 p.m.

"Mr. Turner" held consultation hours at Fahey's Cornwall Hotel in Launceston, Tasmania. *(Tasmaniana Library, SLT)*

daily at Fahey's Cornwall Hotel and was looking for gentlemen who were interested in establishing a genuine Turkish bath or hydropathic institution.[13]

Apparently, Edwin struck out in Launceston, so he moved on to Hobart Town, where he placed the following notice in the *Tasmanian Tribune* of May 8, 1875. "Mr. E. Turner, Hydropathist, Student under Dr. Gulley of Malvern and Smedley of Matlock, Derbyshire, formerly Manager of the Germyn Street Turkish Baths, London and Bathing Palace, Melbourne, will shortly commence practice in Hobart Town." He also placed a similar notice in the *Mercury* on May 8 and 12.[14] Next came a letter to the editor of the *Mercury* that read in part as follows:

> Sir,—In the local column of your last Saturday's issue . . . I observe reference made to the arrival in this city of the popular lecturer and hydropathic physician, Mr. E. Turner, who you assure your readers has come amongst us with the view of staying to practice his profession. I, for one, wish him a hearty success and trust that the community at large will appreciate his talents and learn from his lectures . . . the many highly beneficial advantages attendant upon the practice of hydropathy . . . a few words upon its theory and practice for the benefit of the sceptical and uninitiated may not be out of place in your columns.
>
> Hydropathy, then, is a system of curing diseases common to the human body by the agency of heat, cold water, diet, and exercise.[15]

The letter then detailed at length how disease affects the body and how the body reacts to disease. Signed, "Yours most repectfully, Liberal," the letter writer concludes as follows:

> Hence, whoever suffers from chronic disease can never die a natural death, unless, before it be too late, he resorts to hydropathy for a final cure, which changes the chronic disease by disturbing the corrupt and diseased matter and drives it out of the system by acute eruptions thus changing the chronic to an acute disease, which it cures in the same manner as an acute disease is cured at first, viz., by the water, heat, diet, and exercise treatment of hydropathy.[16]

A week later Edwin made bolder claims in a new advertisement entitled "Hydropathy: Nature's Real Curative Agent." He invited the public to inspect testimonials from "upwards of 371 patients" and noted that he was "formerly the hydropathic attendant upon Prince Alfred, Sir Dominic Daly, Sir Charles Darling, and many other persons of note both in England and these colonies."[17] In total, he placed sixteen notices in the *Mercury* and *Tasmanian Tribune* between May and July 1875.

It appeared that his practice took root in Hobart. On July 1–3, 1875, he placed ads in the *Mercury* seeking a partner. His notice read that he had no objection to one who was desirous of acquiring knowledge of the art of hydropathy.[18]

Further evidence that his practice was going well came on July 12, when a letter to the editor was published in the *Tasmanian Tribune* from A. J. Lumsden, a china and glass dealer. Lumsden paid tribute to hydropathist Edwin Turner for having cured his two-and-a-half-year-old daughter of a large abscess on her head. The writer said that other medical persons declined to treat the child because of her age. His daughter's condition worsened to the point where she lay moaning for hours and was not able to move from the hips down. "His treatment on one or two occasions so alarmed us that we almost decided not to allow him to go on with it," Lumsden said, "but in a couple of days our fears gave place to inexpressible joy on beholding our little one's rapid progress toward recovery."[19]

Next Edwin announced he would be giving a series of public lectures on "Hydropathy Versus Allopathy" (medical practice that combats disease by use of drugs and/or surgery) commencing on August 9. His lectures would be followed by investigation of mesmeric séances, phrenological delineations, and exposure to tricks of legerdemain (magic), all things that interested him.[20] However, the lectures did not come to pass.

Edwin's activities had attracted the attention of Richard Propsting, superintendent of police for Hobart Town. The authorities moved to put an end to Edwin's activities, charging him with breach of the Medical Regulations Act. Edwin had been ordered to appear in Hobart Police Court on August 3. In the case of Propsting v. Turner, the defendant did not appear. Superintendent Propsting reported to the court that Turner had left the colony and requested that the Bench postpone the case. The case was postponed, and a new summons was issued.[21]

The Medical Registration Act required persons practicing medicine to be licensed. In Edwin's defense, he might have maintained that he wasn't actually practicing, merely providing a healthy alternative to medicine. With the memory of his Yatala Prison experience still very fresh, Edwin most likely did not want to risk arguing the point.

The editors of the *Tasmanian Tribune* made the following comment:

> Mr. E. Turner, the itinerant hydropathist, who has recently been practising in our midst with some show of success, has at length said farewell to his numerous patients, and taken his departure, in search perchance of "fresh fields and pastures new." This fact came out at the Police Court yesterday, when a charge of breach of the Medical Regulations Act was preferred against Turner by Mr. Propsting, but when the case was called on, the defendant did not appear, and a fresh summons was accordingly ordered to be issued.[22]

From Tasmania, Edwin returned to Adelaide. It is at this point that Edwin took custody of his daughter. Whether he gained custody of her by fair means or foul is unknown.

The fate of his wife, Ann Pratt Osbaldeston, remains a mystery to this day. Did she leave Edwin, possibly for another man? Did he abandon her in Adelaide when she was critical of his behavior following his release from Yatala Labour Prison? Did he murder her and dispose of her body in such a fashion that it was never found or never identified?

Years later Edwin gave several different versions of the facts surrounding her disappearance. In three articles published in March 1926, two in the *Asbury Park Evening Press* and one in the *New York Times,* he explained it as follows:

> He married in England and while in Australia with his wife and baby, lost his wife, who rode into the Australian wilderness, on an evening canter, and was never found. The doctor believes she was captured and killed by cannibals.[23]

> I went to Australia as a ship's doctor and there met Miss Lewisham, whom I married. We were living in the bushland, and one day when out riding I saw a kangaroo. That night around the campfire I told of my experience. My wife said: "If I saw him, I'd kill the old man kangaroo!"
>
> A short while later one of the porters told me that she had saddled a horse and, with a gun, gone off into the vastness of the bushland. Frightened, I jumped on my mount and started in pursuit. It was very difficult to follow the tracks, which went miles ahead and finally disappeared altogether.
>
> You can imagine the desperate fear that overtook me. I sped back to the camp, cried for the native porters to follow me, and we plunged back into the wilderness. But from that day to this nothing has been seen or heard of the dear little woman who made my early days so happy.[24]

> His next great adventure, he said, was his search for the missing explorer [Leichhardt] in the Australian bush. He referred last night with great feeling to the loss of his first wife on that expedition. "We never learned her fate exactly," he said, "but we always believed that the kangaroos got her."[5]

Clearly this was a fabrication beginning with meeting "Miss Lewisham." German scientist Ludwig Leichhardt went missing during an expedition that took place in 1848. Edwin and Ann Pratt Osbaldeston did not arrive in Australia until 1865. Something had obviously happened to Ann—or he had done something to her—that he did not want to reveal. Perth's *Daily News* conducted an investigation in 1926 into Edwin's claims that he had lost his wife while on a search for Leichhardt. The paper reported that there was no record among the journals in the Mitchell Library in Sydney of Obsbaldeston being with any of the search parties. Further, the paper noted "no white woman accompanied any of the expeditions" that were conducted.[26]

Making this fabrication even more absurd, the *New York Times* reporter obviously did not know much about kangaroos. Death by kangaroo is highly unlikely. Unless threatened, kangaroos generally avoid humans. If provoked they may attack. Kangaroo attacks leave scratches and bruises but rarely result in death. Further, kangaroos are herbivores; they feed on grass, leaves, flowers, and sprouts.

San Francisco

The next chapter of Edwin Turner Osbaldeston's life commenced with his departure from the Australian colonies followed by a sojourn of six weeks in San Francisco. If his accounts are to be believed, his stay in San Francisco was most eventful. From Adelaide, Edwin and his daughter Annie Mabel traveled first to Melbourne and then boarded the *Ellora* to Sydney.[27] From there they embarked on the Australasian Steam Navigation Company's vessel *MacGregor*, which left Sydney on September 25, 1875, bound for San Francisco.

Edwin, calling himself Edwin Turner again, had obtained the position of ship's physician. He recorded the following in his journal:

> Appointed surgeon Friday, September 25th [18]75. Baby with me. Arrived at Auckland Oct 1st stayed 4 hours. Arrived Kandavia [Fiji islands] on the 7th. At Honolulu, Hawaii on the 17th. Introduced to the King R. Kalakaua on Monday 18th & splendidly entertained at the palace. Fine fellow. 11 A.M. had us driven along the 6-mile drive & back. Made an offer if I would cure one case of leprosy.[28]

> I do not like Captain Granger. A fine sailor but lacking in sociability, passengers not pleased, [he's] got an incurable attack, I fear, of the swelled head. So I always make it a rule to avoid if possible any person I do not like or cannot get along with.[29]

Shortly after the *MacGregor* arrived in San Francisco on October 27, 1875, the following testimonial, signed by twenty-five passengers, appeared in the *San Francisco News Letter and California Advertiser*:

> Australian Steam Navigation Company's Mail Steamer "MacGregor," Captain

Granger, Commander. —San Francisco, Wednesday, 27th October 1875. We the undersigned passengers on board the above named ship do hereby desire to signify our approval of Mr. Edwin Turner's conduct whilst acting in the capacity of Ship's Surgeon, and consider that his skill and judgment and pains-taking efforts to secure the comfort and health of his patients, deserve the highest commendation.[30]

Rather than return to Sydney on the *MacGregor*, Edwin elected to remain in San Francisco. Over the course of the next month, he placed numerous advertisements in local newspapers promoting "Dr. E. Turner's Orthopedic Classes." This time he targeted parents with children who suffered from "feeble physiques, deformity, or constitutional debility."[31] As the days went by he placed additional notices and broadened his services and audiences, offering men's and women's classes and even a course in child birthing.

MR. EDWIN TURNER,
Consulting Physician and Surgeon, late Ship's Surgeon, and formerly of Bombay. Residence, 324 Sutter Street. Consultation Hours, 9 to 11 A. M., 2 to 4, 7 to 10 P. M.[32]

ORTHOPEDIC SURGERY.
Dr. Edwin Turner's Orthopedic Classes in process of formation. Applications received at 324 Sutter Street.[33]

DR. EDWIN TURNER,
Consulting Physician and Surgeon, 324 Sutter Street.–Ladies' Orthopedical Classes, Wednesdays at 3:30 P. M., Saturdays at 3 P. M., Gentleman's Classes, Wednesday and Saturday at 7:30 P. M. Juveniles on ladies' days.[34]

DR. EDWIN TURNER,
Consulting Physician and Surgeon Accoucheur, 324 Sutter Street. Orthopedical Surgery Classes.[35]

Edwin's journal entries contain living arrangements for the care of his daughter and himself. He also records a major incident that spilled over from his passage on the *MacGregor*.

Leaving my pet Annie Mabel, who has grown [to be] quite a fine, big girl for her age [9] & very smart & much attached to papa, with Miss Slocum [May Ida Slocomb] [who had been a passenger on the *MacGregor*] & her sister Mrs. [Susan] Swain, a wealthy widow, & Mrs. Elizabeth J. Corbett all of Brunswick House corner of Sixth & Howard streets near Pine & Hyde streets.

My home [in] San Francisco was with a Mrs. Hoff of 324 Sutter Street . . . from whom I rented two apartments $10⁰⁰ per week including the services of a Chinese servant who became devotedly attached to me & my child.

Among the passengers on board the SS *McGregor* . . . was a sporting man named Hughes, though that was only one of several names I learned that he was known by in San Francisco. On ship he was thoroughly hated by all the passengers for his gross rudeness & familiarity with women married or single & his uncouth remarks often got him into trouble.

He tried to strike up acquaintance with me & hung a good deal about the surgery. On one occasion I found him sitting with my baby girl on his knee in the surgery. When I got mad & ordered him to leave & dared him to ever enter again so long as the voyage lasted. He said all right Doc wait until we get ashore.

I was told by some of the passengers to look out for the fellow as he would surely do me harm in some manner & he frequently had said he must have that kid, meaning Annie.[36]

A few days after my landing I was enjoying the company of some newspaper men I had met & we were having champagne in Coates Saloon [37 Sutter?], a highly respectable & fashionable resort, when my Chinese servant hurried in to the booth where we were sitting and informed us that two men had been about the outside of the house & had tried to take away my child. The description of one was that of Hughes & we all decided to hurry to my home when who should come into the place but Hughes accompanied by two other men.

They at first appeared to take no notice of me & my party. But after a few minutes having finished their drinks at the bar Hughes rolled up our way & approaching our table spoke to me & at the same time lifted my glass saying "here's luck doc" & putting it to his mouth began to drink.

The four gentlemen first looked at him & then me. I did not give them a moment to await the result. I was just furious & quickly rising I struck the glass his hand held to his mouth [and gave a] smashing blow. It cut his tongue & lips almost in two. My friends laughed & said "perhaps the bully has had enough."

Hughes swung his hand round & was about to draw his shooter but was covered by . . . two of my friends & he dared not draw at this juncture. The two companions fired & I wonder to this day that my friends and I were not killed.

There was a quick exchange of shots. Hughes was near . . . a wine cask mopping the blood from his mouth & pulling pieces of glass from his lips. When I sneaked round the cask & quickly seized his revolver sticking out of his pocket. He roared like mad & drew another from somewhere behind his neck. I thinking the fellow was disarmed was making back to near the bar where my friends & Hughes men had ceased firing & were having it out in argument. Some thirty shots had been fired & one of Hughes men hit badly, shattering his arm. . . . Broken mirrors, bottles & glasses, & the wine running out of the side of the cask showed where bullets had hit.

As I was making for the party across the big hall Hughes . . . fired not more than 12 feet away at me.

I was near a post & dodging behind returned his fire. My first or second shot cut a furrow all along the top of his head. . . . He crawled towards two more casks nearby when I fired at his . . . hand carrying the revolver & my shot cut the right hand so badly that his thumb hung back by a little skin. He turned & sitting on the floor raised his hands above his head & begged to have the thumb sewn on.

His two mates came to me after putting their revolvers away & wanted to shake hands with me but I said not yet I must know you men better first. With some flattering remark about my bravery & some violent language cast at Hughes, they left the premises walking partly backwards. I called to my friends to secure them until the police could be sent for but they said such things were common in the city & the police were all in with the rowdies.

Hughes continued to yell, "Save my thumb. Save my thumb," & his head & face were streaming with blood. Dr. [Charles W.] Horner happened to be one of our party & with him we made a examination of the wound on Hughes head. It was a scalp [wound] but down to the bone for seven inches in length. [His] thumb would have to come off. . . . Hughes had now fainted & lay on a bench like a dead man. Money in gold had rolled out on the floor.

On my return home my landlady Mrs. Hoff gave me the full account of the men's efforts to abduct my child & I reported the matter to the police but they only appeared to be amused at the affair. One returned & said if I would put up 25 dollars he believed he could get all three men before night. I declined to do anything of the kind.[37]

Woodward's Gardens, San Francisco—allegedly the site of a duel between Edwin Turner and William Dobie
(Photo: San Francisco History Center, San Francisco Public Library, San Francisco, CA; reprinted with permission)

Edwin then described a second incident and a duel that he claimed took place a week later on November 11, 1875. The confrontation was the result of advice Edwin had given to one of his patients, a May Ida Slocomb. The advice in turn upset the patient's fiancé. Given Miss Slocomb's medical condition, Edwin had advised her to postpone her upcoming marriage.

I was looking in the visitors' book . . . of the Grand Hotel [SE corner New Montgomery and Market] when suddenly I was nearly blinded by a man of the name of [William] Dobie [bookkeeper with Greenebaum Bros., 7 Sansome St.] smashing into my right eye a large chew of tobacco. For a few moments I could not see for pain. But when I got steady I was told who did it & the man pointed out to me a person well dressed of about 30 years of age, standing laughing & talking near the door with others.

I went up to him. I was not furious at the time for a great wonder. I fear to get in such conditions because I seem to get blind furious, fear nothing & may do harm of a serious nature to another . . . but this was a deliberate willful assault by a man I had no recollection of ever having seen or heard of before.

As I approached him he scarcely seemed to notice me as I enquired the cause & if he had intended that as an insult or had mistaken me for another person. He replied, "Take it as you please." I replied that he was a dirty, cowardly cur & challenged him to come into the rear premises & I would show him such to his friends.

A revolver muzzle pointing right into my face he had drawn from his sleeve was the next thing. I made a lightning-like movement & knocked his hand up & before he could use it, I had it in my hand but he still held the butt. I put my foot between his legs & he fell to the floor carrying me with him.

After a terrible struggle during which the revolver went off two or three times landing its bullets in the ceiling, I got possession of it. I then covered him & told the cur to get up.

I then challenged him to a fistfight in the rear of the premises. His friends here interfered & said if I wanted satisfaction their friend Mr. Dobie would give me all the satisfaction in a duel at Woodward's Gardens [an amusement park covering two blocks in the city's Mission District].

I enquired of them the cause of the attack on me when they told me that I had advised Miss Slocum [Slocomb] not to marry the man. I had done no such thing. I did not know him . . . before this affair happened. She had been my patient & from the nature of her trouble I had advised her not to marry as she informed me she was going to do shortly, for a year or two at least.

I accepted the challenge and we all proceeded [with] his four friends and two persons who volunteered to stand by me . . . to Woodward's Gardens. . . . All preliminaries were arranged. We both with our seconds decided upon revolvers. Two were laid under a coat & our seconds tossed up whose man should put his hand under the coat & select a weapon.

It fell to Dobie's referee to take the first. They were rather small size of the Colt pattern. They were then loaded being five chambered.

The conditions were that two shots each only were to be fired. Dobie was free of coat, vest, & hat. I remained dressed against the persuasion of my referee. We were instructed to pace five paces from each other by count of the referee & when five was called to turn & fire. This we did & at the word "fire," I turned quickly side ways . . . raising my right hand [and] rested my revolver against the inside of [my] left shoulder. My fire was delivered first but only by a second or two. When I glanced towards my foe he was standing full-faced towards me.

Both our shots had gone wide of the mark. Then according to instructions we stood back to back again & paced off five paces to time given by the referee as before. I resorted to the same tactics, calculating from a straight pacing I should be directly opposite my opponent. . . . As before I was

San Francisco, California (circa 1875) (Photo: San Francisco History Center, San Francisco Public Library, San Francisco, CA; reprinted with permission)

in the lead in delivering my fire. Dobie's shot furrowed through my shirt & coat cuffs of my revolver hand but did no further harm. Mine hit him in the shoulder & was stopped in the rear by the scapula where it had to be cut out afterwards.

When hit he exclaimed, "Oh!" & whether by accident or design, I know not, he fired another shot which passed harmlessly by my head making a singing noise by my right ear.

The affair was then called off & whilst he was being examined I explained my advice to Miss Slocum [Slocomb] & my lack of the least knowledge of who her affianced was. At this he asked why I had not informed him of these facts before & he would have apologized like a gentleman. His friends informed him that I had done so to them but that in the excitement of events they forgot the matter. We then shook hands & I promised to call on him but I could not as our vessel had to sail.

San Francisco is a pretty lively city. The Sand Hill settlement fosters nearly all the rowdy element of the place & men of the most desperate character live about there ready for a small fee to accomplish any devilish thing proposed to them. Many of the notorious Bushrangers of Australia are to be found there, sent over by their respective governments to get rid of them. One Frank Gardner keeps the Twilight Hotel, Kearny St. There are Chinese, Italian, and French settlements of lawless people also there. The authorities are much to blame for allowing persons to carry firearms which appears a universal custom.[38]

Duels were outlawed in California after the 1859 infamous challenge between United States Senator David C. Broderick and former California Supreme Court Justice David Terry in a ravine at Lake Merced,[39] but most possibly could have continued to occur illegally after that.

Broderick and Terry had been good friends and political allies. They had a falling out over the issue of slavery. Both Democrats, Terry wished to extend slavery to California, and Broderick, the leader of the state's Free Soil movement, was strongly opposed.

When Terry lost re-election to the California Supreme Court, he blamed his defeat on Broderick. A feud ensued and escalated with angry words and accusations, and finally the former friends decided to settle the matter with a duel of honor on September 13.[40]

Broderick, who held tight political control of San Francisco, was mortally wounded in the duel. Broderick's funeral turned into a huge demonstration against slavery in San Francisco. As for Terry, he was charged with murder, but his case was dismissed. Interestingly, the California law declaring duels illegal included enhanced penalties if a duel resulted in death.[41]

In the latter half of the nineteenth century, San Francisco did in fact have a well-deserved reputation for lawlessness and vigilante justice. The gold rush of 1849 had brought waves of people to the city, many of whom were looking to make a quick fortune. Gambling, drug use, drunkenness, and prostitution were rampant. City government and the police force were not effective and marred by corruption and graft.

Senator Broderick had come to California from New York City as part of the gold rush. He quickly rose through the political ranks in San Francisco. By 1852, he headed a "vicious" political machine in the city that was notoriously corrupt and rife with "kickbacks" and poltical favors.[42]

As in most of Edwin's recorded accounts, a vein of discernible fact runs through them. Many of the persons and places mentioned in San Francisco have been verified, including the existence of William Dobie and May Ida Slocomb. In fact, Dobie, age 30, and Slocomb, age 21, were married on September 14, 1876 in San Francisco.[43] However, Edwin's accounts were likely exaggerated.

In December 1875, after only six weeks in San Francisco, Edwin decided to take the job as physician on the Australasian Steam Navigation Company's vessel RMS *Mikado* that was soon to sail from San Francisco to Auckland, New Zealand, and then on to Sydney.

My many friends think the voyage on the *Mikado* will benefit me. People begin to go shy of me I notice. Some tell me I act queerly at times. . . . I go on board the *Mikado* in the morning December 9, 1875. We sail at 12 o'clock and expect to reach Honolulu, Hawaii in seven or eight days; then Levuka, Fiji Island in 14 days; Auckland, New Zealand in four and half days; & Sydney, in four & half or five days. We carry mail for the several places, also passengers & merchandise.

As surgeon I am allowed twenty square feet for luggage so I can take something & trade if I like but I have no experience as a businessman. My surgery is small but has two berths & a sofa berth so I shall take baby & she shall have a top berth & the steward will see after the dear. We are taking out the great Cook & Murrhara Circus [Wilson's Palace Circus] with all their outfit animals & people—a vast quantity. They appear a lively crowd. I shall have my hands full I see.[44]

Edwin and Annie Mabel disembarked the *Mikado* in Auckland, not sailing on to Sydney. Their arrival in Auckland was noted in the *New Zealand Herald* along with that of the thirty members of Wilson's Palace Circus and its animals.[45] Edwin made no additional journal entries regarding traveling with the circus.

The Wilson's Palace Circus, organized by California showman John Wilson, included Arabian acrobats, clowns, trained horses, and monkeys. The arrival of the circus caused great excitement in Auckland. The troupe set up a large canvas tent a week after its arrival to perform for as many as 2,500 people. Among the star performers were James Cooke and Ella Zoyara, with their trained horses and daring fetes on horseback.[46 47] (Ella was a man who dressed as a woman.)

NOTES

1. ETO, "Journal" (unpublished manuscript), 95. Siver family history material.
2. State Records of South Australia GRG 54/33 Yatala Labour Prison, Superintendent's Journal, vol. 1, 1 December 1869–31 December 1872.
3. "Larceny by a Bailee," *South Australian Register* (Adelaide), 14 May 1873, p. 3, col. e.
4. Ibid.
5. "Larceny by a Bailee," *South Australian Advertiser* (Adelaide), 14 May 1873, p. 3.
6. Ibid.
7 ETO, "Journal" (unpublished manuscript), 134, Siver family history material.
8 "Turkish and Hydropathic Establishment," *Sydney Morning Herald*, 6 January 1875, p. 1, col. f.
9 "A Certain Remedy," *Sydney Morning Herald*, 30 January 1875, p. 11, col. a.
10. ETO, "Journal" (unpublished manuscript), 135, Siver family history material.
11. ETO, "Journal" (unpublished manuscript), 136, Siver family history material.
12. *Cornwall Chronicle* (Launceston, Tasmania), 30 April 1875, p. 2, col. e.
13. *Cornwall Chronicle* (Launceston, Tasmania), 3 May 1875, p. 2, col. e.
14. *Mercury* (Hobart, Tasmania), 8 May 1875, p. 2, col. e.
15. "Hydropathy," *Mercury* (Hobart, Tasmania), 12 May 1875, p. 2, col. g.
16. Ibid.
17. *Mercury* (Hobart, Tasmania), 15 May 1875, p. 4S, col. g.
18. *Mercury* (Hobart, Tasmania), 2 July 1875, p. 1, col. g.
19. "Hydropathy, To the editor of the Tasmanian Tribune," *Tasmanian Tribune* (Hobart, Tasmania), 12 July 1875, p. 3.
20. *Mercury* (Hobart, Tasmania), 29 July 1875, p. 5, col. c.
21. "Police Court," *Tasmanian Tribune* (Hobart, Tasmania), 4 August 1875, p. 2.
22. *Tasmanian Tribune* (Hobart, Tasmania), 4 August 1875, p. 2.
23. "Held At 93 For Alleged Offense of 45 Years Ago," *Asbury Park Evening Press* (NJ), 27 March 1926, pp. 1–2.
24. "Doctor Refuses to Retreat Under Fire," *Asbury Park Evening Press* (NJ), 31 March 1926, pp. 1–2.
25. "Doctor, 93, To Fight Extradition as Thief," *New York Times*, 29 March 1926, pp. 1 and 3.
26. "Strange Claim: Searched for Leichhardt," *Daily News* (Perth), 21 May 1926, p. 12, col. f.
27. http://mariners.records.nsw.gov.au/1875/09/072ell.htm, accessed 10 December 2008.
28. ETO, "Journal" (unpublished manuscript), 132, Siver family history material.
29. ETO, "Journal" (unpublished manuscript), 100, Siver family history material.
30. *San Francisco News Letter and California Advertiser*, vol. 25, no. 41, 6 November 1875, p. 5, col. b.
31. *Daily Alta California* (San Francisco), vol. 27, number 9351, 10 November 1875, p. 2, col. d.
32. *San Francisco News Letter and California Advertiser*, vol. 25, no. 42, 13 November 1875, p. 5, col. b.
33. *San Francisco News Letter and California Advertiser*, vol. 25, no. 42, 13 November 1875, p. 5, col. b.
34. *San Francisco News Letter and California Advertiser*, vol. 25, no. 44, 27 November 1875, *Postscript to the San Francisco News Letter*, p. 4, col. b.
35. *San Francisco News Letter and California Advertiser*, vol. 25, no. 45, 4 December 1875, *Postscript to the San Francisco News Letter*, p. 6, col. b.
36. ETO, "Journal" (unpublished manuscript), 115–16, Siver family history material.
37. ETO, "Journal" (unpublished manuscript), 116–22, Siver family history material.
38. ETO, "Journal" (unpublished manuscript), 122–29, Siver family history material.
39. *Wikipedia*, s.v. "Broderick-Terry Duel," accessed 14 February 2014, https://en.wikipedia.org/wiki/Broderick%E2%80%93Terry_duel.
40. *Wikipedia*, s.v. "David C. Broderick," accessed 10 September 2016, https://en.wikipedia.org/wiki/David_C._Broderick.
41. *Wikipedia*, s.v. "Broderick-Terry Duel," accessed 14 February 2014, https://en.wikipedia.org/wiki/Broderick%E2%80%93Terry_duel.
42. *Wikipedia*, s.v. "David C. Broderick," accessed 10 September 2016, https://en.wikipedia.org/wiki/David_C._Broderick.
43. "Marriage Records, Dm-Dz," accessed 10 September 2016, http://www.sfgenealogy.com/sf/vitals/sfmardm.htm.
44. ETO, "Journal" (unpublished manuscript), 104–8, Siver family history material.
45. "Per RMS Mikado, from San Francisco," *New Zealand Herald* (Auckland), 3 January 1876, p. 2.
46. "Wilson's Palace Circus," *Auckland Star* (New Zealand), 5 January 1876, p. 3, col. b.
47. "Early Circus Days," *Morning Call* (San Francisco), 8 July 1894, p. 11, cols. a-d.

CHAPTER NINE

A New Life in New Zealand ~ 1876

The *Mikado* docked briefly in Auckland, New Zealand, on January 3, 1876, before continuing on to Australia. Edwin and Annie Mabel went ashore. Like many of the newly arrived immigrants, a fresh start and a new life lay ahead of them in this young country. New Zealand had only been a part of the British Empire since 1840, with the signing of the Treaty of Waitangi between the Crown and the native Maori people. Settlers, mostly from Ireland and England, had come in droves in the two decades following.

With the troubles and disappointments of Melbourne, Ballarat, Adelaide, Hobart, and San Francisco behind him, Edwin set out to establish himself anew. He had been to Auckland before while working on the RMS *MacGregor* and was aware that a Turkish bath had been established there some months earlier. As was his custom, he visited the local newspaper, inviting them to announce his presence.

The *New Zealand Herald* obliged on January 6. The article read, "We understand that Dr. Edwin Turner who has been for some considerable time engaged as surgeon in the vessels of the Australian Steam Navigation Company, intends to practice in Auckland for some months. Dr. Turner is, we believe, well acquainted with the hydropathic system of treatment pursued in America. He has a diploma from Philadelphia, and also one from Edinburgh, and has several testimonials from the passengers who have travelled between America and Australasia as to the care and attention he has shown them."[1]

En route to San Francisco in October, Edwin had visited the newly opened Turkish baths operated by K. D. Sykes on Upper Queen Street in Auckland while the *MacGregor* was briefly docked there. He dashed off a letter to the *Daily Southern Cross* on October 1, 1875, praising Sykes's operation.

Edwin and daughter Annie disembarked on January 3, 1876 in Auckland.
City of Auckland 1876. *Drawn by A. Hutchinson, from a sketch by J. M. Hammett, chromolith. by W. C. Wilson. Auckland; G. T. Chapman, [1876] Ref: D-001-010. Alexander Turnbull Library, Wellington, New Zealand. http://natlib.govt.nz/records/22346990 Printed with permission of the Alexander Turnbull Library / National Library of New Zealand.*

"I have much pleasure in being able to bear testimony," Edwin wrote, "to the excellent manner in which Mr. K. D. Sykes has constructed and fitted his Turkish hydropathic institution here. I consider it equal, as regards the cleanliness and ventilation, to the best institutions of the kind I have visited in London, America, the East, and in Melbourne or Sydney. Indeed, the method of cleanliness and ventilation is, if anything, superior, and all that can be desired by the medical profession. . . ."[2] He went on to praise the operator, the method of shampooing, and the blessings of the Turkish bath. His testimonial was signed, "E. Turner, Surgeon on board the RMS *MacGregor*."

By mid-January Edwin was in the employ of Sykes as a shampooer at his Upper Queen Street establishment.[3] A few days later, Edwin turned up working thirty miles north of Auckland at the Waiwera Hot Springs. This resort was operated by successful trader, farmer, and politician Robert Graham, who, from personal experience, believed in the health benefits of mineral waters and thermal spas. Edwin divided his time between the baths in Auckland and the spa and recorded the following in his journal:

> I am now resident physician at the Honorable Robert Graham's famous Waiwera Hot Springs Sanatorium. I rendered him an important private service in connection with his niece when Surgeon to the *MacGregor* & he gave me this appointment

> at £5/– per week & privileges with board & lodging and use of guns & boats, with a man servant, a native born here. My surgery is a pretty cottage all to myself, Annie Mabel & my man. Climate lovely. I am much sought after by all the sick natives about here & often go to their camps which are well built & cozy with large gardens & peach orchards. One, a Princess & Chief of an important tribe close by, which less than a century ago fought a neighbouring tribe who owned these Springs, conquered them & ate them. . . . I am told, as [late as] 40 years ago most of the tribes of New Zealand were cannibals. She gave 9 acres of peach land as fee.
>
> I have constructed a Turkish & Russian Bath establishment for Mr. K. D. Sykes, a jeweler & watchmaker, on Queen St., Auckland. He has one daughter age 16 & one son, named Clara & Walter. A charming family, I love to visit them.
>
> Have made a great many friends as usual. Chief of them Mr. R. Graham, the Reverend Mr. Chapman, Baptist Minister, who I study with every Sunday night, & Mrs. Mills, his sister. . . . A charming class of wealthy people flock to these Waiwera Hot Springs & Sanatorium.[4]

On January 31 money was taken from the cash box at Sykes's bath house. Edwin was not immediately suspected, but a warning to merchants was reported in the local paper that a thief was in their midst.[5]

In a preemptive move to avoid coming into the crosshairs of local authorities as he did in Tasmania, Edwin placed a notice in the *Daily Southern Cross* on February 18 advising the public that he was not practicing medicine. His notice read, "Wanted to be known that Mr. Turner, Hydropathist, late ship's surgeon, is not practicing as a Medical Doctor, but that the theory of his practice is pure air, exercise daily, dry heated air, and applications of hot and cold waters. Consultation free at the Turkish baths."[6] New Zealand had passed a revised Medical Practitioners Act in 1869 that called for the registration of medical men to be undertaken by the registrar-general who "had power to remove a name from the Register in the event of false registration, or after conviction of felony or misdemeanour, but the Act made no provision for removal for discreditable or infamous conduct in any professional respect."[7]

That same day he also published a notice announcing that he was holding a meeting that evening at Sykes's Baths for "persons favourable to hydropathy" to learn about its principles and practice.[8] The *Daily Southern Cross* gave him an endorsement in a separate article. "His numerous testimonials of a very flattering nature bear undeniable testimony to his skill as a hydropathist, some of them being already from well-known citizens here."[9]

Top: The dock at Waiwera Springs

Above left: The hotel and spa owned by politician Robert Graham at Waiwera Springs. Graham hired Edwin to provide hydrotherapy treatments to hotel guests.

Above right: Waiwera Springs, New Zealand

Accounts of the meeting were reported the next day in the *New Zealand Herald* and the *Daily Southern Cross*. "Those present," the *Southern Cross* noted, "formed themselves into the nucleus of a committee for furthering the cause of hydropathy in this city, and Dr. Turner announced his intention to deliver a course of lectures, beginning in about a fortnight's time, in which he would give the fullest explanation so as to enable every man to become his own doctor."[10] The committee was to be known as the Hydropathic Benevolent Association of Auckland. Edwin told those in attendance that he felt duty bound to inform the public of the benefits of hydropathy to the point that he was substituting it for his former medical practice. He also spoke of "certain interested persons" who had pledged themselves to thwart the introduction of hydropathy in New Zealand.[11]

Several favorable reviews were published in the *Daily Southern Cross* of treatments administered by Dr. Turner at Waiwera Hot Springs. However, Edwin was very displeased that Robert Graham had retained the services of Vincent Mohabeer, a naturalized British subject from India. Mohabeer said that the waters of Waiwera were ideal for curing many ailments and claimed to have returned many to good health, although he had no license to practice medicine in New Zealand. Calling Mohabeer "a notorious, East Indian quack doctor," Edwin threatened to resign his position, and looked into taking a position on a departing ship. There appeared to be little difference between the two men "professionally."

> Mr. Graham consented to a notorious East Indian quack doctor living at the Hotel for a time. I have threatened to resign & have already seen the agents of the New Zealand shipping boat *Glenlora* (Captain LeVisconte) which trades & carries passengers with her sister ship the *Carnatic* between London & N.Z. about becoming Surgeon & they are delighted to have me for either vessel & so are the captains who have often been my guests at the Springs.[12]

Edwin was hired to sail on the *Carnatic* but backed out of the commission at the last minute. He decided in March to leave his daughter in the care of Mrs. Rebecca Stewart, mayoress of the town of Napier, and her daughter Julia for a month to six weeks.

Annie Mabel sailed from Auckland down the coast to Napier with her guardians on the *Colima* on March 28. The *Colima* was due to arrive in Napier in three days but did not appear. A violent storm had come up the coast. The ship sheltered close to shore to wait out the storm. Edwin wrote, "The vessel being saved with difficulty & all lives threatened in one of the customary great storms that occur on these coasts. I thank Almighty God who has been ever most merciful toward me for my child's safe return. Life without her would be an awful dismal blank to me. Indeed, I fear I could not survive her loss."[13] Nonetheless, he quite often left Annie Mabel in the care of others.

Not content to further establish himself in Auckland and at Waiwera Hot Springs, Edwin launched

Annie Mabel Osbaldeston,
Auckland, New Zealand (1876)

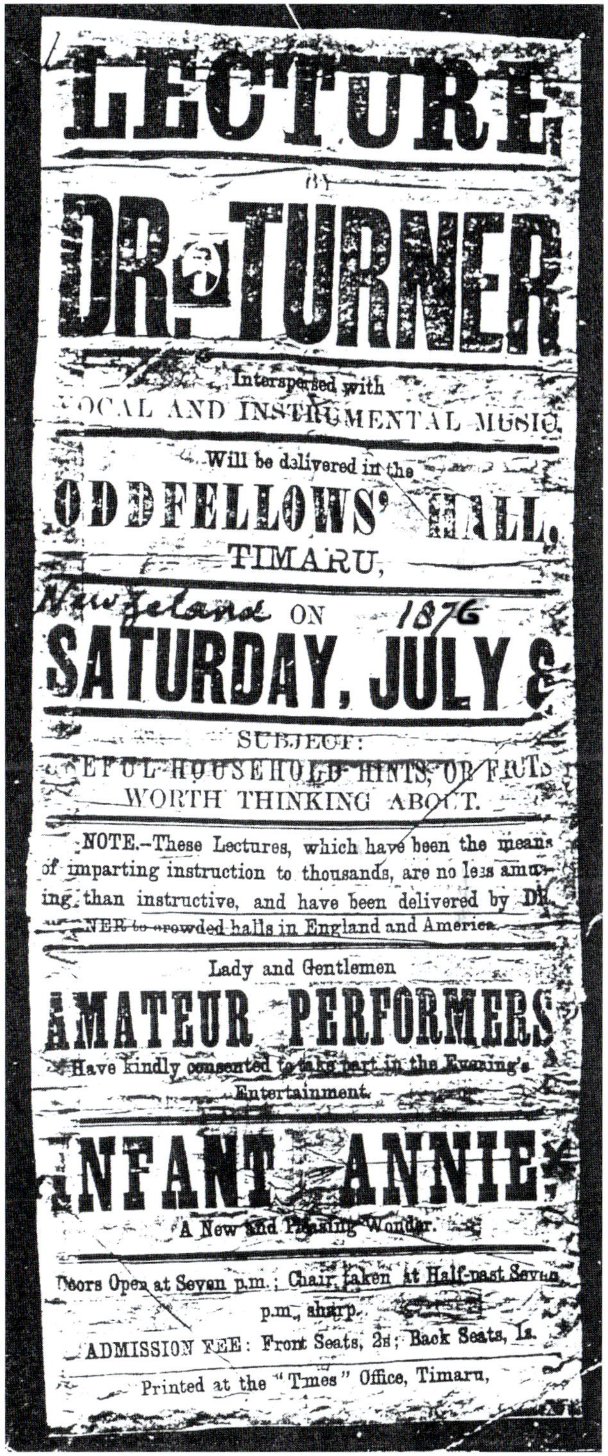
LECTURE
BY
DR. TURNER
Interspersed with
VOCAL AND INSTRUMENTAL MUSIC
Will be delivered in the
ODDFELLOWS' HALL,
TIMARU,
New Zeland ON 1876
SATURDAY, JULY 8
SUBJECT:
USEFUL HOUSEHOLD HINTS, OR FACTS
WORTH THINKING ABOUT.
NOTE.–These Lectures, which have been the means of imparting instruction to thousands, are no less amusing than instructive, and have been delivered by DR. TURNER to crowded halls in England and America.
Lady and Gentlemen
AMATEUR PERFORMERS
Have kindly consented to take part in the Evening's Entertainment.
INFANT ANNIE,
A New and Pleasing Wonder.
Doors Open at Seven p.m.; Chair Taken at Half-past Seven p.m., sharp.
ADMISSION FEE: Front Seats, 2s; Back Seats, 1s.
Printed at the "Times" Office, Timaru.

a campaign to educate the residents of New Zealand on the wonders of hydropathy. He traveled to the settlements of Thames, Wellington, Christchurch, and Timaru in May, June, and July. He was announced in Thames by the *Advertiser* as having come to the town "to try his treatment in cases of scarlet fever."[14]

A few weeks later the *Wellington Post* noted, "A large, well-conducted hydropathic establishment, where the water cure could be carried out on scientific principles, has long been a desideratum in New Zealand." The paper reported that "Dr. Turner, formerly of Bombay, and more lately of Auckland, is endeavoring at present to establish such an institution, and with this object is visiting the several provinces to obtain shareholders."[15]

He spent several weeks in Christchurch, where he announced hours for free consultations, placed advertisements in the local paper, and successfully enlisted the mayor's support. Apparently responding to feedback from potential clients and investors, Edwin began to stress that "his system is not 'the cold water cure' but a warm and soothing method."[16] Here a lecture on Turkish baths was held at the Oddfellows' Hall. The mayor of Christchurch presided and "during the evening several songs were sung by some ladies and gentlemen and a little girl."[17] Attendance was light.

Next stop on his promotional tour was the town of Timaru. Varying his approach somewhat, he planned his lecture with more entertainment and renamed it "Useful Household Hints or Facts Worth Thinking About." He added vocal and instrumental performances and introduced "Infant Annie / A New and Pleasing Wonder." Besides newspaper notices, Edwin had a handbill printed to promote his event on Saturday, July 8.

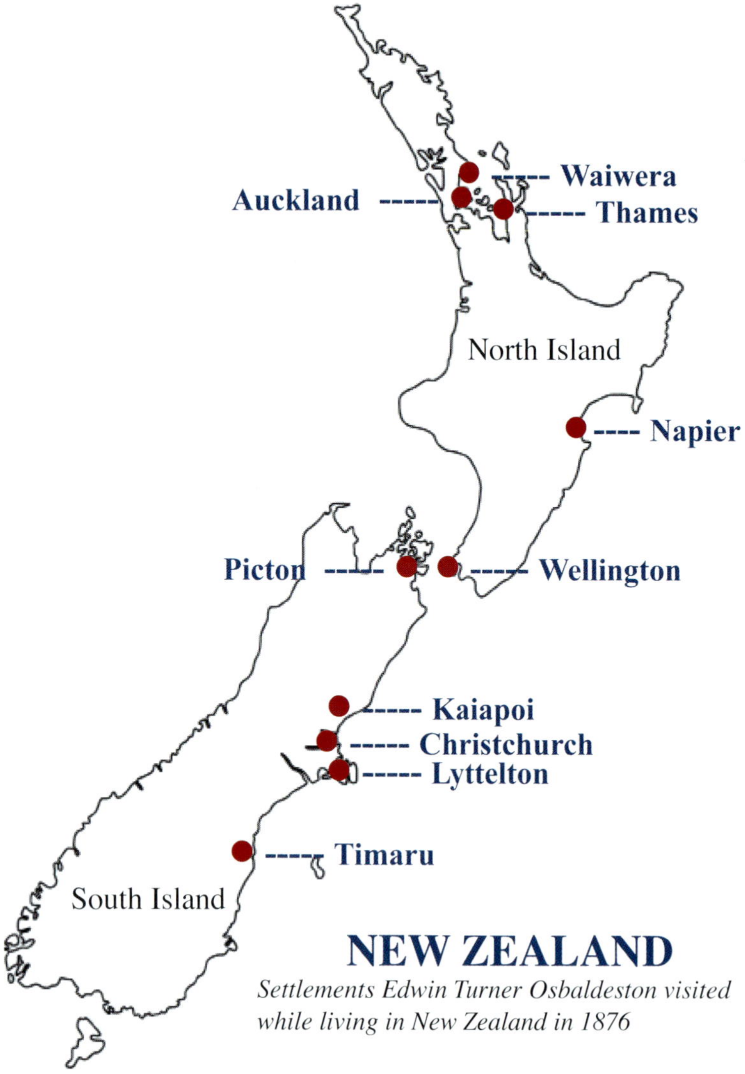

NEW ZEALAND

Settlements Edwin Turner Osbaldeston visited while living in New Zealand in 1876

> LECTURE.—Dr E. Turner announces that he will deliver a lecture on Saturday evening in the Oddfellows' Hall, interspersed with vocal and instrumental music. The subject of the lecture is "Useful Household Hints, or Facts Worth Thinking About." The lecture will have reference principally to hydropathic treatment, a science in which Dr. E. Turner is one of the first men of the day. Some wonderful cures by the application of hydropathy at his hands have been reported, and a gentleman in this district has taken the trouble to inform us personally of a case in which a relative was successfully treated by this method, when all other plans had failed. The lecture, in addition to being instructive and interesting, is also certain to be amusing, as the learned doctor has a very pleasing style with him.[18]

The following Monday's edition of the *Timaru Herald,* announced that Dr. E. Turner's lecture was "unavoidably postponed until Wednesday next."[19] No reason was given.

The day of the lecture a new advertisement was carried in the *Herald,* announcing that Dr. Turner's lecture and vocal and instrumental entertainment was under the patronage of G. Cliff, Esq., ex-mayor and the elite of Timaru. The venue was Turnbull's Hall and tickets were "two shillings and one."[20] The next day the *Herald* reported that "owing to poor attendance at Mr. Turnbull's Hall last evening, Dr. Turner did not deliver his promised lecture."[21] Perhaps in sympathy, the *Herald* printed Edwin's lecture in its edition of July 14.

Edwin made numerous references in his journal to preaching at Baptist churches and outdoor "Song & Praise" meetings during his stay in New Zealand for which he shared in the collections. Perhaps it was the monies from these events that supported his travels and the promotion of his lectures.[22] Then again, perhaps not.

His tour came to an abrupt halt on July 15 when he was arrested for stealing a coat six weeks earlier. The coat wasn't just any coat—it was a Goodi's

(Goudie's) patent, life-preserving, waterproof coat (an inflatable life jacket). It had been taken from fellow traveler John Peters on the steamship *Wellington* on June 1. Since it was an unusual item, the police had been on the lookout for the coat. It turned up in Timaru when local physician Dr. MacIntyre purchased it for £4 pounds (approximately $328 in current value) from Edwin Turner. When he sold the coat, Edwin had told Dr. MacIntyre that he had brought one hundred of these coats to New Zealand from America and had sold all but four.[23]

> **Arrest.**—On Saturday evening last [July 15] Dr E. Turner, the hydropathic practitioner and lecturer, was arrested on a charge of larceny of a coat that was lost some time since from the Wellington steamer. The police have been on the lookout for the coat (which is a peculiar one) from the time that it was lost, and they discovered it in the possession of a gentleman in this town to whom Dr Turner sold it. The prisoner asserts that he purchased the coat from a person in Auckland. He will be brought up before the Resident Magistrate this morning [July 17], and as the information is laid in Christchurch, he will probably be remanded to that place.[24]
>
> **DR TURNER'S CASE.**
> **Christchurch, July 19.**
> **Dr Turner** was brought up before the Resident Magistrate this morning.
>
> **Mr Thomas** appeared for the defence. The evidence taken at Timaru was read over.
>
> **John Peters**, a commercial traveller, said that when on the voyage from Picton to Wellington, and when near Wellington Heads, he missed one of Goodi's [Goudie's] patent life-preserving coats. He left it in the smoking room while he went on deck. The prisoner was in the room at the time, professing to write a letter. When prosecutor returned the coat was gone. He asked prisoner if anyone had taken any luggage out of the room. Prisoner said either a car man or a bus man had done so four or five minutes ago, to which prosecutor replied that could not be as the vessel was not near the wharf. Prosecutor next saw a coat at Detective Feast's office [in Timaru]. He identified the coat produced as the one he missed. It was worth £4 10s. . . .
>
> **Anne [Mabel] Turner, daughter of the prisoner,** said she knew her father had purchased a waterproof coat in Auckland. He brought it home and blew it out with a tube. Witness here blew up the coat in Court the same way as she saw her father blow it up in Auckland.
>
> **Inspector Feast:** She had not seen her father since he was taken away by the police till that morning at Mr Thomas's office, and did not speak about the coat. Inspector Feast desired to call Detective Walker to prove that the prisoner had made a similar statement in his daughter's presence at Timaru to which she had just said in evidence: but his Worship thought that it would be best to remand the prisoner until evidence was obtained from Auckland as to whether coats like the one produced were for sale in Queen Street at the time mentioned by the prisoner when arrested. Inspector Feast said, he could do so, and would ask for a remand to enable him to communicate with the police at Auckland. His Worship granted the request, and prisoner was remanded till Friday.
>
> **Mr Thomas** applied for his client to be admitted to bail. Inspector Feast said that he must oppose the application. One reason for this he might state that when Detective Walker went to Mr Gosling's at Timaru, he saw a gun left there by the prisoner which answered to the description of one stolen from Christchurch.
>
> **Mr Thomas** did not think the Bench should refuse bail, as his client was a gentleman who had occupied a very responsible position, and held many certificates of character. He had come out in medical charge of a large steamship, the *MacGregor*, carrying upwards of 300 passengers, and only the other day received an appointment to the *Carnatic*. He [Mr Thomas] had several testimonials which had been given to his client while acting in a medical capacity on ship board, and would submit them to the Bench.
>
> **Inspector Feast**: They might be forgeries.
>
> **Mr Thomas:** What, when one of them contains a large number of signatures?
>
> **Inspector Feast:** Yes; they might be. Such cases have occurred before.
>
> **Mr Thomas** contended that such a view of the matter was absurd, and again requested the Bench to accept bail.
>
> **Inspector Feast** said that he would strongly oppose it, and might tell Mr Thomas that even were prisoner admitted to bail, he would at once be arrested on another charge; also, that he could produce a man in Court to state that prisoner's name was not Turner but Osbaldiston.
>
> **Prisoner,** addressing the Bench, said that his name was Turner, and that he was a son of Dr Turner, Birmingham. He had brothers in Melbourne or Adelaide, and Lady Francis Turner was his mother. He had not communicated with his family for six years, and, although born in America, was of British descent.

> **His Worship** said that after what Inspector Feast had stated, he could not admit the prisoner to bail. Prisoner was remanded till Friday.[25]

Back in court on Friday in Christchurch, Edwin's story about purchasing the coat was debunked. The Auckland police sent testimony from the Queen Street merchant attesting that he knew Edwin Turner well and that he had never sold him a coat. Further damaging, the Auckland Inspector of Police sent a telegram confirming that the prisoner had been convicted of burglaries in Australia under the name "Osbaldiston" and sentenced to seven years hard labor. Judge Woollcombe said he did not believe the testimony of the prisoner's daughter and had no doubts about Turner's guilt. Edwin was sentenced to one month's imprisonment with hard labor.[26]

Addington Gaol in Christchurch, New Zealand

Both the police and the press took umbrage at Edwin's behavior. Because he had traveled to numerous towns in New Zealand, his arrest was widely covered. The *Canterbury Police Gazette* published a detailed listing of all of Edwin's personal property in the event that anyone reading the publication might notice something that had belonged to them and gone missing.[27]

News accounts referred to Edwin as "the so-called Dr Turner," "the alleged Dr Turner," "the notorious Dr Turner," and finally, "the eminent hydropathist and coat abstractor."[28] The press also reported a sense of betrayal from those who had placed their trust in the hydropathist. "The affair has created a little stir here as several people have reposed confidence in him by suffering themselves to be treated hydropathically," one report said.[29] Another noted the "mutability of human affairs" in recalling how Dr. Turner had a few weeks earlier been lecturing to an influential audience presided over by the mayor of Christchurch.[30] Looking back at the theft of cash in January from K. D. Sykes's Turkish bath in Auckland, it was now suspected that Edwin was the culprit.

> Dr Turner, lately convicted of the larceny of a coat, seems to have been employed at some period in Auckland. In reference to his career there, a Northern contemporary remarks:—"Mr Sykes had his till robbed during the time that Turner was employed at the baths. The offence was then attributed to some petty thief, who had sneaked in during the temporary absence of the custodian, but the recent disclosures are calculated to excite suspicions of a thief within rather than without."[31]

After the completion of his month-long incarceration Edwin was not a free man. He was immediately arrested for the theft of a second coat from a commercial traveler in the City Hotel in Christchurch that took place on or around July 1.

> The so-called Dr Turner, hydropathic lecturer, completed his sentence on Saturday (August 19). He was again arrested on a charge of stealing a coat belonging to a traveller named Cawell [sic]. [Correct name was Cowle.] He is remanded for eight days.[32]

At his hearing on the second charge of larceny in Resident Magistrate's Court in Christchurch on August 21, a debate ensued between Police Inspector Feast and Edwin's counsel. Mr. Thomas, representing Edwin, insisted that his client should not be held because there was no proof that a coat had been stolen. The inspector said that the coat was found in the accused's possession. He requested that Edwin be jailed until such time as the victim (Cowle) could return to Christchurch to testify. The judge agreed that the prisoner should be remanded.

Mr. Thomas then argued for bail, to which inspector Feast asked the bench to require a substantial sum. Bail was then set at £100 (approximately $8,000 in current value) which Edwin could not make. He was taken to Addington Gaol.[33] Although it was not reported at the hearing following his first arrest for stealing a coat, authorities knew that Edwin had been found to have in his possession of a set of skeleton keys used to open bedrooms in various lodging houses where he had stayed.[34]

On the sixth day of his detention, Edwin saw an opportunity to escape the Addington Gaol and seized upon it. Shortly after 11:00 a.m. he was briefly alone in the exercise yard, which was fenced with sheets of galvanized iron. Loosening one of the metal sheets, he obtained a footing, scaled the wall, jumped to the ground, and fled. He was spotted running off by a guard who gave chase but was unable to catch up with the escapee. It was reported that Edwin "displayed great fleetness of foot, managed to get a strong lead, the pace being very smart. He took across some paddocks, and ultimately the officers lost sight of him."[35] Law enforcement organized a search party to capture and bring him back to Addington Gaol.

> THE ESCAPE FROM ADDINGTON GAOL.—Up to a late hour last night no news had reached town of the re-capture of the prisoner Edwin Turner, who escaped from Addington Gaol on last Saturday morning. A tent was robbed on Mr Flemming's run, Ahuriri, between one and five o'clock on the same afternoon, and a loaf of bread and £2 5s stolen. It is known that Turner and a man who has lately been released from Addington Gaol, and with whom he had changed clothes, slept at Mr Parkinson's station on Sunday night. The latter is known to possess a thorough knowledge of the country on the peninsula, and from a conversation that was overheard, their intention seemed to be to make for the Bays and endeavour to obtain a passage in some craft outward bound.[36]

In the meantime, the authorities had been looking after the welfare of Edwin's daughter Annie Mabel. Defense attorney Thomas petitioned the court for the release of Edwin's funds so as to provide child support. Attorney Thomas may also have been looking for compensation for his defense efforts on Edwin's behalf.

> At the Magistrate's Court yesterday morning [August 30], Mr Thomas applied for an order for a portion of the money belonging to "Doctor" Turner, who has not yet been re-captured. . . . The money was intended for the support of Turner's child, for whom it was greatly required. . . . Mr Thomas said that he had rendered professional services to Dr Turner in the full belief that the order would be honoured, and besides this he would urge upon the Bench the necessity for provision for the support of Turner's daughter. Mr Feast said Mrs Lodge, with whom Turner's daughter resided, assured him the previous evening that the child would be taken care of without regard to money—that money or no money, she, Mrs Lodge, would keep the girl. . . . His Worship said he would take care that some provision should be made for the support of Turner's child, but he could not make an order for any of the money to be paid over except for this purpose. . . .[37]

After six days on the run, Edwin was spotted along a road thirty-five miles north of Christchurch, near Kaiapoi. Upon seeing the mounted officer coming towards him, Edwin jumped a fence, ran through an orchard, and was running along a hedge in a crouched position with his hat in his hand. The constable gave chase and caught up with him. Several times he ordered Edwin to stop or he would shoot. Finally, Edwin surrendered, was handcuffed, and taken to the lockup in Kaiapoi. Inspector Feast was notified by telegram that the fugitive had been apprehended.[38]

Returned to court in Christchurch, Edwin objected to the arresting constable's testimony that he had been spotted running along the road before his re-

Edwin in 1876

arrest. Instead, he claimed to have been walking leisurely while looking for a place to hide.[39] When asked by the judge if he had a statement to make, Edwin began by denying that he was some other person (Osbaldiston) and that his escape was not anything but a breach of prison law.

"I do assert, and call God to witness, that I suffered the month's imprisonment for stealing the coat innocently and I have most positive evidence in my possession to show this," Edwin said. "The fact is that I am surrounded by a host of enemies. I am like a sheep at bay with a pack of wolves around me, and there is little mercy for me if I do not get it from you, gentlemen of the Bench,"[40] he continued as if he were the victim.

He claimed that he had escaped due to the desire to see his child and had gone to the house where she was staying, only to find it surrounded by police.[41] As to why he was headed toward Kaiapoi, he explained he went there with the intention of drawing police away from his daughter and that he had planned to double back to Christchurch, visit his daughter, and then turn himself in.[42]

The judge, not impressed with Edwin's discourse, interrupted to state that the more Edwin spoke, the worse he was making things for himself. The judge turned to inspector Feast and inquired as to the status of the witness to the second charge of larceny as he was overdue in coming before the court. The inspector replied that Cowle was a traveler and had promised to appear. In response the judge said he would dismiss the case if Cowle failed to turn up.[43] Edwin was then remanded for another fortnight [fourteen days] for jail breaking.

On October 2, at the conclusion of his sentence, Edwin was back in court for the disposition of the second charge of larceny. Mr. Cowle still had not returned to Christchurch. Defense attorney Thomas reminded the Bench that at the last hearing it had indicated that the case would be dropped if the alleged victim failed to appear. Inspector Feast reported that Mr. Cowle had been ill and unable to travel. Thomas responded that it was not fair to continue to remand the prisoner week after week. Following more discussion, the judge ruled that the prisoner was to be remanded for another fortnight; however, he would be released on his own recognisance after posting £20 to reappear. At that point, Edwin was released.[44]

When his case came up in court again on Monday, October 16, Edwin did not answer to his name. According to Inspector Feast, it was probably not long after his release on bail on October 2 that Edwin—dressed in female attire—had gone to the house where his daughter was staying, collected her, and headed to the nearby port of Lyttelton from where they embarked on a steamer to Melbourne.[45] Edwin and Annie Mabel had spent just over nine months in New Zealand. Once again he had destroyed his opportunities for success.

NOTES

1. *New Zealand Herald* (Auckland), 6 January 1876, p. 2, col. f.
2. *Daily Southern Cross* (Auckland), 2 October 1875, p. 3, col. b.
3. "A Visit to Syke's [sic] Turkish Baths Auckland, and Its Result," *Evening Star* (Auckland), 21 January 1876, p. 2, col. f.
4. ETO, "Journal" (unpublished manuscript), 110–115, Siver family history material.
5. "A Case of Larceny," *Daily Southern Cross* (Auckland), 1 February 1876, p. 2, col. e.
6. Advertisements, *Daily Southern Cross* (Auckland), 18 February 1876, p. 1, col. c.
7. *An Encyclopedia of New Zealand*, 1966, s.v. "Medical Profession," accessed 28 February 2014, http://www.TeAra.govt.nz/en/1966/medical-services/page-6.
8. Advertisements, *Daily Southern Cross* (Auckland), 18 February 1876, p. 1, col. g.
9. *Southern Daily Cross* (Auckland), 18 February 1876, p. 2.
10. "Turkish Baths," *Daily Southern Cross* (Auckland), 19 February 1876, p. 3.
11. *New Zealand Herald* (Auckland), 19 February 1876, p. 2.
12. ETO, "Journal" (unpublished manuscript), 114, Siver family history material.
13. ETO, "Journal" (unpublished manuscript), 110–115, New Zealand, 1876, Siver family history material.
14. *Thames Advertiser* (NZ), 24 May 1876, p. 3, col. a.
15. *Evening Post* (Wellington), 6 June 1876, p. 2, cols. d-e.
16. "Hydropathy," *Star* (Christchurch), 16 June 1876, p. 2, col. c.
17. "Turkish Baths," *Press* (Canterbury), 1 July 1876, p. 2, col. e.
18. "Lecture," *Timaru Herald*, 6 July 1876, p. 4, cols. c-d.
19. "Lecture," *Timaru Herald*, 10 July 1876, p. 3, col. d.
20. *Timaru Herald*, 12 July 1876, p. 3, col. a.
21. "Dr Turner," *Timaru Herald*, 13 July 1876, p. 3, col. f.
22. ETO, "Journal" (unpublished manuscript), 138 and 142, Siver family history material.
23. "Resident Magistrate's Court," *Timaru Herald*, 18 July 1876, p. 3, col. g.
24. "Arrest," *Timaru Herald*, 17 July 1876, p. 3, col. c.
25. "Dr Turner's Case," *Timaru Herald*, 20 July 1876, p. 4, col. a.
26. "Dr Turner's Case," *Timaru Herald*, 22 July 1876, p. 3, col. d.
27. *Canterbury Police Gazette* (Christchurch), no. 15, 1 August 1876, p. 122.
28. "Capture of 'Dr' Turner," *Star* (Christchurch), 1 September 1876, p. 2, col. c.
29. *Press* (Canterbury), 17 July 1876, p. 2, col. c.
30. *Star* (Christchurch), 1 September 1876, p. 2, col. c.
31. "A Late Case of Larceny," *Star* (Christchurch), 8 August 1876, p. 2, col. e.
32. *Evening Post* (Wellington), 21 August 1876, p. 2, col. f.
33. "Larceny," *Star* (Christchurch), 21 August 1876, p. 2, col. d.
34. "Miscellaneous Information," *Victorian Police Gazette* (Melbourne), 29 November 1876, p. 307.
35. "Escape of a Prisoner," *Press* (Christchurch), 28 August 1876, p. 2, col. e.
36. "The Escape from Addington Gaol," *Press* (Christchurch), 30 August 1876, p. 2, col. d.
37. "'Doctor' Turner," *Lyttelton Times* (Christchurch), 31 August 1876, p. 2.
38. "The Fugitive 'Doctor,'" *Star* (Christchurch), 2 September 1876, p. 2, col. c.
39. "Escaping from Legal Custody," *Star* (Christchurch), 2 September 1876, p. 2, cols. c-d.
40. Ibid.
41. Ibid.
42. Ibid.
43. Ibid.
44. "Larceny," *Star* (Christchurch), 2 October 1876, p. 2, col. d.
45. "Larceny of a Coat," *Star* (Christchurch), 16 October 1876, p. 2; *Evening Press* (Wellington), 17 October 1876, p. 2. The same item appeared in *Wanganui Herald*, *Tuapeka Times*, and *West Coast Times* (New Zealand).

CHAPTER TEN

Return to England ~ 1876–1880

Booking passage on a ship to Melbourne, Edwin and Annie Mabel abruptly left Lyttelton, the port of Christchurch, New Zealand, on October 9, 1876. The authorities in Christchurch surely assumed that he would flee and forfeit his bail rather than risk another trial and likely incarceration.

Nine days later the pair were on board the SS *Durham* on their way to London. Though his stay in Melbourne was brief, Edwin did not escape Australia without notice. Both the *Victorian Police Gazette* and the *South Australian Police Gazette* reported in their November editions that "Osbaldiston" had been in the city, attempted to borrow money, expressed interest in going "up country," and was traveling with a young girl.[1]

In his journal he recorded the progress of the trip. The *Durham* reached Cape Horn and sailed through the Straits of Magellan after twenty-five days at sea, reached the Cape Verde Islands on December 6, and arrived in London on December 21. According to his journal, he and Annie Mabel went to Birmingham on December 23. There they spent Christmas Day with Edwin's younger brother Frank and his wife, Sarah, who were living in Smethwick, Staffordshire, northwest of Birmingham. Also living in Smethwick at that time were Edwin's sister Emma, her husband Joseph Vernon, and their sons.

Edwin and Annie Mabel appear to have spent most of the next three years (1877–1879) in England. His notebook gives very few clues as to their daily lives and activities. Edwin did resume lecturing in 1877. His topics were "Explorations & Adventures in New Guinea," "Useful Household Hints & Facts Worth Knowing," and "Mesmerism." More than likely, the former talk would have included tales of saving natives' lives through hydropathy, tribal conflicts, and his involvement with tribal leaders that may have been extrapolated from experiences he'd had in Australia and New Zealand.

Edwin and Annie Mabel sailed to England from Australia on the SS Durham.

There was no mention in his journal of having traveled to New Guinea, a large island to the northeast of Australia. However, he may have visited New Guinea while serving on a ship prior to his sailing to San Francisco and relocating to New Zealand.

Fascinated with alternative medicine and treatments, Edwin had studied mesmerism and for a time endorsed its principles. Decades earlier, German physician Franz Mesmer (1734–1815) had experimented with the use of magnets as curative agents. He developed a theory of animal magnetism. He believed that the human body possessed magnetic forces and that illness occurred when the flow of body fluids was interrupted. Use of magnets could correct the flow and thus return a person to good health.

In the nineteenth century, Mesmer's followers rejected magnetism and applied hypnosis as a form of treatment—the power of the mind over the body.[2] For his lecture, "Practical Illustrations of the Mysterious Power of Mesmerism," Edwin chose people from his audience to hypnotize. He then had them perform various scenes or feats of strength through the power of his suggestion while in a hypnotic trance.

Edwin noted that he gave these talks in Bristol, Cheltenham, Chester, Liverpool, and Birkenhead in England; Dublin, Limerick, and Belfast in Ireland; and the French region of Normandy.

In his journal Edwin claimed to have been the manager of the Longton Hall Hydropathic Institution, Longton Hall Hotel and Sanatorium, West Hill, Sydenham, London. Mr. and Mrs. W. R. Barnett

After his return to England, Edwin went on the lecture circuit. The poster above promoted his speaking engagement on February 12, 1877, in Albert Hall in Bristol, England. He supported daughter Annie Mabel and himself through his lectures when not working in the baths.

There is no record of his travel to New Guinea. However, he may have traveled there while working on one of the mail and passenger ships of the Peninsular and Oriental Steam Navigation Company.

were the proprietors in 1879. Given his tendency to overstate his position, in all likelihood he may simply have been employed as a bath attendant at Longton Hall. However, among his testimonials was one from the Barnetts.

Edwin's life in England was not trouble-free. In August 1879 he was arrested for shoplifting at a clothing store in London. He had asked the clerk to see some children's stockings, and the clerk obliged. Edwin then asked if the clerk had any others that he might see. When the clerk returned with additional stockings, he noticed that two pairs were missing from the first bundle and he had seen Edwin put his hand inside the breast of his coat.

When challenged about the missing stockings, Edwin claimed to be absentminded. He was arrested and appeared in the Worship Street Police Court. Edwin entered the court well dressed with a substantial sum of money in his pocket. He told the magistrate that he was a surgeon who had recently returned from San Francisco with his daughter. He presented a packet of testimonials as proof of his good character. For his defense he claimed that he had lingering effects from sunstroke and that he suffered spells of absentmindedness. The magistrate, impressed with Edwin's explanation and testimonials, and given that he had not left the store with the merchandise, dismissed the case.[3] Several London newspapers reported on his day in court.

Edwin made no mention of this incident in his journal, nor did he write about his family. There were no remarks recorded of his father, Josiah Scudder Osbaldeston. Certainly, he knew his mother, Mary Ann Turner; her husband James Hubbard; and his youngest brother, Julian, had moved to Bristol in 1866.[4]

At the time of the 1871 census, Mary Ann Turner and James Hubbard were living in the Bedminster

ADVERTISEMENTS. 17

LONGTON HALL. HYDROPATHIC ESTABLISHMENT. SYDENHAM. S.E.

LONGTON HALL
HYDROPATHIC ESTABLISHMENT,
And Residence for Patients and Visitors,
WEST HILL, SYDENHAM, S.E.

Longton Hall is within a few minutes' walk of the Crystal Palace and two Railway Stations.

The sheltered position which the establishment occupies renders it eminently adapted as a RESIDENCE for Invalids, and offers advantages not attainable at any establishment so near the Metropolis. The Bath Rooms have been constructed upon the most modern and approved principles, and are under the supervision of a resident physician, and include the Turkish (which has been recently added), Warm and Cold Needle Douche, and Shallow, Warm and Cold Running Sitz, Sulphurous, Vapour, and Medicated Baths of various kinds, Russian-Vapour, Electro-Chemical, Electro-Spinal, &c., &c.

There is an excellent Billiard Room, a Library, Conservatory, and Croquet Lawn. A LIBERAL TABLE is kept, and the domestic arrangements are such as to combine the comforts of a luxurious home with the quiet so essential for the recovery of Invalids.

Patients wishing to enter the establishment are requested to communicate with the RESIDENT PHYSICIAN and Proprietor, DR. ADAMS, M.R.C.P.E., &c.

TERMS PER WEEK.
Board and Residence, with use of all Baths (excepting the Turkish, Electro-Chemical, and Russian-Vapour), from £2 2s. upwards.

section of Bristol. Curiously, the couple were enumerated in the census under the surname Turner rather than Hubbard. James Hubbard's occupation was listed as cane worker and he was recorded as being blind.[5] Mary Ann and her son Julian were no longer living in Bristol when Edwin lectured in the city in 1877.

Mary Ann Turner was committed to the Bristol Lunatic Asylum on July 26, 1876, suffering from senile dementia.[6] It is not known if Edwin visited her while he was in the area. When Mary Ann died on June 23, 1878, it was her married daughter Emma

Vernon in Smethwick, near Birmingham, who was notified by the asylum. Mary Ann was buried in the churchyard of St. John's, in the Bedminster area of Bristol.[7] She was sixty-three years of age.

In other family matters, Edwin arranged to have his daughter Annie Mabel baptized on July 27, 1879, at All Saints Church in Birmingham.[8] He recorded that on August 25, 1879, Annie Mabel attended "Mrs. E. Miles private boarding school, Tonsley Hill, Wandsworth"[9] in South London.

The most significant event for Edwin was meeting twenty-four-year-old Alice Agnes Moore, probably in 1879. Alice Agnes was born and raised in Suffolk, the daughter of a journeyman tailor. As was customary for daughters of working class families, she left home at an early age to work as a domestic servant or maid.

She lived with a family of landed gentry at Yoxford Rookery in Suffolk and then moved with the family to London. There she ended up working at Putney Hospital (on the Thames). For a time she was engaged to a man who was a patient at the hospital.[10]

Edwin told people that he and Alice Agnes were married on December 27, 1879, by the Reverend J. T. Blackmore, Kirkdale, Sydenham, southeast London. However, there is no record of this marriage in the *General Index, Marriages 1879* of the United Kingdom's General Register Office nor in the register of marriages for St. Bartholomew's Church in Kirkdale.[11] It is probable that he claimed he and Alice were married in England in December 1879 for the sake of propriety. Alice became pregnant with his child in December 1879 or January 1880.

His reasons for not marrying her in England may have been because he was still married to Ann Pratt and feared that the authorities might learn that he had already been married once before and would ask what had become of his first wife. If he said that she had died in Australia, they would have asked him to produce her death certificate. There was also the matter that he was a deserter from the Royal Artillery. Registering the marriage might

Top of page: Alice Agnes Moore at age seventeen
Above: Moore family home in Yoxford, England

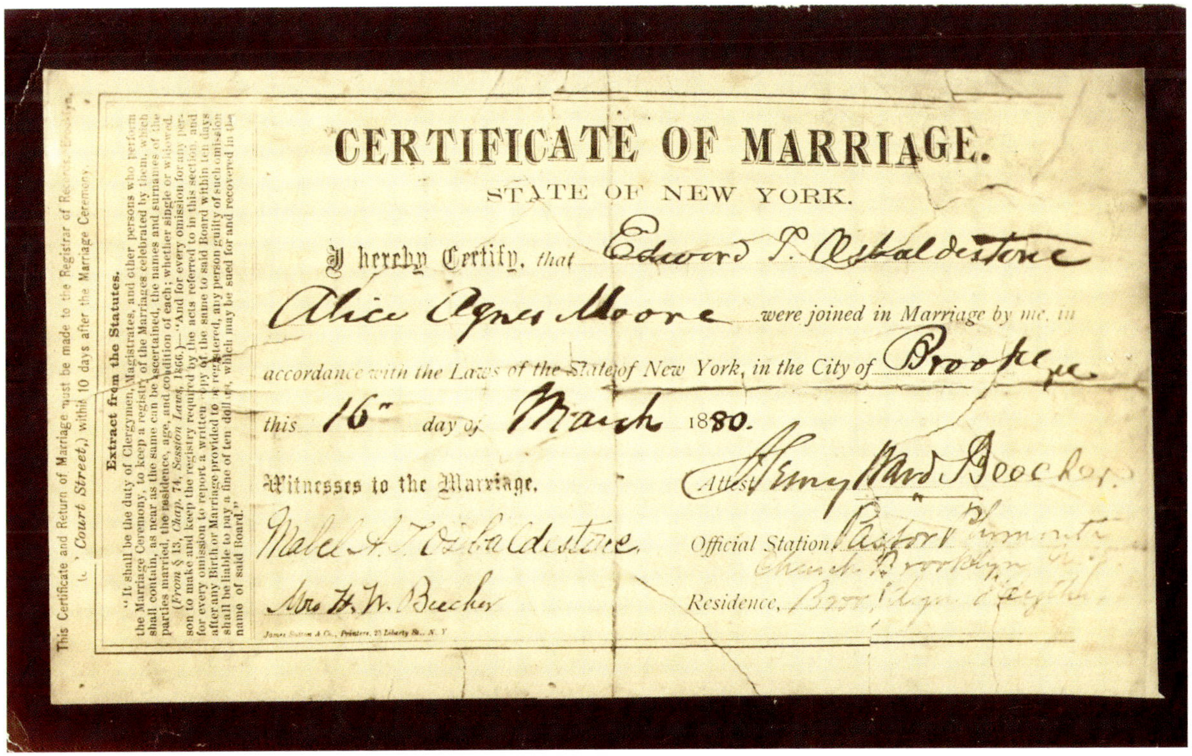

This Certificate and Return of Marriage must be made to the Registrar of Records, ... Court Street), within 10 days after the Marriage Ceremony.

Extract from the Statutes.

CERTIFICATE OF MARRIAGE.

STATE OF NEW YORK.

I hereby Certify, that Edward T. Osbaldestone

Alice Agnes Moore were joined in Marriage by me, in accordance with the Laws of the State of New York, in the City of Brooklyn

this 16th day of March 1880.

Witnesses to the Marriage.

Mabel A. T. Osbaldestone

Mrs H. W. Beecher

Attest Henry Ward Beecher

Official Station Pastor Plymouth Church Brooklyn N.Y.

Residence, Brooklyn Heights

The date on this marriage certificate was changed from May 16 to March 16, 1880 as a matter of propriety.

have brought the kind of attention he did not want. Edwin was in a bind once again. As he so often did when in a predicament, he moved to another playing field. This time it was New York City. Edwin, Alice Agnes, and Annie Mabel sailed from London on the SS *Erin* (in steerage) and arrived in New York on February 26, 1880.

Immigration to the United States was relatively free and easy during the nineteenth century. America's doors were essentially wide open. For decades states had created immigration laws. The United States Supreme Court *(Henderson v Mayor of New York)* ruled in 1875 that immigration was a federal responsibility and that state immigration laws were unconstitutional. Congress, however, was slow to enact immigration controls. Other than passing the Chinese Exclusion Act of 1882 (which also barred convicts, lunatics, and those unable to care for themselves) and the Contract Labor Law of 1885, making it illegal to import unskilled laborers from overseas, it did little to regulate the influx of immigrants immediately following that court decision.[12]

Thus, between 1880 and 1890 over 5.2 million immigrants entered the country. By 1890, 15 percent of the US popuation were foreign born.[13]

The US census of 1880 records Edwin as using the surname Turner. On June 5, 1880, Edward Turner, Alice Turner, and Ann (Annie Mabel) Turner, along with ten other individuals, most of whom were of German origin, were enumerated in a boarding house run by a thirty-seven-year-old Prussian widow named Aurora Vismeski. Her occupation was recorded as "Hygenic Baths Keeper." Edwin gave his occupation as "Surgeon," but it is possible that he was employed as a bath attendant by Mrs. Vismeski. Their address was 56 East Fourth Street in Manhattan.[14]

Edwin and Alice were married on May 16, 1880, in the Brooklyn, New York, home of famed social reformer and abolitionist Reverend Henry Ward Beecher. Witnesses were Reverend Beecher's wife and Annie Mabel. Edwin altered the date on their marriage certificate from May to March for the sake of appearances and to conceal the fact that Alice Agnes was by then several months pregnant.[15]

Surely, it never occurred to him that one of his descendants would discover that on March 16, Reverend Beecher was not in New York City but at a speaking engagement in Ohio.[16 17]

NOTES

1. *South Australian Police Gazette* (Adelaide), 6 December 1876, p. 198.
2. *Wikipedia,* s.v. "Franz Mesmer," accessed 12 September 2014, http://en.wikipedia.org/wiki/Franz_Mesmer.
3. "Police Intelligence. Worship Street: A Surgeon Charged with Felony," *Standard* (London), 21 August 1879, p. 2, col. d.
4. "Had a Life of Adventure," *Detroit Free Press,* 9 January 1898, p. 29, cols. e-f.
5. *Census Returns of England and Wales, 1871.* Kew, Surrey, England: The National Archives of the UK (TNA): Public Record Office (PRO), 1871, class RG10, piece 2507, folio 42, page 24, GSU roll: 835203.
6. Bristol Record Office ref: 40513/C/8. 1875–1879, Female Case Book, vol. 13, 1875–1879, folios 76, 10, 161.
7. "England Deaths and Burials, 1538–1991," database, *FamilySearch,* accessed 5 August 2015, https://familysearch.org/ark:/61903/1:1:JZL3-KTG, Mary Ann Turner, 27 Jun 1878; citing reference it1 p67 n534; FHL microfilm 1,849,446.
8. "England Births and Christenings, 1538–1975," database, *FamilySearch*, accessed 5 August 2015, https://familysearch.org/ark:/61903/1:1:J9GC-DP8, Annie Osbaldeston, 27 Jul 1879; citing Birmingham, Warwick, England, reference item 2 p. 177; FHL microfilm 1,519,861.
9. ETO, "Journal" (unpublished manuscript), 174, Siver family history material.
10. Alice Agnes Moore Osbaldeston's half-sister Emma Moore Flaxman, High Street, Yoxford, Suffolk, England, to Alice Agnes Moore Osbaldeston's eldest daughter, Ethel Turner Osbaldeston, in New Jersey, 8 February 1921.
11. Seen at Lewisham Local History Centre, Central Library, Lewisham, London, England.
12. "A Brief Timeline of U.S. Policy on Immigration and Naturalization," accessed 10 September 2016, http://www.flowofhistory.org/themes/movement_settlement/uspolicytimeline.php.
13. Ibid.
14. "United States Census, 1880," index and images, *FamilySearch,* accessed 20 December 2014, https://familysearch.org/pal:/MM9.1.1/MZ6H-591, Edward Turner in household of Aurora Vismeski, New York, New York, New York, United States, 258; citing sheet 381B, film number 0878, NARA microfilm publication T9, National Archives and Records Administration, Washington D.C.; FHL microfilm 1,254,878.
15. According to his daughter Normandie Alice Osbaldeston Siver, the damage to the marriage certificate was a result of it having been torn up by ETO during a family argument. He then paid to have it repaired and reproduced using a photographic technique.
16. "NYC Brides Record Index," accessed 2 July 2009, http://italiangen.org/records-search/brides.php.
17. "No Place for Beecher," *New York Times,* 17 March 1880, p. 1.

CHAPTER ELEVEN

Starting Over Again in America ~ 1880–1881

In the course of one's life, there are years that can be termed extraordinary, marked by accomplishments, milestones, great change, or even calamity. Such years are the result of decisions, events, circumstances, relationships, place, vocation, etc., that come to shape and define a person. The year 1880 was certainly an extraordinary year for Edwin Turner Osbaldeston.

Mile markers along his life's path that year were his arrival in America, marriage to Alice Agnes, the birth of a second daughter (Ethel), the establishment of a promising practice in the art of massage, and another fall from grace.

In June Edwin left Alice and Annie Mabel in Manhattan and went to the town of Rome in Oneida County, New York, to once again establish himself in the business of the healing arts. Rome, located in the center of the state, held great strategic and commercial importance as it connected Canada and the Great Lakes to the Hudson River Valley and New York City. Situated on the Mohawk River, the largest tributary of the Hudson, Rome was a key stop on an inland trade route. Construction of the Erie Canal had begun there in 1817. Edwin, now promoting the Swedish movement cure, was invited to Rome to attend to a resident of that town.[1]

Originating in the early nineteenth century, the Swedish movement cure gained popularity in the intervening years. Also known as Swedish massage or Swedish movements, it consisted of a series of systematic exercises therapeutically applied to the human body with each exercise or movement having a fixed direction and duration. The treatment involved active and passive movements of the body.

Devised by Per Henrik Ling (1776–1836), the basic techniques were "effleurage," or long, gliding strokes; "petrissage," which required lifting and kneading the muscles; "friction," which consisted of firm, deep, circular rubbing movements; "tapotement," or brisk tapping or percussive movements; and "vibration," which consisted of rapidly shaking or vibrating specific muscles. The active movements required the patient to do a series of exercises. An attendant or operator applied the passive movements.[2]

Ling and his followers prescribed the Swedish movement for treatment of indigestion, nervousness, consumption, and numerous other diseases and as an alternative to medicines. As with hydrotherapy as a curative for disease, a number of physicians viewed the Swedish movement cure as quackery. Nonetheless, it was reported in Rome that "[Edwin] attended a number of our prominent citizens, and by his manipulations appeared to be meeting with considerable success. There is no doubt that his method of treating certain diseases was efficacious and that some of his patients improved under his care."[3]

In short order, Edwin built a following in Rome for his Swedish treatment and massage. As had been his practice when arriving in a community for the first time, he contacted the local newspapers and thereby enumerated his credentials and displayed his testimonials. Before long, his wife and daughter joined him. On October 4, 1880, Ethel Monica Augusta Turner Osbaldeston was born to Edwin and Alice Agnes in Rome.

Troubles began anew a few weeks later with the announcement that former president and Civil War general Ulysses S. Grant and US senator Roscoe Conkling would be appearing in Utica, campaigning for the Republican presidential ticket of James A. Garfield and Chester A. Arthur.

Grant's popularity had waned during the last years of his scandal-plagued administration. After leaving office in 1877, President Grant and his wife, Julia, took a trip around the world that was followed by the public through newspaper accounts. Upon his return to the United States, his public standing had improved.

On Monday, October 25, large crowds had gathered for three daytime rallies and a torchlight parade in the evening with Grant and Conkling. Edwin was among those who went to Utica to see the former president. At some point during the festivities, Edwin stole a horse and wagon belonging to farmer Thomas Allen. Allen had left his rig on the street while attending the parade.[4]

Edwin took Allen's rig to a nearby carriage shop, hitched the horse to a three-spring wagon that had been left there for repairs, and then drove himself to Binghamton, where he sold the outfit for thirty-five dollars and checked into a hotel. Meanwhile, his patients and his family in Rome were left without explanation as to his absence. Upon his return he said he had been on a hunting trip in the wilds. As a reporter later recalled, "He told some persons in town that he had been on a trip to the North

Woods, and as proof of his assertion, showed his hands, which appeared rough and calloused. People would perhaps have believed this story but for the fact that Turner enlarged upon it so greatly. He said he had been in a portion of the wilderness where no white man had ever been before; that he had shot ever so many animals, deer, bears, etc.; and had sold the skins . . . for thirty-five dollars."[5]

On the night of Saturday, October 30, a horse and phaeton belonging to Dr. Edwin Ford were stolen from a livery in Binghamton. The thief had covered a window to block his light and then made off with the goods. The following Thursday a man appeared at Foley's livery stable in Utica with a horse and phaeton matching the description of Dr. Ford's rig. The driver gave his name as Dr. E. T. O'Shaughnessy. That same day he returned to Foley's for the rig, saying that he was going to move his family from Rome to Utica. While he was in Rome, several people reported that they were offered the horse and phaeton for $150.[6]

Returning to Utica on Saturday, November 6, O'Shaughnessy approached William Martin of Martin & Co. Livery, offering to sell him the rig. Martin sensed something was not right and declined the offer. O'Shaughnessy then went to John Foley about purchasing the rig for $150, claiming to be in dire financial straits and needing to liquidate his property. Like Martin, Foley was at once suspicious because he knew the black mare and phaeton had a value greater than the asking price. However, after a woman said to be Mrs. O'Shaughnessy appeared with a fourteen-year-old girl who was upset by the pending sale of her pet, Foley's doubts were erased. He and O'Shaughnessy settled on $125 for the outfit.[7]

Reflecting on the transaction, Foley told a reporter that his reservations about the purchase evaporated because "the fellow was so respectable in appearance, cool, and deliberate, and had kept his promise in regard to moving his family from Rome so promptly." Foley told the same reporter that "O'Shaughnessy spoke of his wife at their boarding place as 'Mrs. Mitchell,' but corrected this slip quickly." Foley also said he saw three or four buffalo robes in the doctor's room.[8]

The Binghamton Sheriff's Office had circulated a flyer in central New York describing the horse and phaeton taken from Dr. Ford. Troubled by O'Shaughnessy's proposition, liveryman Martin contacted Utica police chief James Dwyer. In short order Dwyer paid a visit to Foley's livery stable. Foley explained the transaction and gave the chief a description of O'Shaughnessy. Chief Dwyer arrested Edwin on November 8 for theft. An account of the arrest in the *Utica Morning Herald* the next day praised the chief's handling of the case.[9]

> The police [chief] handled him [Edwin] so skillfully that he obtained the money paid him by Foley from his wife, and Chief Dwyer returned it to that gentleman, who was very grateful. Dr. Ford was notified of the recovery of his property and will be here today to identify it. The thief has several names and probably some of them are correct. He is undoubtedly a professional rascal, and has been operating in other places. It is feared that his wife and possibly his child are acquainted with his operations [or] possibly they have been deceived by him.[10]

Following Edwin's capture, Broome County deputy sheriff S. Foster Black collected his prisoner and took him back to Binghamton to be arraigned. Edwin waived his right to a hearing and, unable to post bond, was placed in the Broome County Jail. He denied stealing the rig but admitted he knew it was stolen.[11] In comparing notes of the arrest, Black and Dwyer discovered that Edwin had purloined not one but two horses and carriages. Dwyer recovered the horse, bridle, and wagon belonging to farmer Allen.

Edwin's arrest was big news in the communities of central New York. The local papers devoted many column inches to the apprehension of the doctor turned horse thief. The media played upon a doctor stealing from another doctor. Certainly, if Edwin had maintained a low profile, the papers would have had less to say on the matter. However, that was not the case.

Upon learning that Dr. Turner was charged with grand larceny, others came forward with suspicions that he was responsible for items that were missing. "At several of the residences where Turner practiced, articles of jewelry, etc., mysteriously disappeared," the *Watertown Daily Times* reported. "At one place a diamond ring and a lady's skirt were missed; at another a gold watch; at yet another, an opera glass. One of our tradesmen missed a sealskin cap after Turner had visited his store."[12] Meanwhile, the *Utica Morning Herald* reported, "Three valuable robes are said to be among the things he offered for sale in Utica. Two of them doubtless belong here [Rome], one of them being the one Mr. Wiggins has been in search of for the past three weeks."[13]

Perhaps the course of events in Rome, Utica, and Binghamton would have been different if investigations into the missing items had been conducted. Some residents were loath to accuse Dr. Turner as it was hard to fathom that he had committed such acts. Once charged with stealing Dr. Ford's rig, the authorities did not bother to charge him for taking farmer Allen's property.

In the case of the missing sealskin cap, the suspicion was so strong that a sworn search warrant was issued of Dr. Turner's rented rooms. The cap was not found. By this time the doctor had left Rome.[14] Without consequences, Edwin was certainly emboldened to continue taking things that did not belong to him.

The newspaper reporters who had met Edwin could not resist commenting on his character.

> He was very fond of talking about himself, what he had done and where he had been. He was a great braggart, and it was his habit of telling of what he had accomplished that first impressed people with the idea that he was not all that he professed to be. He told some very tough stories regarding wonderful cures he had accomplished. These stories were palpably so far from truth as to insult the intelligence of the people to whom he told them.[15]

Another reporter made the following appraisal:

> My first suspicions of the man were received on the evening of a lawn festival, which occurred shortly after the doctor came here. He volunteered to give some recitations and did so. After the festival he brought me a report of the entertainment, which he wished to have in "Rome Matters" the next morning. "By far the greatest attraction of the evening was the entertainment given by Dr. Turner. The worthy doctor's talents as a reciter and actor equals his skill as a physician. His acting as the part of the Miser, in 'Dimes and Dollars,' could scarcely be surpassed," is a selection from this article. The "entertainment" was a failure.[16]

One charge made in news articles did elicit a response from Edwin. It was reported by the owner of the boarding house where Edwin had rented rooms that he treated his wife and children "in a most brutal manner."[17] Another story noted "a roughness in his manner towards his family, which is said to have gone so far as blows."[18] Signed by "Mrs. A. Turner," the *Utica Morning Herald* printed the following letter to the editor as a rebuttal in its edition of November 9:

Broome County Jail, Binghamton, New York *(Paul C. Koeber Co., New York, NY)*

> In justice to the wife and child of this unfortunate man, we print the following:
>
> *To the editor of the Utica Morning Herald:* UTICA, Nov. 8.—Sir: In the article contained in your yesterday's issue entitled "Medical horse thief," an error occurred in the letter from Rome which I am desirous you should correct. My husband never had a child in his charge which he ill treated. The doctor was the child's physician. I and my daughter were its dear guardians and had sole charge of it. It never was at any time ill-treated. I am prepared to state under oath further respecting blows being given me and his daughter. The statement is without foundation, false, a malicious slander; intended as one of those kicks the cowardly inflict upon the fallen. Until my husband fell into this error he was beloved, honored and respected and his papers show what sort of a life he had led, certainly not such a one as merits such a storm of abuse and cruel and unjust calumny as is being showered upon his unhappy head. My husband's too confiding confidence in the honesty and truthfulness of a scoundrel at large has placed him in an unfortunate position. His past career will challenge the minutest inspection.
> Respectfully his wife.
> MRS. A. TURNER[19]

It is highly doubtful that Alice Agnes wrote this letter. Given Edwin's penchant for writing letters to newspapers and his denials of wrongdoing, assigning blame to others, and the level of righteous indignation he could summon, he most likely penned the letter over his wife's signature.

Edwin was in Broome County Jail from Monday, November 8, until the early morning of Monday, December 6, when he and his cellmate made their escape. When arrested Edwin had $700 or $800 on his person. It was theorized in news reports that Osbaldeston's wife on her visits to the jail was given these funds. In turn, she slipped her husband a saw, a revolver, and returned some of the money.[20] On December 1, 1880, Alice Agnes Moore Osbaldeston, baby Ethel, and her stepdaughter, Annie Mabel, left New York on the SS *Italy* bound for Liverpool. Presumably, Edwin had decided that it would be better if his wife and daughters stayed with relatives in England while he worked out how to extricate himself from his current predicament.

Naturally, word of the escape set off another round of news stories. The *Broome Republican* gave a detailed account of the jail breaking.

> Quite a flutter of excitement prevailed in this city Monday, caused by the news that the notorious Dr. E. T. O'Shaughnessy, alias Turner, Osbaldison and various other names, accompanied by Timothy Ahern, of this city, had escaped during the night or very early in the morning, from the county jail. A close examination of the traces left by the fugitives indicated plainly that the manner of their escape was exceedingly well planned and executed. A section in the lower corner of the door of wrought iron bars, situated on the lower floor of the South corridor, and which opens into the jail yard, had been neatly sawed out, cutting through six heavy bars, and making an opening of ten inches by thirteen. The bars being removed, the staple which held the padlock of the solid iron door that closes the same doorway on the outside, was cut through in two places and the door then easily opened.
>
> Access being thus gained to the jail yard the men climbed a small tree and crossed along one of its branches which rests upon the northeast corner of the wall, and attaching to this branch a number of blankets tied together easily slid to the ground and betook themselves to parts at present unknown.
>
> No tools were left behind them, but from the very smooth and precise manner in which the iron bars and staple were severed it is evident that the enterprising Doctor and his accomplice were provided with fine steel saws . . . and he has fully demonstrated the fact that he is thoroughly posted in the use of such implements.[21]

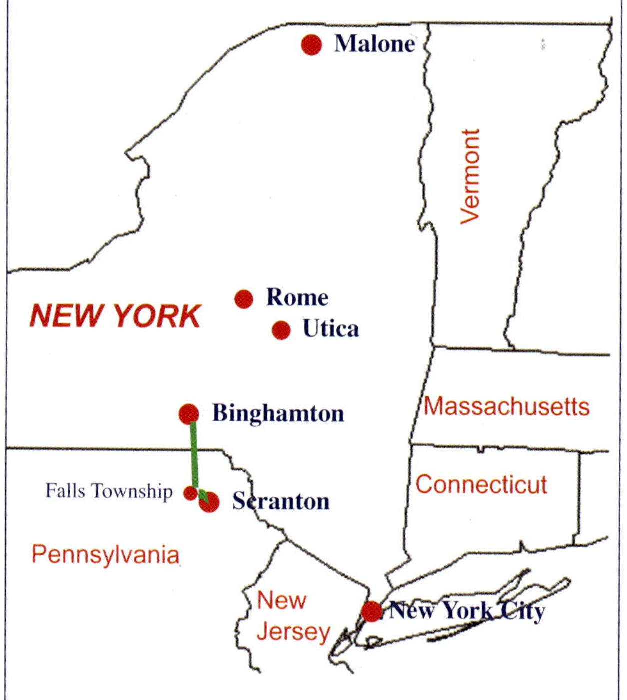

Edwin Turner Osbaldeston's New York ~ 1880–1897

The same news story reported that other inmates at the jail had heard the escape in the early morning hours and that a resident of the city had seen the two escapees on a Binghamton street at 6:00 a.m. The reporter also posited "O'Shaughnessy's personal effects, left behind him in his cell, are rather a mixed lot, and include a package of cookies, paper collars and cuffs, lemons, old shirts, old periodicals, brushes, and [a] comb. On the white-washed wall of the corridor he has inscribed various compositions and caricatures, one of his cartoons representing the District Attorney with a cannon pointing at his head and in quotations underneath, 'Let Justice unite with mercy. There is none perfect, no, not one.'"[22]

Broome County Sheriff's Office offered a reward of one hundred dollars for the capture of either man and alerted police in the surrounding communities to be on the lookout for the horse thief and his partner. Ahern had been jailed on a concealed-weapons charge for carrying brass knuckles.[23]

Six days later, on Sunday, December 12, Edwin and Ahern were recaptured in northeastern Pennsylvania. They were found staying at the farmhouse of George Hufford in Falls Township, Wyoming County, where Edwin had been treating the farmer's sick son in exchange for room and board. Having somehow procured guns, they had told the farmer that they were hunters.

The *Broome Republican* added some mirth to their capture. "Mr. [George] Brown is an expert detective, and it is probable that he has succeeded in securing the much wanted manipulator of the Swedish movement of horses and iron bars, together with his pupil, Ahern, the brass knuckle hero."[24]

Brown had notified Black by telegram that O'Shaughnessy and his "pard" had been captured, but it was a Broome County policeman and a justice of the peace who had actually located them at Hufford's farm. Brown had been asked to come along to assist with the arrest. Brown's reputation quickly went into a tailspin when Edwin escaped by jumping through a washroom window of the Scranton hotel in which he and Ahern were being temporarily held. Ever the opportunist, Edwin had asked to use the lavatory. With the detective only several feet away, Edwin managed to make his exit.[25]

Even though the officers, accompanied by men from the hotel, began a search for him instantly, Edwin successfully escaped into the night. He was not immediately heard from again, managing to put a great distance between himself and his former captors.

Due to a delay in receiving a second telegram advising that O'Shaughnessy had escaped, Deputy Sheriff Black boarded a train to Scranton, only to be disappointed. As for Ahern, he was charged with jail breaking and returned to the Binghamton jail, where he is said to have told many humorous stories of traveling with the Swedish movement man.

Evidently quite pleased with himself for eluding Binghamton Sheriff Bartlett and Deputy Sheriff Black, Edwin wrote them a letter from London months later expressing his regret "that he had been so suddenly called away from his quarters in Binghamton." He apologized that in his hurried departure, he had been unable to bid his friends good-bye. "He inquired solicitously for the health of the sheriff and his family and sent kind regards to the friends he had left behind. He forgot, however, to give his post-office address."[26]

When the British census was taken on April 9, 1881, in the village of Yoxford in the county of Suffolk, England, tailor Josiah Moore had visitors. Staying with him were his married daughter, Alice A. Turner, twenty-six; Alice's stepdaughter, Annie Mabel Turner, fifteen; and Alice's six-month-old baby daughter, Ethel. Edwin reunited with his wife near the end of April or in early May 1881. Evidence for this was the birth of their second child nine months later.

NOTES

1. *Utica Morning Herald* (NY), 11 June 1880, p. 2, col. c.
2. Judi Calvert, "The Swedish Movement Cure," accessed 13 March 2014, www.massagetoday.com.
3. "Dr. Turner in Trouble," *Rome Sentinel* (NY), 9 November 1880; "Dr. Turner. Doings of Another Bogus Doctor Taken in by the Best Families, Exploits as a Horse Thief," *Watertown Daily Times* (NY), 10 November 1880, p. 3, col. d.
4. Ibid.
5. "Dr. Turner in Trouble," *Rome Sentinel* (NY), 9 November 1880; "Dr. Turner. Doings of Another Bogus Doctor Taken in by the Best Families, Exploits as a Horse Thief," *Watertown Daily Times* (NY), 10 November 1880, p. 3, col. d.
6. Ibid.
7. "The Horse Thief. Dr. Ford Identifies His Property and Takes It to Binghamton—Chief Dwyer Finds a Stolen Utica Horse and Carriage in Binghamton," *Utica Morning Herald* (NY), 9 November 1880, p. 2, col. f.
8. Ibid.
9. Ibid.
10. "The Horse Thief. Dr. Ford Identifies His Property and Takes It to Binghamton—Chief Dwyer Finds a Stolen Utica Horse and Carriage in Binghamton," *Utica Morning Herald* (NY), 9 November 1880, p. 2, col. f.
11. Ibid.
12. "Dr. Turner in Trouble," *Rome Sentinel* (NY), 9 November 1880; "Dr. Turner. Doings of Another Bogus Doctor Taken in by the Best Families, Exploits as a Horse Thief," *Watertown Daily Times* (NY), 10 November 1880, p. 3, col. d.
13. "Medical Horse Thief. A New Feature of the 'Swedish Movement Cure'—Arrest of Dr. Turner with Stolen Property in His Possession," *Utica Morning Herald* (NY), 8 November 1880, p. 2, col. c.
14. Ibid.
15. Ibid.
16. Ibid.
17. "Dr. Turner in Trouble," *Rome Sentinel* (NY), 9 November 1880; "Dr. Turner. Doings of Another Bogus Doctor Taken in by the Best Families, Exploits as a Horse Thief," *Watertown Daily Times* (NY), 10 November 1880, p. 3, col. d.
18. "Medical Horse Thief, A New Feature of the 'Swedish Movement Cure'—Arrest of Dr. Turner with Stolen Property in His Possession," *Utica Morning Herald* (NY), 8 November 1880, p. 2, col. e.
19. "A Card from Mrs. Turner," *Utica Morning Herald* (NY), 10 November 1880, p. 2, col. c.
20. "Dr. Osbaldestin Again. The Slippery Customer Who Was Once Arrested in Utica," *Utica Daily Press*, (NY), 19 January 1897, p. 3, col. e.
21. "Broke Jail. Successful Escape of Two Jail Birds — They Saw Their Way Through Iron Bars Undiscovered—Climb a Tree and Scale the Jail Yard Wall—'Gone Where the Woodbine Twineth'—One Hundred Dollars Reward for the Capture of Either of Them," *Broome Republican* (Binghamton, NY), 8 December 1880, p. 8, col. b.
22. Ibid.
23. Ibid.
24. "The Jail Breakers Caught. A Dispatch Announcing Their Arrest at Scranton," *Broome Republican* (Binghamton, NY), 15 December 1880, p. 2, col. b.
25. "Dr. O'Shannesy Loose! He Eludes the Grasp of the Officers of the Law a Second Time," *Broome Republican* (Binghamton, NY), 15 December 1880, p. 8, col. b.
26. "Dr. Osbaldestin Again. The Slippery Customer Who Was Once Arrested in Utica," *Utica Daily Press* (NY), 19 January 1897, p. 3, col. e.

CHAPTER TWELVE

New York—A Period of Prosperity ~ 1881–1894

New York in the 1880s was the epicenter of the Gilded Age. The decades following the Civil War witnessed tremendous advances in manufacturing, transportation, communications, and technology in the United States. It was the dawn of America's modern age and the beginning of the country's transformation from an agrarian society to one based on industry and a more complex brand of capitalism.

The economic boom was fueled by increased manufacturing, westward expansion, and immigration. Large corporations were formed, which significantly changed business and banking operations. The captains of industry and finance accumulated tremendous wealth and with it made great displays of conspicuous consumption. The age symbolized capture of the American dream by self-made men.

There was an underside to the Gilded Age as well. The excesses of the robber barons contrasted sharply with the deplorable living conditions for the unskilled and undereducated in tenements and slums, unsafe and harsh working conditions in mines and factories, the exploitation of children in the workforce, ruthless business practices, unscrupulous speculators, and scandal-plagued politics. In sum, it was an age characterized by greed and guile. The gold that glittered was only a thin veneer.

Returning to New York, Edwin's sabbatical in Great Britain came to a close after five or six months away. Perhaps he thought his letter from London would convince law enforcement in Binghamton to drop their pursuit of the escaped felon. He did not appear to have great concern of being apprehended. In July 1881, with wife and children, he visited Niagara Falls, checking into the Park Place Hotel under the name Dr. E. T. Osbaldeston of New Zealand.[1] His visit was noted in the local paper and several times again in other papers as he made numerous trips to central and Upstate New York.

A brownstone on Forty-Sixth Street in Manhattan similar to the residence of the Osbaldeston family

The Osbaldeston family settled into New York City and lived on Sixth Avenue (and for a time West Forty-Sixth Street).

Following the Civil War, New York's population had exploded, outpacing Philadelphia and Boston as the nation's largest city. By 1880 New York had over nine hundred thousand inhabitants and had developed a cosmopolitan flair. Thousands had left the farms and moved to the city, while wave upon wave of immigrants arrived hoping for a better life and a slice of the new American wealth. In this decade Thomas Edison founded the Edison Illuminating Company that began to bring light to homes, businesses, and streets in New York City. The Brooklyn Bridge, a great engineering feat at the time, opened, and the Statue of Liberty was erected.

There was a bit of irony that the Gilded Age in New York should serve as a backdrop for the next chapter of Edwin's life. While he wasn't a Rockefeller, Vanderbilt, Carnegie, Astor, or Gould, he did share something in common with these titans of business and finance, and he was in part a reflection of the age.

The next dozen years of Edwin's life were ones of relative stability and growth. He settled in Manhattan and, using the name Osbaldeston, began building up a practice as a masseur based on the principles of Swedish movement, primarily serving well-to-do clients. He established the New York School of Training for Massage. Lessons were taught in progressive stages "in the art of massage and Swedish movements; also in the use of portable medicinal baths."[2]

At first he did not include his name in newspaper advertisements, or he used the name of his nephew, Oscar Vernon. In notices for the school that appeared in the New York City directory and in newspapers he claimed that the school was first established in 1862. Perhaps he tied that year to the beginnings of his employment in Turkish baths.

Edwin's claims that his school was the first of its kind in New York City could well be accurate. However, he was not the first to offer massage in New York. Dr. George H. Taylor and his younger brother, Dr. Charles Fayette Taylor, are credited with introducing massage to America. The elder brother started his medical career in 1852 in a hydropathic institution. Months later he opened his own practice in water cure. Brother Charles, upon

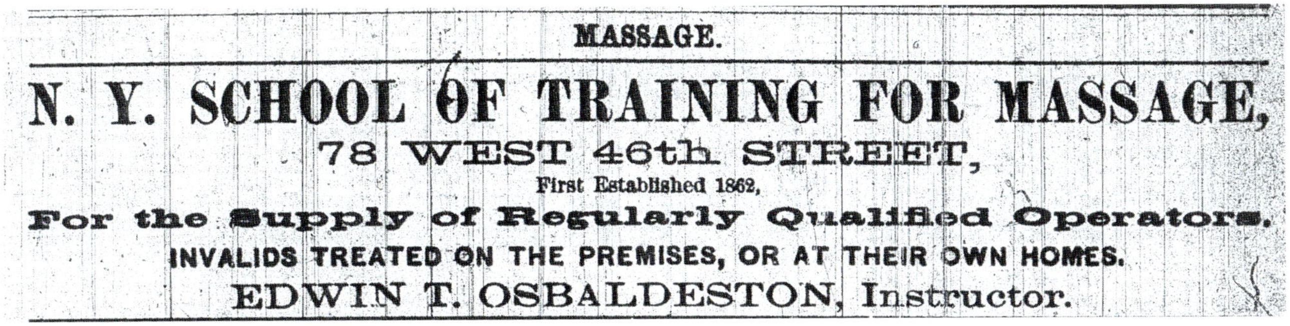
MASSAGE.

N. Y. SCHOOL OF TRAINING FOR MASSAGE,

78 WEST 46th STREET,

First Established 1862,

For the Supply of Regularly Qualified Operators.

INVALIDS TREATED ON THE PREMISES, OR AT THEIR OWN HOMES.

EDWIN T. OSBALDESTON, Instructor.

graduation from medical school in 1856, went to England to study under Dr. Mathias Roth who had authored a book on Swedish massage. He studied Per Henrik Ling's system of Swedish movements.[3]

Two years later George travelled to Sweden to study Swedish movements at the Royal Central Gymnastic Institute in Stockholm. The methods and teachings of Ling continued to be advanced by his disciples at the Royal Central Institute. (Ling died in 1839.) Upon his return to New York, George Taylor opened the Remedial Hygienic Institute (later named Improved Movement Cure Institute) in lower Manhattan. His practice on West 38th Street focused on exercise, hydropathy, and massage for the treatment of various ailments. He published *Exposition of the Swedish Movement Cure* in 1860 to further promote his practice.[4]

Edwin makes no mention of knowing or following the Taylor brothers but clearly they were the forerunners of massage therapy, hydropathy, and the Swedish movement in New York City.

The New York School of Training for Massage was in session from October through May. Summers were usually spent in posh resort towns and vacation retreats such as Saratoga and Richfield Springs, New York, and Newport, Rhode Island—places that were frequented by wealthy urbanites who would be likely candidates for massage treatments.

In 1884 G. P. Putman's Sons printed Edwin's twenty-seven-page book entitled *Massage with Rational Home Gymnastics.* This publication was scant on details on massage technique and instead consisted mostly of self-promotion. Ten pages were devoted to testimonials for Edwin's practice, and three pages warned readers of "the plague of quackery" among massage operators. On the other pages, Edwin discussed the objectives of his school, the program of instruction, the qualifications of a good masseur, the nature of massage and Swedish movements, and the duration and effects of treatment.

He viewed himself as *the* authority on massage. He also did not take kindly to his competition. "Dr. Osbaldeston claimed to have the only right to conduct a massage school in this city. Soon after he opened his school on West Forty-Sixth Street he began to visit different massage schools in the city, and threatened the proprietors with legal trouble if

Cover of Edwin's twenty-seven-page book entitled Massage with Rational Home Gymnastics

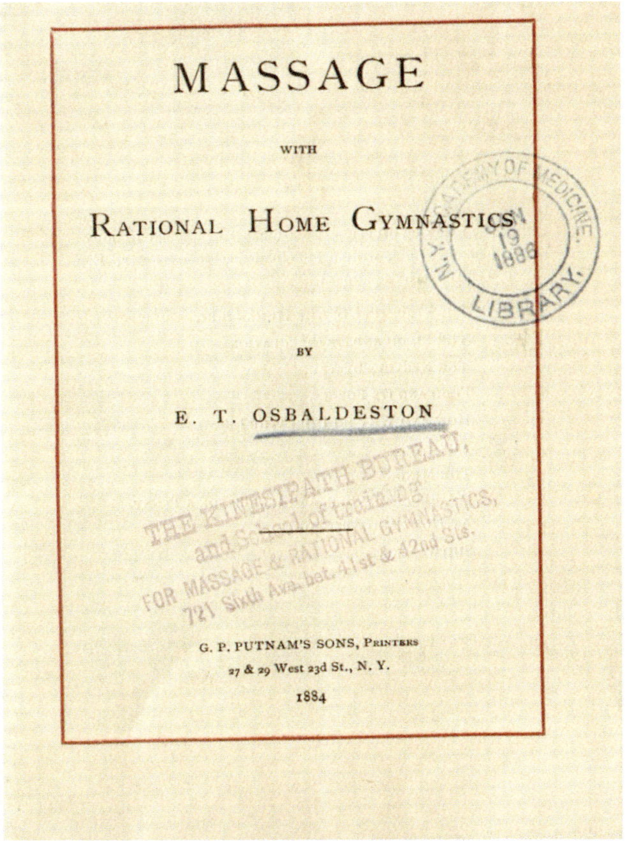
MASSAGE

WITH

RATIONAL HOME GYMNASTICS

BY

E. T. OSBALDESTON

THE KINESIPATH BUREAU, and School of training FOR MASSAGE & RATIONAL GYMNASTICS, 721 Sixth Ave. bet. 41st & 42nd Sts.

G. P. PUTNAM'S SONS, PRINTERS
27 & 29 West 23d St., N. Y.
1884

Title page of Massage with Rational Home Gymnastics

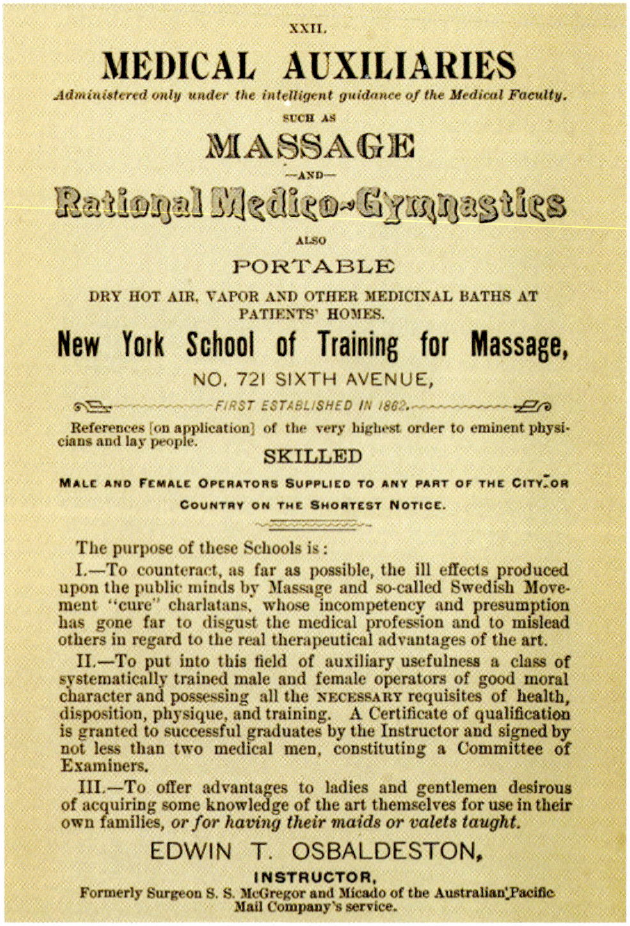
XXII.

MEDICAL AUXILIARIES

Administered only under the intelligent guidance of the Medical Faculty.

SUCH AS

MASSAGE

—AND—

Rational Medico-Gymnastics

ALSO

PORTABLE

DRY HOT AIR, VAPOR AND OTHER MEDICINAL BATHS AT PATIENTS' HOMES.

New York School of Training for Massage,

NO. 721 SIXTH AVENUE,

FIRST ESTABLISHED IN 1882.

References [on application] of the very highest order to eminent physicians and lay people.

SKILLED

MALE AND FEMALE OPERATORS SUPPLIED TO ANY PART OF THE CITY OR COUNTRY ON THE SHORTEST NOTICE.

The purpose of these Schools is:

I.—To counteract, as far as possible, the ill effects produced upon the public minds by Massage and so-called Swedish Movement "cure" charlatans, whose incompetency and presumption has gone far to disgust the medical profession and to mislead others in regard to the real therapeutical advantages of the art.

II.—To put into this field of auxiliary usefulness a class of systematically trained male and female operators of good moral character and possessing all the NECESSARY requisites of health, disposition, physique, and training. A Certificate of qualification is granted to successful graduates by the Instructor and signed by not less than two medical men, constituting a Committee of Examiners.

III.—To offer advantages to ladies and gentlemen desirous of acquiring some knowledge of the art themselves for use in their own families, *or for having their maids or valets taught.*

EDWIN T. OSBALDESTON,

INSTRUCTOR,

Formerly Surgeon S. S. McGregor and Micado of the Australian Pacific Mail Company's service.

Advertisement for the New York School of Training for Massage in the 1890 Medical Directory of the City of New York

they did not close up. For several months he managed to keep several of them really closed up, for fear of him."[5]

An entertaining story appeared in newspapers in August 1892 following another one of Edwin's visits to a competing massage parlor. "Of late he has been making attacks on persons who conduct public houses under the... pretence that they are massage operators. In a Sixth Avenue house, run by Swedish women, the professor sought to expose the sham; but bullets flew so thick in the parlor that one of them cut off the professor's necktie, while two from his own revolver provoked as many screams. The professor has a wounded foot and doesn't know yet how many wounds there are under medical care in the Sixth Avenue house."[6] Personally not opposed to seeking the comforts of women for hire, Edwin took offense when the fine art of massage was sullied by prostitutes posing as masseuses.

Among Edwin's many wealthy and/or famous clients was businessman Jesse Hoyt. Hoyt expanded his father's flour and grain business in the 1850s by purchasing large tracts of Michigan forests in the Saginaw Valley. He established a lumber company and a shipyard and invested in railroads in the Midwest.[7] Prior to his death in 1882, Hoyt had received massage treatments from Edwin. Upon his death he left $1,250,000 of his 7-million-dollar estate to his daughter Mary and an equal amount to his wife. (The remainder of his estate was left to trust funds and other relatives.)

Mary Hoyt, not satisfied with the amount of her inheritance, contested the will on the basis that her father had been ill for five years and was not in his right mind. The case gained considerable notoriety due to the sum of money at issue, Mary's temporary incarceration in an insane asylum, and the noted attorneys involved. (Former secretary of state and New York senator William M. Evarts, Elihu Root, and Joseph Choate were among the lawyers defending the will as written.)[8]

The case dragged through the courts for four years as Mr. Hoyt's state of mind and medical issues were aired and argued. An odd moment midway through the court proceedings came when former senator Roscoe Conkling, back in private practice and representing Mary Hoyt, debated the correct pronunciation of "Osbaldeston" with the opposing counsel.[9] Edwin had been called to testify as to Mr. Hoyt's condition. Finally, in 1886, the court upheld the will as written.

Edwin claimed to have treated John D. Rockefeller, William Rockefeller, William Astor, former presidents Grant, Garfield, Arthur, and Cleveland, and Vice-President William Wheeler.

He said he had treated Ulysses S. Grant on four different occasions. Possible proof that Edwin had visited the ailing former president at Mount McGregor, General Grant's Adirondack cottage home, was found in December 2008 when the Heritage Auction Galleries of Dallas, Texas, held an auction of Americana and political items.

Among the items in their catalogue was a cigar holder purported to have belonged to President Grant. The handwritten note on a tag accompanying the item was penned by Edwin.[10] General Grant had arrived at his cottage from New York City on June 16, 1885. He died there on July 23, 1885, of

Edwin once possessed president Grant's cigar holder as confirmed by a Dallas, Texas, auction house. The note on the tag was penned by Edwin.

The growing Osbaldeston family: Ethel, Geneva, and Edwin Jr. with twenty-year-old Annie Mabel in the center (1887)

cancer of the throat. Due to his illness, he was no longer smoking and thus not in need of the cigar holder.[11] One can only speculate whether this item was given to Edwin or if he purloined it.

Edwin spent the latter part of the 1885 summer season at Spring House, in Richfield Springs, New York, ninety miles from Binghamton. The arrival of "Seignor Osbaldeston" was announced in the *Utica Morning Herald*.[12] In 1887 the *Richfield Springs Mercury*, in its issue of August 25, referred to Edwin's 1885 stay at the hotel:

> Spring House, where he resided as the guest of Mr. Proctor, the proprietor, during the latter part of the season of 1885. His efforts at that time were successful in the organization of a Broom Brigade and Spectre dances for which the doctor appears to possess a special talent. . . .[13]

In addition to the success he was enjoying professionally, another factor in Edwin's decade of stability was the growth of his family. Edwina Agnes Osbaldeston, Alice Agnes and Edwin's second child, was born on January 30, 1882. However, this child did not reach her first birthday. She died of cholera infantum on August 27, 1882, while the family was spending the summer in Newport, Rhode Island.

The couple's third child and first son, Edwin Julian Osbaldeston, was born on May 4, 1883, in the Bijou Hotel at Thirtieth Street and Broadway in Manhattan. Next to arrive was daughter Geneva Agnes, who was born in the family home at 721 Sixth Avenue in Manhattan on June 23, 1885.

On January 22, 1886, Edwin appeared in the Court of Common Pleas for the City and County of New York to be sworn in as a citizen of the United States. As was his habit when it came to filling out forms,

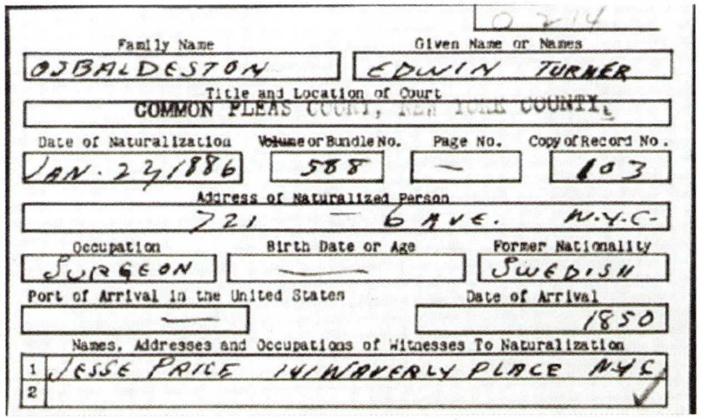
Family Name: OSBALDESTON
Given Name or Names: EDWIN TURNER
Title and Location of Court: COMMON PLEAS COURT, NEW YORK COUNTY
Date of Naturalization: JAN. 22/1886
Volume or Bundle No.: 588
Page No.: —
Copy of Record No.: 103
Address of Naturalized Person: 721 — 6 AVE. N.Y.C.
Occupation: SURGEON
Birth Date or Age: —
Former Nationality: SWEDISH
Port of Arrival in the United States: —
Date of Arrival: 1850
Names, Addresses and Occupations of Witnesses To Naturalization:
1 JESSE PRICE 141 WAVERLY PLACE N.Y.C.
2

Edwin's application for US citizenship in 1883 included outright falsehoods. Citizenship was granted, nonetheless.

National Archives and Records Administration (NARA); Washington, DC; Soundex Index to Petitions for Naturalizations Filed in Federal, State, and Local Courts in New York City, 1782–1906 (M1674)*; Microfilm Serial: M1674; Microfilm Roll: 200.*

he earlier inserted a couple of untruths into the record. In this case he claimed that his former nationality was Swedish and that his date of arrival in the United States was 1850. He did not state his birth date or age. The naturalization process was obviously much more lax in the nineteenth century.

Even before he became a United States citizen, Edwin paid for two of his brothers and his sister to come to the United States. His brother Francis brought his wife, Sarah, and their adopted daughter, Kate. He sponsored his sister Emma, or Emily as she preferred to be called; her husband, Joseph Vernon; and three of their sons, Oscar, Christian, and Alonzo. Youngest brother, Julian, who was single, came on his own.

Edwin taught his siblings and in-laws how to perform massage so they could begin to work soon after they arrived. The Vernons remained in Manhattan. Oscar was listed as secretary to the New York School of Massage for a time. He died unexpectedly in 1885 at age eighteen. Edwin's brother Francis moved to Chicago in 1885 or 1886 and set up in business as a masseur. Julian moved to Ontario, Canada, in 1885, and then relocated to Chicago. He studied medicine in Detroit. After graduating from the Michigan College of Medicine and Surgery in 1901, he returned to Chicago to practice.

In the summer of 1887, Edwin was back in Richfield Springs. The following notice appeared in the local newspaper:

> Mr. Edward T. Osbaldistone, principal of the New York School of Training for Massage, is at the Spring House.[14]

On February 12, 1888, Annie Mabel, then twenty-one, married John Frederick Knowles, twenty-seven, in Manhattan. The wedding came about very suddenly. According to an article in the (New York) *Sun* newspaper, Mabel and her fiancé had not planned to marry for another year or two. However, earlier that day Edwin issued an ultimatum that she must either give up her betrothed or leave his house. Annie Mabel called her father's bluff and left his house.[15] Edwin was possessive of his daughters and had threatened to have Knowles arrested. Instead, it was he who was arrested. Later in court Edwin relayed a different perspective on their marriage.

> Dr. E. T. Osbaldistone was arrested yesterday and taken to the Jefferson Market Police Court, charged with going to the house of Mrs. Victoria A. Meade, and calling that lady names and creating a disturbance.
>
> Dr. Osbaldistone said that all the trouble had been brought about by Frederick Knowles, a nephew of the Meade family, stealing his daughter's affections, and then getting married to her. The Meades were frequent guests at his house, and he treated them in royal style. They thought that his daughter had $3,000 a year, and plotted to get her into their family. It was a mistake to imagine that his daughter had so much money. Now she would not get a cent.
>
> He had forbidden his daughter to keep company with the young man, but during his trip to Atlantic City she was induced to leave his home. He hastened back to this city and did go to the Meades' house to see his daughter Mabel, whom he loved dearly. She had never been a day from him since she was three years old. She had gone all over the world with him. When he was prevented from seeing her he did go to the street and called all the neighbors to witness what kind of house the Meades kept, and that they had stolen away his child. "They stole away my pretty, innocent church-going Mabel," he spoke.
>
> Mrs. Meade and her maiden sister, Miss Stratton, testified that Dr. Osbaldistone did not treat his child as a father should, and they did not believe she was his daughter. Mabel herself had told that he had treated her in a manner that would bring shame to the cheeks of any woman. The accused said he had some of the best people in the land for patients. Justice O'Reilly put him under $500 bail for his good behavior. He is 47 years old. No bondsmen being in court he was locked up.[16]

Annie Mabel

Ethel Osbaldeston had the following to say about her half sister:

> Our own wonderful mother and his first wife's daughter, Annie Mabel, were great friends, Mother only twelve years older than Mabel when [father] married mother.
>
> Mabel helped make our baby garments, and selected some of our names. I was eight and Mabel 21 when she married Fred Knowles. Mabel was an especially lovable character.[17]

One of the last entries in Edwin's journal is a description of an 1888 summer outing:

> I was out with my wife & children on a summer excursion at Daws Farm, Sullivan Co. Hay was put into a large dray & besides ourselves there were four other women & children. The two oxen were being [led by] a boy. I sat in the front. He walked guiding them on the road. He lost control of them & dropped the lines. I knew they were making for a narrow bridge over a deep gully. We were on a narrow road away up on the side of the mountain & I realized the danger we were all in. I scrambled along the pole of the wagon with my hands resting on the bullocks backs. The jolting threw me down to the ground. The wagon passed over me.
>
> I remembered no more until I came to finding myself laying across the laps of some ladies & gentlemen in a carriage. When we reached the farm I was in great agony but remained conscious & assisted them to remove my clothing & roll me in a cold wet sheet & give me an apparent draught of medicine. Fortunately, no bones were broken. In four days I was back attending to my practice in New York City. My wife's presence of mind afterwards saved the lives of all in the wagon by. . . securing the trailing lines & guiding the oxen safely over the narrow bridge.[18]

August of 1888 found Edwin visiting the resort town of Saratoga Springs, New York. Here he had a prominent role in organizing entertainment for the annual midsummer festival held in Congress Park. A description of his participation appeared in the *New York Times:*

> To-morrow will be the great day of the festival. The program will be opened by the entrance of Dr. Edwin T. Osbaldeston of New-York magnificently costumed as the King's Jester. . . . One of the great attractions of the day will be the tableaus or representations of ancient and modern and Biblical scenes under the direction of Dr. Osbaldeston. . . .[19]

Tableaux vivants (living pictures) were very popular in the nineteenth century. Costumed actors or models created scenes in which they did not speak or move. The tableaux were a blend of theater, art, or photography.

Edwin organized a dozen tableaux for the festival in 1888. Among the scenes were the Conquest of Samson, which represented Delilah cutting off the locks of Samson. Other tableaux included the struggle between Cain and Abel, a dying gladiator, and "When Rogues Fall Men Get Their Rights." The actors were dressed in white, donning white makeup to make them appear as statues. Calcium lights were employed to heighten the effect. Edwin opened the festivities appearing as the king's jester.[20]

Scenes from the Saratoga, New York Midsummer Festival of 1888

Top of page: Edwin organized a series of tableaux vivants for the Summer Festival. In this scene, "The Conquest of Samson," he is prone in the foreground.

Lower left: The program was opened by Edwin appearing as the "King's Jester."

Lower right: Another version of the "Conquest of Samson" that Edwin organized as a "living picture"

In the summer of 1893, the Osbaldeston family traveled to Chicago to attend the World's Columbian Exposition. The fair marked the 400th anniversary of the arrival of Christopher Columbus in America. The Chicago World's Fair, with over twenty-seven million visitors, far exceeded previous world expositions. The exposition had a profound impact on art, architecture, sanitation, American industry and entertainment, and the self-image of Chicago. Certainly, the family was dazzled by the size and splendor of the "White City," illuminated with ninety-three thousand incandescent lights. Surely, they enjoyed the amusements of the Midway Plaisance and a ride on the world's first Ferris wheel. And perhaps, they even took in Buffalo Bill's Wild West Show.[21] Only a clear and ruby-colored glass souvenir purchased for Cousin Kate remains of that trip to a fair filled with so many marvels of the day.

The next two children born to Edwin and Alice Agnes were Normandie Alice on July 27, 1887, and then Francis Scudder Osbaldeston, on July 18, 1889.

An article regarding the baptism of the four youngest children appeared in the *New York Daily Tribune* in September 1890. The article noted that Edwin was a "confirmed deist," one who believes in a creator but not in organized religion. His religious beliefs had changed since his days in New Zealand, where he had taken part in Baptist preaching.

Their children's baptisms had become a point of contention between Alice and Edwin as she had Ethel and Edwina baptized when he was not present.

"Mrs. Osbaldeston. . . does not share her husband's views on revealed faith and to her it has always been a matter of bitter mortification that her children had not been baptized. Yielding to the constant persuasion of his wife, however, Dr. Osbaldeston consented to allow his other children to go through the ceremony," the *Daily Tribune* reported.

The baptisms occurred on Sunday, September 28, 1890, at St. Chrysostom's Protestant Episcopal Chapel on Thirty-Ninth Street at Seventh Avenue. Although he yielded to his wife's request, Edwin made light of the baptisms by writing to popular orator of free thought, Robert G. Ingersoll, asking him to be a sponsor of the event.[22] Ingersoll, known as "the Great Agnostic," did not attend the ceremony.

Alberta Victoria, his last child by Alice Agnes, was born in Manhattan on June 7, 1891.

The inscription on this souvenir from the 1893 Chicago World's Fair reads, "To Kate Osbaldeston from Cousins Ethel & Edwin [Jr.]." The reverse side notes place and date.

1888 family portrait: Edwin, Ethel, Geneva, Alice Agnes, and Edwin Jr. with infant Normandie in foreground

Ethel & Edwin Jr. (1888)

Daughter Ethel recalled her father as "a money-maker from the word go. His flair for meeting the best of people—and associating with them was shown by the men of note he knew when we were youngsters. He made big money, always. He simply had no head for finances—so it just dribbled through his fingers or some of his so-called 'friends' were most 'persuasive.'"[23]

> If our Dad had focused on [education] for us, it would have been better than the expensive paintings he was induced to buy—he lost fortunes by poor advice. But we learned a lot from them. The fine library and best of music recordings—and our mother who loved to read—Dickens, Thackery, Shakespeare before we could understand them ourselves.[24] Mother taught me to read and enjoy good literature. . . before I was ten years. Earlier it was Louisa Alcott, Frances Hodgson Burnett, Mark Twain, all Jules Vernes wonder pre science stories.
>
> We had good music too on old fashioned wind-them-up-with a handle music boxes. We were taken to light opera as performed then. Our table manners and curtsies to older people were punishable if not performed correctly.
>
> Mother. . . was patient, kind, good. My Dad always a thoroughbred, kissing the ladies hands, gallantly saluting with his cane, which was carried for style.
>
> At the same time his other self showed up in raging tempers, destruction of articles in the home, after which he would go out and spend lavishly to replace them. Mother must have lived through much mental unhappiness with him—I know I was a frightened child sometimes.[25]

His daughter Normandie recalled the following:

> When I was very young in N.Y.C. (two & a half, nearly three) I was becoming aware of statues (marble statues), oil paintings, many art objects all in a large living room where the piano was. We were locked out of this room, only going in when weekend singing fests were held, Ethel playing old songs & all of us required to join in.
> We were taken to Best & Co. & outfitted in beautiful clothes, leghorn [a wide-brimmed Italian wheat straw hat] flower or ostrich feathered hats, the very best money could buy. Then a fire, no insurance not even on Papa's life.
>
> No business sense at all. Just make money, spend it! So we went to England for three years and on return to America, Papa & Mama had to start from scratch. No savings at all! It just went on that way, over & over

Edwin with Edwin Jr. (1883)

Edwin (1884)

Normandie Alice (1889)

Francis "Frank" Scudder Osbaldeston, age three (1892)

Edwin with daughter Geneva (1889)

& over. My mother could have managed beautifully but never had the chance.[26]

Papa was extremely neat, his clothes well cared for & everything in its place. Mama also took care of lovely things & we enjoyed an immaculate & well aired home. Papa was our thorn in the side as he thought of himself as an absolute ruler.[27]

Pictured here is the Osbaldeston parlor on Sixth Avenue in Manhattan in 1890 with mother, Alice Agnes; son, Edwin (holding dummy); and daughter, Ethel (at piano). The room was heavily decorated with Edwin's art collection. Note: The paintings on the wall are a mix of the works of Barbizon School artists and family portraits drawn by R. Atkinson Fox.

Edwin Builds Extensive Art Collection

During the 1890s Edwin built an extensive art collection. He acquired numerous oil paintings by leading artists of the day, many of whom were connected to or inspired by the Barbizon School in France. These artists were part of a movement towards realism in paintings that included natural scenes, landscapes, and people working in fields and/or on farms. Their works were characterized by loose brushwork, softness of form, and similar shades of light and dark colors. Barbizon artists in Edwin's collection included Jules Bastien-Lepage, Jean-Baptiste-Camille Corot, Narcisse Virgilio Díaz, Jules Dupré, George Inness, Charles Jacque, Émile van Marcke, and Paul Signac. Other significant artists and devotees of realism in his collection were Peter van Bloemen, William Collins, Mauritz de Haas, and Alexander Helwig Wyant.[28] These artists remain highly collectable today, and their works can be found in leading museums around the world.

Artist R. Atkinson Fox (1860–1935)

Another significant component of Edwin's art collection was the work of Robert Atkinson Fox. Fox, a most prolific Canadian American artist and a standout in the "golden age of illustration (1880s to 1920s)," painted no fewer than eighteen portraits of Osbaldeston and Moore family members (his in-laws).

Edwin commissioned Fox to produce oil paintings of himself (three in all), his wife, children, in-laws, and sister Emma. Several of the paintings were done in romantic settings—Ethel in a spring scene, Edwin Jr. as a Greek boy, and himself drawn as a Turk.

Originally from Toronto, Fox moved to New York City in the late 1880s. For years he supported himself as painter of portraits and landscapes. At the turn of the century, Fox left New York and moved into commercial illustration. For the last thirty-five years of his life, his work was highly visible in America as it graced everything from calendars, magazine covers, picture puzzles, and posters to postcards, billboards, and advertisements.[29]

Edwin also commissioned J. H. Forbes to paint several family portraits, including Ethel on a swing. *(See photo of parlor on preceding page.)*

Home Life

Although the photographs show children who appear to be well cared for, the Osbaldeston home frequently lacked harmony. Edwin was a very hard worker and expected all of his family members to behave the same way and, like his own father did, obey his every command. One of the more telling incidents of their family life was reported in the *New York Times* with the headline "Says His Father Is Cruel; Young Boy Goes to Court and Asks for Protection—Badly Bruised and Cut."[30]

> "Please, Sir, I want to give myself up. I want protection from my father." That was what Edwin Osbaldeston, Jr., ten years old, said at the Yorkville Police Court yesterday to Agent Barkley of the Gerry Society (Society for the Prevention of Cruelty to Children). The boy said he was the son of Edwin Osbaldeston, a massage operator and chiropodist, of 78 West Forty-sixth Street, and he told a sensational tale of cruelty at the hands of his father . . . . His father, he said, would impose impossible tasks upon him and then flagellate him because he failed of their performance.
>
> He attended Grammar School No. 69 until three months ago when his mother was taken ill with inflammatory rheumatism. Since then he had helped his father in putting up salves and at the same time his father had insisted upon his continuing along with his studies. Not a day passed, he

Left: At one time Edwin's art collection included The Watering Place *(circa 1850–1885) by Barbizon School artist Émile van Marcke de Lummen (1827–1890).*

This painting (French, oil on canvas) is now in the collection of the Utah Museum of Fine Arts, Salt Lake City, Utah.

(UMFA 1957.003). Painting reprinted with permission from the Utah Museum of Fine Arts.

> said, that he was not treated to a vigorous castigation with an instrument similar to a cat-o'-nine-tails, used in massage. He often ran away to escape the punishment and found a haven with Mrs. Vernon, an aunt, who lives at One Hundred and Twenty-fifth Street and Eighth Avenue. Yesterday morning, he said, his father imposed upon him the task of doing up 160 packages of corn salve, and he was limited in the task until 2 P. M. At the same time he was sent out to find a washwoman which took him until noon. Then, he said, his father directed his attention to the salve, the task still untouched, and reminded him that the job must be completed by 2 P. M. which was impossible.
>
> The boy ventured a remonstrance, whereupon the father flew into a passion and used the "cat" with unwonted vigor. Then it was that, making his escape, the boy hastened to the Yorkville court and sought out Agent Barkley. On hearing this tale, Mr. Barkley examined the boy and found that his feet and his hips were cut and flayed in a horrible manner. Mr. Barkley laid the case before Justice Meade, who promptly issued a summons directing the parent to appear before him tomorrow to make answer to charges of cruelty to children. The boy was committed to the custody of the Gerry Society pending a hearing.[31]

In court Edwin denied the charge, saying that "Edwin [Jr.] is rather a wild boy for his age, but the published statement that he had been cruelly treated and whipped by me is entirely wrong." Professor Osbaldeston, as he was addressed in court, continued, "Two Sundays ago Edwin went out on his wheel and was gone all afternoon. I did not return home until late at night, but the next morning I asked him why he had disobeyed my orders in going out on his bicycle on Sunday and remaining so long. He said he had lost his way on Columbus

Edwin Julian Osbaldeston at age nine (1892)

Avenue." Edwin further explained that as part of his punishment, he told his son to pack one hundred boxes of salve and that, when he returned home, his wife reported that Edwin Jr. had been using bad language to her and his sisters.

It was then that Edwin said he "called him to account for it and decided to punish him. I used a flagella such as we use in the treatment of patients and did not strike him anywhere except about the legs." He attributed the bruises to a quarrel that Edwin Jr. had been in with boys in the neighborhood. "My children," Edwin assured the court, "have a happy home here and I am sure I have never treated them in a cruel way in my life. I believe in parental discipline and am endeavoring to bring up my children in the right way."[32]

The reporter, obviously impressed with his credentials, noted that Edwin "is a veteran of the war and has been a great traveller in his day. His home is decorated with odds and ends from all quarters of the globe. His business brings him in contact with some of the best-known people in the city, and he has the reputation of being one of the foremost massage operators in the country." Edwin Jr. was released to his father.[33]

In later years his sister Normandie would recall, "His [Edwin Jr.'s] head bears the scars—easily discernible when he has a hair cut—scars his father gave him as a child."[34]

Normandie offered the following explanation for her father's temperament:

> The fact is, having so many children was distracting to Papa & a child's destructive ways upset him more than usual. We held his wanderlust down as responsibilities [required] but as I reminded him—we didn't ask to be born. He was older than Mama was so his patience gave out & we were a crowd when it came to travel & lodgings. . . . I doubt Papa ever had much patience, in fact. But he did enjoy a social life—he had good social manners & his clothing was the finest money could buy. He took good care of it too. Always was dressed well & well groomed. On Sundays he wore a high beaver colored hat when he was so prosperous [and] we lived on 46th St. between 6th & 5th Aves.[35]

With such a large family and his wife working as a masseuse as well, help in the home was needed. At the end of September 1893, Edwin put an ad in the Help Wanted columns of the *New York Times* seeking a cook and laundress, also a chambermaid.[36] When the children were very young, the family had employed nursemaids.

Among the distressing incidents that happened as the children were growing up were several fires in their Manhattan homes. The first fire occurred on September 11, 1888, under very strange circumstances.

> What appeared to be a mysterious case of incendiarism was reported yesterday afternoon to Captain Reilly, of the Thirtieth Street Station. Yesterday morning a strong stench filled the three-story brick house No. 721 Sixth-ave., occupied by Dr. Edwin T. Osbaldeston. He thought at first that it came from the sewer, and had the house sprinkled with chloride of lime. At 3 p. m. the doctor discovered flames issuing from the flooring in the hallway on the top floor. A carpenter tore up the boards, and found underneath a quantity of cotton waste, sheeting and rags saturated with oil, burning furiously. It was extinguished.
>
> By order of the doctor the carpenter continued in tearing up the entire flooring of the room. Between the ceiling and flooring the work of an incendiary was found. Across the entire length of the room was a train of cotton batting, sheeting, two newspapers, dated October 24, 1887, and September 10, 1887, all saturated with oil, two bottles of oil and a quantity of parlor matches. Probably an attempt was made to set the house on fire about a year ago, but in some manner was prevented. Detectives Hayes and Brett made a thorough investigation, and came to the conclusion that the matches were set on fire by rats yesterday.[37]

The second fire took place on October 12, 1892. A brief report appeared in the *New York Times:* "9:24 P. M.—78 West Forty-Sixth Street; Dr. Edwin Osbaldiston; damage, $5,000; cause unknown."[38]

> Fire was discovered last night in the cellar of the four-story house at No. 78 West Forty-sixth street. Before the firemen arrived the flames had shot up the dumbwaiter and burst through the rear windows on the top floor. It was feared for a time the blaze would spread to the adjoining houses.

Edwin at the rear of his Manhattan home after digging out from the Great Blizzard of 1888

> A second alarm was sent out and the firemen soon extinguished the flames, but not until the interior of the house had been badly scorched. The building is owned by David Charles, of Troy, N. Y. The upper floors are occupied by Dr. Edwin T. Osbaldeston, whose large collection of curiosities suffered incalculable damage. None of the Doctor's family were home at the time. The damage to the building was estimated at $5,000. Foreman Burke, of a stable in Sixth Avenue, discovered the fire.[39]

Many of the family possessions were lost and his home massage studio was temporarily out of business. Edwin recovered from this misfortune. Yet another house fire a few years later had a different outcome.

Attention Seeking

Although Edwin frequently wrote letters to share his opinions, a letter written to the *New York Herald* voiced his support for the fairer sex but thought the Suffragist League was off track. In another he proffered his opinion of ax murderess Lizzie Borden. Dated August 31, 1892, Edwin shared his unsolicited views as to Lizzie's guilt with Hosea Morrill Knowlton, prosecuting attorney in the case of The Commonwealth of Massachusetts vs. Lizzie A. Borden. (Lizzie was found not guilty.)

> Dear Sir,
> There can be no doubt in the minds of people whose profession is to discover the cause of crime (murders in particular) and the criminals, but that the woman Lizzie Borden is the guilty party, & murderer of her father and stepmother. <u>In my own opinion</u> the <u>woman wore a dress or wrap for the occasion</u> which would require but a few moments to destroy, gloves also. If newspaper accounts are to be relied upon

(of course, I mean the unsensational). The woman is without sympathy or feeling and of that strong determined deep planning nature characteristic of persons who commit such crimes.

Respectfully Surgeon E.T. Osbaldeston
formerly Governor of
Paramatta Convict Prison[40]

Clearly, Edwin had first-hand knowledge of criminal behavior. His promotion from convict to prison governor was his usual way of inflating himself.

Always revelling in a good story, Edwin created a tall tale that newspapers of the day swallowed. Probably as an attention-getting ploy, in July 1893 Edwin placed an ad in the *New York World* in search of a man who was willing to have his stomach opened. (This story may have been inspired by the gastric system research of Dr. William Beaumont decades earlier.) The *World* was known for printing lurid crime reports, reform exposés, and a fair number of sensationalized stories that wildly boosted its daily circulation during the New York "Penny Papers War." The initial want ad read, "Wanted—a man who will be willing for consideration of $5,000 to submit to an experimental surgical operation that may possibly prove fatal." The ad garnered 142 responses within days. The *World* then published an interview with Edwin that in turn was carried by a number of other newspapers.

Claiming that he was acting on behalf of physicians living in Ecuador, Edwin said the experimental surgery entailed cutting a hole in the volunteer's stomach through which the action of gastric juices and the process of digestion could be observed.

"Twice before I have been called upon to furnish a subject on whom these doctors could experiment." Thirty-three applied in 1888 and 127 in 1890, Edwin noted. When asked how the earlier experiments turned out, he reported, "The first man survived, the second died. It was at the time when the bacillus craze was at its height. He was inoculated with the germs of some two score diseases and he died a frightful death." As the tale continued Edwin would not reveal the man's identity.

"I do not care to give his name, for one of the conditions he made was that absolute secrecy should be maintained. But, I may say this much. He was a fighting man, a pugilist by profession, 25 years of age. He is 5 feet, 7¾ inches high. He is all muscles and can easily lift 204 pounds without bending his knees. He has a fierce, bulldog expression."[41]

Edwin said he had shipped the subject off to South America the week before. The reporter then asked to inspect the letters of interest that the ad had drawn. Edwin handed over a bundle. The letters at least were genuine.[42]

A year later a sequel to this story appeared in newspapers across the country. What gave the game away was the fact that Edwin revealed the volunteer's name as Ferdinand Pietrich. Pietrich was his employer in 1866, the owner of the Turkish baths in Melbourne, Australia that had been destroyed by fire. The references to "battlements of a fortress" and "sunstruck" he obviously had borrowed from his days in the Royal Artillery in Malta.

Ferdinand Pietrich, the man who sold himself to South American surgeons, is dead. Here is the story: Last August a man named Osbaldeston advertised in the New York papers for a man who would consent to go down to Guayaquil, Ecuador, and there submit to an experimental operation by two South American doctors. Osbaldeston acted as agent for those physicians. It was illustrative of the hard times that more than 120 answers were received. . . .

Among the 120 persons who answered the advertisement was a well knit, powerful looking fellow who had been a sailor. He was about 5 feet 8 inches in height, weighed about 180 pounds, looked hard and wiry and was active as a cat. Osbaldeston decided that he would do. His name was Ferdinand Pietrich. . . .

Osbaldeston has received information that the operation had been completely successful and that the patient was on the road to recovery when he took to drink. Under these conditions it became necessary to stop the treatment for a time, and in this interval Pietrich while sitting on the battlements of a fortress one morning was sunstruck and died within two hours. He was alone in the world, and it does not appear that he ever received the money for which he had risked his life or in fact anything beyond his travelling expenses.—*New York Letter.*[43]

He may not have realized it at the time, but the decade and a half that Edwin had lived in New York City was his Gilded Age. He had managed to create a comfortable life for himself and his family and had remained mostly free of serious trouble with the law. But alas, his wanderlust would resurface. Beginning in 1894, the Osbaldestons began spending their summers in Malone, in Franklin County, Upstate New York.

Just as Edwin's world was about to change, so was the national economy. The bankruptcy of the Philadelphia and Reading Railroad and the impact of the Free Silver movement ignited the Panic of 1893. The country went into a deep recession that included a run on banks, resulting in the closure of 500 financial institutions, the failure of 15,000 businesses, steep increases in unemployment, a significant decline in the stock market, and thousands of mortgage failures and defaulted loans.[44]

The impact of this economic crisis was not immediately felt by the Osbaldeston family. However, Edwin's next moves would bring the crisis home.

NOTES

1. "Personal," *Niagara Falls Gazette*, 27 July 1881, p. 4, col. a.
2. "Medical," *New York Herald*, 25 November 1883, p. 3.
3. Alan Lewis, "Dr. Taylor's Improved Movement Cure Institute," accessed 10 September 2016, www.oocities.org/unclesamsfarm/drtaylor.htm.
4. Judi Calvert, "The Swedish Movement Cure," accessed 10 September 2016, http://www.massagetoday.com/mpacms/mt/article.php?id=14314.
5. "Osbaldiston Arrested," *New York Times*, 17 November 1896, p. 2.
6. "Not Exactly Like Massage," *Philadelphia Record*, 28 August 1892.
7. "Hoyt, Jesse," in *The Cambridge Dictionary of American Biography*, edited by John S. Bowman (Cambridge: Cambridge University Press, 1995).
8. "The Will of Jesse Hoyt, Surrogate Rollins Declares it Sound," *New York Times*, 29 August 1886, p. 3.
9. "Retorts Scarcely Courteous; Sparring of the Lawyers in the Hoyt Will Case," *New York Times*, 29 May 1884, p. 5.
10. Heritage Auction Galleries, Dallas, Texas, "Political & Americana Auction," December 2–3, 2008, p. 50, item 47183.
11. Beverly Clark, director, Friends of Grant Cottage, e-mail message to Noël Siver, 13 January 2009.
12. "Our Summer Resorts," *Utica Morning Herald* (NY), 21 August 1885, p. 5, col. a.
13. *Richfield Springs Mercury* (NY), 25 August 1887, p. 1, col. d.
14. *Richfield Springs Mercury* (NY), 25 August 1887, p. 1, col. c.
15. "And So They Were Married," *Sun* (New York, NY), 14 February 1888, p. 3, col. a.
16. "Stole the Child Away; Osbaldistone's Lament Over his Daughter's Marriage to Young Knowles," *Press* (New York, NY), 6 March 1888, p. 1, col. b.
17. ETO, "Journal," "Notes by Transcriber, E. T. G. 1962."
18. ETO, "Journal" (unpublished manuscript), 176, 177, Siver family history material.
19. "A Hot Week in Saratoga: Walking Matches Popular but Not Billiards. Features of the Summer Carnival—Receptions and Balls and Other Recreation," *New York Times*, 11 August 1888, p. 2.
20. Ibid.
21. Erik Larson, *The Devil in the White City* (New York: Vintage Books, 2003), pp. 159–160, 222, 235–236, 254, 287, 376–378.
22. "Four Children Baptized by the Bishop," *New York Daily Tribune*, 29 September 1890.
23. Ethel Turner Osbaldeston Groves to Kenneth and Mildred Siver, 15 November 1962.
24. Ethel Turner Osbaldeston Groves to Kenneth and Mildred Siver, 9 September 1962.
25. Ethel Turner Osbaldeston Groves to Kenson Siver, 27 September 1965.
26. Normandie Turner Osbaldeston Siver to Kenson Siver, 8 September 1962.
27. Ibid.
28. *Catalogue of Prof. Edwin T. Osbaldeston's Collection of Oil Paintings & Water Colors,* n.d., Siver family history material.
29. "R. A. Fox Bio," accessed 14 April 2014, www.rafoxsociety.com.
30. "Says His Father Is Cruel. A Young Boy Goes to Court and Asks for Protection—Badly Bruised and Cut," *New York Times*, 6 June 1893, p. 5.
31 Ibid.
32. "Did Not Cruelly Beat His Boy. Prof. Osbaldeston Merely Gave Edwin a Needed Application of the Flagella," *New York Times*, 11 June 1893, p. 5.
33. Ibid.
34. Normandie Turner Osbaldeston Siver to Kenson Siver, 14 March 1963.
35. Normandie Turner Osbaldeston Siver to Kenson Siver, 7 May 1964.
36. "Help Wanted—Females," *New York Times*, 29 September 1893, p. 3.
37. "Incendiary Work Finished by Rats. Discovery of an Attempt Probably Made Nearly a Year Ago to Burn a House," *New-York Daily Tribune,* 12 September 1888, p. 3.
38. "One Day's Fires in This City," *New York Times,* 13 October 1892, p. 5.
39. "His Curiosities Burned," *New York Herald*, 13 October 1892, p. 12, col. c.
40. Fall River [Massachusetts] Historical Society, *The Commonwealth of Massachusetts vs. Lizzie A. Borden, The Knowlton Papers 1892–1893, A Collection of Previously Unpublished Letters and Documents from the Files of Prosecuting Attorney Hosea Morrill Knowlton,* ed. by Michael Martins and Dennis A. Binette (Fall River, MA: The Fall River Historical Society, 1994). Letter HK040 on p. 49. Biographical sketch of ETO on pp. 507, 508.
41. "Taking Big Chances. Surgeon Wanted a Man and Secured Him. Ex Prize Fighter Will Have His Stomach Cut Open. Whether He Lives or Dies $5000 Is the Reward," *Boston Daily Globe,* 14 August 1893, p. 5.
42. Ibid.
43. "Risked Life and Lost. The Man Who Permitted Doctors to Bore into His Stomach," *Auburn Bulletin* (NY), 23 July 1894, p. 3, col. c.
44. *Wikipedia*, s.v. "Panic of 1893," accessed 10 September 2016, http://en.wikipedia.org/wiki/Panic_of_1893.

CHAPTER THIRTEEN

Malone—Edwin & "Mrs. Metzgar" ~ 1894–1897

Main Street, Malone, New York—looking east towards the Congregational Church

Nestled in the foothills of the Adirondack Mountains and close to the Canadian border in Upstate New York sits Malone, a farming community and place that city dwellers visited in the summer for a respite from the noise, pollution, and traffic of their urban existence.

In 1894 the Osbaldestons spent part of the summer in the village. Edwin initially came to Malone to treat a patient by the name of Jennie Shepard. Miss Shepard had been under Edwin's care for several weeks in New York City. Originally, Edwin had planned to remain for a month. Ever resourceful, Edwin went about attracting new clients in Malone. He advertised for new patients and announced that he was starting a class for young ladies on the Delsartian System.[1]

How Edwin came to learn the Delsarte system of expression is not known, but by the 1890s it had become a popular fad in America and throughout the world, and he was ready to profit from it. François Delsarte (1811–1871) was a French musician and teacher who set out to improve drama instruction. He developed a style of acting that drew deeply on emotional experiences in everday situations and connected those feelings with gestures and movements that expressed the same.

His methods became popular with teachers of acting and dance. Delsarte never authored a manual on his techniques, and there was no certification program for anyone who taught his methods.[2] Consequently, as they were passed along, his techniques were subjected to various interpretations, some of which were far removed from anything Delsarte envisioned, including melodramatic posing and gymnastics.

Edwin's version, "Delsarte and medico-gymnastics," as he advertised it, was for "the improvement of health and beautifying the form."[3] [4] His "medico-gymnastics" was an improper American application of François Delsarte. No one seemed bothered by this as sixty misses and young ladies signed up for his class. Their dress consisted of a divided skirt, loose blouse of dark-blue serge, broadcloth leggings of the same color, a yachting cap, and tennis shoes. The course included various exercise routines.

The local paper reported that "Dr. Osbaldeston is an admirable drill master and the work to which he subjects the ladies is calculated not only to give them greater grace of carriage and action, but also a finer development and better health." The same article concluded, "All-in-all, Dr. Osbaldeston's work

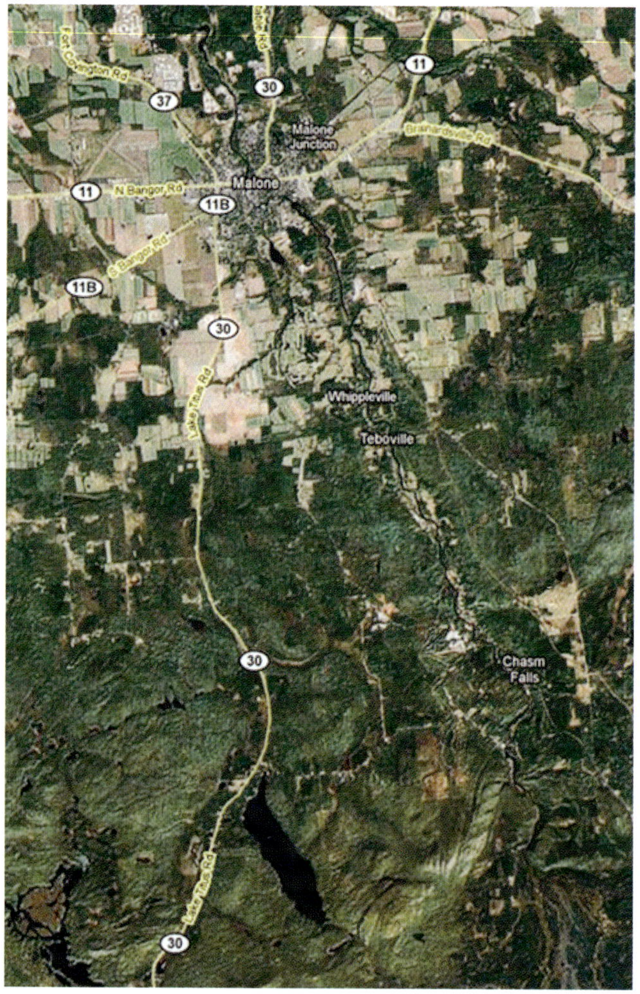

Aerial view of Malone, New York—Lake Titus is in the foreground.

Imagery ©2014 Google, USDA Farm Service Agency, DigitalGlobe, New York GIS, Map data ©2014 Google

on behalf of the ladies is admirable and for it he deserves general and most hearty commendation and thanks."[5] His instruction was nothing short of an exercise class wrapped in Delsarte's name. None-

Lake Titus, south of the village of Malone, New York. Edwin bought property on the lake and named it Camp Mascot.

theless, his pupils appeared satisfied.

In 1894 Edwin purchased a cottage and twenty acres of land on the western shore of Lake Titus, 9.6 miles south of Malone in Franklin County. Returning to the village in 1895, the family began to extend its time there. In addition, he leased what was referred to as the Chateaugay Chasm property, which he planned to turn into a hotel with male and female massage services for locals and guests.[6]

> The Chateaugay *Record* states that Prof. Edwin T. Osbaldeston, of New York, who visited Malone last summer with his family, has leased the Chateaugay Chasm property for the coming year. Extensive repairs and improvements are to be made and there is every prospect that this charming spot will become popular under his management as a sanitarium. Dr. Osbaldeston also owns a cottage site at Lake Titus.[7]
>
> It is expected that Dr. Osbaldeston, who has leased the Chateaugay Chasm property, will open the hotel about June 1st. It is now being repaired.[8]
>
> The Y.M.C.A. gymnasium boys have received their wooden muskets from Dr. Osbaldeston, of New York and are now receiving rudimentary military drill at the hands of a member of the 27th Separate Company. The boys are greatly interested in the work and are making rapid progress.[9]

With mortgage payments to meet on the Lake Titus property and a family to provide for, his ambitions exceeded his ability to deliver. Edwin abandoned the Chateaugay project within a month or so and put his energies into developing the cottage and grounds at Lake Titus.

Edwin had made a good impression on Malone residents, and for a short time in 1895, he rented a wooden frame house on Elm Street in town, where he and his family stayed until moving into the cottage on Lake Titus.

At 1:00 a.m. on Thursday, July 11, 1895, the Elm Street house caught fire. The family had divided its time between the in town residence and the lake cottage. The afternoon before the fire the Osbaldeston family had gone to stay at their cottage. The blaze was raging by the time the firefighters arrived. All of their furniture and household goods were destroyed. The original news report stated that the cause was hard to determine; however, an accelerant was suspected.[10]

After reading the account of the fire in the *Malone Farmer,* Edwin wrote a lengthy reponse to the paper, denying that he stored combustible materials in the house. Instead, he suggested that robbery had been the motive. To give credence to this motive, he cited that trunks that had been upstairs were now on the first floor, curtains and shades were found outside the house, and a neighbor reported seeing two men in nearby woods acting suspiciously.[11] Edwin further stated that a week before, the house had been entered through a basement window, a locked trunk had been forced open, and a painting was missing.

Edwin reported the loss of a number of rare and valuable paintings due to the fire. Overall, he claimed that his loss was "not less than $15,000." These claims were meant to impress the insurance adjuster. For good measure, he added that he had tucked $613 under a rug spread on an upstairs floor.[12] An insurance settlement would help finance his plans for his Lake Titus property.

"The trifling amount of insurance did not cover my most valuable collection of paintings, which were about to be placed on public view as soon as the rooms could be readied to exhibit them," he said. "Some people put their spare cash . . . in the purchase of diamonds, or else bank their monies, and there are people like myself who put their money in pictures and sculpture by eminent artists, taking the surer chances of a rapid increase in value, sometimes to the extent of 500 percent on the original expenditures."

The owners of the home had it insured for $1,700, while Edwin was reported to have coverage for $2,000 on household goods and $25 per painting.[13] The value of his claim was denied. Years later it was recalled that when Edwin attended a meeting with the insurance adjuster to discuss his loss, "he calmly drew a revolver and laid it down on the table before him."[14]

In early 1895 Edwin met a nineteen-year-old woman by the name of Louise Weiss. (Louise also called herself Louisa.) Born in Germany, her father was from Wisconsin and her mother from Germany. Weiss moved to New York in 1891. It appears that she desired to take up massage and enrolled as a student at Edwin's school. When the New York School of Training for Massage recessed for the summer, some of Edwin's patients and students joined his family in Malone. Weiss was one of them.

Many improvements had been made to the Lake Titus property over the summer, including the creation of a park, a new drive from the main road, and the addition of a large dining room and kitchen. The cottage was renamed Camp Mascot.[15]

At the end of the 1895 summer season, Alice Agnes and the children returned to New York City in late October. Before leaving, the Osbaldeston children entertained their peers attending a local school. An article commenting on the improvements to the camp and the end of the season performance appeared in the *Franklin Gazette* on November 1 and was signed simply "L. W." Edwin may very well have written the article as he was in the habit of supplying copy to local newspapers for purposes of self-promotion.

After Alice Agnes and the children departed for New York City, Edwin remained behind for a few weeks ostensibly to attend to a few patients in Malone and neighboring villages. Weiss remained as well. By this time he had become totally infatuated with Weiss and began having an affair with his pupil. The affair became his ruination, ending his period of relative stability, and would cause great anguish for his wife and family.

Yet another fire hit the family home on West Forty-Sixth Street. An explosion occurred on the top floor of the four-story row house at 2:40 a.m. on February 27, 1896. The resulting fire was reported to have amounted to $10,000 in damage. Edwin and his family were asleep when the blaze began but managed to escape without injury.[16 17]

As the affair progressed and Weiss became noticeably pregnant, Edwin's family life became more difficult. There was no mention in his journals or papers of these developments.

In April 1896 Edwin left his wife and six children. He and Weiss moved to Washington, DC, where he placed an ad in the *Washington Post* announcing the founding of a branch of the New York School of Massage.[18] However, it wasn't long before Edwin created new difficulties for himself. Business was slow, so he hatched a scheme to drum up customers by visiting established massage parlors in the city. In a move somewhat similar to his behavior at Manhattan massage parlors, he employed coercion with operators of massage parlors in the District of Columbia. He attempted to force the managers into taking his training course. Within a month Edwin was arrested for obtaining money under false pretenses.[19]

He had approached several massage operators, presenting himself as a representative of the director of the Metropolitan Police. He displayed his credentials and told the operators that they had to take a course from him and obtain a certificate of completion or the police department would put them out of business.

The operator of a salon on New York Avenue paid Edwin $40 for the training. Following the third session, she complained to the police that he had become abusive to her and so sought redress from the department. The scam quickly came to light and charges were filed. At the time of his arrest (May 12, 1896), he expressed great indignation, produced an abundance of testimonials, and denied that he ever indicated that he was representing the police department. The detectives were unimpressed and took him to the station to be booked. Unable to post bail, he was detained in the Sixth Precinct station house for several days.[20]

A reporter for the *Washington Post* interviewed Edwin while he was in custody. The reporter noted that Edwin "could readily be taken for a professional man" and noted that Edwin was "greatly mortified by his predicament and particularly regretted that his family should read about his arrest."[21] Again, he presented his testimonials and credentials and indicated that he had been threatened in writing and by a "burly fellow" who had come to his door some days before—all in an attempt to elicit sympathy and cast doubt that the charge against him had merit. Casting himself as the victim, he laid the blame for his arrest on a conspiracy created by the massage parlor operators to keep him from prying into their methods. There was only brief mention of Weiss in the article, identifying her as the "doctor's attendant."[22]

Edwin's trial was delayed because the head of the Metropolitan Police Department was out of town.[23] Upon posting $500 bond, he visited the chief witness against him, telling her that she had misconstrued what he said and never meant to give the impression that he represented the police.[24] In June the prosecutor dropped the charge against Edwin, ruling that there wasn't enough evidence to bring the case to trial and some of the witnesses were no longer in Washington.[25] It is not known if Edwin had anything to do with their departure. Once again, he had extricated himself from a tight spot.

In the meantime, Alice Agnes and the children moved to Camp Mascot on Lake Titus in late April or early May 1896 and lived there continuously until mid-March 1897. She continued to support her family by running the family business. An announcement of their return appeared in the *Franklin Gazette*.

> Mrs. E. T. Osbaldeston and children are now at Camp Mascot, Lake Titus, for the summer, the New York School of Training for Massage being closed until October 1st. Dr. Osbaldeston is now in the west establishing new schools, and will not join his family here for several weeks.[26]

Having dodged a trial in the District of Columbia and likely low on funds, he returned to Malone. On July 3, 1896, the *Franklin Gazette* reported that "Dr. E. T. Osbaldesten is with his family at 'Camp Mascot,' Lake Titus."

The announcement did not mention that Weiss came with him. For those who inquired, Edwin explained that the heavily pregnant Louise was a young widow and that her name was Mrs. Percy Metzgar. On August 9, 1896, the daughter of Edwin Osbaldeston and Louise Weiss was born at Camp Mascot. They named her Louisa Mascot Osbaldeston. What the children knew of Louise and Mascot was not discussed openly.

Log schoolhouse on Lake Titus (1893)
Franklin County Historical and Museum Society. A Franklin County Family Album *(Brushton, NY: TEACH Services, 2008): p. 215.*

Family life seemed to continue normally for the children. They were involved in school, church, and activities. Ethel attended Franklin Academy in Malone while her siblings attended a country school or the local grammar school. Daughters Ethel and Normandie recalled many happy times at Camp Mascot.

> I remember when we . . . were young how we spent some Winters in Northern N.Y. state and went to school there. We had lots of friends and good times. Most of all we had a little mutt dog, named Mink because of his color. I had just started high school, the others were in one or two lower grade schools. We also attended church. Mink was always in school or church with one or the other of us. Chase him home and he made his way to the next school or church. He was a great "mugger," his varied expressions of woe when scolded made one break down and hug him—but good. Ed's [Edwin Jr.] big stunt was to get me in our sled (cutter they called them), hitch up our mare Topsy, black as coal, then drive me out of town where big drifts skirted the road, drive up sidewise on one so the cutter would turn over sidewise and tip me out along with the thick robes and hot bricks.[27]

> We lived here winter + summer for three (3) years—going to a small school house walking through the woods to do so. Here we had a horse, a calf, a lamb, chickens + a dog—beehives. I made balsam pillows to sleep on + loved them. All kinds of wild animals came to the clearing—deer, raccoons, foxes, porcupines, squirrels. Black bears + wild cats were there but stayed away.[28]

The children thought of the farm animals as pets and were particularly fond of the calf they named "Red." One evening around the dinner table, one of the children commented that Red had disappeared. Their father let them know that Red was what they were eating for dinner. Their reaction was one of revulsion and tears.[29]

These otherwise seemingly happy times would not last for the children. In some respects they were better off without their father's presence, but the absence of the family's chief breadwinner brought hard times. Meanwhile, Edwin and Weiss were about to launch themselves into a highly turbulent relationship that could only be described as a "train wreck."

NOTES

1. *Malone Palladium* (NY), 26 July 1894, p. 3, col. e.
2. *Wikipedia*, s.v. "François Delsarte," accessed 6 March 2014, http://en.wikipedia.org/wiki/François_Delsarte.
3. *Malone Palladium* (NY), 20 September 1894, p. 3, col. b.
4. *Malone Palladium* (NY), 16 August 1894, p. 3, col. b.
5. Ibid.
6. *Franklin Gazette* (Malone, NY), 7 June 1895, p. 3, col. a.
7. *Franklin Gazette* (Malone, NY), 5 April 1895, p. 3, col. a.
8. "Local All Sorts," *Franklin Gazette* (Malone, NY), 24 May 1895, p. 3, col. a.
9. "Local All Sorts," *Franklin Gazette* (Malone, NY), 24 May 1895, p. 3, col. b.
10. "Was Spite or Robbery the Motive," *Franklin Gazette* (Malone, NY), 19 July 1895, p. 3, col. c.
11. "A Mysterious Fire," *Malone Palladium* (NY), 18 July 1895, p. 3, col. c.
12. Ibid.
13. Ibid.
14. *Malone Farmer* (NY), 24 December 1902, p. 5, col. a.
15. The newspaper in which this article, among our family history material, appeared has not been identified. However, a shorter version was published in the *Franklin Gazette* (Malone, NY), 1 November 1895, p. 3, col. d.
16. "Yesterday's Fires," *New York Times,* 28 February 1896, p. 5.
17. *Franklin Gazette* (Malone, NY), 6 March 1896, p. 3, col. a.
18. *Washington Post,* 28 April 1896, p. 5.
19. "Got Money for Faking," *Washington Post*, 13 May 1896, p. 1.
20. Ibid.
21. Ibid.
22. Ibid.
23. "Trial Set for an Alleged Massagist," *Washington Post*, 14 May 1896, p. 3.
24. "Prof. Osbaldeston Out on Bail," *Washington Post*, 18 May 1896, p. 3.
25. "Osbaldestine May Escape Prosecution," *Washington Post*, 11 June 1896, p. 2.
26. *Franklin Gazette* (Malone, NY), 8 May 1896, p. 3, col. d.
27. Ethel Turner Groves to Kenson Siver, 29 January 1964.
28. Note written by Normandie Osbaldeston Siver on the back of a photograph of Lake Titus taken during a June 1936 visit to the lake and cottage.
29. As told to Judith Siver in a conversation with her grandmother Normandie.

CHAPTER FOURTEEN

Alice Agnes Stands Behind Her Man ~ 1896–1897

Imagine the life of Alice Agnes Osbaldeston in 1896—mother to six children, alone in America without her extended family, manager of a household, masseuse in the family business, and wife to a husband with a violent temper, erratic behavior, and a proclivity for criminal activity. Further, Alice's husband was now engaged in an open affair with a woman twenty-one years her junior. He had fathered a child with his mistress, and the mistress and child were living under the same roof with her family.

These factors were certainly more than adequate grounds for divorce, yet Alice Agnes remained with Edwin. In fact, as difficult as things may have been for her, family matters were about to become even more strained in the year ahead. Still she endured.

By today's standards, divorce was very rare and very hard to obtain in the latter half of the nineteenth century. Many couples remained in their marriages because of social stigma (particularly for women) and the societal belief in the sanctity of marriage. For most women, divorce was hard to fathom given that when she married, her property, earnings, and rights were given over to her husband. Laws of the times favored men. Men ran the government and the courts. A man also could more easily obtain a divorce than a woman. Where a wife had to prove the grounds for divorce, the husband did not.

While the budding women's rights movement had made some headway in terms of property ownership for wives and expansion of the grounds for divorce (drunkenness and cruelty), there was no universal standard for women in the matters of divorce in the United States. Societal norms were changing slowly. The fight for women's suffrage was underway, but even women's right to vote would take decades to accomplish. The Nineteenth Amendment to the US Constitution was not ratified until the latter half of 1920.

Three percent of all marriages in America ended in divorce in the years immediately following the Civil War. By the 1890s the divorce rate doubled to 6 percent. In the context of the times, alarm was sounded over this increase. State legislatures began to consider new laws to make divorce harder to obtain.

In the early 1900s, during Theodore Roosevelt's administration, the divorce rate then stood at 8 percent.[1] A concerned President Roosevelt spoke out on the issue, "Questions like the tariff and the currency are literally of no consequence whatsoever when compared with the vital question of having the unit of our social life, our home, preserved," he said. Roosevelt likened the rise of divorces to suicide of the race.[2]

In the fall of 1896, Louise Weiss and Edwin moved from Camp Mascot to a house on Webster Street in Malone. This move would seem to make family life a bit less awkward for Alice Agnes. However, Alice Agnes was known to have stayed at this house as well. Perhaps the nine-mile trek over a rough road from Camp Mascot to town or the proximity of the Webster Street house to schools for the children necessitated the in-town residence.

Edwin (1896)

That fall Edwin received an invitation to lecture at McGill University in Montreal, arriving there on November 6 with "Mrs. Metzgar," his assistant. They visited hospitals to give demonstrations of massage, and he made a presentation to twenty-nine physicians.

The night before leaving for Montreal, Edwin and Louise stopped at Fay Brothers department store in Malone. They chose to enter the store during the dinner hour when only one member of staff would be on duty. Edwin asked the lone clerk to see some carpets that were kept on the second floor of the store. Meanwhile, with the clerk distracted, Weiss helped herself to a cloak valued at fifty dollars, two skirts, and a dress pattern. Apparently, she wanted some new clothes for their trip.[3]

The Fay brothers missed the merchandise and heavily suspected Edwin because he had been in the store several times in recent days. They filed a report of the theft of their merchandise with Malone authorities. Malone constable Martin Donohoe went to Montreal in search of the pair, hoping that he would find Weiss wearing the stolen items. He had a little difficulty locating them at first, but through persistence he learned where they were staying and that they were giving a lecture at Victoria Hospital on massage for the nursing staff.

Donohoe and a Montreal dectective attended the lecture on November 13 and saw that the clothes Weiss was wearing matched the description of the missing items from Fay Brothers. Following the lecture, Edwin and Weiss were arrested and taken to the police station. There they saw and recognized Constable Donohoe. Some words were exchanged, and Edwin struck the constable. Montreal police then restrained Edwin and placed him in chains.

The Fays were wired that arrests had taken place, and a request was made for one of the brothers to come to Montreal to make a positive identification of the stolen merchandise. Irwin W. Fay complied and appeared in court the next day. Both Edwin and Weiss loudly protested their arrest and claimed that a "shameful outrage had been committed upon them." Mr. Fay positively identified the cloak and skirt. Later, Weiss confessed that she had taken the items and what was not with her was back at the house on Webster Street in Malone.[4]

On November 16 the Webster Street house was searched, and additional items taken from the department store were found. Edwin and Weiss were advised that they could return to Malone voluntarily with Mr. Fay and Officer Donohoe or they would be remanded to jail to await extradition. Edwin said he would await extradition. Both were remanded to the city jail for eight days. After a few days in jail, Edwin changed his mind. The judge advised him that his first decision would stand.[5]

The Fay Brothers department store was not the only place in Malone with missing items. Farmer Fred Amsden reported that a pair of rubber wading boots had disappeared from his home. He said that Dr. Osbaldeston had been treating his father and suspected Edwin would know something about the missing boots. Upon learning of the arrest in Montreal, Amsden visited the house on Webster Street and collected his waders.[6]

Meanwhile, back in Montreal, court proceedings continued. The original eight-day stay was extended while the paperwork for extradition to New York was processed. On Monday, November 23, Edwin and Weiss appeared in Extradition Court. Irwin Fay testified to the identity of his goods and to the manner in which they were stolen. Constable Donohue said he found additional items during a search of the house on Webster Street.[7]

A week later, finding the evidence sufficient for extradition, the transfer was approved. However, Edwin and Weiss were given fifteen days to appeal extradition and remained in custody.[8] Since they did not file an appeal, the pair was scheduled to be turned over to Malone authorities on December 14. However, a problem arose. Montreal authorities were demanding $242 to cover court costs, transportation, and housing of the prisoners since November 13. Malone did not have the funds to cover the expense. If the fee were not paid, the prisoners would be set free in Montreal. Fay Brothers initially agreed to pay one hundred dollars toward their return. Malone still could not come up with the remaining $142. Finally, a deal was struck whereby Fay Brothers would pay the full fee and be reimbursed by the village council at a later date.[9] [10] [11]

The arrest and return of Dr. Osbaldeston and Louise Metzgar (Weiss) were big news in the village of Malone. A crowd gathered at the train station on January 7, 1897, to watch them disembark and be whisked off to jail.[12] Because he had been belligerent, Edwin appeared before the onlookers with hands and feet shackled. The prisoners were kept in separate quarters so that they could not compare stories.

The *New York Times* had reported Edwin and Weiss's arrest in Montreal and the *Malone Palladium* had provided frequent updates to residents. Reading the account of Edwin's arrest in the *Times*, retired Brooklyn masseur Thomas Denny sent a letter to the Malone chief of police regarding Edwin and his siblings. Obviously not a fan of Edwin's, Denny warned the police chief that Edwin was an escaped convict from Australia. A number of assertions in the letter were incorrect, including, "He assumed the name 'Osbaldeston' upon reading 'Rob Roy' by Sir Walter Scott, thereby making his real name, which is Turner, his middle name. . . ," wrote Denny.[13] Denny's letter was reprinted in the *Malone Palladium*, adding to the lore of Osbaldeston.

Edwin was arraigned on Saturday afternoon, January 9. He pleaded "not guilty" to the charge of grand larceny. His wife, Alice Agnes, daughter Ethel, and son Edwin were present in the courtroom as the *Franklin Gazette* reported.

> Owing to other business before Police Justice Earle's court the examination of Dr. Osbaldeston did not take place until Saturday afternoon. He was then brought

From left to right—Franklin County Jail, Clerk's Office, and Courthouse, Malone, New York. Weiss was held in a small cell on the second floor of the jail.
Franklin County Historical and Museum Society, A Franklin County Family Album *(Brushton, NY: TEACH Services, 2008): p. 158. Photograph by Frank Spencer, Malone, NY.*

before the court charged with grand larceny in the second degree. The court room was packed with spectators at the time, as this case has aroused general interest and many were possessed of a curiosity to see the prisoners. The Dr. has lost considerable flesh since his arrest at Montreal several weeks ago, but though pale from confinement, faced the court with a confident air. He had retained Hon. John I. Gilbert and G. H. Main as counsel and when arraigned plead not guilty. District Attorney Paddock requested that bail be fixed at $1,000 but this was opposed by defendant's counsel and the court finally decided upon $700 as the amount of bonds. The district attorney was assisted by M. A. Martin at the examination. Mrs. Osbaldeston and a son and daughter were present and sat by the side of the Dr., it being the first time they had seen him since his arrest. After the agreement upon the amount of bail the hearing was adjourned until January 22d at 10 in the forenoon. . . .[14]

On Monday evening Dr. Osbaldeston secured bail in the requisite sum of $700, Justice of the Peace E. J. Mannix going upon the bond, and he was released from custody. This is as far as the proceedings have gone and the result of the adjourned hearing January 22d is awaited with interest by a large number of citizens of Malone, who have become interested in the case.[15]

Weiss was arraigned the following Monday and also pleaded "not guilty." Her examination date was set for January 22 as well. However, no bail was set for her, and she remained in custody. Her defense was going to be based on kleptomania.[16] All this time Alice Agnes had been caring for Mascot, the child of her husband's mistress.

While he was out on bail Edwin took the opportunity to compose a seven-hundred-word reply to the letter of Thomas Denny and submitted it to the local police chief. In his letter, published on January 21 in the *Malone Palladium*, Edwin defended his family lineage and name, although he claimed his grandmother as his mother.

"I presume that none who have read the letter could form any other impression than that the man is an idiot or a rascal, actuated by some knavish prompting of revenge or petty jealousy," Edwin exclaimed. He further suggested that Denny's motivation in writing the letter was revenge for having been exposed as a "massage freak and imposter" by Edwin numerous times.[17] It is telling that freshly released from jail his priority was to devote time and energy to defending his honor over a letter written to the chief of police.

On Friday morning, January 22, Police Court justice Earle called Edwin's name on the charge of grand larceny in the second degree. To the surprise of his counsel, he did not appear. Franklin County district attorney Paddock then asked the court to declare his $700 bail bond forfeited. The bond had been backed by the title to the twenty-acre Camp Mascot on Lake Titus.[18] Edwin had just traded his freedom for his wife and children's security.

Besides the likely possibility that he was facing more time in jail for his role in the department store larceny, there was the matter of the old charges in Binghamton for jail breaking and stealing a horse and carriage. District Attorney Paddock had written to Broome County authorities to ask if Edwin was still wanted in Binghamton. However, on the same day that he mailed his letter to Deputy Black, he also asked Edwin how he would like to return to Binghamton, thus cluing Edwin that he would surely face additional time beyond the resolution of his Malone trial. By the time Deputy Sheriff Black reached Malone, Edwin had already been gone for two days.[19] Black would not forget this.

In Edwin's absence, Justice Earle then proceeded with the hearing for Louise Weiss/Metzgar on charges of grand larceny. First witness was Irwin W. Fay, who testified as to the items missing from his store and having seen them in Mrs. Metzgar's possession in Montreal. Additional testimony included her confession and the items found at the Webster Street home. On the witness stand, Weiss did not deny stealing the items. Her case was bound over to a grand jury and would be heard in May. Her bail was also set at $700. Unable to post a bond, she was remanded to jail.[20]

From northern New York State, Edwin made his way to Manhattan. In February word filtered back to Malone that Edwin had been to see the German consul.

> District Attorney Paddock has received information that Dr. Osbaldeston recently called on the German consul in New York and tried to induce the consul to intercede with the authorities in behalf of Mrs. Metzgar, whom he represented to be a German citizen. A photograph of the doctor was sent to the consul, together with a statement of facts in connection with his case, and if he should renew his call he will quite likely be arrested.[21]

Alice Agnes and the children stayed in Malone for almost two months after Edwin jumped bail. She made an attempt to sell Camp Mascot, hoping to raise funds beyond the $700 bond obligation, but received no takers for the property. Winter was not an ideal time to market the camp property. The state of the national economy following the Panic of 1893 may also have been a factor. Camp Mascot had a mortgage lien. After auctioning off all of their furnishings, she and the children (including baby Mascot) left for New York City on Tuesday, March 16. Camp Mascot then became the property of Captain E. J. Mannix, thereby reimbursing him for his forfeited bail bond.[22]

Louise Weiss ("Mrs. Metzgar")

Weiss continued waiting in the Malone jail for her next court appearance. A grand jury was to be impaneled on May 10. To fill her time, she did housework in the jail and helped out in the kitchen. As the only female inmate, she was confined alone in a small cell on the second floor. From early evening until morning, she was locked in her cell. During the day she was allowed to come to the dining room and kitchen. The sheriff left the jail early on the morning of April 17 to run an errand. The other staff member on duty unlocked her cell at 6:00 a.m. and then went out to the stable to work. With her keepers otherwise occupied, she walked out through the office. At 6:45 a.m. she was on a train bound for Montreal. The ticket agent did not recognize her. The one person on the train who did did not attempt to block her escape. Her absence was discovered three hours later.[23] She left a note for the district attorney:

> To Mr. F. G. Paddock:
> Sir: To be in this suspense is too awful for me to stand any longer, and I think that I have already suffered more than my case demands, as I am dying by inches in here. I beg your forgiveness, and please do not chase me as you would a wild deer. I am mad for want of being again with mother. Good-bye, and God bless you.
> Louisa[24]

In her letter she made no mention of her daughter. From Canada, Weiss made her way to Manhattan, where she was reunited with Edwin.

The *Malone Palladium* editorialized the following:

> While it is unfortunate that one who was unquestionably guilty of the crime with which she was charged should escape punishment, and especially so in view of the trouble and expense involved in securing her, there is a quite general feeling that the principal criminal, whose tool and victim Mrs. Metzgar undoubtedly was, having forfeited his bail bond and escaped the punishment which he undoubtedly deserved, it would be small satisfaction to see her convicted while he goes free. Taxpayers can have the satisfaction of knowing that the forfeited bail bond . . . more than reimburses the county for the expenses that have been incurred in the case.[25]

With the whole cast of characters from Camp Mascot reassembled in Manhattan, travel plans were being made to further distance themselves from the upstate authorities. Edwin, Alice Agnes, their children, Weiss, and Mascot would set off for Europe as soon as their affairs could be settled in New York City and passage arranged. To leave the door open for their return to America, they created a paper trail of sorts. It was decided to have the baby baptized. According to Edwin the baptism of his daughter Louisa Mascot took place at St. Paul's Chapel, Trinity Parish, Broadway, New York, on May 6, 1897.[26][27] Agnes filed for United States citizenship on May 19, followed the next day by Weiss.[28][29]

How long Edwin and Weiss could remain on the run was debatable. Authorities in Malone could have pressed a search for the pair. However, it had only been a few months back that Edwin and Weiss were almost freed in Montreal due to lack of funds to cover the costs associated with extradition. Further, since both had spent time in jail, the stolen merchandise had been returned, and shoplifting was not considered a major crime, was it worth going after them? After a time, Edwin decided it would be better to keep moving rather than stay in Manhattan. But then he faced the balancing act

The Osbaldestons fled to England on the American Line's SS St. Louis *in June 1897 while Weiss and Mascot went on a separate ship to Europe.*

between Alice Agnes, their six children, Weiss, and Mascot. Louise's mother had already sent money for passage to Germany for her daughter and granddaughter.[30] Edwin decided to take Alice Agnes and their children to England. On June 2, 1897, the Osbaldestons sailed from New York on the American Line's SS *St. Louis*. They arrived in Southampton, England on June 10, 1897.[31]

Years later Ethel recalled the time in England happily and as a sightseeing adventure. She made no mention of their father fleeing the law. From a child's perspective, it was a holiday. That was most likely how she chose to remember it. She wrote the following:

> When we were children our parents took us on many wonderful trips. To England—and while there—to much that was historical or well known. . . . In London, we spent many hours visiting such places as the Tower of London, where we saw the Royal jewels, the room where the little King and his brother were smothered by their cruel, wicked uncle. Their little bodies were put in a large ornamental urn, which we saw when we visited Westminster Abbey. There we saw so much of England's history, the tombs (with effigies) of Kings and Queens and their families. The place and throne where they have crowned many of their rulers. . . .
>
> We arrived in London . . . the day old Queen Victoria celebrated her 60 years reign. We sat in a cab while waiting to get across London, and watched the colorful brilliant procession. We saw Queen Victoria, too. She died a few years later. We visited the House of Parliament, and used to sit around the lovely parks where the Royal children played nearby. We used to watch the important ceremony of the changing of the Guard. King Edward used to watch this too, over the garden wall of Marlborough House. . . .[32]

Queen Victoria's Diamond Jubilee procession placed the Osbaldestons' arrival in London on Tuesday, June 22, 1897.[33] Queen Victoria died on January 22, 1901.

> When we lived in London, we used to spend quite a lot of time in the Abbey and the Tower for sightseeing. It was like going to the Museum of Natural History in New York, but more interesting of course. We lived near enough to walk to the Palaces and Abbey, but had to take a tram to the Tower.[34]

From London the children of Edwin and Alice Agnes went to live with or near her relatives in Suffolk and Norfolk. Again, the children saw it as an adventure and had many happy memories of living with their English relatives. Ethel described the arrangement as follows:

> When we were small and all went to England to live for a while all our English relatives wanted at least one or two of Mother's children so she divided them up, two [Norma and Frank] to [her half sister] Aunt Emma [on a livestock farm], one [Geneva] to [her sister] Aunt Annie, one [Alberta] to [her half brother] Uncle Arthur. Ed [Edwin Jr.] and I kept house in Great Yarmouth together and all of them came to visit us often.[35]

Now safely in England, Edwin could not resist several displays of his contempt for authority and indignation over his victimization by those in Malone. As was his custom, Edwin wrote to his "tormentors" and to the editor of the *Malone Palladium.* The editor of the paper only quoted portions of his missive as he indicated "the greater portion of it is not of a character for newspaper use." The *Palladium* reported that Mr. Osbaldeston protested the gross injustice done him in coupling his name with Mrs. Metzgar's. "As a man constantly before the public notice, holding a high position in my special profession, and prosperous beyond the prospects of other practitioners, all knew I had no occasion to lend myself a willing hand to thefts of any kind." Edwin claimed that Mrs. Metzgar absolved him of guilt and when she committed the thefts it was due to postpartum depression. He reported that she was now working as a companion to a lady and would rather visit Hades than America. Edwin wrote that he was traveling not for fear of anything but because he was suffering from chronic melancholia and heart trouble and wished "to finish this now soon to end life."[36] Most likely he was suffering more from melodrama than melancholia.

From England Edwin went on his own to Germany and lived with Weiss and their daughter, Mascot, at Louise's mother's home in Oberstein, in the Rhineland-Palatinate area of western Germany. He remained there for about five months.[37] They also traveled and worked together in Germany during that time, performing massage treatments. From Wiesbaden, Edwin wrote to the Fay brothers in Malone.

> Fay Brothers were much surprised Friday morning by the receipt of a letter from Dr. Osbaldeston, written and mailed at Wiesbaden, Germany. The letter invited them over to Germany [along with] Constable Donohue and the other officials connected with the Osbaldeston case. From the tenor of the letter the doctor does not seem to have been driven insane, or to have skipped his bail here on account of anything said in the Malone newspapers, as was intimated in court at the time. On the contrary, he seems to be flourishing on as grand a scale as when he first came to Malone. He claims to have lately attended Prince [Otto von] Bismarck, in the absence of his regular masseur, and to have also treated the Duke of Saxe-Coburg and Duke Frederick Paul.—*Farmer* [38]

This letter was reminiscent of the letter he sent from London to Sheriff Bartlett in Binghamton in 1881 after breaking out of the Broome County jail.

Edwin returned to England from Germany in 1898. In the February 5, 1898, issue of the medical journal *The Lancet,* there was an acknowledgement of receipt of a letter from "Dr. E. T. Osbaldeston, Lond." While he was in London, Edwin visited the Public Record Office in Chancery Lane on March 28, 1898, in an effort to obtain information from Admiralty records regarding his maternal grandfather, Royal Navy lieutenant Charles Pye Turner.

On November 5, 1898, after seventeen months in England, Alice Agnes Osbaldeston and her six children left Southampton on board the SS *St. Louis.* On their arrival in New York on November 12, they passed through Ellis Island.[39] Edwin was not on the ship with them. (In 1913 Alice Agnes would make one last trip to England to visit her relatives.)

Edwin had caused a great deal of turmoil for his family over the past two years. Why Alice Agnes remained with her husband will never be known. For certain, she loved her children and they adored her. She may have feared that she would lose her children if she divorced. In those times, that typically happened to women who left their husbands. Worse, she may have suffered from "battered wife syndrome," blaming herself for her husband's outbursts and fearing physical abuse or death at his hands. Conversely, much of the time, Edwin had been a good provider for his family and offered security. Or perhaps she simply loved Edwin with all his idiosyncrasies and misdeeds. His absence in the coming years would provide a degree of relief but also bring the strain of raising her children alone.

As for Edwin's feelings towards Alice Agnes, he stated the following, "My wife possesses naturally some of the most admirable traits of a woman's character—a faithful, loving wife and mother, strongly imbued with the instincts of benevolence, and sympathy, ever willing to sacrifice, comfort, and go to the aide of others needing her services."[40] Edwin's words were a rare expression of empathy but also a telling double standard of the sexes.

The dutiful and loyal wife, Alice Agnes Moore Osbaldeston, in 1907

NOTES

1. Audrey M. Jones, "Historical Divorce Rates," accessed 24 March 2014, www.lovetoknowdivorce.com.
2. Glenda Riley, *Divorce: An American Tradition* (Lincoln, NE: University of Nebraska Press, 1997), p. 115.
3. "Dr. Osbaldeston in Trouble Again," *Malone Palladium* (NY), 19 November 1896, p. 3, col. c.
4. Idid.
5. Ibid.
6. *Malone Palladium* (NY), 19 November 1896, p. 3, col. b.
7. "That Charge Against a Masseur," *Montreal Daily Star,* 23 November 1896, p. 8.
8. *New York Times*, 29 November 1896, p. 6.
9. *Malone Palladium* (NY), 17 December 1896, p. 3, col. c.
10. *Malone Palladium* (NY), 24 December 1896, p. 3, col. b.
11. *Malone Palladium* (NY), 31 December 1896, p. 3, col. b.
12. "Dr. Osbaldeston in Malone. Shackled Hand and Foot During the Journey," *Herald* (Potsdam, NY), 15 January 1897.
13. "The Osbaldeston Case," *Malone Palladium* (NY), 26 November 1896, p. 3, col. c.
14. *Franklin Gazette* (Malone, NY), 15 January 1897, p. 3, col. b.
15. Ibid.
16. *Malone Palladium* (NY), 14 January 1897, p. 3, col. c.
17. "Dr. Osbaldeston Replies to the Letter of Thos. Denny," *Malone Palladium* (NY), 21 January 1897, p. 3, col. c.
18. "The Osbaldeston-Metzgar Case," *Malone Palladium* (NY), 28 January 1897, p. 3, col. a.
19. "New Jersey Governor to Deny Extradition of Black's Prisoner," *Binghamton Press* (NY), 29 March 1926, p. 1, col. b.
20. "The Osbaldeston-Metzgar Case," *Malone Palladium* (NY), 28 January 1897, p. 3, col. a.
21. *Malone Palladium* (NY), 11 February 1897, p. 3, col. b.
22. *Franklin Gazette* (Malone, NY), 14 May 1897, p. 3, col. c.
23. "Mrs. Metzgar Escapes from Jail," *Malone Palladium* (NY), 22 April 1897, p. 3, col. a.
24. "A Woman Escapes from Jail," *New York Times*, 18 April 1897, p. 1.
25. "Mrs. Metzgar Escapes from Jail," *Malone Palladium* (NY), 22 April 1897, p. 3, col. a.
26. Edwin T. Osbaldeston, in State Prison, Saarbrücken, Germany to US Embassy, Berlin, Germany, 24 September 1902. Department of State, US Embassy, Germany. Record Group 84, UD Entry 24, vol. 261, folios 511–516. National Archives at College Park, College Park, Maryland.
27. Whitey Flynn, achivist technician, Trinity Wall Street, in an e-mail message to Noël Siver, 22 January 2015, stated that Edwin and Louise's daughter was baptized as Louisa Mascot Osbaldeston at St. Paul's Chapel on May 6, 1897.
28. National Archives at New York City; *US District Court for the Southern District of New York (121–122);* ARC Number: *5324244*; ARC Title: *Petitions for Naturalization, 1793–1906*; Record Group Title: *Records of the Immigration and Naturalization Service*; Record Group Number: *85*. Ancestry.com. *New York, Petitions for Naturalization, 1794–1906* [database online]. Provo, UT, USA: Ancestry.com Operations, Inc., 2013.
29. New York State and Federal Naturalization Records, 1794–1929. Circuit Court, Southern District, vol. 002–003, 10 December 1894–17 July 1899. www.ancestry.com. Record for Louisa Osbaldeston, dated 20 May 1897.
30. "Mrs. Metzgar Escapes from Jail," *Malone Palladium* (NY), 22 April 1897, p. 3, col. a.
31. Ancestry.com, *U.K., Incoming Passenger Lists, 1878–1960* [database on-line] (Provo, UT, USA: Ancestry.com Operations Inc., 2008). Original data: *Board of Trade: Commercial and Statistical Department and successors: Inwards Passenger Lists*. Kew, Surrey, England: The National Archives of the UK (TNA). Reference BT 26/115/38, p. 11.
32. Ethel Turner Groves in Florida to Kenson Siver in New Jersey, 30 March 1957.
33. "The Diamond Jubilee. Celebration in London. The Queen's Procession," *Times* (London), 23 June 1897, p. 9.
34. Ethel Turner Groves in Florida to Kenneth and Mildred Siver in New Jersey, 3 June 1953.
35. Ethel Turner Groves in Florida to Kenneth and Mildred Siver in New Jersey, 13 June 1953.
36. *Malone Palladium* (Malone, NY), 15 July 1897, p. 1, col. a.
37. Information from an article in the newspaper *Nahethal-Bote* (Oberstein, Germany), 6 May 1902. Courtesy of archivist Manfred Rauscher of Stadtarchiv Idar-Oberstein, e-mail message to Noël Siver, 7 February 2008. Translated by Noël Siver.
38. "Miscellaneous Items," *Adirondack News* (St. Regis Falls, NY), 11 December 1897, p. 1, col. f.

39 www.ellisisland.org. Also seen on www.ancestry.com.

40. ETO wrote these words about Alice Agnes on the back of his certificate of naturalization as a US citizen, which is among our family history material.

CHAPTER FIFTEEN

The Free Fall to Ruin ... & Back ~ 1897–1903

Exactly when Edwin, Weiss, and Mascot returned to the United States is not clear. In December 1897 the trio was still in Germany. Edwin recalled that they had lived for five months at Weiss's mother's home in Oberstein and had traveled in Germany promoting massage.

For certain, by the spring of 1899 they were back in New York City.[1] Alice Agnes and her children had remained in England until November 1898. At some point the husband, wife, mistress, and children were reunited in the city.

One thing is certain, Alice Agnes had had enough of Weiss by May of 1899. She sent a telegram to the sheriff of Malone asking if he cared to secure Weiss as she was in New York. The sheriff hesitated in deciding to come to the city and arrest her. The general feeling in Malone was not to bother as they were happy to be rid of her and the Osbaldestons. Word had also been received in Malone that Dr. Osbaldeston had returned to New York.[2]

The United States census of 1900 recorded Edwin twice. He was listed on June 6 as residing with his wife and six children at 7 West Sixty-Third Street in Manhattan.[3] In all probability he was listed as the head of the household even though he was absent from the home. Edwin was also enumerated on June 1 that year as living at 6016 Penn Avenue in Pittsburgh, Pennsylvania, with a woman he claimed to be his wife and whose name he said was Alice, twenty-four, born in June 1875, and their daughter Louise, four, born in August 1895. He claimed that all three of them were born in England and had immigrated to the United States in 1896. He also stated on his census return that both he and his wife were physicians.[4] (Weiss was born in January 1876 and Mascot in August 1896.) Perhaps he gave this misinformation in an attempt to mislead anyone seeking his whereabouts. More than likely, it was in keeping with his habit of not responding truthfully on government forms.

Edwin taught exercise classes at the Gusky Hebrew Orphanage in Pittsburgh.

It is not known why they chose to move to Pittsburgh in 1899. (A center of manufacturing, the city had doubled in population in the past two decades to over 320,000 people.) It may have been to distance themselves from authorities in New York in case a sheriff decided to come looking for them. Another possible reason was Pittsburgh had a sizable German community.

An advertisement for teaching the Delsartian method, physical culture, and general massage appeared in the *Pittsburg Post* in March 1900. Instruction was offered at the Penn Avenue address.[5] Edwin taught fencing to wealthy residents and, ironically, to city policemen. By September that year, the Pittsburgh police force was receiving lessons in physical culture and "Delsartian grace" under his direction.[6] He also taught physical culture classes in the public schools. Establishing himself once more in business, he opened a sanitarium that included baths and Swedish movements. It was reported that he regaled acquaintances with his experiences of life abroad.[7] All indications were that he had successfully rebuilt his business.

His name appears in the Pittsburgh city directories for 1900 and 1901. Among the places where Edwin taught exercise classes in 1901 and 1902 was the Gusky Hebrew Orphanage and Home. Located on the outskirts of the north side of the city, it was the city's first Jewish orphanage.[8] The orphanage had been founded by wealthy widow Esther Gusky in memory of her late husband, Jacob. (Jacob Gusky had been the owner of Pittsburgh's first large department store.) Short notes about the progress of the children in Edwin's classes appeared in *The Jewish Criterion* newspaper.[9]

In 1901 Weiss, who was thirty-eight years younger than Edwin, began to tire of him. In addition, her widowed mother, who was still in Oberstein, Germany, was having difficulties with a grasping son-in-law over family property matters. As a result Weiss decided to visit her mother and take daughter Mascot along. They sailed from New York on September 18, 1901, on the Red Star Line's SS *Kensington*.

Weiss told Edwin that she would return by Christmas, but Christmas came and went, and then so did the start of the new year. She then wrote that she would return at the end of January.

Extremely possessive of Weiss, Edwin grew increasingly anxious over her absence. He had heard from friends he had made in Oberstein that Weiss had been convinced not to return to Pittsburgh. She was to stay in Oberstein and take the position of housekeeper for well-to-do widower Eduard Wild. Whether it was true or not, he said that he also received word that Weiss had been "semi-intoxicated" with Wild at a New Year's Eve party that had been arranged by Louise's mother.

He was further informed that Weiss had announced she had divorced Edwin and that she had been advised that her marriage to Edwin would not be considered legitimate in Germany. This news sent him into an emotional frenzy. According to Edwin, he wrote to Weiss to confirm what he had heard. He also placed advertisements in the Oberstein newspaper to contradict the statements about their marriage. Edwin and Weiss had never legally married, but he considered her his wife by virtue of living together. To him, she was his common-law wife without consideration that he was still married to Alice Agnes.[10]

As Edwin told it, following the newspaper advertisements, Weiss wrote him "abominable letters" filled with coarse language. She referred to Mascot as their "bastard" child. She said that if he came to Oberstein, he would be lynched and that the *Bürgermeister* had given orders to the gendarme to arrest Edwin.[11] Naturally, Edwin would not be warned off by such threats. Even more incensed by the absence of his mistress and their daughter, Edwin decided to go to Germany. He applied for a passport on February 13, 1902, and one was issued the following day.[12] (Edwin had become a naturalized citizen of the United States on January 22, 1886.)

Among Edwin's preparations for his trip to Germany was target practice. He was insanely jealous and convinced that his mistress had been seduced by another man.

> Three months ago he told a friend his wife had left him, taking his five-year-old daughter, and going back to her Prussian home. She had practiced massage abroad and claimed to have been an attendant of the late Empress of Austria. Osbaldeston feared the wiles of an old lover at Oberstein, especially as his wife wrote that she would never return to America. Then the professor quit the sword and began practicing with the revolver. He put a paper heart on the wall of his gymnasium. Soon he was able to puncture it at every shot. He told the landlord he was working to be able to kill the man who took his wife.[13]

On April 9, 1902, Edwin sailed from New York to Antwerp, Belgium, as a cabin passenger on the Red Star Line's ship SS *Southwark*. He claimed that his son Edwin was with him, and there is some evidence that this was the case.[14] Following his arrival at Antwerp on April 20, Edwin made his way to Luxembourg. There he had business cards printed in three languages (English, French, and German) with his photograph on the back.

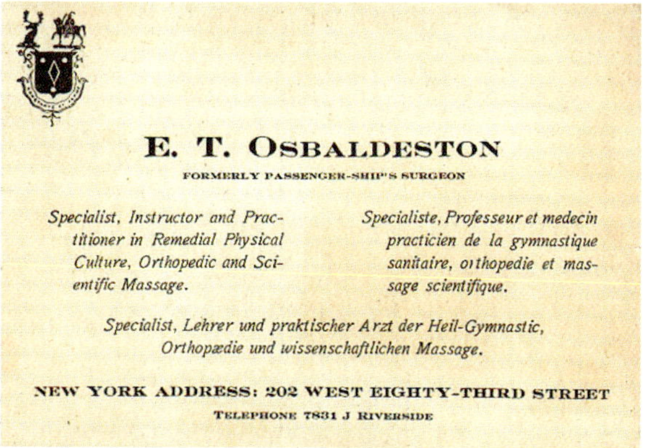

Above: The front side of the business card Edwin had printed in three languages in Luxembourg in April 1902.

Left: The back side of the business card contained this photo.

In Germany Edwin found accommodation at the Hotel de Post in the town of Kirn, northeast of Oberstein. Seven and a half months had passed since he had seen his mistress and child. He was distraught over the failure of Weiss to return and the acrimonious exchanges that had taken place in the interim. Finally on Saturday, May 3, 1902, he took the train to Oberstein, where he met with Louise's employer, Eduard Wild, the owner of a small gun-manufacturing company. They met at the home of a third party. Edwin's account of the meeting follows:

> I had resolved to act upon the advice of others & see the man Wild personally & find out if he was a victim of Frau Weiss [mother of Louise] & Louisa or not. . . . That remarkable interview took place at Herr F. Raber's home in Oberstein on Saturday night, May the 3rd. The man's candor with me very much impressed me and those present with the fact that he was not so much at fault as the women in the case; he possessed a desire to be rid entirely of the despicable affair and hoped that I had come to take the wife back to the United States. I informed him that I had come wholly and solely in the interests of our child. . . .[15]

The village of Oberstein, Germany

The final showdown came on Monday, May 5. The tension surrounding his domestic situation brought out the worst in Edwin. Of all of Edwin's misdeeds the events of this day would mark the lowest point of his behavior and bring tragic consequences. Initially there were two versions of what took place on May 5—Edwin's version and the version published in the Oberstein newspaper. The Oberstein accounts differ greatly from Edwin's. Translations of the four articles that appeared in the *Nahethal-Bote* newspaper follow:

> **Local and Miscellaneous News.**
> Oberstein, 6 May. Yesterday afternoon around 4 o'clock a terrible murder was committed here, news of which spread like wildfire through the city and moved the populace with excitement. The American Edwin T. Osbaldeston came on the 3:10 train from Kirn to here, proceeded to the house of the carbine manufacturer Eduard Wild and killed him with three revolver shots; in addition he inflicted on Wild's workman [Wilhelm] Baumhardt a serious injury with another shot. Regarding further details we are able to publish the following: Osbaldeston is a man well known by people here, since in 1897 he spent a longer time here with his wife Louise née Weiss and practiced massage treatments. Last year his wife together with their child left him in New York, came here and in spite of repeated requests did not return to him. Finally it is said that Osbaldeston still just wanted his child, a girl, back, and when this was also denied him, he set out on a trip here, in order to take her away from the mother. The latter was to be found since two months as a housekeeper at Eduard Wild's. A discussion between Wild and Osbaldeston took place on Saturday in which Wild apparently rejected that Mrs. Osbaldeston be induced to surrender the child. Osbaldeston, who had taken lodging in Kirn, encountered, when he arrived yesterday afternoon at Wild's house, his child in the street and took her himself, but since she cried, on the urging of passersby he let her go in the house. Then Wild appeared in the corridors and after short words with Osbaldeston was shot at close range. Two bullets penetrated . . . the arm and the chest, while the third bullet that was fired, when Wild was already lying on the ground, in the back pierced the heart and immediately brought about his death. When Baumhardt rushed to the aid of his employer, the American discharged . . . two more shots, of which one hit him in the neck.
>
> As Osbaldeston threatened everyone who

came near him with the revolver, no one else approached him and so he escaped unmolested to Winterhauch [large forest south of Oberstein], where the people who later followed him no longer found him. In the meantime, all places in the vicinity were informed by the police by telegram of the murder with the result that Osbaldeston could be arrested already towards evening. He approached Baumholder [a village 12 km south of Oberstein] and wanted to buy headgear for himself in a village shop, as he had lost his hat in the attack. Immediately a crowd surrounded the store and here his arrest succeeded. After the corresponding telegraphic communication with the local mayoralty arrived, our two gendarmes drove to Baumholder from where they brought the prisoner here this morning and delivered him to the local prison. The murder can now quickly find its atonement. It is so much the worse in its consequences as Wild, who was a widower, leaves behind 5 children and as Baumhardt, who has a numerous family to support, will be incapacitated for a long time, if his severe wounding does not have still worse in its wake.[16]

Local and Miscellaneous News.
Oberstein, 7 May. The murder in Wilhelmstrasse dominated of course also today public interest and discussion. Towards Osbaldeston as well as his wife people are extremely angry and everywhere, where the crowd was considerable, she is pursued with curses and not misunderstandable gestures. In the interrogation as well as in the postmortem of Wild's corpse Osbaldeston is said to have displayed great cold-bloodedness and calm; he is alleged to have acted only in self-defense. The corpse postmortem revealed that the one bullet which Wild received in the back had pierced the heart. This morning the judicial examinations resumed and a detailed visit of the crime scene was carried out. The condition of the seriously wounded worker Baumhardt remains until now unchanged.[17]

Yesterday afternoon the body of the deceased carbine manufacturer Eduard Wild was buried. A large carriage provided him an escort to the churchyard where in addition a crowd of the curious had also turned up. Mrs. Osbaldeston left our city on Wednesday, 7 May 1902. In the evening she proceeded to Nahbollenbach [today a suburb of Idar-Oberstein] and boarded the train there.[18]

The second victim of the murder that the American Osbaldeston committed on 5 May in Wilhelmstrasse has now also died from his injury: factory worker Wilhelm Baumhardt, who in the murder affair received a shot in the neck, from where the bullet was brought into the lung, after heavy suffering died yesterday at midday. Baumhardt is 30 years old; he leaves a widow and 5 children. As the deceased manufacturer also left 5 children, so by Osbaldeston's act 10 children have become orphans.[19]

Edwin spent the night of May 5 in the village of Baumholder from where the Oberstein gendarmes transferred him to the jail in that city. From Oberstein he was taken to the state prison at Saarbrücken on May 7. Upon his incarceration in Saarbrücken prison, he wrote to the United States Consulate in Mainz. The consulate received his letter on May 12 and replied the same day. He was offered the name of a defense counsel, but Edwin had already retained someone else. The head of the consulate had little sympathy for Edwin. In June the Mainz Consulate received a letter from Ethel Osbaldeston in New York inquiring as to the whereabouts of her father.

On September 24, 1902, after four and a half months in prison, Edwin wrote a twelve-page, five-thousand-word, rambling letter to the United States Embassy in Berlin. (The opening paragraph of this letter appears below. The remainder is paraphrased afterwards.)

States Prison Saarbrücken
Königlich Gefängnis
September 24th 1902

The Honorable
The United States Minister to Germany
Berlin

Honorable Sir:
On the ninth of last April I sailed from New York City as cabin passenger with my son on board the S.S. *Southwark* of the Red Star Line Arriving at Antwerp on the 20th.
I came with three objects in view:
I, for my health having been a severe sufferer from an attack of Melancholia in its worse form for a long time previous. The result of sunstroke in years previous and more recently from to close application to my profession (overwork) and domestic calamities.
II–To go into practice in Wiesbaden for which purpose I applied for & obtained before leaving the United States a two-year leave of absence passport.
III–With the view of taking legal steps before the Bürgermeister of Oberstein where my wife Louise was residing as she said as "housekeeper" to another man. She having previously on September 18th 1901 obtained my consent to come . . . ostensibly [to assist] her mother Frau Louise Weiss of Oberstein in a civil action to recover property from her son-in-law Herr Albert Haupt of the Weiss Hotel there. [And, finally, to] show that she was an unfit person to have the care of and bringing up of our young daughter, (age six years the 9th of last August) Louisa Mascot.[20]

As proof that Weiss was his wife, he created a portfolio of documents upon which she had indicated her marital status. One was her application for naturalization as a citizen of the United States drawn on May 20, 1897. A second was Mascot's baptismal record recording the child's mother as Louisa Osbaldeston. The third paper was an oath she had taken in court in Oberstein regarding the transfer of property rights. To free his child from Weiss, he prepared a pamphlet entitled "An Appeal to the Mothers of Oberstein." In it he outlined her past life and her current affair with the man Wild—all intended to prove she was an unfit mother.[21]

In the letter he then outlined his version of the sequence of events on May 5. As the train approached Oberstein that afternoon, the house of Eduard Wild was pointed out to him. From the station, he walked to Wild's house, and as he approached, he saw a woman and girl in the street. He was not sure who the woman was as she darted into the house, but he was sure the girl was Mascot. He ran forward and raised Mascot in his arms. "As I was caressing my child a great, country ruffian sprang from his cart and seizing me for an instant by the coat, began to talk, yell, and gesticulate."

Edwin said he then showed the man that he was armed but that it made no difference as he pushed and yelled louder. The disturbance brought workers from Wild's carbine company to the street, and a crowd of onlookers gathered. From there Edwin said that he wasn't sure what happened. It was a blur of words and faces. Fearing the crowd, the menacing man, recalling Weiss's threats, hearing Wild talking, "and a dozen conflicting things ran through my mind. By this time I was like a mad bull at bay. I emptied my shooter. Herr Wild, being the nearest and doing most of the talking, got fatally hit first. I cannot see that I was the most serious at fault. Herr Wild was more use to me alive rather than a dead man."[22]

In his letter to the ambassador, he summarized his defense. While he admitted he lost intelligent control of himself, he felt that he should be granted mercy because he is a benevolent person, one inclined to forgive, had young children, had marched with Garibaldi, and later fought in the American Civil War. (Edwin was in Malta and England during these events.) Further, he was not trespassing or injuring others' property, had not rushed from Antwerp like an assassin, had had business cards made, and burdened himself with luggage and baggage. He wrote a full page on his professional accomplishments and used more than a page to drop the names of all the famous people he had treated.[23]

And he placed blame on Weiss. "Ever since I made the acquaintance of Frau Louisa," he wrote, "things have been going back on me. . . ." But then he said it was not really her fault. "She is in all . . . respects very superior to the majority of women of her standard and possesses a wonderful influence over men. All coming in contact with her feel the charm of her manner and have hard work to resist its effect on them. They become haunted by night and day with her presence. . . ." He said the spell she cast on him had caused his practice to decline. He claimed he had been earning $7,000, and as high as $11,000 a year, before he met her. Afterward, he had never gone far above $4,000.

Consistent with his self-defense in past troubles, Edwin blamed others—the country ruffian who seized him, Weiss who enticed him, Herr Wild for talking. In truth, Weiss had been his ruination but it was he who had gone willingly in pursuit of her. Once again, Edwin cast himself as the charitable man wronged by others.

He felt that if what had happened had taken place anywhere but Oberstein, and were not tainted by the trouble between Weiss and himself, it would have been viewed as justifiable homicide. He closed his letter complaining that he had been waiting in suspense and solitude for months for his case to be heard. And finally, he asked the ambassador to use his official influence to see that the trial goes forward in October and not be delayed again.

> ***"She [Weiss] is in all . . . respects very superior to the majority of women of her standard and possesses a wonderful influence over men. All coming in contact with her feel the charm of her manner and have hard work to resist its effect on them. They become haunted by night and day with her presence. . . ."***
>
> **— Edwin Turner Osbaldeston**

On September 29 the United States Embassy in Berlin sent Edwin's letter to the consulate in Mainz, requesting it to "look into this matter at once and let the Embassy know if you think that the gentleman has a valid claim upon it and is being treated unjustly."[24] Mainz consul Walter Schumann was very aware of Edwin's case and someone who was not taken in by Dr. Osbaldeston. Schumann replied to the embassy as follows:

> Replying to the Embassy's letter of Sept. 29, regarding the case of one Edwin T. Osbaldeston, now held for murder of two men at Oberstein a.d. Nahe, I beg to say that Osbaldeston, immediately upon his arrest in May last, addressed a letter to this Consulate, setting forth the facts in the case, in a similar manner as contained in the letter addressed to the Embassy, which is returned herewith, and requesting the name of a lawyer at Saarbrücken who would undertake his defense. We sent

him the name of a lawyer who was willing to take his case, but before this lawyer was able to communicate with Osbaldeston, the latter had already retained Herr Rechtsanwalt Lanser, No.I Dudweiler Str. St. Johann-Saarbrücken, who sent the enclosed photograph and two pamphlets to this Consulate for inspection, which I beg to submit to the Embassy as you may best judge Osbaldeston's character thereby. These pamphlets, with the photographs they contain, speak for themselves! Comment seems unnecessary! In my mind Osbaldeston is either a totally depraved being, lacking every sense of honor or shame, or else a lunatic, for such only could spread such vile literature.

> As regards the case itself, Osbaldeston admits having shot into the crowd with intent to kill. He killed two men. He is now represented by, as it seems, a competent lawyer, and I have no reason to believe that the courts will not give him a fair trial. On receipt of the Embassy's letter, I communicated with Herr Rechtsanwalt Lanser, and beg to enclose the latter's reply herewith. In my mind the case promises to be such a filthy one that I see no reason for the intervention of the Embassy.[25]

In his acknowledgement of receipt of Consul Schumann's letter of October 3, embassy secretary John B. Jackson stated, "The Embassy agrees with you in the opinion that, under the circumstances and for the present at least, the case is not one in which diplomatic action is necessary."[26]

Flashing forward twenty-four years, on March 30, 1926, Edwin told newspaper reporters that his trip to Germany had been an "affair of honor" and that he had fought a "duel" for the woman he loved. He went on to say, "For this affair I was arrested and brought to trial. After the hearing, and on order of the Kaiser of Germany, I was given the freedom of any German city that I might choose. For sixteen months I enjoyed unbridled hospitality. I was feted and treated with the consideration given royalty, and finally, after the American ambassador, a Mr. Tower, intervened, secured my release."[25]

The only speck of truth in this illogical tale was the name of the American ambassador. It was neither an "affair of honor" nor a "duel." At close range he shot an unarmed man in the back, killing him, and fatally wounded a bystander. Their deaths left ten children fatherless. Edwin expressed no remorse or shame. Instead, he cast himself as a hero.

On November 20, 1902, Edwin wrote a fairly similar but shorter letter to the new United States ambassador to Germany, Charlemagne Tower Jr. The letter began by asking for a fair trial and reporting what had transpired since his last letter to the ambassador.

> Letter No 1.
>
> Königliches Gefägness
> Saarbrücken
> November 20, 1902
>
> To The United States of America
> Ambassador Extraordinary
> To Germany ————
>
> The Honorable Charlemagne Tower:
>
> Herewith I most respectfully desire to inform you that I am a prisoner in the above named Institution and petition you in your official capacity to use your influence with Judge Herr Seibert, and Herr Heckelsberg I. Staatsanwalt of Saarbrücken to grant me a fair trial which I am entitled to—by Judge and Jury.
>
> I make this application on the grounds that a certain *semi* local government official informed me a week ago that I would not be tried at all but sent to the Bonn Provincial Hospital for life –
>
> On September 29th I was kindly sent there six weeks for examination by the said Judge Seibert and returned here on November 9th feeling less nervous.
>
> On my return, the said *semi* official also informed me that Dr. Pellmann the Director had written during the first week I was at the hospital to a person in Saarbrücken that he Dr. Pellmann considered me insane, and that this fact was again communicated to my Frau Louisa W. Osbaldeston against whom I formerly made serious charges verbally and in print of extreme immoral conduct supported by a very large quantity of undeniable proofs including a sworn to descriptive document by Mrs. Alice Agnes T. Osbaldeston of 7 West 63rd St. New York City and who followed & exposed Louisa to many places in the United States and even to England.[28]

The letter continued for several more pages repeating much of what was stated in his letter of September 24. Meanwhile, the German consul in New York was called upon to assist with fact-finding for the upcoming Osbaldeston murder trial. Its inquiry moved to Malone, where the residents were treated to yet another round of the exploits of Edwin and Louise. The Syracuse *Post Standard* reported the following:

> Malone, Dec. 19.—Rudolf Dalson, a lawyer, residing in New York city, accompanied by Berthold Schmidt, a stenographer, representing the German Consul General of that city and the Superior Court of Germany, has been in Malone for the purpose of looking up history, character and habits of one "Dr." Edwin T. Osbaldeston, and also a woman named Louise Metzgar, both of whom made a precipitate exit from Malone

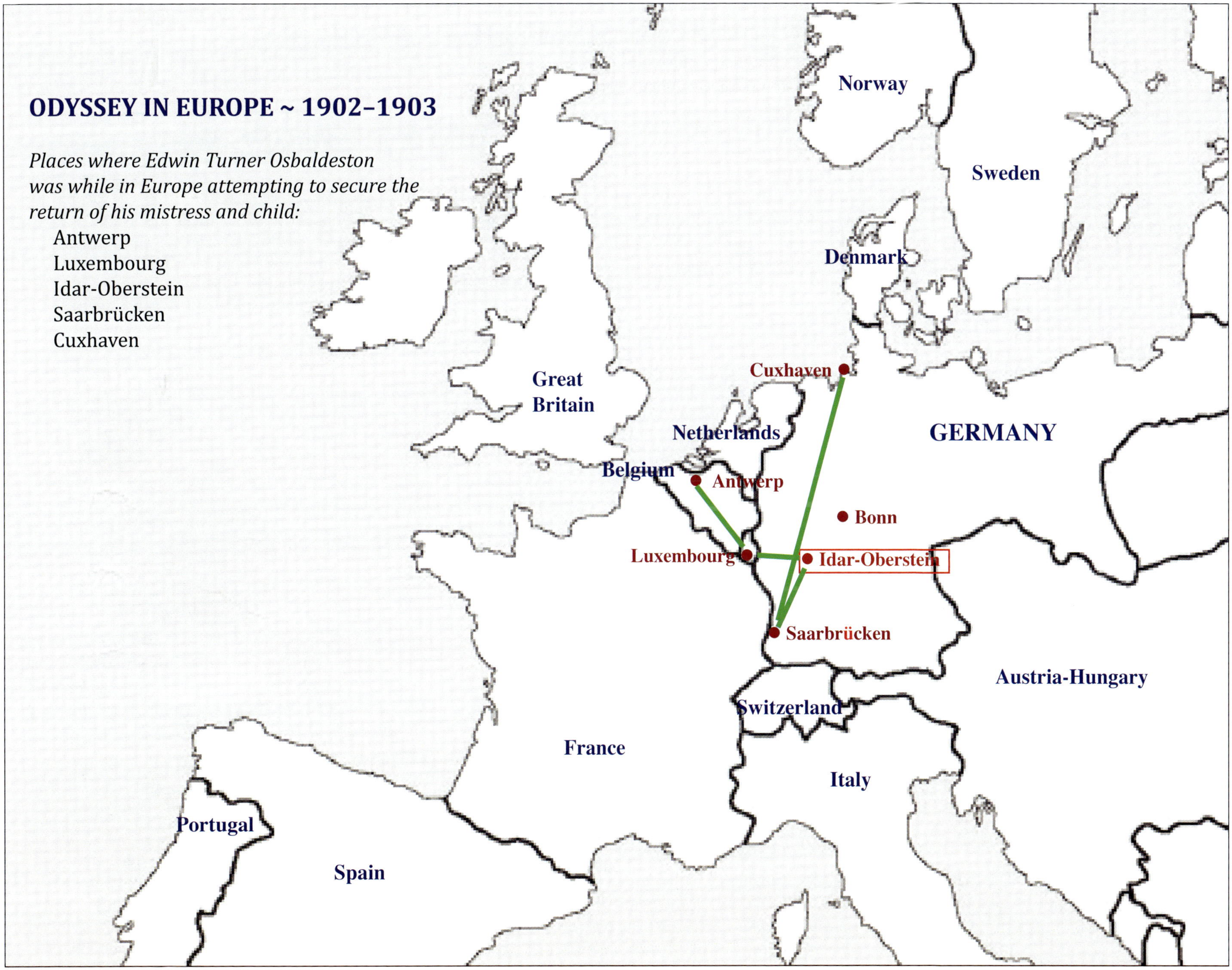

ODYSSEY IN EUROPE ~ 1902–1903
Places where Edwin Turner Osbaldeston was while in Europe attempting to secure the return of his mistress and child:
Antwerp
Luxembourg
Idar-Oberstein
Saarbrücken
Cuxhaven
Norway
Sweden
Denmark
Great Britain
Cuxhaven
Netherlands
GERMANY
Belgium
Antwerp
Bonn
Luxembourg
Idar-Oberstein
Saarbrücken
Austria-Hungary
Switzerland
France
Italy
Portugal
Spain

> in 1897. At present Osbaldeston is said to be in prison in Saarbrutek [sic], Prussia, charged with the murder of two men, one a wealthy man named Wilde [sic].
>
> It is alleged that the Metzgar woman followed Osbaldeston in Europe, where she met Wilde [sic], who became infatuated with her, leading to insane jealousy on the part of Osbaldeston, who is alleged to have murdered Wilde [sic] on that account. The attorney referred to has been taking depositions here relative to what is known of Osbaldesten and the woman. The career of both in Malone was short. They were arrested and placed in jail on a charge of stealing goods from Fay Bros.' store. The woman managed to escape, while Osbaldeston succeeded in obtaining bail in the sum of $700, which he promptly jumped and "skipped the country." He had not been heard of since until this report of his incarceration in Germany was made known here.[29]

In 1926 a Malone judge would recall having been told by the consular agent who visited the city in 1902 that under Prussian law the punishment for the alleged crime (murder) was decapitation by the sword.[30]

As Edwin had stated in his letters to the United States consul and ambassador to Germany, once he collected his daughter at Oberstein, he had planned to relocate to Wiesbaden, one of Europe's oldest spa towns famous for its hot springs, to reestablish his practice. He carried a large sum of money to Germany for this purpose. After his arrest these funds were deposited in a German bank by his defense counsel. Upon learning this, the families of the victims used legal means to seize the funds, jeopardizing Edwin's ability to pay his lawyer.[31]

The German court ruled on June 8, 1903, that Edwin was insane, but rather than commit him to an asylum, it preferred to have him deported. He was released from prison on June 26 and resided at Hotel Bristol in Saarbrücken until arrangements for his deportation were completed. Edwin, eager to leave the country, ran into a bureaucratic difficulty. Once more he turned to the United States consul and ambassador for assistance.

THE PITTSBURG PRESS.

LATEST NEWS
CLOSING STOCK QUOTATIONS

PITTSBURG, PA., TUESDAY EVENING, JUNE 24, 1902—SIXTEEN PAGES — ONE CENT

TWO MEN SLAIN BY A DOCTOR AND TEN CHILDREN HIS VICTIMS

How Prof. Edwin T. Osbaldesten Satisfied His Terrible Thirst for Blood of Edward Wild, of Oberstein, Germany—He Sends Money to Orphan Children From Prison.

News of the murders of Eduard Wild and Wilhelm Baumhardt reached Pittsburgh weeks later. On June 24, 1902, the Pittsburg Press *ran an illustrated, front-page story on the matter. The coverage was in keeping with sensationalized news of the penny press. Early reports misspelled Edwin's last name and gave the wrong middle name. The paper's masthead appears above and the illustration is on the following page. (Note: From 1891 to 1911 Pittsburgh dropped the "h" in the spelling of the city's name.)*

The court required that he be escorted to the point of embarkation by the local police. The local police informed Edwin that it did not have the authority to deploy an officer to a far-away port.

In his letter to the consul dated June 29, he stated, "It is therefore suggested to me that I write my country's representatives . . . to send a person here for that purpose all expenses incurred therewith to be defrayed out of my available funds, I would gladly go myself and report to the local police at the port of sailing but that is not permissible. Failing to find such aide the police say they have no other alternative than to place me in some lunatic hospital, a worse fate than the guillotine & of the two I would prefer the latter rather than be constantly haunted with the knowledge that my large family of young children . . . continue to suffer from my absence. . . ."[32]

The consul in Mainz wrote to Edwin in Saarbrücken on July 6 and July 8 regarding his trip to the seaport. Edwin's name appeared on the passenger list for the Hamburg-American Line's SS *Moltke* that was scheduled to sail from Cuxhaven, the port of Hamburg, to New York on July 23, 1903. However, instead of leaving Germany on that ship, he sailed two days later on board the North German Lloyd's SS *Prinz Sigismund*. He arrived back in New York on August 8, 1903.

Although he was leaving Germany under the most personally advantageous circumstances given his offense, Edwin continued to obsess over Weiss. Prior to leaving Germany, Edwin had sent a threat-

HOW E. T. OSBALDESTEN, OF PITTSBURG, KILLED TWO MEN IN OBERSTEIN, GERMANY, ON MAY 5.

ening letter to Weiss, who was now back in Pittsburgh. After the murder of Eduard Wild, she was held partly to blame for his demise. She fled Oberstein and returned to America.

Weiss married thirty-year-old William Frank Lucas on June 11, 1903, in Beaver, a town thirty-four miles northwest of Pittsburgh popular for weddings. Lucas had a daughter from a previous relationship. She reported the threats to the Pittsburgh authorities. Stories about the threats appeared in several newspapers. Edwin had claimed that he would be arriving in Philadelphia on the SS *Westernland* on July 28.

> Believing they had within reach a man accused of enslaving a Pittsburg girl with a marriage certificate she says was forged, detectives hunted from cabins to steerage through the steamship Westernland when she arrived from Liverpool at her wharf yesterday afternoon.
>
> They were unsuccessful, however. They could find none among the passengers answering the description of Theobald Osbaldesten [sic] the man sought. Osbaldesten, it seems, had written that he would sail on the Westernland, but when the hunt for him was over the searching party gave expression to the opinion that he was trying to throw his American acquaintances off the track.
>
> The woman he claims as his wife declares she is Miss Louise Day [should be Weiss] and not Mrs. Osbaldesten. She asserts that when he is arrested she purposes prosecuting him.
>
> **Shot Man For Her**
> The couple lived together in Pittsburg until about one year ago. Then Osbaldesten went to Germany and shot a man whom he accused of breaking up his home. Since that time Miss Day [Weiss] has declared they were never married legally; that alleged proofs of their marriage sent to Germany to help in getting Osbaldesten out of trouble were false and that she would make trouble for the man if he returned.
>
> A few days ago she gave out this statement to a newspaper for publication concerning assertions reported to have been made by Osbaldesten:

Kept Her Prisoner

"I personally reply that all reports, letters and statements made by Osbaldesten are without foundation. He has no claim on me whatever as I was kept a prisoner by him as long as we were together. He made me work at times as in slave days. The papers which he produced in the courts of Germany alleging that I was his wife were all forged. I will uncover his doings to the public as soon as he lands. . . ."[33]

His obsession with Weiss continued after he arrived in New York from Germany. The day after his arrival, Edwin mailed a package to Weiss/Lucas containing pieces of the bloodstained shirt and bullet-pierced cloth said to have been from Eduard Wild. (It was reported that the evidence in the Wild and Baumhardt murder cases was returned to Edwin by German authorities when he was released from jail.)[34]

The note that accompanied the pieces of shirt stated in part, "The scene of the trouble has been removed to America and will have to be gone over again."[35] Understandably, Lucas took this as a threat on his life and went to police. A warrant was issued in Pittsburgh for the arrest of Osbaldeston.

During the two-week period of August 15–29, 1903, the Pittsburgh and New York newspapers followed the story, often reported with dramatic headlines.

The *Pittsburg Post* and the New York *Sun* reported that Mrs. Frank Lucas had barricaded herself in her home at 6319 Broad Street in Pittsburgh, fearing death at the hand of an assassin. Professor E. T. Osbaldeston had written from Germany that he was coming to Pittsburgh to claim Mrs. Lucas as his wife.

In addition to the threats, Edwin mailed copies of the inflammatory pamphlet that he had published, and originally sent to people in Oberstein, to discredit Weiss as an unfit mother and wife. Lucas sought the assistance of United States postal authorities on grounds of libel and sending obscene materials through he mail. (Several reporters had indicated the contents of the brochure were not fit for publication.) The Pittsburgh postmaster declined to rule on the claim and forwarded the complaint to postal officials in Philadelphia, and later to Washington, DC. No charges were ever filed against Edwin for mailing obscene materials.[36]

Pittsburgh police monitored the arrival of trains into the city and guarded the Lucas home.[36] Edwin denied sending threatening letters to Weiss. He said he was only coming to Pittsburgh to collect his daughter.

In an article published in the *Pittsburg Press* on August 19, Louise stated the following:

> With regard to Osbaldeston, he has been bothering people in Germany for 18 months. Evidently, he is out of his mind, otherwise he would not write such crazy stuff. He will not fool my husband, Mr. Lugas [sic], as he seems to have done with German authorities. He is a most peculiar man, at one time seeming altogether rational, but suddenly he will act very strangely.
>
> To me, it is odd that he is not afraid to continue writing such matter now, as I would think he would have enough trouble in Germany, without stirring up more here. I did not have the least apprehension as far as he was concerned, until I received the threatening letter and the bloody exhibit. On receipt of that, however, I had to take precautions, and my husband will see that they are protected.[38]

Louise's husband retaliated.

> Pittsburg, Aug. 24.—Frank W. Lugas [sic] last night closed his Broad Street home and took his family to New York, where he will have a settlement with "Prof." E. T. Osbaldesten, who has been annoying Mrs. Lugas [sic] through the mails.
>
> Before going Lugas [sic] told neighbors that he visited Osbaldesten in New York last week while absent from Pittsburg. He said he informed the Professor that he was a newspaper reporter. The Professor talked freely of his plans relating to Mrs. Lugas [sic], and the irate husband finally placed his card in Osbaldesten's hand and a pistol under the Professor's nose and advised him that if he ever annoyed Mrs. Lugas [sic] again he would be killed.
>
> Lugas [sic] told his neighbors he was going to New York to prosecute Osbaldesten and he would be home about Sept. 1.[39]

Edwin would recall this meeting with Lucas as a cordial chat over a few glasses of wine.[40]

On Lucas's return to New York City, he sought to have Edwin prosecuted. Tipped off by a reporter that Lucas was arriving in New York, Edwin fled the city for Asbury Park. Next, Frank and Louise secured a search warrant of Edwin's residence. There, in the presence of a constable, they took documents relating to Louise from a trunk belonging to Edwin and two paintings of Louise.[41]

In the midst of the news reports, one thoughtful reporter for the *Pittsburg Gazette* realized that Edwin had been referring to Louise as his "common-law" wife. He suggested that Edwin should be charged with bigamy in New York since he had not obtained a divorce from his "real wife."[42] Nothing came of that suggestion.

Having been told he would be arrested if he went to Pittsburgh, Edwin had the good sense to remain in New York. Either that or his family members prevailed upon him not to go there. And so he ended his ties with Louise Weiss and returned to Alice Agnes. However, he could not resist writing one more letter. In mid-September the Pittsburgh police received a missive from Edwin abusing Louise and stating that he will be in Pittsburgh "before winter has well started."[43]

When informed of the latest letter and that it was postmarked in New York, Frank Lucas asserted, "He doesn't dare go there as the police are watching for him." He further proclaimed that Edwin was in Asbury Park.[44]

Questions remain. Was Edwin really insane? Had his overwrought emotional state driven him to revenge and murder? Did he feign mental illness to escape more difficult consequences? For certain, Edwin was in denial over his actions.

Several weeks after arriving in New York, Edwin was interviewed by a reporter for the *Syracuse Journal*. The article contained many errors of fact, and it appeared that the reporter accepted everything Edwin purported as the truth. The *Journal* headline said it all, "Reads Like One of Hope's Novels; Dr. Osbaldesten of New York Tells a Story of Love, Feud and Blood. Left his Wife, Lived with Another, She Estranged, Her Admirer Shot by Him."[45]

Edwin put a new spin on the events of 1902 and 1903 that romanticized the ugly truth. He told the *Journal* it was Wild who had threatened him in a letter, saying that he would be lynched or shot in a duel. When he saw Mascot outside Wild's house, he was clubbed on the head from behind as he bent down to hug his daughter. With the threatening mob gathered before him, he fired at its leader and then again. Wild lay dead. He then turned the revolver on himself, determined to die rather than be bowled over by the mob, but the mob dispersed. He sought the protection of the *Bürgermeister*, who told him that the sympathies of the town were with him, and for his protection was placed in Saarbrücken Castle.

When Louise Weiss attempted to leave town, her carriage was mobbed by the townspeople, and she abandoned her flight. She then became repentant and begged Edwin to give her his love again and promised to return to him. It was determined by the emperor that Edwin had fired in self-defense. Louise and daughter were sent to America. Upon his release from the castle, he was feted at a banquet by the townspeople for his bravery. As he departed Germany, he was given an envelope and told not to open it and when he reached America to send it to his wife (Weiss). After Weiss received the envelope, he learned that it contained the bloody shirts of the men he had killed in self-defense.[46]

Surely, that was how Edwin wanted to remember the episode. Once again he donned the veil of the victim, hoping to escape judgment and condemnation for his actions. In his delusional state, he had found a sympathetic reporter who was only too willing to provide that cover. In all probability, Edwin had worked his persuasive powers on the reporter who accepted the tale without fact checking. Anyone who had been victimized by Edwin would doubt the veracity of the story. Many readers may have been entertained by the tale and even admired the man who survived the ordeal. As for his family, they distanced themselves from Weiss, Mascot, and the deaths of Wild and Baumhardt.

In any event, Germany had rid itself of a problem, and Edwin had yet again dodged the most serious consequences—in this instance execution—for his criminal behavior. Once more, Edwin was a free man.

NOTES

1. *Franklin Gazette* (Malone, NY), 26 May 1899, p. 3, col. b.
2. *Malone Palladium* (NY), 25 May 1899, p. 3, col. b.
3. "United States Census, 1900," database with images, *FamilySearch*, accessed 7 August 2015, https://familysearch.org/ark:/61903/1:1:MSV5-YZ7, Edwin Osbaldeston, Borough of Manhattan, Election District 9 New York City Ward 19, New York County, New York, United States; citing sheet 8B, family 211, NARA microfilm publication T623 (Washington, DC: National Archives and Records Administration, n.d.); FHL microfilm 1,241,102.
4. "United States Census, 1900," database with images, *FamilySearch*, accessed 7 August 2015, https://familysearch.org/ark:/61903/1:1:MS1P-F2G, Edwin Osbaldeston, Precinct 1 Pittsburgh city Ward 20, Allegheny, Pennsylvania, United States; citing sheet 1A, family 5, NARA microfilm publication T623 (Washington, DC: National Archives and Records Administration, n.d.); FHL microfilm 1,241,361.
5. "Personal," *Pittsburg Post*, 18 March 1900, p. 23, col. e.
6. "Police Becoming Men of Grace," *Pittsburg Press*, 30 September 1900, p. 7.
7. Dispatch from Pittsburgh published in *Malone Farmer* (NY), 18 June 1902, p. 4, col. b.
8. "Gusky Home and Orphanage," accessed 18 March 2014, http://www.jewish-history-hhc.org.
9. "Gusky Home Notes," *Jewish Criterion* (Pittsburgh and Philadelphia), 3 May 1901, p. 10, col. b; 24 May 1901, p. 3, col. b; 12 July 1901, p. 9, col. c; 25 October 1901, p. 9, col. c; and 21 February 1902, p. 9, col. a.
10. Edwin Turner Osbaldeston, State Prison, Saarbrücken, to US Embassy, Berlin, 24 September 1902; vol. 261, folios 511–516; US Embassy, Berlin, Germany. Miscellaneous Correspondence; July 1, 1902–December 31, 1902; Records of Foreign Service Posts of the Department of State, 1788–1964, Record Group 84, UD Entry 24; National Archives at College Park, College Park, Maryland.
11. Ibid.
12. National Archives and Records Administration (NARA); Washington DC; NARA Series: *Passport Applications, 1795–1905*; Roll #: *592*; Volume #: *Roll 592 - 01 Feb 1902–28 Feb 1902*; Ancestry.com. *U. S. Passport Applications, 1795–1925* [database on-line]. Provo, UT, USA: Ancestry.com Operations, Inc., 2007.
13. Dispatch from Pittsburgh published in *Malone Farmer* (NY), 18 June 1902, p. 4, col. b.

14. Edwin Turner Osbaldeston, State Prison, Saarbrücken, to US Embassy, Berlin, 24 September 1902; vol. 261, folios 511–516; US Embassy, Berlin, Germany. Miscellaneous Correspondence; July 1, 1902–December 31, 1902; Records of Foreign Service Posts of the Department of State, 1788–1964, Record Group 84, UD Entry 24; National Archives at College Park, College Park, Maryland.
15. Edwin Turner Osbaldeston, State Prison, Saarbrücken, to US Embassy, Berlin, 24 September 1902; vol. 261, folios 511–516; US Embassy, Berlin, Germany. Miscellaneous Correspondence; July 1, 1902–December 31, 1902; Records of Foreign Service Posts of the Department of State, 1788–1964, Record Group 84, UD Entry 24; National Archives at College Park, College Park, Maryland.
16. Article that appeared in the newspaper *Nahethal-Bote* (Oberstein, Rheinland-Palatinate, Germany), 6 May 1902. Courtesy of archivist Manfred Rauscher of the Stadtarchiv Idar-Oberstein, e-mail message to Noël Siver, 7 February 2008. Translated by Noël Siver.
17. *Nahethal-Bote* (Oberstein, Germany), 7 May 1902. Courtesy of archivist Manfred Rauscher, Stadtarchiv Idar-Oberstein, e-mail message to Noël Siver, 7 February 2008. Translated by Noël Siver.
18. *Nahethal-Bote* (Oberstein, Germany), 9 May 1902. Courtesy of archivist Manfred Rauscher, Stadtarchiv Idar-Oberstein, e-mail message to Noël Siver, 13 February 2008. Translated by Noël Siver.
19. *Nahethal-Bote* (Oberstein, Germany), 23 May 1902. Courtesy of archivist Manfred Rauscher, Stadtarchiv Idar-Oberstein, e-mail message to Noël Siver, 7 February 2008. Translated by Noël Siver.
20. Edwin Turner Osbaldeston, State Prison, Saarbrücken, to US Embassy, Berlin, 24 September 1902; vol. 261, folios 511–516; US Embassy, Berlin, Germany. Miscellaneous Correspondence; July 1, 1902–December 31, 1902; Records of Foreign Service Posts of the Department of State, 1788–1964, Record Group 84, UD Entry 24; National Archives at College Park, College Park, Maryland.
21. Ibid.
22. Ibid.
23. Ibid.
24. John B. Jackson, secretary, US Embassy, Berlin to Walter Schumann, consul, US Consulate, Mainz, 29 September 1902; vol. 185, folio 37; US Embassy, Berlin, Germany. Miscellaneous Correspondence; Outgoing, September 19, 1902–April 1, 1903; Records of Foreign Service Posts of the Department of State, 1788–1964, Record Group 84, UD Entry 24; National Archives at College Park, College Park, Maryland.
25. Walter Schumann, consul, US Consulate, Mainz to Andrew D. White, ambassador, US Embassy, Berlin, 3 October 1902; vol. 261, folios 509–510; US Embassy, Berlin, Germany. Miscellaneous Correspondence; July 1, 1902–December 31, 1902; Records of Foreign Service Posts of the Department of State, 1788–1964, Record Group 84, UD Entry 24; National Archives at College Park, College Park, Maryland.
26. John B. Jackson, secretary, US Embassy, Berlin to Walter Schumann, consul, US Consulate, Mainz, 6 October 1902; vol. 185, folio 76; US Embassy, Berlin, Germany. Miscellaneous Correspondence; Outgoing, September 19, 1902–April 1, 1903; Records of Foreign Service Posts of the Department of State, 1788–1964, Record Group 84, UD Entry 24. National Archives at College Park, College Park, Maryland.
27. "Strain Telling Upon Old Crimean Veteran," *Asbury Park Evening Press* (NJ), 30 March 1926, p. 2, col. a.
28. Edwin Turner Osbaldeston, State Prison, Saarbrücken, to Charlemagne Tower, ambassador, US Embassy, Berlin, 20 November 1902; vol. 261, folio 720; US Embassy, Berlin, Germany. Miscellaneous Correspondence; July 1, 1902–December 31, 1902; Records of Foreign Service Posts of the Department of State, 1788–1964, Record Group 84, UD Entry 24; National Archives at College Park, College Park, Maryland.
29. "Osbaldeston in Germany. The Doctor Said to Be in Prison. Charged With Murder," *Post Standard* (Syracuse, NY), 20 December 1902, p. 14, col. e.
30. "Osbaldeston Was Once of Malone," *Watertown Daily Times* (NY), 29 March 1926, p. 8, col. e.
31. "Germans Seize His Money. American Accused of Murder at Oberstein Loses Means of Defense," *Logansport Morning Journal* (IN), 24 October 1902, p. 1, col. b.
32. Edwin Turner Osbaldeston, Hotel Bristol, Saarbrücken to Secretary, US Embassy, Berlin, Germany, 29 June 1903; vol. 264, folio 618; US Embassy, Berlin, Germany. Miscellaneous Correspondence; 1903, O-Z; Records of Foreign Service Posts of the Department of State, 1788–1964, Record Group 84, UD Entry 24; National Archives at College Park, College Park, Maryland.
33. "Says That He Enslaved Her; Police Seek Man Whom Girl Says Kept Her a Prisoner. Denies She Was Wife," *Telegram* (Syracuse, NY), 29 July 1903, p. 4, col. d.
34. "Osbaldeston Sends Note of Death," *Pittsburg Post,* 15 August 1903, p. 1.
35. Ibid.
36. "Has Appealed to the Postal Authorities," *Pittsburg Press*, 17 August 1903, p. 1.
37. "She Fears Assassination. Former Husband of a Pittsburg Woman Writes That He Is Coming to Kill Her," *Sun* (New York, NY), 16 August 1903, p. 1, col. e.
38. "Lugas' Appeal May Succeed," *Pittsburg Press*, 19 August 1903, p. 1.
39. "Letter Writer Threatened," *New York Times,* 25 August 1903, p. 2.
40. "Trip Was Not Fruitful," *Pittsburg Gazette*, 29 August 1903, p. 2.
41. "Lugas Makes Search of Osbaldeston's House." *Pittsburg Press*, 29 August 1903, p. 2.
42. "Moving with Caution in Osbaldesten Case," *Pittsburg Gazette*, 22 August 1903, p. 12.
43. "Osbaldesten Writes Again," *Pittsburg Gazette*, 16 September 1903, p. 6.
44. Ibid.
45. "Reads Like One of Hope's Novels; Dr. Osbaldesten of New York Tells a Story of Love, Feud and Blood. Left his Wife, Lived with Another, She Estranged, Her Admirer Shot by Him," *Syracuse Journal* (NY), 19 August 1903, p. 3.
46. Ibid.

CHAPTER SIXTEEN

Return to New York City ~ 1903–1919

The saying "There's no such thing as bad publicity except your own obituary" could certainly apply to Edwin Turner Osbaldeston. Fallout from the tragic events in Germany appeared to have minimal, if any, impact in New York on Edwin. In effect, he had "gotten away with murder" and his life resumed following what had been a temporary detention.

Once back in the city, he began rebuilding his practice as a masseur. The pattern was the same—he was up, he was down, he was back up again. Edwin did not resurrect the New York School of Training for Massage but taught and performed massage. Without Weiss and Mascot, his life returned to what would be considered "normal" for him. He was reunited with Alice Agnes and his family. His children were growing up and the older ones beginning to move on.

Among his clients in late 1904 was fifty-eight-year-old Brodie L. Duke. Duke, along with his half brothers James and Benjamin, had entered their father's tobacco company W. Duke, Sons & Co. in North Carolina. Similar to the consolidation taking place in many other American industries, in 1890 the Dukes bought out four other tobacco companies to form the behemoth American Tobacco Company. That year American Tobacco produced 90 percent of all cigarettes made in the United States.[1]

Following an acrimonious divorce from his second wife earlier in the year, Brodie Duke had become involved with Alice Webb, a scheming woman who wanted him to help her buy a tobacco plantation in Nacogdoches, Texas, that she had optioned. Webb's

Alice Webb Duke

Tobacco mogul Brodie L. Duke

friend, Agnes Desplaines, introduced Edwin to Duke and Webb. Edwin had known Desplaines for years, having treated her previously. Edwin went to the Hotel Winton, 110th Street and Park Avenue, Manhattan, where they were staying and treated all three of them.

After a couple of visits, Edwin became convinced that the two women were taking advantage of Duke, who was an alcoholic.[2] Alarmed, he contacted Duke's half brother Benjamin to advise him of his suspicions. The *New York Times* reported Edwin's involvement in the matter.

> **SAYS MRS. DUKE IS MRS. POWELL.**
> The doctor [Edwin] said his next meeting with Mrs. Duke occurred on the evening of Dec. 9. Mrs. Desplaines came to his home in a carriage just before 11 o'clock and told him she had a good patient for him. He was taken to the Hotel Winton. Here he was introduced to a woman as Miss Webb, and was surprised to recognize in her the Mrs. Powell of years ago.
>
> "Look here, doctor," the woman said, pointing to a man in bed: "Here is a patient worth having. He is a member of the Duke family, the wealthy tobacco men. He is Brodie L. Duke, the power behind the throne, who has gotten the Dukes all the money they have. He is worth $20,000,000 in his own right. We are going to get married."
>
> Dr. Osbaldeston said he found Mr. Duke under the influence of drugs. He was very weak. "I worked with him until after 3 in the morning," he said. "When I was through Mrs. Desplaines mixed something in two glasses. The fluid in one glass looked like milk, that in the other like whisky. She poured the contents of both glasses together and gave it to Duke, who in a few minutes fell back on his pillow, his jaw dropping and the man breathing hard."
>
> On the day before the marriage, Dr. Osbaldeston said, he called again to give Mr. Duke the usual massage treatment, but found him so low that he insisted upon having a medical practitioner called in. The next day, in the evening, when he returned he was told by Mrs. Desplaines that Miss Webb and Mr. Duke had gone down town to get married.
>
> "I expressed surprise," said Dr. Osbaldeston, "and told Mrs. Desplaines that I feared there would be trouble. She said: 'There won't be, if you keep your mouth shut. You are too talkative, anyhow, and don't mind your own business enough.'"
>
> On the day after the marriage Dr. Osbaldeston said he called again, and that Mrs. Duke met him at the door and held a little book up for him to look at. The book

> contained the marriage certificate.
>
> "Now, address me as Mrs. Duke, worth $20,000,000," he says the woman told him. "Oh, my God, what have I not gone through and suffered this last few weeks to get to this. I can't tell you, but now, thank God, it is all over."
>
> The doctor said she told the same thing to Dr. [Maurice] Sturm, who called shortly afterward, and to several of the servants about the hotel.[3]

Benjamin Duke, who had been staying at the Hoffman House in New York, had Edwin meet with his lawyers to relate what he had witnessed. Due to Brodie Duke's alcoholism and a string of failed investments, his half brothers had removed him from control of the American Tobacco Company.

The Duke family reacted very negatively to the news of the marriage of Brodie L. Duke and Alice Webb on December 19, 1904. Duke had given a number of prenuptial promises and promissory notes to Webb. Just before the couple were married she had cashed a $4,000 check from Brodie, which was added to the $15,000 in notes that he had signed.[4]

The family immediately set the wheels in motion to have the marriage annulled. First, family lawyers obtained a court order for his commitment to a sanitarium, pleading that he was temporarily insane due to intoxication.[5] As part of the legal proceedings, Edwin was called on to provide testimony to the District Attorney's office.

> Assistant District Attorney Lord will examine several witnesses in connection with the case today. . . . Among the persons Mr. Lord questioned yesterday were Dr. Maurice A. Sturm of 1620 Madison Avenue, who attended Mr. Duke and his bride both before and after the wedding, and Dr. E. T. Osbaldeston of 7 West Sixty-Third Street, a masseur, who also attended them and Mrs. Agnes Desplaines professionally.
>
> Dr. Osbaldeston, it was said, told the Assistant District Attorney that when he saw the woman who afterward became Mrs. Duke she said to Duke that she was the daughter of William H. Webb, the philanthropist who founded the Webb Academy and Home for Shipbuilders on University Heights. She also said, according to Dr. Osbaldeston, that she was a relative of the Vanderbilts and of Dr. W. Seward Webb.
>
> Dr. Osbaldeston came to the District Attorney's office late in the afternoon and remained in the Criminal Courts Building closeted with Mr. Lord, for more than an hour, and was instructed to return again today for further examination. When he left the building he was accompanied by several county detectives to make sure that nobody could approach and question him.[6]

For Edwin this experience was a bit of role reversal. The woman calling herself Alice Webb was obviously a fraud. William H. Webb, the New York shipbuilding tycoon and philanthropist, had two sons and no daughters. Edwin recalled meeting the new Mrs. Duke five or six years earlier when she went by the name of Alice Powell and was sharing a flat on West Sixty-Fourth Street with Desplaines, whom he had known for even longer. He said at the time Webb/Powell/Duke was connected to a man who operated a number of sporting establishments in the city and Long Branch, New Jersey.

For the assistant district attorney, Edwin recalled his conversation with the woman Webb/Powell after she had been introduced to him:

> "Doctor, possibly you don't know it, but I am a relative of the Vanderbilts."
>
> "Oh, indeed," the doctor replied.
>
> "Yes," Mrs. Duke said, "and Dr. Seward Webb is my cousin."
>
> "Now, how can that be?" the doctor answered. "Gen. Webb was my patient, and I knew all his children as they grew up, but I cannot place you."
>
> "I don't care whether you believe it or not," said the woman then, "but W. H. Webb is my father."
>
> "What are you talking about?" the doctor says he said. "He is my patient at the present time. My children gave the first library to the Home for Shipbuilders he founded on University Heights."[7]

W. Seward Webb had married a Vanderbilt and may have been Edwin's patient in 1905, but William H. Webb certainly was not. He had died in 1899. As for donating a library, that was highly unlikely and there was no documentation of that. The exchange was a verbal volley between two grifters. Alice Webb/Powell/Duke, for the moment, stuck to her story.

Sobered up, Brodie Duke sued for divorce on the grounds that he had no recollection of ever marrying the woman. Edwin's testimony helped secure the divorce, which was finalized in April 1906. Duke married for a fourth time in 1910.

Left: At age seventeen daughter Geneva married Frederick Miller. Left center: Normandie married James Siver of Albany, New York. Center right: Daughters Alberta, Ethel, and Geneva

Edwin's Children Come of Age

In his own family, daughter Geneva married widower Frederick B. Miller on January 28, 1903, while Edwin was imprisoned in Germany. A hotel manager, Miller was forty-five and Geneva, seventeen. Months earlier Geneva had left home to become a chorus girl and was reportedly abducted by a man known as Kid Levinson. After the fuss subsided, she returned home unharmed two weeks later.

At the time, Miller happened to live down the street from the Osbaldestons. When Edwin returned he made it known that he did not approve of the marriage and began harassing Miller by showing up at his workplace and creating a scene. Miller twice lost his employment as a result. He finally had enough and sought the assistance of the court. Miller wanted Edwin's sanity examined. He wrote to Alice Agnes that if she would bring Edwin to court, and if his mental state warranted it, he would help her place Edwin in an asylum and drop the harassment charges. Instead, Miller was arrested for libel.[8] Eventually, the harassment stopped. Geneva remained married to Miller until his death in July 1926.

Next daughter to marry was Normandie, who wed James Henry Siver, of Albany, on June 20, 1908. Always very possessive of his daughters, this time Edwin did not appear to have any objections. Siver was two years younger than his bride, who was twenty-one at the time of their nuptials. Perhaps Edwin approved of the union as Norma (the name she preferred to be called) was similar in temperament to her father, strong-willed and opinionated. She was not known to be meek.

Their only child, Kenneth Ludbrooke Siver, was born on May 22, 1909. The Sivers lived in Manhattan for a couple of years before James took jobs in Schenectady, New York, and later East Orange, New Jersey, creating a good distance between his family and the menacing father-in-law.

The youngest daughter, Alberta, had a turbulent relationship with her father. Her sister Normandie

Alberta Osbaldeston at seventeen (1908)

recalled her at fourteen as a sad, rebellious teen. "She longed to develop her great talent instead of becoming a household drudge. . . . She was often beaten—her hair pulled savagely [by her father]. . . ." She also recalled, "Alberta was so talented and so beautiful. She had beautiful, large brown eyes and light golden hair that curled slightly. She showed great talent for painting and drawing at four and five years of age."[9]

In the United States census of 1910, Alberta, who was eighteen, gave her occupation as "actress" and her industry as "theatre." In June that year she had a role in *The Barnyard Romeo*, described in *Leslie's Weekly* as "a Viennese musical satire on 'Chantecler' at the American Roof Garden."[10] She used the stage name Alberta Ludbrook. (Ludbrook was a family name on her mother's side.) Alberta was also a model, appearing in magazine advertisements and on the cover of the September 1911 issue of *Cosmopolitan*. While climbing out a window in order to leave the house without her father knowing it, Alberta slipped, fell, and broke her left leg. The broken bone did not heal properly, and this left her in pain and/or with a limp.

At the end of February 1914, Alberta married artist/illustrator Philip Plaistridge in Philadelphia. She was twenty-three and he, twenty-eight. She married Plaistridge to escape her father. They sailed from New York to Europe on May 2, 1914, on the SS *Minneapolis*. A fellow passenger was noted landscape and marine artist Charles Paul Gruppé. Alberta traveled with Gruppé to study painting in Holland.

She experienced some success as a young artist. The *Twenty-Sixth Annual Exhibition of American Oil Paintings and Sculpture* of the Art Institute of Chicago included her painting titled *Bay of Fundy,* and a year later the Art Institute's *Exhibition of Water Colors, Pastels and Miniatures by American Artists* featured her watercolor *The Lowlands.*[11] [12]

The *Atlanta Constitution* noted, "Mrs. Alberta Ludbrook Plaistridge, who has charge here of the Gruppé collection being shown in Edison Hall, under the auspices of the Atlanta Art Association, is distinguished in the world of art, not only as an artist, the protégée of Gruppé, but as a woman whose beauty has been interpreted by Harrison Fisher for magazine illustrations, and by Aimé Dupont in his studies in artistic photography."[13]

Philip and Alberta Plaistridge sailing to Europe in 1914

Alberta painting in a stream

Alberta as photographer's model

Alberta and Philip separated after a few months of marriage. Interviewed in 1951 for *Collier's* magazine, Plaistridge claimed he had never married. In 1928 he retreated to rural New Hampshire, where he lived an existence similar to that of Henry David Thoreau. On a twenty-one-acre, heavily wooded plot, he built a cabin and several outbuildings, including a blacksmith shop. Plaistridge was an artist in his own right but never had a gallery show or an exhibition. He painted hundreds of New England landscapes. He sold his paintings mostly to tourists who drove by a roadside stand he constructed to showcase his art. Plaistridge also repaired guns and furniture and was only interested in making enough money to maintain his solitary existence.[14]

In 1936 Plaistridge produced the illustrations for

Elmer Keith's book *Big Game Rifles and Cartridges*.[15] These illustrations are the only works of his known to have been published. He died at his home in 1973.

Like Alberta, Edwin Jr. also dropped the surname Osbaldeston. He changed his name from Edwin Julian Turner Osbaldeston to John Edwin Turner but to friends and family was known as Ed. In 1901 he joined the New York National Guard, drilling at the armory at Sixty-Second Street and Columbus Avenue. For a time he assisted his father as a masseur.

In 1907 he married Jean McDonald in Rochester, New York. The union produced one child, a son

This untitled watercolor is one of the few paintings by Alberta that has survived. She signed her works "A. Ludbrook," an adaptation of her maternal grandmother's maiden name, Ludbrooke.

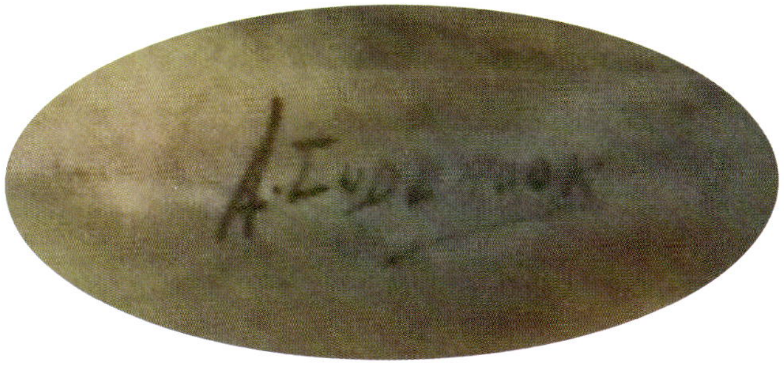

Edwin Jr. worked for a time as a chauffeur.

Edwin Julian Turner Osbaldeston in 1906 at twenty-three

named Donald. Ed worked for several years as a chauffeur to a wealthy family in Canandaigua, New York, and accompanied his employers to Europe on a lengthy tour. He visited Gibraltar, Cannes, Monte Carlo, Nîmes, Paris, Bern, Amsterdam, and Liverpool. Ethel was afforded a similar opportunity in 1913 with an all-expenses-paid trip to Europe for three months with the Haley Fiske family. Ethel served as companion to Mrs. Fiske, who was suffering from a heart condition.

Later Ed worked as a machinist for the Sargent and Greenleaf company in Rochester, the maker of a wide variety of locks and padlocks. Ed befriended a company salesman named Roy Bogart. As it turned out, their friendship was one he would later regret. Ed purchased a home in Rochester, and Bogart was invited to board with Edwin, Jean, and son Donald. (Bogart's wife had been committed to a mental institution.) Jean and Bogart began an affair. Ed left the home as the situation became unbearable. He returned to New York City heartbroken.

After holding a few jobs as a clerk, younger brother Francis (Frank) left New York for Chicago in 1914. There he met divorcée Olive Teel Bilky of Baraboo, Wisconsin. They married in October 1914 but later learned that their marriage was not legal as Olive had not been divorced for a full year as required by law. In September 1915 Frank and Olive married a second time and then a third time in December of that year.

Frequently arguing over money, their marriage was rocky for many years. Olive's family money and his spending of it were at the root of many of their problems. Frank was said to have copied his father's explosive style when dealing with domestic issues. Olive filed for divorce in 1923 but didn't follow through with it, fearing Frank's temper. Olive claimed domestic violence and cruelty as reasons for seeking a separation. Six years later Olive filed again. They divorced in 1929, only to mend their relationship and marry for a fourth time later that year. Like his brother Ed, Frank had what amounted to an eighth-grade education. He worked in sales before starting a series of businesses. Unlike his father, he had the ability to manage money.

Francis Scudder Osbaldeston and Normandie Alice

Above: Sons Francis and Edwin with Alice Agnes in 1911 in New York. Right: Ethel in 1913 in Bad Nauheim, Germany, working as traveling companion.

The year 1919 would be a year of change and passings for Edwin and the country. On January 6, former president Teddy Roosevelt died in his sleep at the age of sixty at his Sagamore Hill home on Long Island. Although World War I had come to a close two months before the new year dawned, the months ahead would see unrest in the United States as a wave of labor strikes and riots hit the country. The Eighteenth Amendment to the Constitution went into effect, authorizing Prohibition, and the Nineteenth Amendment won approval, guaranteeing suffrage to women.

Two of Edwin's siblings died in 1919. First, his sister Emma, widow of the late Joseph Vernon, died at the home of her son Alonzo in Buffalo on February 20. Edwin and his sister had been very close when they were children. He had helped the Vernons get settled in America. Her death affected him greatly. On November 13 their eldest brother, Major Frederick Turner, died in Bournemouth, England, at the age of eighty-seven. His death was due to injuries sustained from a fall from an upstairs window of his home.

Edwin's older brother, Major Frederick Turner

As his children were moving on, Edwin began spending more and more time in Asbury Park, New Jersey. Edwin and Alice Agnes were living apart. Edwin was residing in an old building on Broadway at Eightieth Street, New York City.[16] His wife was sharing an apartment with their daughter Ethel on 135th Street. Alice Agnes had also lived part-time in 1919 and 1920 with her daughter Normandie, son-in-law James H. Siver, and grandson Kenneth, who had moved from Schenectady, New York, to East Orange, New Jersey.

With his building slated for demolition, Edwin was preparing to move full-time to Asbury Park. However, he almost did not make it out of the building alive. In early April his nephew Christian Vernon came over to his residence at 2245 Broadway to help his eighty-one-year-old uncle pack. After laboring for a few hours, Christian felt tired and lay down for a nap. He woke up a while later and, feeling chilled, put on an overcoat and went back to sleep. Waking again after another hour, he felt extremely ill, rose, and passed out. Both Christian and Edwin had been overcome by carbon monoxide poisoning. They were rescued, revived, and taken to Knickerbocker Hospital.[17] From Manhattan Edwin moved to the New Tenney Hotel in Asbury Park.

Edwin outside the New Tenney Hotel in Asbury Park

NOTES

1. *Wikipedia*, s.v. "American Tobacco Company," accessed 29 March 2014, http://en.wikipedia.org/wiki/American_Tobacco_Company.
2. "Jerome on Duke Case, May Go to Grand Jury; Bridegroom Still in Sanitarium—Bride in Seclusion. Detectives Seek Woman; Physician Who Attended Mr. Duke Says He Looked as if under the Influence of Drugs," *New York Times*, 11 January 1905, p. 16.
3. Ibid.
4. Gary B. Borders, "The Tobacco Queen of Texas," accessed 2 November 2014, http://garyborders.com/pages/category/tales.
5. "Duke, Brodie Leonidas," accessed 30 March 2014, www.opendurham.org.
6. "Jerome on Duke Case," *New York Times*, 11 January 1905, p. 16.
7. Ibid.
8. "Wants Father-in-Law Shut Up; So Miller's Mother-in-Law Has Him Arrested for Writing Letter," *Sun* (New York, NY), 3 December 1904, p. 3.
9. Excerpt from letter from Normandie Osbaldeston Siver to Judith Siver, 8 June 1962.
10. *Leslie's Weekly* (NY), 23 June 1910.
11. Art Institute of Chicago, *Catalogue of the Twenty-Sixth Annual Exhibition of American Oil Paintings and Sculpture, November 14 to December 25, 1913* (Chicago: Art Institute of Chicago, 1913), 222.
12. Art Institute of Chicago, *The Twenty-Seventh Annual Exhibition of Water Colors, Pastels and Miniatures by American Artists, May 13 to June 13, 1915* (Chicago: Art Institute of Chicago, 1915), 211.
13. "'A. Ludbrook,' Noted Model, in Charge of Gruppé Paintings Shown Here," *Constitution* (Atlanta, Georgia), 20 May 1917, p. B10.
14. John W. Randolph, "He Leads the Life He Loves," *Collier's*, 16 June 1951, pp. 26–27, 60.
15. Elmer Keith, *Big Game Rifles and Cartridges*, drawings by Philip Plaistridge (Onslow County, NC: Small Arms Technical Publishing Company, 1936).
16. *Deaf-Mutes' Journal* (Mexico, NY), 17 April 1919, p. 3, col. b.
17. Ibid.

CHAPTER SEVENTEEN

Final Years in Asbury Park ~ 1926–1929

Edwin had settled into a fairly quiet existence in Asbury Park—that is until the Broome County lawmen came calling. From time to time his daughters came to visit him, but mostly Edwin was living on his own.

He had made his permanent home in Asbury Park at 801 Railroad Avenue (now Memorial Drive) near the intersection with Asbury Avenue. Railroad Avenue was in the center of the city and just eight blocks from the resort town's famous boardwalk.

The *New York Times* described Edwin's home as a "two-room hut he had constructed of soap boxes and similar material." Another news article noted that it had a tin roof and that it was "scarcely larger than a couple of joined piano cases."[1] Edwin described his home differently: "It is a cozy little place. . . . You see how the sun streams in this window? It makes the room warm even in the coldest days of winter. And in summer there are so many flowers and pretty little gardens nearby where I can work."[2]

Once the excitement of his arrest in the spring of 1926 waned, Edwin resumed his day-to-day existence in Asbury Park. Walking to the pier, visiting the local cemetery, tending small gardens, screening films at the local movie theaters (where he had a lifetime complimentary pass), participating in town events, and retelling of adventures past, filled his days. Having alienated his family, their visits were few. The media attention he received subsided, but he was far from forgotten. Edwin continued to get more than his share of attention, especially considering his age and activities. As a reporter for the *Asbury Park Evening Press* said, "Dr. Osbaldeston was good copy."[3] In truth, Edwin was a celebrity in Asbury Park, one of those persons the media follows seemingly just because they breathe or sneeze. Then, too, Edwin still had the ability to create news.

Edwin sporting Crimean War medal on his lapel (circa 1928)

Thus, when S. Foster Black's birthday rolled around in October 1926, Edwin sent him greetings and made peace with the sheriff who had dogged him. In a telegram to Binghamton, Edwin wrote, "As a token of amity toward Deputy Sheriff Black upon his eighty-second [should be eighty-third] birthday, I hold in abeyance all thoughts of damage suits against him. I forgive the injustice done me. Will you please express to him my wish that he live long and prosper."[4] The *New York Times*, New York *Sun,* and other papers saw fit to carry this development in their pages.[5]

The newspapers also regularly reported on Edwin's health. On what Edwin believed was his birthday (December 27), the *New York Times* reported "Osbaldeston Hale at 94."[6] Conversely, Edwin's hospitalization in March 1927 at St. Luke's Hospital in New York City was mentioned in numerous papers. The *New York Evening Post* reported the veteran of the Crimean War, Garibaldi's Red Shirts, and the Australian bush "was doing well today despite the sudden paralytic stroke."[7] The *New York Times* noted, "Last summer Dr. Osbaldeston, who is a Crimean War veteran, was hale enough to organize a Robin Hood Archery Club in Asbury Park, and on his birthday last December he was reported still spry. At that time he announced that he expected to reach the century mark."[8] The *Times* further noted, "It was said that his illness probably was due more than anything else to the effects of old age. He is said to be much improved and no longer confined to bed."[9]

In May 1928 he suffered an attack of vertigo that made the newspapers, as did bruises he sustained when knocked down by hurricane winds the following September.[10] [11] His daughter Ethel came to visit him in early May of 1928 upon her return from an extended stay in England. Ethel spent several weeks in Asbury Park looking after her father. An ambulance had been called to his home on May 2, but the paramedics decided not to take him to a hospital. After Ethel arrived she had him admitted to Ann May Hospital. He was released, and she remained with him until the end of May. Edwin recorded her visit.

Daughter Ethel Monica left me alone again today, Monday May 28th. Her visit unexpected came like a legendary angel's visit, stayed about three weeks. Mr. & Mrs. Frick of Sewall Ave. gave us a special dinner, & . . . [not legible].

Daughter Eth took charge of my lone caboose & squared up fine as I was too ill. Her coming really saved my life close on ending after leaving the Ann May Hospital & weak almost too weak to speak or walk or see correctly.[12]

With death on his mind, Edwin had a new will drawn up by attorney Charles Cook, who had represented him during the threat of extradition to New York. Although Ethel was present, he left all his possessions to daughter Geneva and named Geneva the executrix of his estate. (Perhaps Ethel requested not to serve as the executrix due to her travel plans and Geneva was more in need as she was unemployed at the time and widowed. Following the death of her husband, Geneva had given up her apartment in Manhattan and was living with Normandie and James Siver in River Edge, New Jersey.)

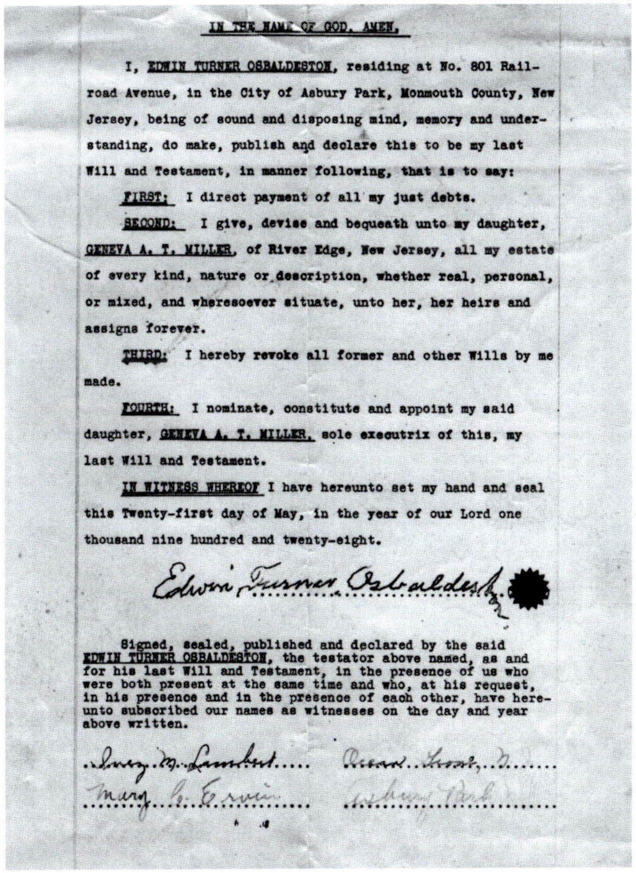
IN THE NAME OF GOD, AMEN.

I, EDWIN TURNER OSBALDESTON, residing at No. 801 Railroad Avenue, in the City of Asbury Park, Monmouth County, New Jersey, being of sound and disposing mind, memory and understanding, do make, publish and declare this to be my last Will and Testament, in manner following, that is to say:

FIRST: I direct payment of all my just debts.

SECOND: I give, devise and bequeath unto my daughter, GENEVA A. T. MILLER, of River Edge, New Jersey, all my estate of every kind, nature or description, whether real, personal, or mixed, and wheresoever situate, unto her, her heirs and assigns forever.

THIRD: I hereby revoke all former and other Wills by me made.

FOURTH: I nominate, constitute and appoint my said daughter, GENEVA A. T. MILLER, sole executrix of this, my last Will and Testament.

IN WITNESS WHEREOF I have hereunto set my hand and seal this Twenty-first day of May, in the year of our Lord one thousand nine hundred and twenty-eight.

Edwin Turner Osbaldeston

Signed, sealed, published and declared by the said EDWIN TURNER OSBALDESTON, the testator above named, as and for his last Will and Testament, in the presence of us who were both present at the same time and who, at his request, in his presence and in the presence of each other, have hereunto subscribed our names as witnesses on the day and year above written.

Edwin's last will and testament

In June he began looking for an undertaker. Even this made the news as it was reported that he was shopping around for a bargain and wanted a cremation and plain box. He received a bid for $150 but hoped to "get himself put away for one hundred dollars."[13] He joked that he wanted cremation because he didn't want to face the prospect of being buried alive.

Previous to this bout with mortality, Edwin had added a new fitness routine to his daily walks. In what his daughters termed "an embarrassing stunt," he began climbing a railroad signal tower that had been newly erected near his home. Once again the showman, he didn't just mount the tower, he performed acrobatics thirty-five feet above the ground. As he climbed he stopped to lower his body headfirst and performed five sit-ups with his legs

This photo of Edwin climbing a railroad semaphore across from his home in Asbury Park appeared in the St. Louis Post-Dispatch *on January 15, 1928.*

wrapped around the rungs. He began this routine in November 1927 and announced a special performance for his birthday in December, complete with white summer suit, bow tie, and Crimean War medal.

> A crowd gathers every morning at 10 and every afternoon at 5:30 to observe the erect figure of the nonagenarian, with white hair flowing and red necktie breaking out to the breeze, ascend the signal tower. At each rung beyond ten feet from the ground Dr. Osbaldeston lowers himself five times in a sitting position and on reaching the top, locks his legs in the rungs and throws his body backward until it is dangling downward. Then he raises himself slowly and doffs his hat to the admiring crowds.
>
> "It is comparatively simple," the doctor explained, "and it is the best exercise in the world for all the muscles. Through it I continue to keep my body in good form and my muscles supple as in youth. . . ."
>
> "I pursue my exercises and hobbies with no spirit of bravado," said the doctor. "Through my long life I have been blessed with the power of endurance."[14]

Edwin's signal tower acrobatics garnered national headlines. "Dauntless at 95, Skins a High Cat and Tells Stories," the *Helena Daily Independent* of Montana proclaimed.[15] "Has 95th Birthday Atop Railroad Semaphore—54 Feet High," exclaimed the *Indianapolis News*.[16] "Does Acrobatics at 95 to Amuse His Friends," said the *New York Times*, while the *Dallas Morning News* reported, "Still Climbing at 95th Birthday."[17] [18] The *Binghamton Press* chimed in with "Dr. E. P. T. Osbaldeston, Nemesis of S. Foster Black, Demonstrates His Spryness on 95th Birthday."[19] There was no comment from the New York and Long Branch Railroad on this use of its semaphore.

Giuseppe Garibaldi, on landing in Marsala, Sicily, in 1860 (Expedition of the Thousand). *Painting (1861) by Girolamo Induno. (National Museum of the Risorgimento, Turin, Italy)*

Every Memorial Day during his years in Asbury Park, Edwin sold poppies on a street corner to raise funds for the American Legion and Veterans of Foreign Wars. He was joined in this activity by local schoolchildren. Even though he was still recovering from an illness, 1928 was no exception. One would expect nothing less from a decorated war hero. The *New York Times* reported, "Although he had returned but a few days ago from the hospital, where he was taken following a breakdown, Dr. Osbaldeston was the first to appear on the street this morning with 'poppies.'"[20]

Since 1926, in virtually every story about Edwin, readers were reminded that the aged doctor had been arrested on a forty-five-year-old charge for stealing a horse and buggy along with a reiteration of his war record. He was often referred to (and it went unchallenged) as the oldest living veteran of the Crimean War. The war stories had been told so many times that Edwin and everyone else believed them. Who wouldn't want to be associated with the bravery of the daring, charismatic Garibaldi and the heroism of those who fought in Crimea against the Russian army?

Giuseppe Garibaldi was one of the most widely known and internationally acclaimed figures of the nineteenth century. Unlike most military leaders of the time, he did not come from the aristocracy. He was the son of a fisherman and one who never forgot his humble beginnings. He shunned the trappings of success and power when they came his way in later life.

Referred to as a "hero of two worlds," his popularity was rooted in his efforts to liberate the oppressed in Uruguay, Brazil, and Italy. In his long fight for the unification of Italy, Garibaldi was twice exiled from his homeland and condemned to death in absentia. His appeal was further enhanced by his travels to far-flung places around the globe—Peru, New Zealand, Australia, Morocco, among other lands. Most of all, he was the charismatic general that led the Risorgimento, the social and political movement that freed the peasants from French and Austrian occupation.[21] Even in his failures, the working classes of the world embraced him as one of their own.

Immensely popular in Great Britain, where citizens had helped to finance his campaigns of 1860 in Italy, Garibaldi arrived there in April 1864 to thank the people for their support. As he was mobbed everywhere he went, it was estimated that he drew an unprecedented crowd of five hundred thousand in London's Trafalgar Square. His popularity alarmed the establishment and Queen Victoria. Public appearances by British royalty had not drawn crowds that large.[22]

> Britain was in the grip of Garibaldi-mania. By 1864 a veritable Garibaldi cult was in full swing. There were mementoes in abundance. You could acquire Garibaldi sheet-music, popular portraits, Staffordshire figures, linen labels, medals, handbills, invitations, broadsides, and *cartes de visite* galore. And at least two moving panoramas had been painted—one that was being exhibited by the panorama proprietor, Moses Gompertz, and another that was associated with the name of Burford.[23]

Garibaldi was highly regarded in the United States as well—particularly revered in the nation's Italian American immigrant communities. And he had ties to New York and New Jersey. The general had spent a year of his exile on Staten Island (1850–1851). These same communities raised the funds needed to erect the landmark fountain and statue of Garibaldi in New York's Washington Square Park. President Abraham Lincoln thought so highly of his military abilities that he offered Garibaldi a commission in the Union Army in the early days of the Civil War, an offer Garibaldi declined.[24]

Thus, it was that Edwin claimed association with Garibaldi. As a performer, Edwin absorbed the history created in the general's wake and made a part of it his own. Unfortunately for Edwin, the closest he ever came to being at the side of the great liberator was to be stationed hundreds of miles to the south on the island of Malta. Rather than bravely fighting in the battles at Gaeta, Milazzo, and Calabria, he performed routine guard duty at a British outpost in the middle of the Mediterranean.

Bust of Giuseppe Garibaldi in Palermo, Italy

The way he wished to remember it, and be remembered, was recorded in his journal.

> It is a long time since I made notes, not since I was discharged cured from Ricasler [Ricasoli] Hospital Valetta Harbour Malta. Have seen active service for 7 months with Garibaldi at the Siege of Gaeta [November 5, 1860 to February 13, 1861; 45 miles northwest of Naples, on the Gulf of Gaeta], & afterwards at the battle of Aspremonte [Aspromonte]. Was well received & appointed by the General at Caperia [Caprera, a small island off the north coast of Sardinia] his island home. He has two sons; bright boys. Minotti [Menotti], the eldest, bids fair to become as brave & famous as his illustrious father. And one daughter a sweet little miss named Anneta who spoke English with me like her father fluently. The General is a widower.[25]

The Battle of Aspromonte was waged on August 29, 1862. At this time Edwin was a deserter from the Royal Artillery and just days away from meeting his first wife, Ann Pratt, in Acock's Green in Birmingham, England.

The same, of course, was true of Edwin's claim of service in the Crimean War. In response to Russian demands to protect Orthodox populations in the Ottoman Empire (including the Holy Land) and due to Russia's occupation of what is now Romania and the mouth of the Danube River, the Turks had declared war on their neighbor to the north in July 1853. Nine months later France and Great Britain sided with the Turks and joined the conflict.

At the time Edwin was fifteen years old living in Birmingham. He must surely have remembered the wave of nationalistic pride that washed over Britain as Her Royal Majesty's troops and ships battled the Russians. Major engagements of the Crimean War were fought on the Alma River—the most famous being the Battle of Balaklava.

Here a brigade of British soldiers was ordered to charge a heavily fortified Russian position. The battle was immortalized by Alfred, Lord Tennyson in the narrative poem "The Charge of the Light Brigade."

> Cannon to right of them,
> Cannon to left of them,
> Cannon in front of them
> Volley'd and thunder'd;
> Storm'd at with shot and shell,
> Boldly they rode and well,
> Into the jaws of Death,
> Into the mouth of Hell
> Rode the six hundred.

Flash'd all their sabres bare,
Flash'd as they turn'd in air,
Sabring the gunners there,
Charging an army, while
All the world wonder'd:
Plunged in the battery-smoke
Right thro' the line they broke;
Cossack and Russian
Reel'd from the sabre stroke
Shatter'd and sunder'd.
Then they rode back, but not
Not the six hundred.[26]

Tennyson's poem is an ode to bravery in the face of death. His verses alternate between the nobility of serving country and the brutality of war. These were themes that appealed to Edwin. He wished to be associated with the dashing horsemen of the Light Brigade and the bravery they exhibited in battle. Many of those who fought and died in the Battle of Balaklava were eighteen, nineteen, and twenty years old.[27] Edwin joined the Royal Artillery at age twenty in 1859.

In a bit of historic irony considering Edwin's attempt to secure a pension from the British War Office, those who survived the Crimean War had been all but forgotten by 1890. Rudyard Kipling took up the plight of the real veterans of Crimea in his poem "The Last of the Light Brigade."

There were thirty million English
who talked of England's might,
There were twenty broken troopers
who lacked a bed for the night.
They had neither food nor money,
they had neither service nor trade;
They were only shiftless soldiers,
the last of the Light Brigade.

They felt that life was fleeting;
they knew not that art was long,
That though they were dying of famine,
they lived in deathless song.
They asked for a little money to keep
the wolf from the door;
And the thirty million English
sent twenty pounds and four![28]

After this poem was published, it was largely ignored and not found among the most famous works of Kipling. Neither did it come to light in 1926 during the media coverage of the man claiming to be the oldest veteran of the Crimean War living in what some termed was a "shack by the railroad tracks."

Edwin had not been a captain in the British artillery, directing eighty men and the fire of six guns in the Crimean War. Nor had he seen service in the Boer War, the American Civil War, or the Boxer Rebellion or been on a search party in the Australian bush for the lost Leichhardt expedition. He lacked a formal education and had not earned a medical degree, nor was he a descendant of the British nobility. He would have loved to have led the life of adventure and military accomplishment of Garibaldi and relished the fame and adulation that the general received. Likewise, it was the battles that he favored and not the humdrum of military training or duty. The best he could do was wear someone else's medal and keep the sacrifice of those who served in these conflicts alive by his retelling of them.

Another summer passed in Asbury Park. Edwin told reporters that he had received a document from an office in London clarifying his birth date. He announced that he wasn't ninety-five but ninety-nine years old and his birthday wasn't December 27 but July 27.[29] The origin of this photostat wasn't clear to anyone, and the handwritten notation on it made it suspect. Regardless, Edwin was elated by this news. He had declared numerous times that he wanted to live to be one hundred. In truth, he was ninety. His birth date was July 11, 1838.

Regardless of what age he believed himself to be, Edwin grew tired of living his life. He feared the infirmities of old age and found it harder and harder to create situations where he was the center of attention.

In late January 1929, Asbury Park policeman Alfred Giles found him unconscious in his house on Railroad Avenue. Edwin had attempted suicide by turning on the gas jets. He was revived and taken to Ann May Hospital. Ethel visited him frequently while he was in the hospital and stayed with him for a few days after his release. On February 18 Edwin made good on ending his life. He did not go to bed that night. Instead, he put his bed and his little house in tidy order and sat up toying with his old .32-caliber revolver. He had left a note with instructions for dealing with his remains with a local undertaker. Sometime after midnight he shot himself first in the neck. That first bullet made a clean passage through his body and came to rest in a trunk across the room. It did not bring death.

Still conscious, Edwin fired again. This time the bullet entered his chest, about an inch above his heart. After that it appeared that he rested the gun on a chair and his head upon a pillow on the floor as he bled out. His body was discovered by patrolman Frank Rowland at 3:20 a.m. The officer had noticed a light was still burning in the tiny house on Railroad Avenue and went to check on the aged resident. As usual, the door was unlocked; he entered and discovered the ghastly scene.[30]

Later that day, across all eight columns of the *Asbury Park Evening Press,* the banner headline in bold block letters screamed, "DR. OSBALDESTON KILLS SELF WITH REVOLVER." The subheads told the rest of the story, "Famed Nonagenarian Found

Dead in Shack; Bullets Thru Neck And Over Heart End Life—Sent Note to Undertaker Few Hours Before—Suicide Is Laid to Brooding."[31]

Two days earlier Edwin had sent a package containing a pair of blue pajamas and a note to a mortuary requesting that his body be placed in a plain box, cremated, and his ashes be spread in the Atlantic Ocean off the Asbury Park fishing pier. The note read as follows:

> Being in my right mind and in good health, but nevertheless afflicted with extreme age and its infirmities, following my lifelong rule in making full preparations for any course which I intended to pursue, I take this opportunity of writing you and request that in the event of anything serious in the form of death occurring to me you will take sole charge and comply with my wishes in such an event.
>
> First, I have decided that there is to be no interference with my desire to be cremated by anyone. My body to be dressed in a light silk pair of pajamas which I will supply. The body to be placed in a plain box to be convenient for the crematory to handle.
>
> With regard to invitations to the funeral, I have given none and leave you to use your own discretion in the matter.
>
> Upon receiving the ashes from the crematory, it is my wish that you notify the veterans on Sewall Avenue and select a party for the final taking off at the end of the fishing pier on the boardwalk. Further than this I have nothing to suggest but leave it to your best judgment to carry out my wishes.
>
> When the passing comes, these are in outline my own wishes. No funeral gloom, corpse gazing, tears, black raiment, graveyard grimness. Think of me withdrawn in the dimness. Remember all the best of my past moments and forget the rest. I would wish my children, relatives, and friends to observe this when I die.[32]

The *New York Telegram*, in a lengthy article noting the passing of Dr. Osbaldeston, ruminated as follows:

> But no man could explain why he should have killed himself, this scampish old yarn-spinner whose self-announced age varied between 94 and 99, according to the degree of his spirits; who cavorted on high bars and railroad semaphores, and loved to tell his extravagant tales and vowed to live another fifty years.
>
> True, he had seemed in these last few months, since a stay in two hospitals for futile treatment for arteriosclerosis, to be less gallantly enamored of life; he had even gone about visiting the local undertakers last summer bullying and bargaining over burial and cremation prices.

ASBURY PARK EVENING PRESS

FORTY-THIRD YEAR NO. 41. ASBURY PARK, N. J., MONDAY, FEBRUARY 18, 1929. PRICE THREE CENTS

DR. OSBALDESTON KILLS SELF WITH REVOLVER

FAMED NONAGENARIAN FOUND DEAD IN SHACK

Bullets Thru Neck And Over Heart End Life—Sent Note To Undertaker Few Hours Before—Suicide Is Laid To Brooding.

Restrained From Suicide By Reporter 5 Years Ago

This banner headline in the Asbury Park Evening Press *announced the death of Edwin Turner Osbaldeston on February 18, 1929. The paper ran extensive coverage on Dr. Osbaldeston's life and burial wishes on pages 1, 2, and 15 (four related stories in all). Coverage of Dr. Osbaldeston's passing continued for days after his death.*

Several New York City newspapers ran articles on Dr. Osbaldeston's death. Numerous other newspapers, both in the United States and abroad, also carried news of his passing.

But even last week he made his customary daily parades, ancient tam-o'-shanter over one eye, pipe in the corner of his mouth, carnation in frayed buttonhole; he called at the post office for the mail he almost never received, and conferred dignified greetings upon those whose smiles were friendly. . . . He had been particularly fond of the story of how he, as gallant a young British artillery officer as any Osbaldeston who ever fought for king and glory, had attacked four Russian troopers in the battle of Balaklava in the Crimean War, and had slain three of them before his sabre had broken at the hilt. "This silver plate in my head, sir," he always said, tapping it with a forefinger, "is my souvenir of that bloody day. Ten months I lay in a hospital, sir, and knew nothing. Then I came to with this plate in my skull."

He always denied vehemently that the plate was achieved in less romantic fashion, that he was the "Professor" Edwin T. Osbaldeston who [actually] got his pate cracked fighting rival masseurs in New York in the 1880s. . . .

For as far as his war adventures were concerned—his eyewitness account of the charge of the Light Brigade, and his romantic friendship with Florence Nightingale, and the rest of those gaudy incidents—did he not have tangible proof in the greasy old silver Crimean War medal pinned to his overcoat?[33]

His obituary in the *New York Times* began simply, "His zest for life quenched at last by the burden of his ninety-odd years, Dr. Edwin Pye Turner Onslow Osbaldeston shot and killed himself this morning in the tiny shack by the railroad tracks where for many years he had lived alone with his memories."[34]

NOTES

1. "Doctor Refuses to Retreat Under Fire," *Asbury Park Evening Press* (NJ), 31 March 1926, p. 1.
2. "Strain Telling Upon Old Crimean Veteran," *Asbury Park Evening Press* (NJ), 30 March 1926, p. 1.
3. "Nonagenarian's Life Like That of Hero in Fiction," *Asbury Park Evening Press* (NJ), 18 February 1929, pp. 1–2.
4. "Forgives Old Sheriff," *Sun* (New York, NY), 23 October 1926, p. 1, col. b.
5. "Aged Physician Makes Peace with Sheriff," *New York Times*, 24 October 1926, p. 16.
6. "Osbaldeston Hale at 94," *New York Times*, 28 December 1926, p. 21.
7. "Aged Veteran Stricken," *New York Evening Post*, 1 March 1927, p. 8.
8. "Dr. Osbaldeston Ill," *New York Times*, 1 March 1927, p. 27.
9. Ibid.
10. "Dr. Osbaldeston Ill at 94," *New York Times*, 3 May 1928, p. 20.
11. "Wind Damage High at Shore Resorts," *New York Times*, 21 September 1928, p. 23.
12. Notes by ETO in family history files of Kenson Siver.
13. "Sidelights," *Courier* (Brookfield, NY), 20 June 1928.
14. "Physician of 95 Becomes Acrobat," *Waterloo Evening Courier* (IA), 24 November 1927, p. 5.
15. "Dauntless at 95, Skins a High Cat and Tells Stories," *Helena Daily Independent* (MT), 5 January 1928, p. 7.
16. "Has 95th Birthday Party Atop Railroad Semaphore—54 Feet High," *Indianapolis News*, 7 January 1928, p. 25.
17. "Does Acrobatics at 95 to Amuse His Friends," *New York Times*, 28 December 1927, p. 11.
18. "Still Climbing at 95th Birthday," *Dallas Morning News*, 27 January 1928, p. 2.
19. "Dr. E. P. T. Osbaldeston, Nemesis of S. Foster Black, Demonstrates His Spryness on 95th Birthday," *Binghamton Press* (NY), 28 December 1927, p. 1.
20. "Osbaldeston Leads Sale," *New York Times*, 27 May 1928, p. 25.
21. *Garibaldi: Great Lives Observed*, ed. Denis Mack Smith (Englewood Cliffs, NJ: Prentice-Hall, 1969), pp. 1–2.
22. Ralph Hyde, "'The Campaigns of Garibaldi': A Look at a Surviving Panorama," November 2004, accessed 14 April 2014, www.library.brown.edu.
23. Ibid.
24. *Garibaldi: Great Lives Observed*, p. 6.
25. ETO, "Journal" (unpublished manuscript), 26–27, Siver family history material.
26. Alfred, Lord Tennyson, "The Charge of the Light Brigade," stanzas three and four, 1854.
27. "The Lives of the Light Brigade: The E. J. Boys Archive," accessed 14 April 2014, www.chargeofthelightbrigade.com.
28. Rudyard Kipling, "The Last of the Light Brigade," stanzas one and two, 1890.
29. "Osbaldeston Says He's 99," *New York Times*, 28 July 1928, p. 15.
30. "Dr. Osbaldeston Kills Self with Revolver," *Asbury Park Evening Press* (NJ), 18 February 1928, p. 1.
31. Ibid.
32. Ibid.
33. "Dr. Osbaldeston a Suicide, Scorned Death 99 Years," *New York Telegram*, 18 February 1929.
34. "Osbaldeston Ends His Life by Bullets," *New York Times*, 19 February 1929, p. 25.

CHAPTER EIGHTEEN
Edwin Unmasked

Most of Edwin's instructions regarding his remains and funeral arrangements were followed. Daughters Ethel, Geneva, and Normandie arrived in Asbury Park within hours to handle their father's affairs. His sons Ed and Frank did not make the trip to New Jersey. The daughters requested privacy and made only one public comment, thanking those who offered condolences. An *Asbury Park Evening Press* reporter was shooed away by one of the sisters when he stopped by 801 Railroad Avenue to inquire as to the arrangements.[1]

The funeral, closed to the public, consisted of a small ceremony held at the Burtis Funeral Home in Asbury Park. The bill for the undertaker came to $180, not quite the price Edwin had negotiated the summer before.[2] Edwin was cremated and his ashes scattered at sea.[3] Over the decades, their father had put his children through a great deal. It is doubtful they could have withstood a funeral attended by a community that viewed him in a totally different light. They knew more than the public knew and more than the media reported. His suicide was his final selfish act.

Edwin was a public figure in Asbury Park. A number of residents of the city felt shut out by Professor Osbaldeston's family. They wanted to express their grief over the loss of one of their own. There were those who viewed him as a lonely old man who was living on the edge of poverty. Some questioned what appeared to them as a lack of family support or caring for the gregarious old gent who had become a town fixture.

In response to these concerns and statements that had been reported in the newspapers, son Frank (Francis) wrote a letter to the editor of the *Asbury Park Evening Press* that was published on March 8, 1929. The letter, while thanking the people of Asbury Park for their kindness, denies that the professor's family didn't watch out for him. Frank asserted that his father was an independent man and wouldn't have lived any other way.

The most interesting aspect of the letter is the mention of family loyalty and duty. And in that fashion Frank dutifully and loyally defends his family and his father. He termed the horse theft charge "ridiculous" and an attack on his father's honor. The letter leaves his father's image intact as seen by the people of Asbury Park—an image that was perpetuated by the reporters of the *Asbury Park Evening Press* and by Edwin himself.

The only hint that all was not always well is Frank's statement, "True, there have been family differences. . . ."[4] Frank, like his sisters, declined to reveal family secrets. In keeping with their Victorian upbringing, family matters were not discussed openly and double standards were the norm. His letter to the *Evening Press* follows:

> Editor, the *Press:*
>
> The members of Dr. E. T. Osbaldeston's family sincerely appreciate the careful investigation which prompted the *Press* to defend our father at a critical moment in his life [his rearrest in 1926 on an old jail-breaking charge]. That "good copy" was sacrificed for "exact copy" is commendatory in these days of exaggeration.
>
> A reluctance to proffer a thank you, or an interview, is explained by fathers' [sic] statement: "you children cannot answer,

Edwin stands in front of one of his small gardens on the side of his home on Railroad Avenue in Asbury Park.

'yes' or 'no' to something supposed before you were born, further, if I desire to become my brothers' [sic] keeper I assume an individual right to do so." Without that advice a sense of hurt in that if the exalted position he enjoyed in his profession did not secure him honor, reputation, and respect that his age commanded, why add more.

If being careless in business matters, above the other fellow's opinion, or being willing to share a last crumb, or being reckless in giving ground, constitutes failure, then father did fail. However, if refusing charity from any source and insisting upon independent thinking spells success, he deserves a monument.

True, there have been family differences but bitterness or rancor never entered the affairs of the Osbaldeston family. Tension is perhaps natural in a family when [the] principals [sic], loyalty and duty, become thirteenth and fourteenth commandments. Fathers' [sic] friends in Asbury Park would twitter at the thoughts of him in an old man's home, or puttering 'round the home of some in-law. Loyalty was so ingrained in his family that no member would voluntarily place him in a dependent position.

It's the picture of Dr. Osbaldeston without a family despite the fact it spoils "good copy" that I want to destroy. This, in justice to three women whose hearts and sentiments are highly developed. These daughters have for years watched every move and been at beck and call, stelthly [sic] doing all in their power for a strong-willed disciplinarian whom we forgot had grown old.

Dr. Osbaldeston leaves in addition to three daughters, two sons who also feel that the people of Asbury Park have been wonderfully kind. Surely, the thought in back of "judge not, least [sic] we be judged" is exemplified in your city.

The article in the *Press* to the effect that father's remains should be disposed of as he expressed decided the family in a difficult problem. However, it is but symbolic of his life that the sorrows of the living should not be enhanced by morbidness.

The purpose of this letter being to correct the impression Dr. Osbaldeston died without family and to do justice to those who might suffer thru that report upon suspicion of neglect, or indifference, I wish merely to add:

In the sense that a humanitarian and philosopher and we might call him an individualist, is alone in the world, our father had no family. However, from the standpoint of practicability, helpfulness and resourcefulness in helping, his family, especially the daughters, have been and are very much in the flesh.

Assuring you that a correct report would be much appreciated and assuring you that if it made any difference the writer could sit down and tell you by the hours stories of kindness which were an everyday duty for our father to perform. However, alive he would never take the time to tell you that ever since that ridiculous story of the horse-thief and right up until his death, life had lost all of the joys of living for him. Absolutely, those who knew him and especially the members of his family knew that he felt that he had been attacked in his one vulnerable spot, on a question of honor, without that life became a burden.

You will understand that writing this letter has been difficult and why interviewing my sisters results in nothing more than annoyance. Nothing more remains to be said or done, but we are appreciative to the *Press* who have been most careful.

Frank T. Osbaldeston
President, Mission Products Co.
Chicago[5]

The lingering question: who was the real Edwin Turner Osbaldeston? The simple answer is that he was an extremely complex being. There are many more questions than answers regarding his personality and how he was molded. Was he destined from birth to engage in criminal behavior? Was his upbringing the root cause for his insecurities and insatiable need for validation? Did the environment of his early years shape him to believe that he had to do whatever he had to do to survive? Or do the answers lie in the debate of nature versus nurture?

He was born into an English household with a goodly amount of stress and dysfunction. His father was cold, stern, dictatorial, and an alcoholic with a mean temper when inebriated. The family moved numerous times while he was growing up, and it struggled financially. His father had been sentenced to a debtors' prison at one point because he was unable to pay his bills. Edwin and his brothers and sisters were illegitimate. Perhaps worse, his mother was his stepsister. In this era a great social stigma was attached to illegitimacy.

As he grew up, Edwin had to compete for the attention of his parents in a household where there were seven or eight other children at any given time. Edwin was close to his grandmother; however, she left the home when he was six years old.

Many things can be said about the man. Quite obviously, Edwin suffered from major character flaws, starting with deep insecurity and low self-esteem.

His insecurities drove the need to appear superior or to represent himself as something he was not. In order to cover his false representations, he became a compulsive or pathological liar. He lied incessantly and with great facility. He demonstrated no remorse or embarrassment about lying. When caught in a lie or a criminal act, he attempted to turn the tables, painting himself as the victim—essentially creating another lie. Clearly, he believed his lies and became outraged and indignant when challenged about his claims.

Because he relocated frequently, he regularly encountered new people. Many, on meeting Edwin for the first time, took him at face value and were not immediately aware that he was untruthful. To others, he held out hope for a cure for their ailments. Add charm, gracious manners, false sincerity, good grooming, nice attire, and bold confidence to the lie, and it was easy to be taken in.

Edwin developed mendacity to a finely honed skill, and in turn used it to take advantage of others. It was only when he went too far in his claims that people became suspicious. There were any number of instances where he overplayed his hand, casting doubt on his credibility. Such was the case when he explained away his absence from Rome, New York, as a hunting trip. His exaggerations of the wild game he killed and the remoteness of the wilderness were too much to believe. Many times he forgot the details of his lies and changed his story.

This was very evident in 1926 when S. Foster Black caught up with him in Asbury Park and day after day he spoke with reporters. His comments varied from interview to interview when relating the same event in his life history. It was no wonder that his attorney wanted to take Edwin out of the spotlight. (His client could sufficiently damage his own defense.) And then there were those times when he just got carried away, telling tale after tale. In several interviews that followed his signal-tower acrobatic routine, he spun whole new yarns. In speaking once again of his heroism in battle, to underscore his bravery and strength, Edwin claimed he once saved a swimmer who was being pursued by an eighteen-foot shark. He said he dove in the water with a knife and, after a long struggle, slew the giant fish.[6]

Could his extensive record of thievery be blamed on kleptomania? Not likely. People suffering from kleptomania steal to steal. They achieve satisfaction or a release from taking things. Most of the items that Edwin stole were for financial gain or personal use. In Adelaide, for example, much of what he purloined was used to furnish his own home. Items such as the anatomical and physiological charts or the pair of burlesque shoes he could employ in his practice or performances.

Unquestionably, Edwin's behavior certainly would find a place on the spectrum of obsessive-compulsive disorder, but not to the extent of kleptomania. Then again (and perhaps in contradiction), pyromania is a disorder psychologically related to kleptomania. Were the multiple fires in Edwin's life deliberately set by him? Safe to say, very few people in their lifetimes could rival the number of household fires Edwin experienced. (In addition to the fires reported in previous chapters, the Tenney Hotel in Asbury Park was destroyed by fire in 1913, while Edwin was a guest and helping to manage the property.[7] In 1919, The Lodge in Neptune City, New Jersey, was also destroyed by fire while Edwin was a guest. The Lodge fire was deliberately set.)[8] However, no proof was found that he had a hand in the blazes. If he were responsible for the fires, what scant evidence existed suggested financial gain through insurance fraud and not a lack of impulse control.

Narcissistic behavior was Edwin's major character flaw. There is a direct correlation between pathological lying and narcissism. The American Psychiatric Association's *Diagnostic and Statistical Manual of Mental Disorders* defines narcissistic personality disorder (NPD) as characterized by "a pervasive pattern of grandiosity (either in fantasy

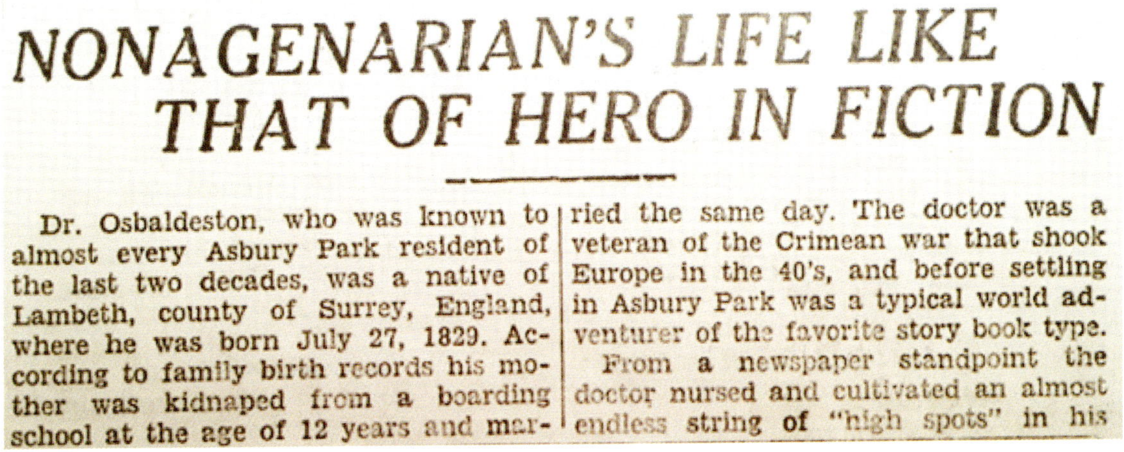

NONAGENARIAN'S LIFE LIKE THAT OF HERO IN FICTION

Dr. Osbaldeston, who was known to almost every Asbury Park resident of the last two decades, was a native of Lambeth, county of Surrey, England, where he was born July 27, 1829. According to family birth records his mother was kidnaped from a boarding school at the age of 12 years and married the same day. The doctor was a veteran of the Crimean war that shook Europe in the 40's, and before settling in Asbury Park was a typical world adventurer of the favorite story book type.

From a newspaper standpoint the doctor nursed and cultivated an almost endless string of "high spots" in his

This story, with its ironic headline, appeared at the bottom of page 1 in the February 18, 1929 edition of the Asbury Park Evening Press. *The article continued for another twenty-three column inches on page 2. Almost all of what was reported in the article on Edwin's life was untrue.*

or actual behavior), a need for admiration, and lack of empathy that begins by early adulthood and is present in a variety of contexts."[9]

People with this disorder often believe they are of primary importance in everybody's life or to anyone they meet.[10] The American Psychiatric Association identifies nine symptoms of narcissistic personality disorder. The true narcissist possesses five or more of the following traits:

- has a grandiose sense of self-importance (e.g., exaggerates achievements and talents; expects to be recognized as superior without commensurate achievements)
- is preoccupied with fantasies of unlimited success, power, brilliance, beauty, or ideal love
- believes that he or she is "special" and unique and can only be understood by, or should associate with, other special or high-status people (or institutions)
- requires excessive admiration
- has a very strong sense of entitlement (i.e., holds unreasonable expectations for especially favorable treatment or automatic compliance with his or her expectations)
- is interpersonally exploitative of others or situations (i.e., takes advantage of others to achieve his or her own ends)
- lacks empathy; demonstrates an unwillingness to recognize or identify with the feelings and needs of others
- is often envious of others or believes that others are envious of him or her and covets others' success, advantages, or possessions
- shows regular displays of arrogant, haughty behaviors, or attitudes[11]

Throughout his life there were many, many specific examples of Edwin's behavior that can be attached to the symptoms listed above. Repeatedly, Edwin's journal accounts differ widely from published newspaper reports and other evidence. He recorded great accomplishments and described himself as a hero, an authority, the savior, the most popular, the man in charge, and so forth. So convinced was he of his self-importance that it never occurred to him that the constant self-aggrandizement undermined his credibility. His collection of testimonials was a vital avenue for the validation he craved.

Other manifestations of his narcissism were vanity and showmanship. Besides commissioning three portraits of himself, Edwin had scores of photographs taken at a time when portrait photography was much less common. He also spent lavishly on clothing and material goods when he had the money. When not, he resorted to theft. He needed to be the center of attention. In addition to his constant self-promotion, lectures, and entertainments, he created spectacles. Whether climbing a semaphore, marching in a parade on Fifth Avenue, or out for a stroll in a top hat and walking stick, he desired to be noticed. People in Malone remembered the time he engaged a man on the street who had a good-sized horse. Edwin bet the man a dollar that he could lift his horse entirely off the ground. The bet was accepted and a crowd gathered. Edwin crouched down under the horse and balanced the animal on his back, all four hoofs dangling in air.[12] It was the sum of Edwin's behavior and not isolated incidents that defined his character issues.

Persons with NPD are very sensitive to criticism and may be easily offended. The veneer covering their self-esteem is very thin. "Although they may not show it outwardly," the American Psychiatric Association states, "criticism may haunt these individuals and may leave them feeling humiliated, degraded, hollow, and empty." In turn, they mask these feelings by reacting with disdain, rage, or defiant counterattack.[13]

Berkeley, California, clinical psychologist Dr. Jonathan Rousell noted that Edwin's behavior is consistent with pathological narcissism. "[His] rapidly vacillating sense of self that defends against perceived slights and even minor injuries to self-esteem through both self-aggrandizing behavior and the tendency to devalue and attack others, with minor provocation," Dr. Rousell stated.[14]

Dr. Rousell further states, "We can see the outward portrayal of a dramatic, charming, brash character, and an inner depleted, shame-prone, envious sense of self, with the outer self being used as a desperate defense against the inner sense of inferiority and hatred of anything that served to associate him with being less than profoundly exceptional."[15]

Such was the case in Ballarat when a Turkish bath patron who had repeatedly attempted to schedule a massage questioned Edwin on the hours he kept. Edwin immediately took offense at what he perceived as criticism and proceeded to curse and physically assault the customer. He felt no remorse or empathy for the customer and, in his resignation letter, defended his behavior, stating in effect that his actions had been justified.

He took his defense a step further by stating that he was looked upon as "an interloper and a nuisance." Frequently, Edwin's distorted reality is difficult to fathom. His interactions with Tom Bastard, the manager of the baths in Adelaide, were a prime example. First, Edwin insisted that Bastard hire him. When Bastard refused, Edwin assaulted and attempted to drown him. Next, Edwin filed false charges against Bastard and made false testimony when the case went to court. Incredulously, Edwin later admitted to Bastard that he had lied in court and told the manager he would make amends if allowed to work in the baths.

In his journal and in letters and interviews, he mentioned suffering from bouts of melancholia and depression. Narcissistic personalities experience dark moods stemming from feelings of inferiority. Other than to blame some of his behavior on melancholia, Edwin never discussed his true feelings or the basis for his depression. Instead, he concealed his feelings of shame, inferiority, and self-loathing with grandiosity or with rage, indignation, or self-pity. His self-righteous reactions to the offenses he committed were well documented. He took the position that his accusers did not know his station in the community or his importance. When caught, he begged his accusers to take pity upon him because one so "great" had fallen.

"Adding to this sense of indignant self-righteousness and callousness was a 'halo of poetry and romance,' an attempt to cast himself as a kind of folk hero, a mythologized self-image that helped him rationalize his continued acts of selfishness and greed," Dr. Rousell observed.[16]

These claims were so absurd as to rightly be derided. At these times he feigned concern for wife and children in an attempt to manipulate the authorities. In reality, much of the time his family suffered abuse at his hands.

Certainly on some level Edwin knew right from wrong, yet he committed criminal offenses most of his adult life. His rap sheet included theft, shoplifting, military desertion, assault, disorderly conduct, intimidation, extortion, adultery, resisting arrest, jail-breaking, domestic violence, child abuse, family abandonment, practicing medicine without a license, obtaining money under false pretenses, falsifying legal documents (uttering and publishing), suspicion of arson, and murder. In today's world he would have faced long sentences as a repeat offender. The murders of Eduard Wild and Wilhelm Baumhardt alone should have resulted in life in prison.

Why he was so criminally inclined could be ascribed to his lack of socialization as a child, lack of formal education, family dynamics, economic factors, behavior disorders, and even genetics. In part, his criminality can be linked to defiance of authority. He derived pleasure in confounding those in control. Escaping captivity and taunting police officials in letters were illustrative of his contempt for authority and his feelings of entitlement.

In the perspectives of psychoanalysts Sigmund Freud, Heinz Kohut, and Otto Kernberg, NPD is rooted in early childhood and parenting. Freud believed all children see themselves as the center of their universe. When confronted with the realities of life (in normal development), the child gains a more realistic sense of self. Building on Freud's work, Kohut theorized that a child grows out of primary narcissism when parents provide opportunities for mirroring and idealization. If parents fail at this, then the child may fail to pass through that stage of development and continue to hold a grandiose and unrealistic sense of self while remaining dependent on the approval of others.

Kernberg took the view that NPD is rooted in cold or distant parents who have failed to nurture their child. As a defense against the depriving parents, the child develops a hyperinflated and grandiose sense of self.[17] A link can be drawn between Edwin's adult behavior and his childhood. Again, Edwin's father was cold, stern, and aloof.

Both Kohut and Kernberg agree that troubled child-parent relationships before the age of three will carry over into adult life and disorders rooted in those years become hard to treat in maturity. The narcissists' feelings of superiority and what they view as a lack of appreciation and/or "stupidity" of others can create a barrier to treatment. Meanwhile, adult narcissists have a history of unsatisfactory relationships with others throughout their lives while having a conflict-ridden dependence on others for validation. This, in turn, causes lifelong swings between feelings of grandiosity and worthlessness.[18]

Perhaps the most noteworthy reason that Edwin engaged in a life of crime was the lack of significant consequences. The worst punishment he faced was at Yatala Prison, and even then, the punishment was mild in comparison with the large number of offenses he had committed prior to confinement. In a life spanning ninety years and six months, he spent less than seven years incarcerated. Edwin managed to get away with a great many of his misdeeds. Further, prosecutors repeatedly failed to try him for a number of his offenses. As examples, most of the thefts he committed in Adelaide never went to trial, including items taken from Prince Alfred and Government House. He was not charged for stealing farmer Thomas Allen's horse and rig in Utica or for his assault on Detective Donohoe in Montreal. His assault on Thomas Bastard in Adelaide was laughed out of court. He skipped trial in Tasmania for violating the Medical Registration Act and forfeited bond in Christchurch on the theft of a second coat and in Malone on the shoplifting charge.

Charges were dropped for lack of evidence in the cases of intimidation and obtaining money under false pretenses in Washington, DC. The charge for shoplifting socks in London was dismissed, as was the child-cruelty complaint involving his ten-year-old son in New York City. Edwin was able to sway the judges in these cases with the pretense of his social standing and wealth. Conflicts with and violence against the operators of competing New York massage parlors went unpunished. In many other instances, no charges were filed or his offenses went unreported.

Even Frederick Miller's plea in 1903 to have Edwin judged insane and committed to an asylum failed.

The court and Alice Agnes would not go along. Instead, the tables were turned and Miller, who had been harassed by Edwin and lost employment because of it, was charged with libel.

Military desertion, skipping bail, and escaping from jail had worked in his favor. Authorities in Christchurch, New Zealand; Hobart Town, Tasmania; and Malone, New York, never went in search of Edwin when he left town before his next court appearance. The person most determined to see Edwin face justice was Deputy Sheriff Black. Edwin's long trail of crimes had mounted steadily following his escape from the Broome County jail. By the time the lawman got his man, it was too late for Edwin's victims and for Deputy Black. In totality, the volume of Edwin's misdeeds that resulted in little or no consequence was truly staggering.

Edwin did possess redeeming qualities. He was outgoing, charming, well-mannered, and personable, not to mention physically attractive. He was also smart, quick-witted, resourceful, and a risk taker. He applied these qualities for good and evil.

"Hardworking" and "energetic" are also words that could be ascribed to Edwin. He placed himself in new situations and surroundings and fearlessly set about making a go of it. He saw the value in physical fitness and a healthy diet. Edwin's lifelong interest in health and medicine was mostly self-taught. Although medical science was making significant advances in the nineteenth century, much of practiced medicine of the day remained in the application of unproven theories and "quack" remedies. The treatments he learned through associating with contemporaries in medicine (either as a patient or practitioner) reflected much of what was believed at the time. Coffee as an antidote for typhus, for example, was a widely held belief. Advances in germ theory, bacteriology, pharmacology, surgery, and sanitation came in the later years of his life.

In business he demonstrated an ability to stay in tune with the latest trends, be they mesmerism, the Swedish movement, or the Delsarte system of expression. Over and over again he demonstrated the ability to build a successful business. He varied his services according to the needs of the market. When applied as a positive force, Edwin was quick to realize customer or client needs. His ideas for improving and advancing the Turkish bath experience were sound. He also understood promotion, publicity, and showmanship and how to employ all three for his personal advancement. Most of all, he was a very good salesman.

Coming from the same home environment, his brothers and sisters managed to lead productive lives. His sister Emma was successful in the massage business. Older brother Frederick had a long, distinguished career in the British military, and youngest brother, Julian, became a well-respected physician in Chicago. None of his siblings gained the notoriety that Edwin managed to acquire.

Somewhat of an exception to this was Edwin's younger brother Francis (1849–1904). After having been brought to the US and taught massage by Edwin, Francis moved to Chicago and set himself up in business there. The services he advertised were massage, Swedish movement cure, and home gymnastics.

Probably inspired by Edwin, Francis also engaged in self-promotion. An individual whose name Francis included in his list of patrons took exception to this. Dr. Charles Gatchell published the following letter:

> I have no sympathy with any one who attempts to build himself up by casting slurs upon others engaged in his line of business, as he does in a circular recently issued. He intimates that others are "imposters," "frauds and charlatans," and speaks of their methods as "clumsy rubbing and pinching and the grotesque twisting and pulling of joints." Worse than this he speaks of "some women" as being "impostors and adventuresses, without skill in the art of medical manipulation, who employ its name merely to cloak practices of immorality and not infrequently schemes of blackmail."
>
> There are many worthy women in Chicago engaged in the practice of massage, and no man who uses such language as this, leaving the reader to make his own application, is worthy [of] the confidence or support of the profession. No gentleman would do such a thing. If this fellow cannot command patronage on his own merits, he does not deserve it after having been so brutal as to slander, by imputation, many women of our city who are gaining an honest and honourable livelihood in the practice of their profession.
>
> Three years ago I received one treatment at his hands, but was so little satisfied with it, and so disgusted with his arrogant pretensions, that I never recommended a patient to him, and have never seen him since. Hence his claim that I am "one of many physicians patronizing" him is false.[19]

At some point Francis also alienated his younger brother Julian, who was a physician practicing in Chicago. On January 19, 1892 Julian published an ad in Chicago's *Inter Ocean* newspaper that included the sentence, "I have no connection with any one calling himself Francis Osbaldeston."

Francis Turner Osbaldeston died of morphine poisoning on March 2, 1904.

Edwin's younger brother, Francis Turner Osbaldeston

So much is known about Edwin because he sought notice. Between his antisocial behavior and his self-promotion, an incredible record was left in his wake. The journal he kept for many years is both fact and fiction.

In death he wished his heirs to remember him for his adventures, travels, bravery, career accomplishments, associates, and so forth. In sum, he wanted to leave an impressive legacy. So much so that in later years, he rewrote parts of his journal to further embellish his life. As a character who knew instinctively when it was time to move his game to the next locale, surely he never dreamed that the man he purported to be would be so unmasked. The image of nobility, accomplishment, and social standing that he fought so hard to build and maintain has been laid bare. While many of his later-life contemporaries and persons in the media were amused by Edwin, viewing him as harmless, or were willing to give him a pass, here his story ends, and he does not get off scot-free.

Truly, Edwin Turner Osbaldeston had an adventurous, extraordinary life. His travels alone were noteworthy in an era when many people in the course of their lives never left the county or shire in which they were born. He advanced hydrotherapy and massage when these treatments were in their infancy. While it has long been recognized that the myriad of health benefits originally attributed to these treatments by Edwin and others were false, massage and Turkish baths are still popular for what they are.

The veracity of all the wealthy and famous he claimed to have treated is not certain, but enough is known to be able to confirm that he did have an elite clientele and that he was quite successful in his profession when he remained on course. He proved that he could lead a successful life and earn a good living. He just was unable to sustain his success. The demons that haunted him eventually interferred.

It could also be said that he lived a very full life, not an honest life but one filled with a myriad of experiences. His life touched upon many of the events, societal forces, political events, and innovations and progress that defined his time. Aside from the names of persons he dropped to impress and had never met, Edwin crossed paths with a great many people who left a mark on history.

Had he avoided criminal activities, his family could have been proud of his honest accomplishments and his elevation from a working-class Englishman to a middle-class American. And finally, he was genuinely a product of the Victorian age. He lived a life of double standards. There was the person he pretended to be and the person he truly was.

NOTES

1. "Dr. Osbaldeston's Cremation Wish to Be Carried Out," *Asbury Park Evening Press* (NJ), 19 February 1929, p. 1.
2. Ethel T. Groves, Funeral Notes, Siver family history material.
3. "Dr. Osbaldeston Kills Self With Revolver," *Asbury Park Evening Press* (NJ), 18 February 1929, pp. 1-2.
4. "Timely Watch Kept Over Osbaldeston, Son Says In Telling of Father's Life," *Asbury Park Evening Press* (NJ), 8 March 1928, p. 4.
5. Ibid.
6. "Does Acrobatics at 95 to Amuse His Friends," *New York Times*, 28 December 1927, p. 11.
7. *Asbury Park Evening Press* (NJ), 2 Ocotber 1913, p. 2b.
8. "Loot Wine Stock, Then Fire House," *Asbury Park Evening Press* (NJ), 29 September 1919. p. 2g.
9. "Narcissistic Personality Disorder," in The American Psychiatric Association, *Diagnostic and Statistical Manual of Mental Disorders*, 5th ed. (Arlington, VA: American Psychiatric Publishing, 2013), pp. 669–670.
10. "Narcissistic Personality Disorder Symptoms," accessed 20 April 2014, http://psychcentral.com/disorders/narcissistic-personality-disorder-symptoms.
11. "Narcissistic Personality Disorder," pp. 669–670.
12. "Dr. Osbaldeston Heard From. Charged with Theft in Binghamton 45 Years Ago," *Malone Farmer* (NY), 31 March 1926, p. 1, col. 5.
13. "Narcissistic Personality Disorder," p. 671.
14. Excerpt from e-mail from Dr. Jonathan Rousell to Noël Siver, 3 September 2015.
15. Ibid.
16. Ibid.
17. "Narcissistic Personality Disorder," *The Gale Encyclopedia of Mental Disorders* (Detroit, MI: Thomson & Gale, 2003), pp. 644–645.
18. Ibid.
19. Charles Gatchell, "A Card," *The Medical Era: A Monthly Journal of Medicine*, 4–5 (August 1886–December 1887), p. 121.

EPILOGUE

Ethel was the last of Edwin and Alice Agnes's children to marry. For many years, as the oldest child after Annie Mabel left home in 1888, Ethel had assisted her mother in caring for her younger siblings, especially during her father's many absences. In the 1910s she worked in New York City for an insurance company as a clerk and then began training to become a nurse. As her parents aged, it was she who frequently looked after her mother and father.

For some time Ethel had been seeing a man by the name of Harry Hatzel. Hatzel was ten years older than she, divorced, and had two teenage children. By profession he was an accountant, led a stable existence, and was well liked by Alice Agnes.

Harry Hatzel at Niagara Falls

Although they were engaged, their relationship didn't seem to be going anywhere. Then Ethel met Donald Duncan Stewart. Stewart loved the ladies. Their meeting was by chance. On November 16, 1919, Ethel, thirty-nine, was standing outside St. Mary's Hospital in East Orange, New Jersey, waiting for an overdue streetcar. Stewart approached and struck up a conversation. Four years younger than Ethel, Stewart was lean, square-jawed, handsome, and a very smooth talker. Ethel was smitten and the relationship took off. In January 1920 Ethel and Stewart became engaged.[1]

If there were any early warning signs about Donald Duncan Stewart, Ethel failed to see them. The charming Stewart came along like a sleek, new sports car, leaving the clunky family sedan that Hatzel represented in the dust. Now the jilted suitor, Hatzel naturally viewed Stewart in a totally different light, readily spotting the imperfections and impracticalities of the new model.

Seeking an ally in his fight to hold Ethel's affections, Hatzel went to Edwin to advise him of the man with whom his daughter had begun an affair. This led to the infamous confrontation between Stewart and Edwin at the New Tenney Hotel in Asbury Park.

With her emotions run amok, it was easy for Ethel to dismiss the concerns of Hatzel and her father. Instead, she proceeded to deepen her relationship with the charming new paramour. The ride that Stewart would take her on over the next three years rivaled, and in some respects exceeded, any of her father's escapades.

To begin with, Stewart's real name was Robert Allan Brown(e). He failed to mention that he was married—twice. Not twice, as in twice divorced, but a man married to two women at the same time. Born in Scotland, Stewart immigrated to the United States in 1904.

He entered the clergy upon his arrival in the United States and was ordained as a Presbyterian minister in 1908. A year later he married Agnes Carruth in Norwalk, Connecticut. The couple had sons born to them in 1910, 1911, and 1913. Meanwhile, his ministry took the young family to New Jersey, Texas,

Ethel in the early 1900s

Arizona, and California. Agnes Carruth Browne would recall during her marriage to Stewart: "Stewart [the boys' father], while he was a minister used to run around with women and pass bad checks." She also said that "he was using drugs all the time."[2] By 1913 the Browne family had moved to Chico, California. There, ironically, Stewart became involved in the temperance movement and was appointed to lead a regional office of a statewide prohibition campaign. Stewart was credited with ridding a number of California towns of their "red light" districts and was the lyricist for the song "We'll Make California Dry."[3]

Reverend Browne

This tune was the official campaign song of the California Dry Federation, which was behind the November 3, 1914, referendum to end the sale of alcohol in the state. Sample lyrics: "The fight is on, oh Christian workers. And our Lord, He leads the way; The cry rings out with triumphant shout, we'll greet a brighter day."[4] The referendum failed.

That same year, Stewart made the acquaintance of Mrs. Maude Hendricks of Hayward, California, through his work in the temperance movement and as a traveling minister. Hendricks was the wife of an engineer on the Southern Pacific Railroad. Her marriage was not solid and she became seriously infatuated with Stewart. As their affair progressed, she offered to divorce her husband. After Stewart refused to marry her, Hendricks committed suicide on December 29. She left a note implicating Stewart in her demise. Four days later he was arrested in connection with her death.[5] Charges were later dropped for lack of sufficient evidence.[6] The scandal that followed her death resulted in Stewart being summarily defrocked by the church. His wife and sons sought refuge in New Jersey for two months. At the urging of a former parishioner, Agnes reconciled with her husband in March.[7] The reconciliation was brief.

With the cover of the cloth pulled from him, Stewart deserted his wife and children and returned to the East Coast in an attempt to put the scandal behind him. He drifted from city to city and job to job, never in one place for very long. And he continued to meet and charm women.

In Wilmington, Delaware, he encountered Mary Barbara James. Stewart would later recall, "She was 28 years old and quite an attractive woman. It seems that she had some sort of trouble with her family and had hidden herself away to bear her suffering alone. Our moods brought us to a sympathetic understanding of each other and I soon realized that she was madly in love with me. I held no infatuation for her but because of my loneliness I decided to propose marriage to her."[8] Their marriage took place on November 8, 1918, without the benefit of a divorce from Agnes Browne.

He was no longer Robert Allan Maclaren Browne; instead he used the alias Donald Alan Stewart. Although he turned out to be a marrying man, it was at this point that Stewart began to enjoy the pursuit more than the kill.

Donald Duncan Stewart (Robert Allan Browne)

He continued to meet women and fill a notebook with their names, addresses, and phone numbers. At some point in 1919, he left Mary James and was living in Newark, where he would add Ethel to his growing list of conquests. Mary James, however, followed him to New York in late November but left in January following an argument. During this time he remained in contact with Ethel.

Ethel was a strong-willed, independent, and bright woman. In the face of Donald Duncan Stewart, as he now called himself, these character traits dissolved. In February Stewart convinced Ethel to quit her job so she could be free to marry. Stewart allegedly took a position in an auto-supply company where in lieu of compensation he would be taught the business and receive room and board. Ethel began financially supporting Stewart and took a job as a housekeeper/nurse to a former patient to make ends meet. (By April 22 she had given him over $1,100.)

At his urging she agreed to give up her apartment on 135th Street in Manhattan by February 28 and sell many of her things, along with sending some items to Stewart to store. The loss of her home, possessions, and former job created a great deal of anguish for Ethel. To reassure her, Stewart wrote numerous love letters. "I sometimes wonder at my love for you but, Oh Pet of My Heart, I do love you. If only you knew the plans I am making for our future I know the worried look would leave your face. As God lives no one can separate us or come between us. I love. I love you! I love you! I am all yours." He signed the letter, "Your Devil Man Donald."[9] In another letter he wrote the following:

> Dearest One and Baby Mistress:
> Please excuse pencil because I find I must

use it in view of the fact that I have no ink. I am writing this in order to make you very glad. Next Monday or Tuesday I wish you to try and get a few hours off during the day and we will go down and get the license. On the following Saturday, we will be quietly married. I will explain more fully on Saturday when we meet.

I feel that I can make you obey me more fully as your husband and master than otherwise. You must obey me. I will kill you if you do not!

I love you, love you, love you!

I shall be a strict and exacting master, but you can depend on my love and faithfulness. I know how to be faithful to one woman. I also feel that you will be much happier if we are married so I will consent to it. I want my baby to be dressed as her master loves to have her dressed.

Goodnight, my beloved one. I will call you on the phone tomorrow afternoon and find out how you are.

A thousand, thousand kisses to my darling Ethel.

From your own, Donald[10]

She termed him a "masterful lover" but otherwise had lingering anxiety and doubt about her situation. In response, Stewart advanced the wedding date. On March 6 he applied for a license, and they were married that evening. He asked her to keep their marriage a secret for business reasons. In April he quit his position with the auto-supply company, sold her furniture, and pawned a number of her remaining belongings.[11]

Later that month Ethel discovered a letter in Stewart's bag from Mary James. The letter, signed "As ever wife, Mary," informed Stewart that she had contacted a lawyer and would be starting proceedings against him and made a veiled demand for money.[12]

Naturally, Ethel demanded an explanation from Stewart and accused him of not legally being her husband. For the next two days, Stewart fashioned a plausible story. He claimed that Mary kidded him as being his wife when she was really his sister-in-law—the wife of his deceased brother Billy. He swore to Ethel that she was the only wife he ever had and offered to have Mary sign a statement that she had never been his wife or had any claim on him.

Ethel wanted to believe him; her anger subsided. On April 29 he made arrangements to meet her for dinner at 7:00 p.m. He stood her up but got a message to her to meet him at 9:00 p.m. He stood her up again. At midnight when Ethel finally returned to the rooming house where he occasionally stayed with her, she discovered that Stewart had taken his trunk and one of hers and run off.[13]

Here began Ethel's quest to learn the truth about Stewart. Fueled by anger at his duplicity and her stubborn nature, she first visited the East Orange police chief to report Stewart. Next, she called on Stewart's former landlady, who informed her that she (the landlady) had lent him large sums of cash and even pawned her diamonds for him. The landlady knew Mary James and provided many details of Stewart's relationship with this woman, how he had left her and returned several times.

On June 1 Ethel traveled to Wilmington, Delaware, to inspect firsthand the marriage license of Donald Stewart and Mary James. She confirmed that they were indeed married.

On June 15, 1920, her investigation completed, Ethel filed an affidavit with the State of New York, County of New York that charged Donald Duncan Stewart, a.k.a. Donald Alan Stewart, with bigamy. She provided a copy of the marriage licenses, photographs of Stewart and James, statements from ministers who had conducted the ceremonies, and other evidence. Some weeks later Stewart would reunite with Ethel, and the warrant was never served.[14]

Repeating a similar pattern with other women in his life, Stewart returned and then left several times. During this period he was drinking heavily and using drugs. His drug of choice was morphine. With full knowledge that he was seeing other women, Ethel forgave him and continued to give him money, some of which went to Mary James to quiet her threats. Underneath it all, she said she loved him and felt that she could change him.

She explained her behavior to a *Los Angeles Times* reporter accordingly:

> I met Donald, married him, and loved him long before I became aware of his past. . . . Then, after taking my money, my clothes, and even my trunk, Don deserted me. In a fit of woman's rage I swore out a complaint charging him with bigamy after I had checked up on his escapades.
>
> Some weeks later my husband returned to me. He confessed to me that he was a drug addict. He told me of the fight that he was having against his craving for liquor. He told me that when he was in the grip of drugs or whisky he was not responsible for his actions and that his escapades always had been the outcome of a debauch.
>
> Donald told me that I was the only woman he really loved, that if I would help him in his fight against slipping to the bottom he would be able to straighten out his bigamous marriages and with my help could again become a man.

> I was unable to quash the warrant which I had caused to be issued, so Donald and I fled from New York State and believing he would keep his promises I went to work in other cities to assist him in his battle to redeem himself.[15]

Her belief in standing by her man may have come from the example set by her mother. In spite of her desire to see her husband redeem himself, she knew that he smoked cigarettes incessantly, could drink a quart of whiskey without showing it, regularly used "filthy" language, and held "strange" beliefs about women. She also knew that he could be a most reverent, cultured, and educated person. Sadly, many more episodes of unfaithful and criminal behavior were to be endured.[16]

Stewart spiraled further out of control in 1921. It was a busy year for him. In February, under the name Donald Allister Duncan Stewart, he married Bertha Ellen Grannis in Indianapolis. His new wife remained in Indianapolis while he took a job in Detroit selling stock for the Border Cities Home Construction Corporation. He defrauded his newest mother-in-law by cashing a check for $1,250 and sold the car that he had borrowed from her. In addition, he took $1,200 from his brother-in-law before disappearing. In Detroit on April 3, 1921, Mary Barbara James Stewart gave birth to a daughter fathered by Stewart. The child's name was Margaret Harriett Mitchell. The parents' names were recorded as Mary and D. D. Mitchell.[17] Mitchell was an alias.

In June he began courting Detroit Public Schools art teacher Gertrude Von Lopik. Von Lopik saved herself from further heartache by breaking off their engagement, but not before Stewart had relieved her and her relatives of $2,480.[18]

Next stop on the marriage train was Boston. Here on September 24, under the name of Donald Allen McGregor, he married Norma Lillian Ehrenzeller. He'd met Norma earlier in the summer at a resort hotel where he was pretending to be a man of leisure. Norma's mother was charmed by him as well. Before skipping out on Ehrenzeller, he managed to relieve her of $1,500 and her parents of $1,000.[19]

There were reports of his activities in other cities. If Stewart was alone, he would lodge at a rooming house, pay rent initially, and then apply his charms to the landlady in exchange for rent. If he was with a female companion, he would rent a small flat. He liked to spend a lot of time in bed during the day, go out to movies at night, call for mail at general delivery, and read newspapers at local libraries to see if his name appeared.[20] Stewart laid the cause of his behavior on the death of Maude Hendricks. He said he was haunted by her memory. "Every night since that tragedy the woman's wraith has trooped with stealthy, accusing footsteps outside my door. Women used to say I had fascinating ways. They were the ways of desperation. Anything to counteract that creeping presence," said Stewart.[21]

Back in Indianapolis the Grannis family hired the Pinkerton Detective Agency to locate Stewart and bring him to justice for bigamy and fraud. In the course of the agency's investigation, it uncovered that Stewart "held a mystifying control over most of his many assorted wives long after he had deserted them."[22] Even his first wife, who had divorced Stewart on grounds of desertion, did not express malice toward him. Agnes Browne was skeptical that her former husband would remain on the right path but, in a letter to Ethel, expressed hope. "I am convinced that there is a wonderful change in him," Agnes wrote, clearly unaware of his latest marriages. "I hope and pray that it will be permanent."[23] To Ethel he explained his absences as business trips.

Aware that he was wanted for embezzlement and fraud, Donald kept moving. His next stop was planned for Sierra Madre, California, near Los Angeles. Here he had a plan to purchase and renovate a rest home. For this he would need considerable capital. He had met a wealthy woman from Sierra Madre in New York and had her in mind to assist him in the venture.

Shortly before leaving for California, he wrote to Ethel.

> Sweetheart o' Mine & Beloved of Beloveds:
>
> Oh, but I am a lonesome Master this morning. Was it yesterday or a year from yesterday since I last saw you?
>
> Now, sweetheart, I do love you all right. I was so worried about you yesterday. I do so love you, my darling mistress, that it seems to me that every sorrow of yours is a knife thrust in my heart. I never dreamed I could love anyone as I love you.
>
> You may think at times that I am too autocratic and masterful, but the girl who possesses a love and heart-beats of such a man as I am must also realize that the joy of being loved comes only through the power of submission. I am true to you now and I shall always be as long as I am your master and own you body and soul.
>
> I shall require three hundred more dollars. This amount will positively be the last I shall call on you for. I shall want fifty dollars on Wednesday night, another fifty next Saturday, and the remainder by the end of next week. Please do not worry about this matter and go out and do your best. This money is absolutely needed, but I will explain more fully on Wednesday night.
> I send you all my love and affections, my darling and beloved sweetheart.
>
> Your very, very own,
> Donald[24]

Ethel and Stewart took a train out to Los Angeles in the spring of 1922. Stewart had maintained a regular correspondence with the woman from Sierra Madre, sending love letters indicating that he was single. He urged the woman to obtain a divorce from her husband and marry him. The woman was making arrangements to advance Stewart $100,000 to purchase and rebuild the Sierra Madre rest home.

Before the transaction could be finalized, Pinkerton detectives swooped in on June 20 and arrested Stewart and Ethel. The Sierra Madre woman told the detectives that she thought Stewart was a good businessman and that he would wisely invest her money. She declined to press charges. Ethel was charged as an accomplice to Stewart's fraudulent schemes. Both were held in Central Los Angeles City Jail.[25] Before they had arrived in California, charges of fraud and bigamy had been filed in Boston by the Ehrenzellers.

Following their arrests, the Pinkerton Agency detectives went through Ethel's papers, finding a diary and numerous letters. They initiated a national search for additional victims and permitted reporters from the *Los Angeles Times* to read her papers. Intimate details of Ethel's life were published in a series of articles written by *Times* reporters that were then picked up by the wire services and reported in papers nationwide.

The story of the bigamist rogue and the women who fell victim to his charms received wide coverage. Stewart would later say that Ethel was educated and talented. "For the first time since my banishment from the pulpit I did feel that my desire for vengeance on women was ill-founded. I did not fall in love with her (Ethel) as I know love, but there was a great attraction. She was in love with me, however, and my education and personality seemed to appeal to her ideal of a man. The idea of bigamy never entered my mind, but after a short courtship I cast discretion to the wind and proposed to her."[26]

Stewart and Ethel were to be extradited to Massachusetts to face charges there. The attorney representing Stewart went before a judge demanding a writ of habeas corpus (a "show cause" hearing to determine the legality of detaining a person). The attorney argued that his client had been held for ten days without any charges filed. The judge agreed, discounting the telegrams from the Boston Police Department as they did not constitute a fugitive warrant.

Because the Los Angeles authorities failed to produce proper proof of charges against him, he was released from custody on July 1.[27] He was told that as soon as the technicality was corrected, he would be charged and rearrested. Stewart's attorney told authorities and the media that his client would remain at a local hotel until authorities arrived from Boston.[28] Stewart did not wait around. He disappeared before the warrant arrived.

Ethel was not so fortunate. Her request for a writ of habeas corpus did not move as swiftly. She was charged with conspiracy in the theft of $2,500 from Norma Ehrenzeller and was held in lieu of a $20,000 bond. She was detained in Los Angeles until taken to Boston, where she denied the charge.[29] Again, unable to post bond, Ethel remained in Boston's Charles Street Jail from August 9 to mid-October, when the charge was dropped. She had spent fourteen weeks in jail to Stewart's ten days. Despite her love for him, Stewart had made a fool of her once again. Ethel's case was officially closed in December, when she received notice that the district attorney had "nolle prossed" the complaint.[30]

It had been an emotionally trying three years for Ethel and her family. Aside from the disastrous affair with Stewart, cousin Christian Vernon died in 1920 followed by Alice Agnes in East Orange, on January 8, 1921. She had been in declining health for several years.

Two months later—on March 7—Alberta Victoria, the youngest child of Edwin and Alice Agnes, committed suicide in Hot Springs, Arkansas, where she had gone for treatment. Alberta had been depressed due to the death of her mother, the breakdown of her marriage to Philip Plaistridge, and the constant pain she experienced in her left leg that had not healed properly.

Alice Agnes with grandson Kenneth Siver in 1918 in East Orange, New Jersey

The third family member to die in 1921 was Edwin's youngest brother Julian, the physician. While riding his bicycle from his home in Chicago to the house of a patient on Sunday, August 21, he was struck by a car and knocked to the pavement. His injuries were fatal.

From Boston, Ethel moved back to New York City, regained her senses, and put Donald Duncan Stewart behind her, including having her marriage to him annulled. In the next few years, she took several long trips ostensibly to put the scandal behind her.

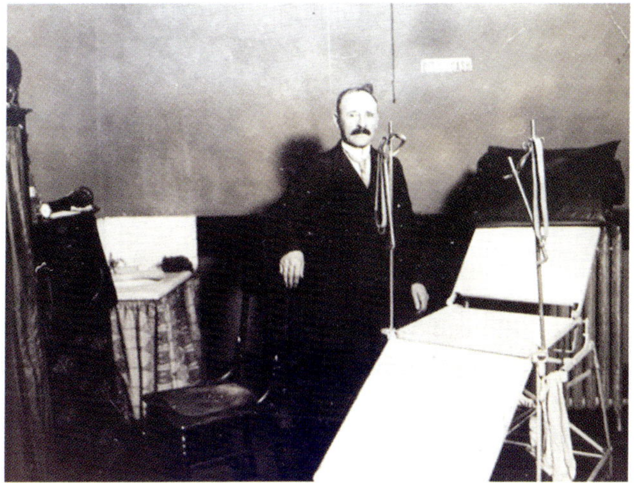

Dr. Julian Osbaldeston, Edwin's youngest brother

In the Northwest she met Arthur Thomas Groves. She married Groves on May 9, 1925, in Tacoma, Washington. An Englishman who had been working in Alberta, Canada, Groves had come to Seattle to visit an aunt. He was twenty-eight and Ethel forty-four at the time of their marriage. In July they drove from Seattle to New York in his new Ford, camping out as they went. The couple stopped in Chicago to visit her brother Francis and sister-in-law Olive.

Ethel and Groves sailed to England in August 1925. For a time she and Groves were living in Birmingham. Ethel returned to the United States in June 1927, thus having missed her father's rearrest in March of 1926 in Asbury Park. In October 1927 she returned to England and remained there until the following May.

Arthur Thomas Groves

Above: Ethel and Arthur sailing to England in 1925
Below: Arthur and Ethel Groves on a stop on their cross-country drive from Seattle to New York in 1925. They stopped in Chicago to visit Frank and Olive.

FINAL NOTES

Josiah Scudder Osbaldeston
(Edwin's father)

Not much is known about Edwin's father's later years. Josiah and his wife Mary Ann Lewis Turner parted ways in 1844 after twenty years of marriage. They never divorced. Josiah never married his stepdaughter, Mary Ann Turner (Edwin's mother). The Church of England's "Table of Kindred and Affinity" forbid it (as it did sexual relations between such a coupling). Mary Ann Turner, who gave birth to seven children by Josiah, left him around 1860. In the 1861 census, Josiah was listed as living in Staffordshire and working as a bookseller. He does not appear in the 1871 and later census records. On his 1884 marriage certificate, his son Frederick Turner listed his father as Josiah Turner, gentleman, deceased. Prior to her death in 1878, Mary Ann Turner Hubbard was an inmate in the Bristol Lunatic Asylum.

Mary Ann Lewis Turner Osbaldeston
(Edwin's grandmother)

Edwin's grandmother, Mary Ann Lewis Turner Osbaldeston, died in Oxford in 1857 of heart disease.

Charles Edward Osbaldeston
(Edwin's brother)

Edwin had no known contact with him after 1867 and no information has been found after that date.

Annie Mabel Osbaldeston Knowles
(Edwin's first daughter by his first wife)

Annie Mabel married John Frederick Knowles in New York City in 1888. She remained close with her half sisters and brothers, although she never had children of her own. Despite her father's objections to her marriage to Knowles, their marriage was

Annie Mabel Osbaldeston Knowles

happy. She died in 1913 after a long illness with Frederick at her side. Six months later Knowles died at the age of fifty-two.

Louise Weiss Lucas

(Edwin's mistress)

With Edwin finally out of her life, Louise and husband Frank (Franz) Lucas lived in peace for a while in Pittsburgh and then moved to Europe, where Frank worked as a chef and Louise was able to assist her mother who had lost her property in the family battle that had begun years before in Germany. Louise sent daughter, Mascot, to school at Dooresele Abbey in Ghent, Belgium. In 1915, Louise and Frank returned to Pittsburgh as Mascot's ballet career took off. In 1916 they relocated to New York City and assumed child care of their granddaughter Alexandra Vesely (see below). Sometime in the early 1930s, Louise and Frank separated and were officially divorced in 1934. By this time Louise had moved to Daytona Beach. She died there on July 14, 1951, of a cerebral hemorrhage at the age of seventy-five.

Louisa Mascot Osbaldeston

(Edwin's daughter by his mistress)

Of all of Edwin's children, Mascot was the most successful professionally. She lived with her mother and stepfather in Pittsburgh, where she began taking dance classes. (She had received gymnastics training from Edwin as a little girl.) Later, Mascot attended school in Ghent, Belgium. In 1914, while visiting her mother and stepfather in England during a school holiday, she was introduced to Russian ballerina Lydia Kyasht, who took her on as a student. Mascot learned enough ballet basics to pass an audition for the dance company of Anna Pavlova in London. (Pavlova was the most celebrated ballet dancer of the day.) To sound more Russian, Mascot adopted the stage name of Mascot Moskovina. She traveled the world for four years with the Pavlova Dance Troupe and then formed her own company and toured North and South America. In 1928 she moved to Daytona Beach, Florida, and established a dance school there.

Her romantic life was more difficult. In 1915 she married fellow dancer Louis Vesely. Later that same year she gave birth to daughter Alexandra Vesely. After the couple divorced, she married Thomas During and had a second daughter (Patricia During) in 1929. Two more marriages would follow: in 1940 (Ralph Cline); and 1950 (Louis Drukker). During World War II she gave up her dance studio to work in Washington, DC, for the War Production Board. She returned to Daytona Beach in 1948 and dabbled in real estate. She died on September 27, 1980, at the age of eighty-four.

S. Foster Black

(Broome County, New York deputy sheriff and later sheriff)

The celebrated lawman died of a stroke on January 20, 1928, at the age of eighty-four. "Binghamton knew S. Foster Black since the War of the States as sheriff of the county, US marshall, deputy sheriff, and private detective. His name always struck terror in the haunts of crime. Unafraid of man or devil, with a highly developed, almost uncanny ability to find the guilty man, Black was a successful hunter of violators of the law," the *Binghamton Press* noted.[31] On the other hand, his obituary in the *New York Times* carried the headline, "Osbaldeston's Foe Dead; S. F. Black Who Served 50-Year-Old Charge, Dies at 84."[32] Edwin sent condolences to Black's family.

Martin C. Donohoe

(Malone, New York detective)

The Malone, New York peace officer and detective died on November 17, 1928, at the age of seventy-four. His obituary mentioned his role in the apprehension of Edwin and Louise Weiss. Edwin outlived both lawmen.

Donald Duncan Stewart (Robert Allan Brown)

(Ethel's bigamist husband)

After jumping bail in Los Angeles, Stewart disappeared for a time. Using the name Reverend Donald A. Mitchell, he married divorcée Ruby Gardner Lynch in San José, California, in 1923. On February 18, 1927, he was arrested in Detroit on the 1921 charge of theft of funds from Gertrude Von Lopik. He was found guilty and sentenced to five to ten years in Michigan's Jackson State Prison. The US Census of 1930 recorded Stewart as a clerk in the prison's medical office. He was released from Jackson State Prison on May 16, 1931. Nothing else is known about Stewart as, more than likely, he changed his name once or twice more.

Geneva Agnes Turner Osbaldeston Miller

(Edwin's daughter)

Although her father had opposed her 1903 marriage with widower Frederick Miller, the couple were happy together. Miller died on July 1, 1926. Geneva never remarried. She worked for many years as a sales clerk and then, in the 1940s, as

Geneva and Normandie in 1936, visiting the grave of sister Edwina Agnes in Newport, Rhode Island

manager of a bookstore in Manhattan. She was known for her gentle disposition and kind manner. She traveled occasionally with her sisters. In 1952 she retired to St. Petersburg, Florida, and died there on April 7, 1954. She was sixty-eight.

Ed (center) with grandson Pete Turner and son Donald (Photo taken in Montreal in September 1940)

While working for his brother Frank's construction company in Chicago, Ed fell off a ladder in 1938, seriously injuring his spine. Pictured above he is wearing a leather brace. He never fully recovered from this accident. Ethel moved to Chicago to care for Ed.

John Edwin Turner (Edwin Julian Turner Osbaldeston)

(Edwin's son)

After his marriage dissolved, Ed moved to New York City. He was emotionally shaken by the loss of his wife, son, and home and had trouble finding work but finally took a job in Texas. In 1930 he relocated to Chicago, where he went to work for his younger brother Frank. In 1938 he fell off a ladder at a construction job and broke his back. He had numerous health issues for the remainder of his life. He never remarried.

His former wife, Jean, died in 1940 of a heart attack. His son, Donald (1908–1980), was the leader of a dance band orchestra that played for many years in the Mount Royal Hotel in Montreal. Donald had one son, Donald Peter Turner (known as "Pete"), born in 1934. A professional photographer, Pete Turner is recognized as one of the first mas-

Ed, Norma, and Frank in Gulfport, Florida (circa early 1960s)

ters of color photography. Many leading magazines, including *National Geographic,* commissioned Pete for his photography. He was also retained to do numerous covers for record albums and published several books of his photography, among them *Pete Turner African Journey* and *The Color of Jazz.*

In the 1940s Ed moved to Florida, where he shared a home with his sister Ethel. He had multiple health issues during his final years. Ed died in St. Petersburg, Florida, at the age of eighty on December 2, 1963.

Normandie Alice Turner Osbaldeston Siver

(Edwin's daughter)

Norma and husband, James, were married for fifty-four years. They had one son, Kenneth (1909–1984), and were grandparents to his five children (Noël, Judith, Kenson, Alison, and Karen). Kenneth had a successful career in the insurance industry working as a salesman for Liberty Mutual. Jim worked for many years for Sunshine Biscuits as a sales representative and Norma was a homemaker. They retired to Gulfport, Florida, in 1960. Jim died

Norma and grand-nephew, photographer Donald "Pete" Turner in Florida in 1961

on November 22, 1962, of arteriosclerosis. Normandie died of a heart attack on October 9, 1965, at the age of seventy-eight.

A homemaker all her adult life, Norma had numerous interests, including reading, painting, fishing, and nature studies. Until her retirement to Florida, she maintained a home in New Milford, New Jersey, and a cottage on Upper Greenwood Lake, New Jersey. Overall, she was dissatisfied with her station in life. She wanted more out of life than being a housewife and was envious of those who were better off than she.

Of her parents she said, "[Mama] earned her place in heaven I am so sure. Papa, at the end was a lonesome, aged man embittered because he could not make the fortunes any longer. Spendthrifts always end up saying 'If I had only done it differently.'"[33] In another letter she wrote, "If you & your family read my father's diary—remember he was really a doer, & did many interesting things in his early life. . . ."[34] Normandie and her siblings never discussed their father's criminal past with younger members of the family. They did, however, mention his violent temper and wanderlust. Norma clung to the belief that her father was descended from British aristocracy.

Frank (age 29) and wife Olive Teel (age 25) Osbaldeston

Francis Scudder Turner Osbaldeston

(Edwin's son)

With the help of his wife, Frank started a number of businesses after relocating from New York City to Chicago. He founded the Turner Sales Company, which marketed Belinda's Joy (a washing compound).

Frank marketed Belinda's Joy.

Following that, he established the Mission Products Company, which produced dried and candied fruits. He also began Turner Building Service, a home-repair and building-cleaning business. The company's copyrighted slogan was, "Give us a ring—we'll fix that thing!" Frank hired his older brother Ed to work in his businesses. He shuttered his dried-fruit company due to Mafia interference.

Frank and Olive retired to St. Petersburg, Florida, in 1950. Olive died of arteriosclerosis in 1958.

Above: The crew of the Turner Building Service in Chicago (Ed on the left and Frank seated in suit)
Below left: Frank and Olive in Florida in the 1950s Below right: Ethel in 1951 at her front door on 15th Avenue S.

Frank died on June 5, 1968, at the age of seventy-eight. Frank was the last family member with the surname Osbaldeston. Frank and Olive had no children.

Ethel Monica Turner Osbaldeston Groves

(Edwin's daughter)

Her marriage to Arthur T. Groves did not last. They were legally separated in March 1928. Ethel did not marry again. In 1938 she moved to Chicago to care for her brother Ed after his serious injury. She and Ed retired to Florida in 1940. They lived in St. Petersburg and traveled together for the remainder of their days. As Ed's health continued to fail, Ethel took care of him. She died on June 25, 1968, twenty days after Frank passed, at the age of eighty-seven.

Ever the caregiver, she was the last of Edwin's children by Alice Agnes. In her final years she suffered four strokes and each time willed herself to move and write again. Right until the end of her life Ethel kept up with current affairs and maintained a sharp wit.

In later years Ethel, Ed, Geneva, Normandie, and Frank never spoke of Louise Weiss or Mascot. Even in their vivid recollections of their days in Malone, they did not mention the mistress and the daughter born to her. More than likely, they knew of their half sister's international acclaim as a ballerina. Or perhaps they did not recognize the name Mascot Moskovina.

The drive between St. Petersburg and Daytona Beach, Florida, takes about two and a half hours. There is no evidence that they ever had any contact after their parting in 1897. Perhaps it was best for all that this piece of their family history remained in the past.

Ever the caregiver, Ethel was the third of Edwin's children. She worked as a nurse for many years.

NOTES

1. "Diary Reveals Waning Love," *Los Angeles Times*, 23 June 1922, sec. 2, p. 1, col. e.
2. "Waning Faith Revealed," *Los Angeles Times,* 23 June 1922, sec. 2, p. 12, col. e.
3. "Reformer is Jailed. Stewart Held a Bigamist," *Los Angeles Times*, 21 June 1922, sec. 1, p. 1.
4. S. Maxwell and R. A. M. Browne, "We'll Make California Dry" (Los Angeles: Campaign Song Dept., California "Dry" Federation, 1914.)
5. "Former Pastor Taken by Cops," *Escanaba Daily Press* (MI), 19 February 1927, p. 3.
6. "Ex-Minister Has Four Wives, Police Assert," *Los Angeles Times*, 22 June 1922, sec. 1, p. 1.
7. "Rev. R. A. M. Browne Reunited to Wife," *Oakland Tribune* (CA), 17 March 1915, p. 1.
8. "Unfrocked Minister Tells More of His Sensational Marriage Career," *Indiana Evening Gazette* (Indianapolis, IN), 25 February 1927, p. 12, col. a.
9. "Was 'Masterful Lover,'" *Los Angeles Times*, 24 June 1922, sec. 2, p. 3.
10. Ibid.
11. "Diary Reveals Waning Love," *Los Angeles Times*, 23 June 1922, sec. 2, pp. 1 and 12.
12. Ibid.
13. Ibid.
14. "Wife Swore to Bigamy Charge," *Los Angeles Times*, 23 June 1922, sec. 2, p. 12, col. h.
15, "Tells of Losing Fight," *Los Angeles Times*, 23 June 1922, sec. 2, p. 12, col. g.
16. Ibid.
17. "Mrs. Osbaldeston Describes Second Wife of Stewart," *Los Angeles Times*, 23 June 1922, sec. 2, p. 12, cols. a-b.
18. "Not Bigamist Says Stewart," *Los Angeles Times*, 25 June 1922, sec. 1, p. 11.
19. "Ex-Minister Says He Can't Pick Legal Wife," *Los Angeles Times*, 23 June 1922, sec. 2, p. 12, col. b.
20. "Was 'Masterful Lover,'" *Los Angeles Times*, 24 June 1922, sec. 2, p. 3.
21. "Vampire Ghost Drove Ex-Pastor into Bigamy, Is His Defense," *Gettysburg Times* (PA), 29 July 1922, p. 4.
22. "Ex-Wife Still Trying to Aid," *Los Angeles Times*, 24 June 1922, sec. 2, p. 3.
23. Ibid.
24. "Was 'Masterful Lover,'" *Los Angeles Times*, 24 June 1922, sec. 2, p. 3.
25. "Stewart's Arrest Nips Huge Loan from Woman," *Los Angeles Times*, 24 June 1922, sec. 1, p. 7.
26. "Preacher-Bigamist Continues Remarkable Story of His Crimes," *Indiana Evening Gazette* (Indianapolis, IN), 24 February 1927.
27. "Court Orders Stewart Freed," *Los Angeles Times*, 2 July 1922, sec. 1, p. 7.
28. "Stewart to Be on Hand for Arrest," *Los Angeles Times*, 4 July 1922, sec. 2, p. 5.
29. "Mrs Stewart Held in Bail of $4000; Denies Conspiracy with Husband to Steal," *Boston Daily Globe,* 11 August 1922, p. 4.
30. Lawyer Guy W. Cox of the Boston law firm of Cox and Bacon to Mrs. Ethel Stewart, 22 December 1922.
31. "S. Foster Black," *Binghamton Press* (NY), 21 January 1928, p. 6, col. b.
32. "Osbaldeston's Foe Dead; S. F. Black Who Served 50-Year-Old Charge, Dies at 84," *New York Times*, 21 January 1928, p. 17.
33. Normandie Alice Osbaldeston Siver to Kenson Siver, 8 September 1962.
34. Normandie Alice Osbaldeston Siver to Kenson Siver, 7 May 1964.

Frank and Olive Osbaldeston resided at 1634 N. McVicker Avenue in Chicago for many years before retiring to Florida. Here the siblings (rear) Ed and Ethel, (front) Geneva, Normandie, and Frank gather for a reunion in 1935.

APPENDIX

Edwin Turner Osbaldeston Family Crest

One manifestation of Edwin's need to appear superior to others was his pretense that he was descended from English aristocracy. He created a family crest that incorporated elements of the coat of arms of the Osbaldestons of Lancashire, England. The coat of arms and the motto CONSTANTE ET FERME ('Constant and Firm' or 'Perseverance and Decision') had been used by the Lancashire Osbaldestons since at least the thirteenth century.

At left: Edwin had his Osbaldeston coat of arms embroidered and framed, The crest measures eight inches high by five-and-a-half inches wide.

Above: A wooden block of the coat of arms that was either applied to wax and used as a seal or inked and reproduced.

At right: The coat of arms was incorporated into an embossed seal for the New York School of Massage.

Osbaldeston Family Artifacts

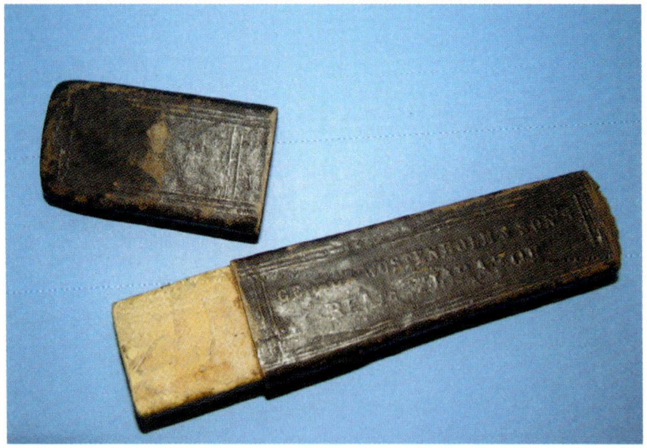

Opera glass and case

This John Barber razor belonged to Edwin. He kept the razor in a case for a George Wostenholm & Son's Real Razor (upper left). Wostenholm & Son's was England's greatest manufacturer of cutlery.

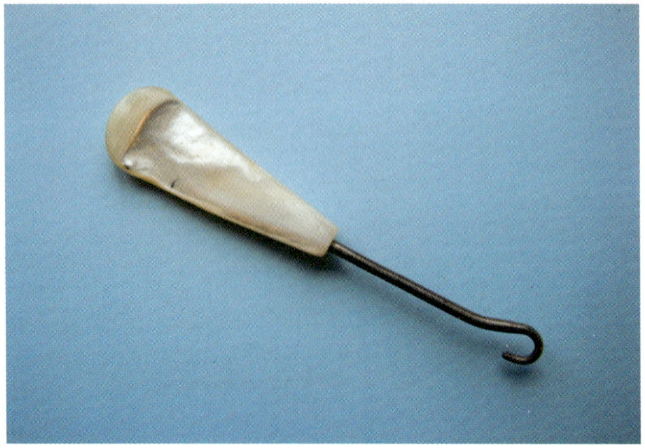

Middle: A pair of Edwin's scalpels with wooden handles

Lower: A buttonhook with a mother-of-pearl handle

A carved bone or ivory stiletto sewing tool. The pointed end screws into the the interior of the handle for storage.

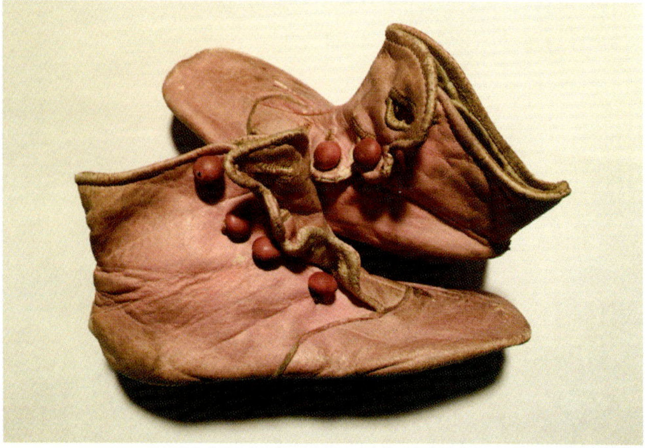

First booties belonging to youngest son Francis Scudder Osbaldeston

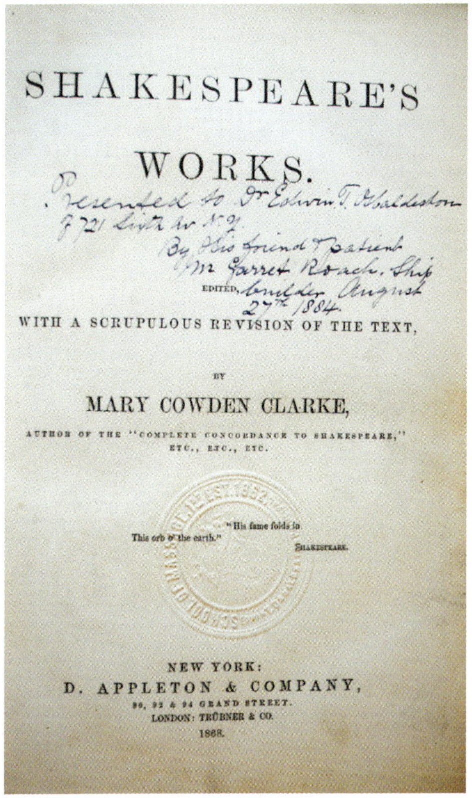

SHAKESPEARE'S

WORKS.

Presented to Dr Edwin T. Ossaldeston
of 721 Sixth Av N.Y.
By his friend & patient
Mr Garrett Roach. Ship
builder August
27th 1884.

EDITED,

WITH A SCRUPULOUS REVISION OF THE TEXT,

BY

MARY COWDEN CLARKE,

AUTHOR OF THE "COMPLETE CONCORDANCE TO SHAKESPEARE," ETC., ETC., ETC.

"His fame folds in
This orb o' the earth."
SHAKESPEARE.

NEW YORK:
D. APPLETON & COMPANY,
90, 92 & 94 GRAND STREET.
LONDON: TRÜBNER & CO.
1868.

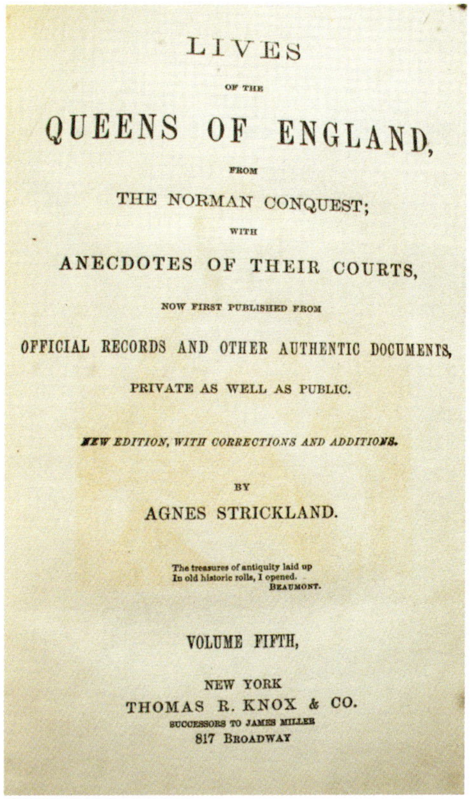

LIVES
OF THE
QUEENS OF ENGLAND,
FROM
THE NORMAN CONQUEST;
WITH
ANECDOTES OF THEIR COURTS,
NOW FIRST PUBLISHED FROM
OFFICIAL RECORDS AND OTHER AUTHENTIC DOCUMENTS,
PRIVATE AS WELL AS PUBLIC.

NEW EDITION, WITH CORRECTIONS AND ADDITIONS.

BY
AGNES STRICKLAND.

The treasures of antiquity laid up
In old historic rolls, I opened.
BEAUMONT.

VOLUME FIFTH,

NEW YORK
THOMAS R. KNOX & CO.
SUCCESSORS TO JAMES MILLER
817 BROADWAY

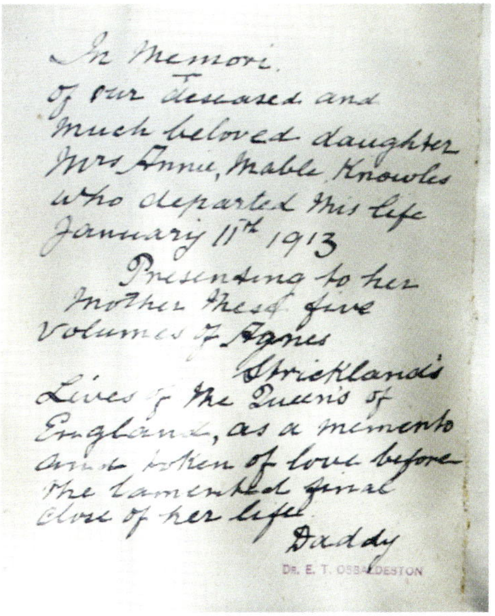

In memori
of our deceased and
much beloved daughter
Mrs Annie Mable Knowles
who departed this life
January 11th 1913
Presenting to her
mother these five
volumes of Agnes
Strickland's
Lives of the Queen's of
England, as a memento
and token of love before
the lamented final
close of her life
Daddy

DR. E. T. OSSALDESTON

Above: Shakespeare's Works *was given to Edwin as a gift by Garrett Roach in 1884. Roach was a wealthy New York ship builder who had been a patient of Edwin's. Roach died in 1888.*

Upper right: The title page of the five-volume series Lives of the Queens of England. *This set of books was given to Annie Mabel by her husband, Frederick Knowles, as a Christmas present.*

Lower right: After Annie Mabel died in 1913, Edwin gifted Lives of the Queens of England *to Alice Agnes with this dedication.*

Far right: An untitled print by landscape and marine artist Charles Paul Gruppé. Daughter Alberta studied under Gruppé.

One of the items Edwin marketed at the turn of the century was the paper powder book. When sheets from the book were applied to the skin it would serve to remove dirt and grease from the face. The makers of this product claimed that use of the perfumed sheets were a tonic to the skin, a cure for pimples, a method to remove blackheads, and could serve as an aftershave. "It imparts a cool sensation without clogging pores," the makers claimed.

Left: Two views of a decorative brass box that may have been used for storage of jewelry, coins, pins, etc.

Top: Written in ink on fabric, the inscription in the photo case is much faded but appears to read, "Edwin Turner Osbaldeston, Surgeon Hobart Town, Tasmania 1876 To my dear daughter Annie M, Daddy" As he did many times in later life, Edwin may have written this inscription at a different point in time. He was in Tasmania in 1875, not in 1876.

Below: Spoon belonging to Alice Agnes Moore—note initials on handle

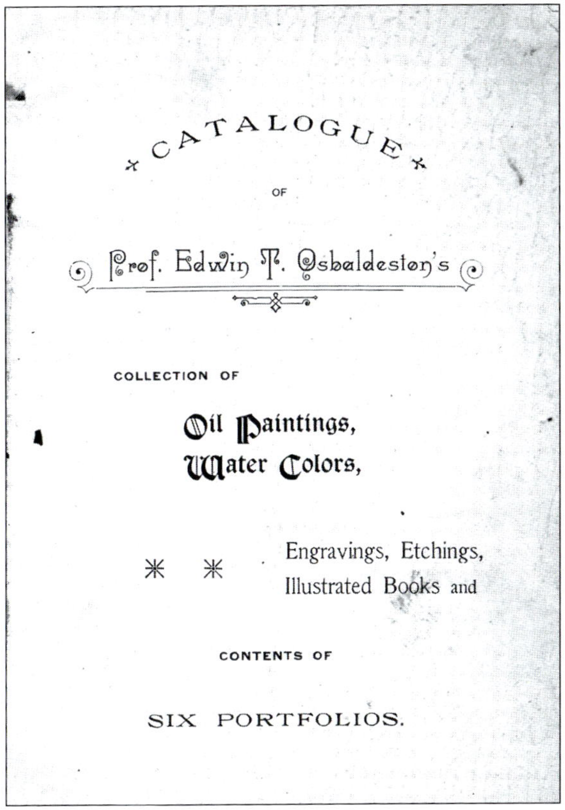

CATALOGUE

OF

Prof. Edwin T. Osbaldeston's

COLLECTION OF

Oil Paintings,
Water Colors,

Engravings, Etchings,
Illustrated Books and

CONTENTS OF

SIX PORTFOLIOS.

Above: Cover of an undated catalogue of Dr. Osbaldeston's art collection

Left: Alberta Osbaldeston was the model for the cover of the September 1911 edition of Cosmopolitan *magazine.*

Edwin Turner Osbaldeston's Family Tree

William Osbaldeston, III = Maria Smith
Grandfather
b. before 24 Feb. 1764
d. 28 Sept. 1821

Maria Smith
Grandmother
b. ca 1769
d. 12 Jan. 1850

Charles Pye Turner, Sr. = Mary Ann Lewis
Grandfather
b. before 6 June 1772
d. 12 Aug. 1820

Mary Ann Lewis
Grandmother
b. ca 1787
d. 11 Dec. 1857

|

Mary Ann Turner
b. 22 May 1815
d. 23 June 1878

Charles Pye Turner, Jr.
b. 17 March 1817
d. 22 Sept. 1889

|

Josiah Scudder Osbaldeston ≠ Mary Ann Turner
Father
b. before 10 May 1797
d. ?

Mary Ann Turner
Mother
b. 22 May 1815
d. 23 June 1878

Frederick Turner
Brother
b. 1832
d. 13 Nov. 1919

Edwin Turner Osbaldeston
b. 11 July 1838
d. 18 Feb. 1929

Emma Turner Osbaldeston
Sister
b. ca 1841
d. 20 Feb. 1919

Charles Edward Turner Osbaldeston
Brother
b. ca 1844
d. ?

Francis Turner Osbaldeston
Brother
b. ca 25 Dec. 1849
d. 2 March 1904

Ann Maria Turner Osbaldeston
Sister
b. ca 1851
d. 18 Oct. 1856

Julian Alexander Turner Osbaldeston
Brother
b. 12 Dec. 1854
d. 21 Aug. 1921

Married Joseph H. Vernon
Brother-in-law
b. 23 July 1838
d. 24 Nov. 1901

|

Edwin T. Vernon (1862–1874)
Oscar T. Vernon (ca 1866–1885)
Christian E. Vernon (1867–1920)
Alonzo A. Vernon (1872–?)
Nephews

Edwin Turner Osbaldeston = Ann Pratt
First wife
b. Sept. 1844
d. ?

|

Frederick Josiah Osbaldeston
Son
b. 12 May 1864
d. 24 May 1864

Annie Mabel Osbaldeston = John Frederick Knowles
Daughter
b. 18 May 1866
d. 11 Jan. 1913

John Frederick Knowles
Son-in-law
b. July 1860
d. July 1913

Edwin Turner Osbaldeston = Alice Agnes Moore
Second wife
b. 28 Sept. 1854
d. 8 Jan. 1921

Ethel Monica Turner Osbaldeston
Daughter
b. 4 Oct. 1880
d. 25 June 1968

Married
Donald Duncan Stewart
Son-in-law
b. 18 Nov. 1884
d. ?

Married
Arthur T. Groves
Son-in-law
b. 16 March 1897
d. Fall 1969

Edwina Agnes Turner Osbaldeston
Daughter
b. 10 Jan. 1882
d. 27 Aug. 1882

Edwin Julian Turner Osbaldeston (John Edwin)
Son
b. 4 May 1883
d. 2 Dec. 1963

Married
Jean McDonald
Daughter-in-law
b. 6 Jan. 1885
d. 7 June 1940

Donald E. Turner
Grandson
b. 31 March 1908
d. 1 Jan. 1980

Donald Peter "Pete" Turner
Great grandson
b. 30 May 1934

Geneva Agnes Turner Osbaldeston
Daughter
b. 23 June 1885
d. 7 April 1954

Married
Frederick Miller
Son-in-law
b. 29 Dec. 1855
d. 1 July 1926

Normandie Alice Turner Osbaldeston
Daughter
b. 27 July 1887
d. 9 Oct. 1965

Married
James H. Siver
Son-in-law
b. 30 June 1889
d. 22 Nov. 1962

Kenneth L. Siver
Grandson
b. 22 May 1909
d. 5 June 1984

Married
Alice Kneeland Grain
b. 6 April 1913
d. 24 Aug. 1998

Married
Mildred A. Lautenberger
b. 27 Jan. 1916
d. 31 Dec. 1980

Noél G. Siver b. 18 Dec. 1941
Judith C. Siver b. 10 May 1944
Kenson J. Siver b. 11 Nov. 1945
Alison Turner Siver b. 13 Jan. 1947
Karen Jean Siver b. 8 March 1948
Great grandchildren

Francis Scudder Turner Osbaldeston
Son
b. 18 July 1889
d. 5 June 1968

Married
Olive Teel Bilky
Daughter-in-law
b. 13 Jan. 1893
d. 18 Jan. 1958

Alberta Victoria Turner Osbaldeston
Daughter
b. 7 June 1891
d. 7 March 1921

Married
Philip Plaistridge
Son-in-law
b. 10 April 1886
d. 4 April 1973

Edwin Turner Osbaldeston ≠ Louise Weiss
Mistress
b. 12 Jan. 1876
d. 14 July 1951

Mascot Louise Osbaldeston
Daughter
b. 9 Aug. 1896
d. 27 Sept. 1980

Married
Louis Vesely
b. ca 1885
d. ?

Alexandra de Vesely
Granddaughter
b. 23 Dec. 1915
d. 10 Aug. 2014

Married
Thomas Patrick During
b. ca 1880
d. ?

Patricia Mascot During
Granddaughter
b. 29 June 1929
d. 15 May 2010

Married
Ralph Hoover Cline
b. 29 April 1894
d. 18 Feb. 1964

Married
Louis Drukker
b. 2 May 1882
d. Dec. 1968

INDEX

E

F

G

HOYT PUBLIC LIBRARY
One of Dr. Osbaldeston's patients was New York business tycoon Jesse Hoyt. Hoyt made a fortune through his investments in Michigan forestry, minerals, and railroads. In appreciation to the City of Saginaw the Hoyt Foundation built the Hoyt Public Libary. Architects Van Brunt and Howe of Boston created the building with a Romanesque exterior featuring large limestone blocks, red sandstone trim, intersecting dormers, a bell tower, and arched entrances. The interior was done almost exclusively in oak. (Photo: Hoyt Public Library, Saginaw, Michigan)

H

I — J

FRANKLIN ACADEMY
Malone, New York
Edwin and Alice Agnes's oldest child Ethel attended the Franklin Academy in Malone while the family had homes in town and at Camp Mascot on Lake Titus.

K

L

M

N

O

Ethel's onetime gentleman friend, Harry Hatzel, rides the Express wagon with Kenneth Siver at the handle. (Circa 1913)

ABOUT THE AUTHORS

Great-granddaddy, "Professor" Edwin Turner Osbaldeston helped write this extraordinary life story.

Noël G. Siver

Noël Siver divides her time between conserving freshly excavated material on archaeological excavations in the Middle East and Mediterranean, copyediting, hiking, and family history research.

She is an ace at archaeological jigsaw puzzles and also has finely honed research skills that serve her well when undertaking genealogical and biographical detective work. She has been researching the life and crimes of her English great-grandfather, Edwin Turner Osbaldeston, the subject of this volume, since 1996.

Noël's degrees are in Spanish, library science, and archaeological conservation. Her publications include *Surveyors of Persian Art: A Documentary Biography of Arthur Upham Pope and Phyllis Ackerman* (1996); "Preparations for Field Conservation," *SSCR Journal*, 13 (July 2002); "Pope, Arthur Upham," *Encyclopaedia Iranica* (2004); and contributions to the forthcoming volumes *Excavations at the Cappadocia Gate*, Kerkenes Final Reports 1; and *Excavations at the Palatial Complex*, Kerkenes Final Reports 2.

When not on travels about the world, Noël resides in Berkeley, California.

Kenson J. Siver

History, writing, and politics have been long-time interests of Kenson Siver.

He had a bond with his great-aunt Ethel. They exchanged letters for many years and he was fascinated by the stories she told of her youth and her parents. Upon her death Ken took possession of the family history materials that Ethel had kept.

As a teacher and administrator in the Southfield (Michigan) Public Schools for forty-five years, Ken taught English, journalism, and American history. He held administrative posts as information director and deputy superintendent of schools.

He has authored three Southfield histories—*Southfield Faces the Crucial Decades* (1987), *A Brief History of Southfield* (for elementary schools) (1996), and *Southfield: The History of Our City in its 50th Year* (2009). In 2015, he also served as editor and contributing author for the commemorative book documenting thirty years of service by Southfield's Martin Luther King Jr. Task Force.

He served on the Southfield City Council from 2001 to 2015. In November 2015, he was sworn in as the sixth mayor of Southfield.

He holds a bachelor's degree from Oakland University (Rochester, Michigan) and a master's and doctorate degrees from Wayne State University in Detroit.